INDIA AND TAIWAN
A Reality Check

INDIA AND TAIWAN
A Reality Check

CHARLES LI

KW Publishers Pvt Ltd
New Delhi

CHENNAI CENTRE FOR CHINA STUDIES

www.c3sindia.org

The Chennai Centre for China Studies (C3S), registered under the Tamil Nadu Societies Registration Act 1975 (83/2008 dated 4th April 2008), is a non-profit public policy think tank with the following objectives.

- Carry out in-depth studies of developments relating to China with priority to issues of interest to India such as
  1. Geopolitical, economic and strategic dynamics of India-China relations.
  2. China's internal dynamics.
  3. The Sino-Indian border issue.
  4. China's relations with South Asian countries.
  5. Prospects of Sino-Indian economic and trade relations.
  6. Future evolution of China's politics and its impact on India and the world.
  7. China-India-ASEAN relations.
  8. China's emerging role in SAARC.
  9. Growing importance of South India for Chinese interaction and economic investment.
  10. India-China-Southeast Asia cultural links.
- Suggest viable solutions/policy alternatives on the basis of studies to the strategic planners and decision makers in India on issues of bilateral, regional and global importance.
- Create public opinion, particularly in South India, on the implications arising out of China's emergence as a leading global power.
- Provide a forum for dialogue with China scholars in India and abroad and give space for expression of alternate opinions on China-related topics.
- Provide a sound data base for research on China with special attention to tapping information available in Chinese language material, so as to benefit scholars, media and think tanks in India as well as rest of the world.
- Address the requirements of the business community in India, particularly informing them about the nature of emerging business opportunities and problems while dealing with China.
- Liaise with think tanks specialising on China, both in India and abroad, with the objective of exchanging views.
- Organise lecture discussions and seminars on topics of current interest.
- Interact with institutions of higher learning in South India to create awareness about developments in China.
- Bring out publications relating to China—books, edited volumes, monographs and occasional papers.

ISBN 978-81-982677-6-4 Paperback

Published in India by Kalpana Shukla

KW Publishers Pvt Ltd
4676/21, First Floor, Ansari Road, Daryaganj, New Delhi 110002
Phone: +91-11-43528107
Email: kw@kwpub.in • www.kwpub.in

Printed and bound in India.
Quiinkit Infotech Pvt. Ltd., Gurugram

Dedicated to
My Parents

Contents

Preface

The relationship between India and Taiwan, once a peripheral topic in academic discourse, has garnered heightened attention in recent years. This increased focus can be attributed, in part, to significant geopolitical events such as the Doklam military stand-off in June 2017 and the Galwan River Valley incident in June 2020, which have underscored the strategic role that Taiwan can play for India. Despite being a comparatively small nation with a population of 23.5 million, Taiwan holds considerable significance for India, extending beyond its prowess in information and communication technology manufacturing.

This book seeks to elucidate the multifaceted dimensions of the Indo-Taiwanese relationship and provide a comprehensive understanding by exploring the historical connections, political constraints, and opportunities for collaboration. It delves into the evolving dynamics of bilateral relations and underscores the potential for mutual benefit in various sectors. Furthermore, the book sheds light on the emerging trends and prospects for cooperation between India and Taiwan, addressing key questions regarding mutual interests, collaborative opportunities, and the significance of cultural exchanges.

While scholarly attention on Indo-Taiwanese relations highlights Taiwan's significance as a key player in the global semiconductor industry and its potential to bolster India's economic and industrial advantages. However, there is a dearth of comprehensive publications offering a holistic perspective on the Indo-Taiwanese relationship, encompassing historical background, contemporary dynamics, and future prospects. This book seeks to address this gap by providing insights gleaned from diplomatic interactions and engagements, offering a nuanced analysis of the evolving bilateral relationship across various domains including trade, investment, culture, education, and technology.

Despite challenges such as political sensitivities and diplomatic constraints, the findings suggest a positive trajectory for bilateral relations, marked by growing mutual understanding and cooperation. By leveraging their respective strengths and fostering deeper engagement, India and Taiwan can capitalise on shared interests to achieve common goals. Although challenges persist, proactive diplomacy and strategic initiatives are crucial to unlocking the full potential of their relationship in the years ahead.

July 1, 2024 **Charles Li**

Foreword

I first met Dr Charles Li in October 2015, when he was serving as the Director-General of the Taiwan Council Chennai, India. I was immediately struck by his honesty, engaging diplomatic skills, and genuine courtesy that extended beyond protocol. Every time I visited his office, he always had plans to visit colleges and universities to meet with students. He frequently welcomed educationists from different professional background—medicine, engineering, technical education—as well as officials from public and private institutions. His tireless engagements and dedicated work ethic impressed me as those of a professional committed to engaging with India and representing his country with genuine dedication to building and expanding the ties between India and Taiwan. We met at regularly to discuss and exchange ideas about school education systems, colleges and universities in India and Taiwan. Dr LI welcomed politicians, medical professionals, technicians, business entrepreneurs, teachers and students with the same respect and dignity, without distinction. I found that everyone was special to him and his mission to create interest and generate and spark discussion about Taiwan was evident in all his engagements.

He is fascinated by the culture and history of India and would often discuss the ancient and classical ties between India and China. We used to talk about the travels of Hiuen Tsang in 630 A.D. in India and the journey of Bodhi Dharma during the late 5th century CE. We also travelled together to the ancient city of Kanchipuram in Tamil Nadu to trace the roots of Bodhidharma by visiting a site dedicated to his honour and memory. By this time, I had come to understand that DR Charles Li was not a high flying diplomat with superficial pretensions, decorative words, and artificially cultivated traits. I realised that I was engaging with a dedicated professional with scholarly instincts and a forward looking approach to building ties between India Taiwan, his homeland. An opportunity arose for me to invite Dr Charles Li and his wife Madam Esther to attend a Tibetan dance and music festival on March 26, 2017 in Chennai, Tamil Nadu, which featured narratives of cultural history and performances of simple yet beautiful folksongs by the Tibetan Institute of Performing Arts. It was a moving and beautiful evening, filled with the art, culture, dance and music from the forgotten country of Tibet.

After the dance and music performance, Madam Esther and Dr Charles Li met me near the stage to share their joy and appreciation for the artists. Madam Esther, being an artist, had more to say with moisture in her eyes, while Dr Charles Li, as a diplomat said less. Yet they both spoke the same language of peace, freedom and justice. Madam Esther suggested that it would be wonderful for Dr Charles Li to pursue an academic and scholarly journey in India. He soon joined the PhD programme at the University of Madras as a research scholar. We discussed the subject and research area aligned with his personal and professional interests. His professional quest to strengthen ties between India and Taiwan, coupled with his lifelong interest in India, guided us in to selecting the study's focus on issues and challenges in India Taiwan relations, with a futuristic vision and commitment. We met regularly to discuss the subject and develop the study. I had found him exceptional in following casual conversations and specific instructions regarding the book reviews, methodology, chapter design, and footnote style, all without compromising on the time schedule. This was a valuable learning experience for me as well, teaching me about the importance of hard work, motivation, time and discipline. Dr Li soon emerged as a model scholar and became a benchmark for other research scholars in the department. We continued to meet even after the submission of his PhD thesis to share and discuss our common interests, until COVID-19 separated us in our respective countries. It was a great privilege and honour to mentor a research scholar of his academic commitment and personal integrity. At the time of his PhD award I told him that his wife deserved even greater appreciation for her patience and selfless support, as it was equally her dream to see him earn his doctorate in International Relations.

I have observed and learnt several extraordinary qualities in Dr Charles Li, particularly his hard work and commitment to meet timelines for both work and research. He is among the few individuals I have encountered in my academic life who demonstrate such remarkable motivation, dedication, respect for time, and a disciplined approach to work and life. Alongside Commodore Seshadri R Vasan, Director General of the Chennai Centre for China Studies (C3S), Chennai, India, Dr Charles Li stands out for these qualities. I am proud and delighted to learn about the publication of this book and was honoured to write a brief note for it expressing my sincere appreciation to Dr Charles Li and his wife Madam Esther for her vision, support, inspiration, and for serving as a source of encouragement throughout this journey. I have also heard Dr Li speak about his childhood, family, dreams as a school boy, and his passion for public service, which shaped life and career. He has remained true and grateful to his family and for all the paths he has taken in life—indeed a rare quality that I wish to acknowledge with great respect. This book is a timely work, offering vision, hope and profound arguments that are difficult to ignore. It encourages us to explore further the prospects and challenges in the bilateral ties between India and Taiwan, presenting insightful reasoning grounded in realities. The time has come for India to acknowledge and appreciate what India and Taiwan can offer one another, paving an era of peace, progress, and mutual development. Dr Li is undoubtedly one of the finest exponents of the potential for building the present and future ties between India and Taiwan. This book is a testimony to his vision and competence in advancing the relationship between our two countries and taking them forward.

5th October 2024

Prof. **Ramu Manivannan**
Professor and Former Head
Department of Politics & Public Administration
School of Politics and International Relations
University of Madras, Chennai-600005, India.

Message from Director General C3S

Add on from the depths of my heart!

– Commodore R S Vasan IN (Retd.)

Readers would be wondering as to what this new heading after the traditional foreword and the Author's note is. I said I will use this heading in a break from the traditions of publishing. Honestly, after that wonderful foreword by Professor Ramu I can hardly add anything more in terms of adding to the honest appreciation of a seasoned diplomat and now a Scholar of eminence. A few months ago, I had the privilege of visiting Professor Ramu Manivannan a very dear friend at the Garden of Peace a school run by him at Vellore. During my visit, I noticed a plaque commemorating the visit of another dear friend, Dr Charles Li, along with his wife, on 26th February 2019. I had the honour and pleasure of meeting and interacting with Dr Li during his memorable tenure as DG TECC in Chennai.

We got around to discussing Dr Li and I was delighted to hear that he had completed a book and had earned his PhD too. This was not at all surprising, given his passion and commitment to promoting bilateral interests and fostering people-to-people connections. He was outspoken, well-meaning and highly respected in the academic and intellectual circles during his stay. I had numerous opportunities to interact with him both formally and informally and he came through as a very genuine friend of India who wanted both countries to work to achieve shared prosperity and progress. His initiatives to engage with the students and industries in Southern India was an effort to bridge the technical and academic gaps that existed due to the way that India and Taiwan evolved over a period of decades.

On the proposal by Dr Ramu to undertake publishing of this book under the aegis of Chennai Centre for China Studies (www.c3sindia.org), I readily agreed to take on this task and C3S is very happy to be able to do this honourable task.

'The book India and Taiwan: A Reality Check' indeed is a labour of love from Dr Charles Li who has brought his keen sense of observation, analytical ability and a desire to contribute to the vibrant relations of the two countries in the form of a book that traces the historical ties, examines the bilateral context of great relevance in the challenging environment in today's challenging environment with China (PRC) leaving no stone unturned to unify Taiwan by force. In this context, there has been an honest effort to analyser the One China Policy and its impact on relations with Taiwan. The synergy that exists due to the convergence of India's Look East Policy with the New Southbound Policy would make it a common goal to work for the future. Dr Li has clearly brought out the difference in approach of the Chinese Confucius centres which have a dubious agenda as part of the influence operations and the Taiwan's Education Centres who are committed to enhancing educational and skill levels of Indian students and technical workers.

The author has made an honest assessment of the present standoff between India and China in the Himalayas, the conflicts in South China Sea, and the emerging challenges in the Indo-Pacific, along with Tibet-related issues and the challenges faced by Tibetans both with in the occupied territory of Tibet by China and refugees in India .

The chapter on Taiwan and India has critically undertaken a SWOT analysis, examining Taiwan's high technology and Industrial capabilities that can complement India's new focus on self-reliance. Utilisation of Taiwan's core strengths to augment the de-risking challenges in the global supply chains have been critically analysed.

Additionally, the nature of quasi diplomatic relations between two democracies has also been analysed in depth identifying the strengths and limitations of such arrangements. With the support of the Indian government, think tanks, academia and more importantly the people of India there are many opportunities for both the countries to elevate the relations to that of a priority strategic partnership.

The book ends on a positive note regarding the emerging ties, strong bonds between the two countries, a desire to work together especially in the post-Covid scenario that has transformed the global landscape. The policy recommendations stem from Dr Charles Li's extensive as a diplomat and with his wide ranging expertise in different parts of the world. This work will undoubtedly contribute to understanding the dynamics of the dynamics shaping the evolving relationship between Taiwan and India which would serve the long-term interests of the two countries as both explore new areas of cooperation and collaboration.

It is an honour for the Chennai Centre for China Studies to publish this seminal work by Dr Charles Li and I have no doubt that it will bridge the gap that exists in understanding the bilateral relations in the context of evolving global challenges. To me, it represents a 'Win–Win' for both the countries who are willing to explore new paradigms of bilateral relations that would contribute to security, stability, and prosperity aligning with the vision of Security and Growth for all in the region (SAGAR). This book is a must-read for all the libraries, think tanks, educational institutions, and policymakers in both countries who would be better equipped to work on parameters to catalyse relations between the two nations.

Let me take this opportunity to wish Dr Charles Li all success in all his future endeavours knowing how determined he is to contribute to and shape the success story of the beautiful relationship between India and Taiwan.

Author's Note

In my childhood, the idea of studying abroad felt like a distant dream that occasionally crossed my mind whenever I watched airplanes soaring through the sky. Growing up in a picturesque township nestled between two majestic mountain ranges in eastern Taiwan, I cherished spending weekends and holidays immersed in nature's wonders—a stark contrast to the textbooks and classrooms of my school days. Learning English in my hometown was quite challenging, given the limited resources available. By the time I reached junior high, I realised I was struggling with the basics of English—pronunciation, vocabulary, grammar, and conversation were all daunting tasks. It was a dark period where I felt lost, with no light at the end of the tunnel. However, a pivotal moment came when I found the courage to seek advice from my new English teacher.

With a warm smile, my teacher suggested I borrow the vinyl records of English textbooks from the academic affairs office and listen to them diligently. It was a revelation. I eagerly borrowed the records, bought a portable record player, and spent hours during winter vacation immersed in listening, repeating, and understanding every word and sentence. This dedicated effort not only put me back on track but also ignited a passion for English that would shape my future. Despite the allure of quality high schools in nearby cities, I chose to stay in my hometown and secured a place in the prestigious Provincial Yuli Senior High School, ranking among the top three in the entrance examination. The following three years were a blend of academic achievement and cherished moments with my parents, as I became increasingly aware of the inevitable separation that college life would bring.

My journey of learning English did not end there. I continued honing my skills by reading magazines, listening to radio programs, and subscribing to an English newspaper called China Post. These habits became part of my daily routine, fuelling my curiosity and preparing me for future opportunities. I persisted in learning English throughout high school by reading English magazine from local book shops and listening to English teaching programs on the radio each week, at a time when neither computers nor internet service was available. Additionally, I subscribed to China Post in my second year of high school. According to my uncle who was a postman at the time, I was one of only two subscribers in town, the other being an English teacher of my senior high school. I thoroughly enjoyed reading China Post for many years. In 1986, after entering my third year of work at the International Telecommunications Administration, I passed the exams to become a Master's programme researcher at the Graduate Institute of European Studies at Tamkang University. Later that year, I passed the two-phase exams and became to join the 20th batch of Taiwan's career diplomats.

After completing a year-long English training program in London in 1988, followed by a twenty months of service at the Ministry of Foreign Affairs in Taipei, I was assigned to Grenada in the Eastern Caribbean in 1990, then to Los Angeles in southern California, USA in 1993, then back to the Ministry of Foreign Affairs in Taipei in 1996. In early 1998 I had an extraordinary honour to serve at our London office and did not expect my tour in London to last for seven years, until I returned to Taipeiin 2005 Unexpectedly, at the end of 2006, I was assigned to lead an ad-hoc team to St. Luca in the Eastern Caribbean and successfully accomplished an almost impossible mission of resuming diplomatic relations with the Government of St. Lucia in 2007. I continued to serve there as the Minister at our Embassy until I was re-assigned to Jakarta, Indonesia, also Minister at our office in 2010. During that time, I completed my on-line Juris Doctor degree, which I had started in 2002. In 2013, I returned to the Ministry in Taipei, and once again, I had an unexpected opportunity to study at the Kennedy School of Government at the Harvard University in Boston, USA. I participated in a four-week intensive Senior Executive Program, which marked my first experience studying on the campus of a prestigious American university. My classmates included senior executives from the US Federal and State governments, military and academic elites, diplomates and civil servants from like-minded countries. What I gained from the programme significantly enhanced and refined my capabilities as a senior Taiwanese diplomat. I remain truly grateful to the Senior Executive Program at the Kennedy School of Government, Harvard University for this invaluable experience!

It was in 2015 when I first encountered Indian culture when I was assigned as the Consul-General at our Chennai Office in Tamil Nadu which covers five states in Southern India, Sri Lanka and the Maldives. At that time, I did not expect to remain in Chennai for more than three years. During my time there, I made good friends, built valuable social networks, enjoyed delicious cuisine, initiated new projects of mutual interest, explored new frontier for our bilateral relations, visited Taiwanese manufacturing facilities, and reflected on the prospects for future collaboration between India and Taiwan.

Southern India is known for its rich cultural diversity, with each state possessing distinct linguistic, cultural, and historical traditions. Tamil Nadu, Andhra Pradesh, Telangana, Kerala, and Karnataka form a mosaic of cultures, with Tamil, Telugu, Malayalam, and Kannada being the predominant languages. In contrast, the Hindi-speaking belt of North India showcases differing cultural practices and historical influences. Tamil Nadu, with its ancient Dravidian roots, has a culture deeply embedded in its history, language, and religion. Tamil is one of the oldest classical languages in the world, with a literary tradition spanning two millennia. It includes works such as literature, Thirukkural, and the epics Silappatikaram and Manimekalai. The language boasts a rich poetic and literary tradition, with a strong focus on grammar and poetics as outlined in ancient texts like the Tolkappiyam. Tamil Nadu is also renowned for its temple architecture, with notable examples like Meenakshi Amman Temple, Brihadeeswarar Temple, and Rameswaram Temple. During my four-and-half year tenure in Chennai, I frequently visited the Kapaleeshwarar Temple in Mylapore, which remains one of my cherished experiences.

The state Tamil Nadu celebrates numerous festivals, including Pongal, a harvest festival, which reflects its agrarian heritage. Bharatanatyam, one of the oldest classical dance forms, originates from Tamil Nadu. Tamil cinema, particularly Kollywood, is a major cultural export and has a significant influence on popular culture. Tamil cuisine features a variety of rice-based dishes, with dosa, idli, and sambar being globally recognised, all of which my family and I thoroughly enjoyed. The cuisine is distinguished using spices, coconut, and tamarind.

Telugu culture, found in Andhra Pradesh and Telangana, is distinguished by its rich artistic heritage and historical significance. Telugu, often referred to as the 'Italian of the East' for its melodic nature, boasts a vast literary tradition. The language holds classical status and is renowned for its poetry and religious texts. Notable works include the Mahabharata by Nannaya, Tikkana, and Errana, and the devotional poems of Annamacharya. The region is home to magnificent temples such as Tirumala Venkateswara Temple and Thousand Pillar Temple. Festivals like Ugadi and Sankranti are celebrated with great fervour. Kuchipudi, a classical dance form, originates from Andhra Pradesh. Telugu cinema, known as Tollywood, plays a major role in the Indian film industry. Telugu cuisine is famous for its spicy and flavourful dishes, including biryani, pappu, and pickles. The use of tamarind and chili is prominent in their cooking.

Kerala, a state that I unfortunately did not have the pleasure of visiting, is often referred to as 'God's Own Country'. Its unique culture is shaped by its geography, history, and the coexistence of diverse religions. Malayalam is the official language, with a rich literary tradition that includes works like Ramacharitam, Manipravalam poetry, and modern novels. The state also has a strong tradition of journalism and print media. Kerala is known for its religious diversity, encompassing Hinduism, Christianity, and Islam. Significant festivals celebrated with great fervour include Onam, Vishu, and Christmas. The state is home to famous temples such as Sabarimala and Padmanabhaswamy Temple, as well as historic churches and mosques. Classical dance forms like Kathakali and Mohiniyattam originate from Kerala, while traditional arts such as Kalaripayattu and Theyyam are integral to its cultural heritage. Kerala cuisine is diverse, focussing on rice, coconut, and seafood. Popular dishes include appam, puttu, and various seafood curries. Coconut oil is widely used with spices like black pepper and cardamom.

Living, traveling and experiencing the cultural diversity of Southern India, represented by Tamil, Telugu, Malayalam, and Kannada cultures, I could sense their commonalities and differences with the Hindi-speaking belt in the North, each with its unique characteristics and traditions. India's ability to maintain political stability and harmonious racial relations amidst this diversity is supported by its democratic framework, constitutional provisions, institutional mechanisms, and inclusive policies, which can be complicated and difficult for foreigners to fully grasp. Through fostering cultural integration, promoting economic and social development, and ensuring robust legal protections, India continues to navigate the complexities of its diverse cultural and linguistic landscape, building a cohesive and stable society.

Conducting in-depth research has been a natural extension of my curious character, and over time, gradually became a key part of my professional responsibilities. However, despite earning an MA degree in Taiwan in 1991, I never had the opportunity to pursue a PhD abroad. Destiny arranged an unmissable path for me, leading me to India, where God opened a window of golden opportunity for me to relocate in Chennai, Tamil Nadu, in 2015. From that point onward, I always aspired to research India and explore how Taiwan could play a meaningful role in India's economic development, firmly believing that India has the potential and momentum to become a new industrial and economic powerhouse at a pace beyond imagination in the coming decade. After hosting numerous Taiwanese delegations and participating in various investment forums organised by the state governments of southern India, I developed the conviction that India is the ideal destination for Taiwanese investors seeking to establish manufacturing and business hub outside of China. During my tenure as Consul-General of Taiwan's office in Chennai, I also became convinced that Taiwan could complement India's efforts to emerge as the next global leader in information and communication technologies (ICT), especially in mobile phone manufacturing and shoemaking industries. As the Indian government unveiled a series of key policy guidelines, such as 'Look East'", 'Act East', 'Invest in India', 'Digital India', '*Atmanirbar Bharat*', I could personally witness the positive momentum and transformation taking place in India. More specifically, I saw the emerging trend in the relations between India and Taiwan. I told myself that someone needed to document and conduct in-depth research, from Taiwan's perspective, on the remarkable milestones achieved in bilateral relations since the Indian government broke diplomatic ties with the Republic of China (Taiwan) in 1949 and established diplomatic relations in early 1950. And I found that there was no one more suitable for this task than myself—a senior Taiwanese diplomat stationed in Chennai, Tamil Nadu—fully convinced of the complementary nature of the relationship between India and Taiwan and passionate about pursuing this research. Life has taken me on a remarkable journey, leading me from Taiwan to various parts of the world, including the UK, the Caribbean, the United States, and back to the UK, with periods spent working in Taipei. It was during my time abroad that my interest in India blossomed, and in 2015, I was drawn to Chennai, Tamil Nadu, in 2015, where I saw immense potential for collaboration between India and Taiwan. Over the years, I have observed the evolving dynamics between the two countries, particularly in economic development and technological advancements. Believing in the complementary strengths of both countries, I eagerly immersed myself into research and advocacy, elaborating on the promising prospects for bilateral relations and mutual growth. As I reflect on my journey—from a dreamy-eyed child to a seasoned diplomat with a passion for cross-cultural exchange and cooperation—I feel deeply grateful for every twist and turn that shaped my path and led me to where I am today.

It all began with an invitation to the Tibetan Cultural Show in 2017 performed by the students from the Tibetan Cultural Academy in appreciation of the Indian government's kindness and support for Tibetan settlements in India, allowing the Tibetans community to preserve their culture for sixty years. After enjoying the first-ever Tibetan cultural performance I had seen, I was deeply moved and impressed by the exquisitely colourful costumes, dance and history of Tibet. That evening, I immediately shared my feelings about the show with Professor Ramu Manivannnan. At the end of our conversation, I enquired about the availability of the PhD Program in Political Science at the University of Madras. Just a few weeks later, with the prompt assistance and guidance of Professor Manivannan, I successfully submitted all the required certificates and documents to apply for a position of PhD Research Scholar at the Department of Politics and Public Administration, University of Madras.

The University of Madras, established in 1857, is one of the oldest and most prestigious universities in India and the first in Tamil Nadu. Its reputation as a well-established and distinguished academic institution .is founded on several factors, including its rich history, academic excellence, research contributions, and notable alumni. The PhD program at the Department of Politics and Public Administration is recognised for its rigorous curriculum, experienced faculty, and significant contributions to the field of political science and public administration. This makes it an excellent choice for students aspiring to pursue advanced research and build careers in academia, policy-making, and public service.

The University of Madras offers over 230 courses across 87 academic departments of post-graduate teaching and research, organised under 18 schools along with 121 affiliated colleges and 53 approved research institutions. These cover a wide range of disciplines including social sciences, sciences, humanities, medicine, and management. The University of Madras and Anna University—the other major university in Chennai focused on engineering and technology—have established themselves as pillars of higher education in Tamil Nadu and India. Their contributions to academic excellence, research, cultural enrichment, and technological innovation have had a profoundly impacted the region's development and continue to shape the future of higher education in India.

I had made frequent visit to the University of Madras, specifically to the Department of Politics and Public Administration for joint events and maintained cordial working relationship with the professors and research scholars involved. After years of up-the-hill effort on my research topic on the chosen topic–The Emerging Ties between India and Taiwan— despite of the challenges posed by the COVID-19 pandemic, I had the greatest privilege of being awarded a PhD degree by the University of Madras in June 2022. I know there are only a few Taiwanese scholars have earned PhD degrees from Indian universities, but I am very likely Taiwan's only alumnus and PhD awardee from the University of Madras in Chennai, Tamil Nadu— and achievement of which I am extremely proud and honoured!

Immediately after I have been awarded the PhD degree, Professor Ramu Manivannnan encouraged me to update and enrich my thesis so that I can publish it as a book, as there is yet to be a comprehensive book, either in India or in Taiwan, that systematically examines with comprehensively the relations between India and Taiwan in a systematic way like my thesis does. Therefore, I have continued to rewrite, update and enrich the contents of my thesis up to mid-June 2024, although tight schedules and travel requirements have prevented me from dedicating as much time to it as I liked. Finally, I believe it is time to submit the entire draft to the publisher in India in July 2024, as the target readers are primarily Indian. My initial intention to clarify and present accurate versions of key issues, that counter the propaganda from the PRC, such as 'China', 'One-China Policy', 'he Republic of China (Taiwan)' 'Taiwan Independence', 'border disputes between India and China', 'Tibet', 'South China Sea', and the 'peace and security of Taiwan Strait'. In addition to expressing my views on these topics, I also aim to advocate for the bilateral and regional interests that India and Taiwan share and, more essentially, to explore the future prospect for the two countries.

I wish to emphasise that I am deeply indebted to Professor Ramu Manivannan, the former Head of the Department of Politics and Public Administration of the University of Madras, for his tireless guidance and instruction on maintaining steady progress over the years from November 2017 to June 2022 and beyond. I am particularly grateful for his attentive advice and insights, provided step by step during our meetings, both on weekdays and weekends, often late into the night during the last six months, as the deadlines for submitting the synopsis and the PhD thesis approached. Without his professional guidance, academic expertise and kind encouragement throughout the journey, I would not have been able to complete my PhD thesis as scheduled. Moreover, Professor Manivannan encouraged me to publish a book based on the thesis upon my passing the Viva Voce and suggested a simple and fitting title for it. I remain profoundly grateful to Professor Manivannan and Madame Manivannan for their unwavering support, friendship, love, and warmth, which made me feel like their family.

I extend my heartfelt gratitude to my fellow Research Scholar Sathish Kumar, now also a PhD awardee of the University of Madras, and to Mr. Sumit Bothra, who is likely a PhD research scholar of the University of Madras, as well as to Mr. Laurent Liu, Miss Kaiyun Peng and many other unsung heroes who contributed their time and efforts to support my research., Their help in encouraging my work. Purchasing books in Taiwan, visiting libraries and bookstores to locate useful archives and data, submitting progress reports, payment receipts, the Synopsis and my PhD thesis—the foundation of this book—especially at a time when the COVID-19 pandemic was affecting us all, in and travel to Chennai had become nearly impossible. I am also grateful to Mr. Terry Chen for his kindness and efficiency in promptly providing me with the most up-to-date data on bilateral trade and investment between India and Taiwan whenever requested. Their timely assistance has been invaluable and is appreciated!

Completing a Ph.D. and publishing this book without interrupting my diplomatic career is a monumental achievement, but it is not a journey one embarks on alone. It requires immense support, understanding, and sacrifices from loved ones. As I reach this significant milestone, I am filled with profound gratitude towards my family—particularly my mother, wife and children—whose unwavering support and sacrifices have been the bedrock of this accomplishment. First and foremost, my job requires me to work far away from my mother. Meeting with her occasionally and spending a few hours chatting away refreshes and reinvigorates my will to move forward, to honour her. The steadfast encouragement from my wife has been my greatest source of strength. Her belief in my abilities, even during times when I slowed down progress, has been a beacon of hope. She took on countless additional responsibilities, allowing me the time and space I needed to immerse myself in my research and demanding workload. Her patience and understanding during late nights, missed family events, and the stress that accompanied this journey have been extraordinary. She has been my cheerleader, and my rock. Without her emotional and practical support, this achievement would have remained a distant dream.

The love, support and patience from my sons and daughters-in-law have been truly remarkable. I know there were many moments over the years when my attention was diverted, and my presence limited due to the demands of my official duties and studies. Yet, they showed unwavering support, understanding the importance and urgency of my work, even when it meant sacrificing precious family time and chatting moments of conversation. Their constant concerns about the progress of my research and the draft of this book often rekindled my enthusiasm and reminded me of the broader impact of my efforts. Their pride in my achievements has been a constant source of motivation, encouraging me to strive harder and aim higher.

The journey to a PhD and further to the publishing of this book is not just about the academic challenges; it is also about managing the emotional rollercoaster that accompanies such a rigorous pursuit. There were moments of intense pressure, setbacks, and self-doubt. Through it all, the unconditional love and support of my family provided the solace and motivation I needed to persevere. They shared in both the struggles and triumphs of this journey, making this achievement a shared victory.

I am deeply grateful for the sacrifices each of them has made. The missed vacations, the quiet understanding during periods of intense focus, and continual encouragement have not gone unnoticed. Each act of support has been a step forward on this path. Their contributions have been as vital as the research itself, and for that, I am eternally thankful.

As I celebrate this accomplishment, I am acutely aware that it is a testament to our collective effort. The PhD degree and by extension this book, are not just mine; they are ours. They symbolise our resilience, commitment, and love. I am profoundly grateful for their unwavering support and for being my pillars of strength and for making this journey possible. I dedicate this achievement to them all!

October 2024 in Taipei, Taiwan, R.O.C. **Charles Li**

Abbreviations

AI	Artificial Intelligence
AICTE	All India Council for Technical Education
APEC	Asia-Pacific Economic Cooperation
APS	The Foundation on Asia-Pacific Peace Studies
ARF	ASEAN Regional Forum
ASEAN	Association of Southeast Asian Nations
ASPI	Australian Strategic Policy Institute
BECA	Basic Exchange Cooperation Agreement
BIA	Bilateral Investment Agreement
BIMSTEC	The Bay of Bengal Initiative for Multi-Sectoral Technical and Economic Cooperation
BRI	Belt-and-Road Initiative
BRICS	Brazil, Russia, India, China, and South Africa
CBI	China-Burma-India Theatre of war
COMCASA	Communications Compatibility and Security Agreement
COVAX	COVID-19 Vaccines Global Access
COVID-19	Coronavirus Disease 2019
CPEC	China-Pakistan Economic Corridor
DPP	Democratic Progressive Party
DTAA	Double Taxation Avoidance Agreement
EAS	East Asian Summit
EU	European Union
FDI	Foreign Direct Investment
FICHET	Foundation for International Cooperation in Higher Education of Taiwan
Foxconn	Hon Hai Technology Group

FTA	Free Trade Agreement
GCTF	Global Cooperation and Training Framework
GDP	Gross Domestic Product
HADR	Humanitarian Assistance and Disaster Relief
ICAO	The International Civil Aviation Organisation
ICMR	Indian Council of Medical Research
ICT	Information and Communication Technology
IHR	International Health Regulations
IISS	International Institute for Strategic Studies
INPR	Institute for National Policy Research
INSTC	International North-South Transport Corridor
INTERPOL	The International Criminal Police Organisation
IOR	Indian Ocean Region
IoT	Internet of Things
ISRO	India Space Research Organisation
IT	Information Technology
ITA	India-Taipei Association
ITRI	Industrial Technology Research Institute
JIIA	Japan Institute of International Affairs
KMT	Kuomintang Party
LAC	Line of Actual Control
LEMOA	Logistics Exchange Memorandum of Agreement
LEO	Low Earth Orbit
MOU	Memorandum of Understanding
MSME	Micro, Small and Medium Enterprises
NGO	Non-Governmental Organisation
NIV	National Institute of Virology
NSPO	National Space Organisation
ODM	Original Design Manufacturer
OEM	Original Equipment Manufacturer
ORF	The Observer Research Foundation
PoK	Pakistan-occupied Kashmir
PSMC	Powerchip Semiconductor Manufacturing Corporation
Quad	Quadrilateral Security Dialogue

RCEP	Regional Comprehensive Economic Partnership
R&D	Research and Development
SAARC	South Asian Association for Regional Cooperation
TAITRA	Taiwan External Trade Development Council Taiwan
ICDF	Taiwan's International Cooperation and Development Fund
TECC	Taipei Economic and Cultural Centre
TFD	Taiwan Foundation for Democracy
The ROC	The Republic of China (1912-1949 in China) (Since 1949 in Taiwan)
The PRC	The People's Republic of China (since 1949)
TSMC	Taiwan Semiconductor Manufacturing Co. Ltd.
UAV	Unmanned Aerial Vehicle
UMC	United Microelectronics Corporation
UNCLOS	United Nations Convention on the Law of the Sea
UNFCCC	United Nations Framework Convention on Climate Change
UNGA	United Nations General Assembly
UNSC	United Nations Security Council
US	The United States
UK	The United Kingdom
WHA	World Health Assembly
WHO	World Health Organisation
WMA	World Medical Association
WPRO	Western Pacific Regional Office
WTO	World Trade Organisation

Definitions

'Taiwan': This term broadly refers to the Republic of China (ROC) established in 1912, nowadays commonly known as Taiwan, which comprises the Island of Taiwan, Pescadores of Penghu, islets of Kinmen, Matsu, Green Island and Orchid Island, among others. To avoid political controversy or ambiguity over the international legal identity of the Republic of China, this thesis refers to it as Taiwan or ROC (Taiwan) throughout.

'China': Today the term refers to the People's Republic of China (PRC) established in 1949. The PRC assumed the China seat from the Republic of China (ROC) in the United Nations Security Council (UNSC) as a Permanent Member in 1971, replacing the Republic of China (ROC). However, in certain academic publications and from the perspectives of Taiwan's few diplomatic allies, "China" means the Republic of China (ROC).

'The New Southbound Policy': A set of policy guidelines initiated by President Tsai Ing-wen of Taiwan during her inauguration in May 2015 to enhance cooperation and exchanges between Taiwan and 18 countries in Southeast Asia, South Asia, Australia and New Zealand. It is a 'people-centred' policy aimed at promoting a new model of economic development that is conducive to regional growth and prosperity. The policy enhances bilateral cooperation in the following areas:

- **Economic Collaboration**: Strengthening cooperation with target countries in supply chains, domestic demand markets, and infrastructure projects.

- **People-to-people Exchanges:** Deepening bilateral programs for scholars, students and industry professionals.
- **Resource sharing:** Promoting bilateral and multilateral cooperation in culture, tourism, medical care, technology, agriculture, and small and medium-sized enterprises.
- **Regional Links:** Building systematic bilateral and multilateral cooperation by enhancing negotiations and dialogue framework with partner countries.
- **'Look East Policy'**: Since 19992, India has regarded South Asian and Southeast Asian countries as important trading partners,alongside the United Kingdom and other European countries. In alignment with this policy, the Indian government has undertaken significant measures to expand trade interactions and has developed several substantial bilateral and multilateral trade relations with these countries.

'Act East Policy': This is a diplomatic initiative by the Indian government to promote economic, strategic, and cultural relations with the Asia-Pacific region at various levels. India's eastward momentum since 1992 has underscored the significance of the Asia-Pacific in its contemporary international relations. 'Act East Policy' and 'Look East Policy' represent two successive phases in the evolution of India's engagement with this region. Since Prime Minister Narendra Modi launched the 'Act East Policy' in 2014, India has expanded its economic strategy to enhance trade and investment relations with the Southeast Asian countries. The policy further extended to Japan, South Korea, and Australia, encompassing political, strategic, and security dimensions.

'Taipei Economic and Cultural Centre in India (TECC)': Established in Delhi in 1995, the TECC serves as an 'unofficial' representative of Taiwan's interests in India and has effectively promoted bilateral relations with the support of the Ministry of External Affairs of India. It is headed by a senior career diplomat of ambassadorial rank from the Ministry of Foreign Affairs of the ROC (Taiwan). In 2012, a TECC branch office was opened in Chennai was set up in 2012 to cover the five southern states of India, led by a senior diplomat of Consul-General rank. Both India and Taiwan agreed to establish Taiwan's third office in Mumbai in mid-2023.

'India-Taipei Association (ITA)': The ITA has served as India's 'unofficial' representation in Taipei, Taiwan, and has been the counterpart of Taiwan's TECC in Delhi since 1995. It is headed by a senior career diplomat from the Ministry of External Affairs of India, designated as the Director-General,who is effectively regarded as India's de facto 'Ambassador' to ROC (Taiwan).

'Make in India': Prime Minister Narendra Modi launched the Make in India initiative on September 25, 2014, to encourage multinational and domestic companies to manufacture their products in India and transform the country into a global manufacturing hub. The initiative aims to raise the manufacturing sector contribution from 16 percent to 25 percent of the Gross Domestic Product (GDP) by the year 2025. To support this goal, several new policy guidelines were introduced to promote foreign direct investment (FDI), implement intellectual property rights and develop the manufacturing sector. This was followed by other contemporary programs, such as, 'Digital India', 'Startup India'.

'One-China Policy': This term originates from the PRC's 'One-China Principle' which essentially demands that governments and major international organisations recognise the PRC or the ROC as the sole legitimate government of all of China, including Taiwan and its outlying islands. The contemporary version of the 'One-China Principle' has been defined and refined by the PRC in order to block the ROC (Taiwan) from gaining diplomatic recognition or participating in any international organisations, especially specialised agencies under the United Nations. This has been enforced since PRC assumed the China seat on the UN Security Council as a permanent member in 1971. The principle asserts that the PRC is the 'sole legitimate representative of China, that 'Taiwan is part of China', and that any matters concerning Taiwan must be consulted with and approved by the PRC. Consequently, countries adopting various versions of the 'One-China Policy commit to refraining from diplomatic engagements with ROC (Taiwan).

1
Introduction

"Taiwan is not a card to be played. It is an opportunity to be grasped."
–Madhav Das Nalapat

India-Taiwan relations have been a rarely touched upon theme across all walks of life in India; it has never attracted as much attention in the country as it does now. Over the past few years, the question of why Taiwan matters to India has frequently reported and discussed in the Indian media.

Since the early 2000s, India;s rapid economic expansion, driven by factors such as liberalisation, globalisation, and a burgeoning middle class has not only elevated India's status as an economic powerhouse but has also increased its influence in global decision-making forums. India's large and youthful population, often referred to as a demographic dividend, has been a significant contributor to its economic success. This demographic advantage has not only fuelled domestic consumption but has also attracted foreign investment and attention from global stakeholders. Consequently, India has emerged as a key player in geopolitics.

Section 1: India's Evolving Global Position

India's sustained economic growth and its remarkable demographic dividend have been pivotal factors in its emergence as a key player in geopolitics. These aspects have not only propelled India's domestic progress but have also significantly enhanced its influence and standing internationally.

Economic Growth and Demographic Dividend

Economic Growth: India has experienced robust economic growth over the past two decades. According to World Bank data, India's GDP growth rate averaged over 7 percent per year from 2000 to 2023, making it one of the fastest-growing major economies globally.

Emergence of a Middle Class: India's sustained economic growth has led to the emergence of a sizable middle class with increased purchasing power. This expansion of the middle-class expansion has fuelled domestic consumption, driving demand for goods and services and contributing to economic diversification.

Foreign Direct Investment (FDI): India's long-term efforts towards integration into global trade networks through trade agreements, export promotion, and participation in international forums have boosted exports and facilitated access to global markets. More importantly, India has attracted substantial FDI over the past two decades.

Global Trade Integration: India's integration into global trade networks, achieved through trade agreements, export promotion, and active participation in international forums has boosted exports and provided greater access to global markets.

Infrastructure Development: India's investments in infrastructure projects, including transportation, energy, telecommunications, and urban development, have improved connectivity, productivity, and quality of life.

Demographic Dividend: India's outstanding demographic dividend cannot not be overstated:

- **Youthful Population:** India has a large and youthful population, with a median age of around 28 years, according to the World Bank (2020). This demographic dividend presents opportunities for a dynamic workforce, innovation, entrepreneurship, and sustained economic growth.
- **Labour Force Participation:** India's labour force participation rate is significant, with a diverse workforce contributing to various sectors such as information technology (IT), manufacturing, agriculture, healthcare, and services.
- **Skill Development:** India's initiatives focused on skill development, vocational training, education, and technology adoption have enhanced

human capital and productivity, aligning with India's demographic advantage.

- **Urbanisation and Consumption**: India's urbanisation trends have led to an increased urban population and changing consumption patterns, driving demand for housing, infrastructure, consumer goods, and services.

India's economic growth and demographic dividend are instrumental in its emergence as a global economic power, influencing trade, investment, and economic policies both regionally and globally. This economic growth not only enhances India's soft power by showcasing its economic potential, innovation capabilities, market opportunities, and investment attractiveness, but also Amplifies this soft power, coupled with diplomatic initiatives, to strengthen India's global influence and partnerships. India's economic growth facilitates regional connectivity, infrastructure development, trade corridors, and integration initiatives positioning the country as a key player in regional cooperation and development. Furthermore, it also fortifies India's strategic alliances with major powers, regional blocs, and international organisations, fostering collaboration in areas such as defence, technology, energy, and climate change.

Foreign policy Shifts and Strategic Partnerships

India's foreign policy has undergone significant shifts in the past two decades, evolving from a predominantly non-aligned stance during the Cold War to a more proactive and strategic approach in the 21st century. A key aspect of India's foreign policy has been the cultivation of strategic partnerships with major powers such as the United States(US), Russia, Japan, and countries in the European Union (EU). These partnerships have encompassed areas such as defence cooperation, trade, technology transfer, and geopolitical alignment.

The Indo- US strategic partnership has witnessed significant growth, with cooperation in defence, counterterrorism, trade, and technology becoming increasingly prominent. The signing of the Civil Nuclear Agreement in

2008 marked a milestone in Indo-US relations, signalling a deeper level of engagement and cooperation between the two countries.

India's engagement with other major powers, such as Russia and China, has also been carefully calibrated to balance its strategic interests and maintain regional stability. Despite occasional tensions, India has sought to cultivate constructive relationships with these powers while asserting its own interests and priorities on the global stage.

Regional Dynamics and Connectivity Initiatives

India's geopolitical influence is also shaped by its role in regional dynamics, particularly in South Asia and the broader Indo-Pacific region. As the largest country in South Asia, India plays a pivotal role in shaping the political, economic, and security landscape of the region. Its relationships with neighbouring countries, including Pakistan, Bangladesh, Sri Lanka, Nepal, and Bhutan, have a significant impact on regional stability and cooperation.

India's efforts to enhance connectivity and infrastructure development in the region through initiatives such as the 'Neighbourhood First' policy, the International North-South Transport Corridor, and the Asia-Africa Growth Corridor have further strengthened its regional influence. These initiatives aim to promote economic integration, connectivity, and cooperation among countries in South Asia, Southeast Asia, and Africa, positioning India as a key player in regional development and connectivity projects.

Multilateral Engagement and Global Governance

India's engagement in multilateral forums and global governance structures has also contributed to its growing influence in geopolitics. As a founding member of institutions such as the United Nations (UN), the World Trade Organisation (WTO), and the BRICS (Brazil, Russia, India, China, South Africa) grouping, India actively participates in shaping global norms, policies, and agendas. India's candidacy for a permanent seat on the UN Security Council (UNSC) reflects its aspiration to play a more prominent role in global governance and decision-making. Its contributions to peacekeeping operations, climate change mitigation efforts, and development assistance programs underscore its commitment to global cooperation and collective action in addressing pressing global challenges. By leveraging its economic potential, fostering strategic alliances, addressing security concerns, and actively participating in global governance, India has positioned itself as a significant actor in shaping the geopolitical landscape of the 21st century.

Current India's international status

The year 2023 marks a significant juncture in India's journey, with its growing influence and multifaceted advancements shaping its status in the international arena. India's economic trajectory has been nothing short of remarkable in recent years. From April 2023, India became the most populous country with a population of 1.43 billion, according to the UN with a land area of 3.3 million sq km (For details, refer to Annexures 1 and 2) The International Monetary Fund confirmed that India replaced the United Kingdom (UK) to become the world's 5th largest economy in 2022 and is expected to surpass Japan and Germany to become the 3rd largest in 2027. For several years India has been the 2nd largest telephone market and holds the 3rd largest pool of scientific and technical manpower globally. India also ranks among the top three global economies in terms of the number of digital consumers, with its market size projected to reach USD 400 billion by 2023-24. It is widely expected that India will achieve 900 million internet subscribers by 2025.

In 2023, India continues to be one of the world's fastest-growing major economies, sustaining a GDP growth rate of 7.2 percent fuelled by strong performance in the services sector and robust consumption, which outpaced nearly all developed nations. India's GDP touched the USD 3.75 trillion mark in 2023. India's burgeoning middle class and its domestic market potential remains unmatched. Key sectors such as IT, pharmaceuticals, and manufacturing have played pivotal roles in driving this growth.

The government's emphasis on economic reforms, ease of doing business, and the 'Make in India' initiative has attracted FDI and bolstered the manufacturing sector. Furthermore, initiatives like 'Digital India' have propelled the technology sector to new heights, enhancing India's global tech influence. However, challenges such as income inequality, unemployment, and infrastructure bottlenecks persist, necessitating sustained efforts to ensure inclusive and sustainable growth.

On the political front, India's democratic credentials remain strong. The government's commitment to upholding the rule of law, freedom of speech, and minority rights continues to be a cornerstone of India's global image. India's foreign policy outlook has evolved significantly, focusing on fostering stronger ties with both traditional and non-traditional allies. The 'Look East Policy' and 'Act East Policy' have deepened India's engagement with Southeast Asia and East Asia, enhancing economic and strategic linkages. In the realm of strategic affairs, India's military capabilities and partnerships have garnered international attention. India's defence modernisation efforts have driven indigenous technological advancements, particularly in nuclear deterrence, missile technology, and space exploration. The successful testing of advanced missile systems and the establishment of a dedicated Space Warfare Command exemplify India's commitment to safeguarding its security interests. The evolving security landscape in the Indo-Pacific region has positioned India as a pivotal player in maintaining regional stability and prosperity. The QUAD alliance, comprising Australia, India, Japan, and the US has gained prominence as a regional security framework, emphasising maritime security, infrastructure development, and humanitarian assistance. Collaborative efforts with the QUAD partners and enhanced defence cooperation with countries like France have bolstered India's strategic influence. The Malabar naval exercises, joint military drills, and intelligence-sharing mechanisms underscore India's commitment to collective security efforts.

Counterterrorism measures remain high on India's strategic agenda, given its history of facing terror threats. Collaborative efforts with international partners, including intelligence-sharing and joint operations, demonstrate India's determination to combat transnational terrorist networks. However, the ongoing challenge of terrorism demands a comprehensive approach that encompasses not only security measures but also socioeconomic development and countering radicalisation.

India's diplomacy has been proactive in addressing global challenges such as climate change and terrorism. The country's role in international forums like the UN and its commitment to the Paris Agreement underscore its determination to contribute to global solutions. However, geopolitical tensions with neighbouring countries, such as China and Pakistan, continue to influence India's foreign policy decisions, necessitating a delicate balance between cooperation and assertiveness.

The success of India's lunar mission Chandrayaan-3 on August 23, 2023 is not only a milestone for India space mission, but also for global space research. The lunar rover Pragyan left The Vikram lander, roamed the south pole of the moon and detected the existence of sulphur and other elements, including aluminium, calcium, iron, chromium, titanium, manganese, oxygen, and silicon… etc. This mission makes India the 4th country in the world, only after the US, Russia and China, to have ever landed on the moon. India's space technology has proven to be one of the front runners, achieving new milestones by launching its first solar study mission in September 2023. This mission has marked a remarkable achievement in India's space exploration history.

At the beginning of 2024, India stands at a pivotal crossroads in its global journey, characterised by remarkable economic growth, dynamic political engagements, and strategic advancements. Its expanding economic prowess, political maturity, and strategic partnerships have elevated its status on the global stage. India's efforts to maintain regional stability, uphold democratic values, and contribute to global solutions underscore its evolving role as a responsible and influential player.

Nevertheless, India's journey forward is indeed marked by challenges, including addressing internal socio-economic disparities, managing complex regional dynamics, and ensuring sustainable development remain crucial imperatives. As the global landscape continues to evolve, India's ability to navigate these challenges while leveraging its strengths be instrumental in defining its future trajectory. This approach will shape India's enduring impact and contribution on the world stage.

Section 2: Taiwan's Strategic Position to Complement India's Strength

Taiwan is an island country covering an area of 36,000 sq km off the southeast coast of Chinese mainland. (For details refer to Annexures 1 and 3) Its official name is the Republic of China (ROC), which has been in existence since 1912 following the revolution on October 10, 1911, when it replaced the Ching Dynasty and became the first republic in Asia. Its 23.5 million hardworking and peace-loving people have managed to transform Taiwan into a full-fledged democracy from decades of totalitarian rule under Martial Law[1] till May 1987 after the government relocated to Taiwan from mainland China in 1949, and when the People's Republic of China (PRC) was established. Taiwan has strengthened its democratic system since 1988, during the presidency of Lee Teng-hui, holding its first-ever direct presidential election in 1996 and achieving its first peaceful transfer of power in 2000 from the Kuomintang (KMT) to the Democratic Progressive Party (DPP). This, demonstrated that Taiwan, as part of the broader ethnic Chinese community, could effectively implement the principles and values of democracy and uphold the rule of law. With limited natural resources, Taiwan's economy relies heavily on trade and bilateral investment. Since the early 1990s, Taiwan's outbound investment has expanded, initially focussing on China. In 2026, Taiwan's new Southbound Policy further redirected investment towards Southeast Asia, enhancing economic diversity and reducing over-reliance on China..

India's 'Look East Policy' and later rebranded as the 'Act East Policy' initially targeted ASEAN countries and expanded to encompass wider regional engagement. While these policies also paved the way for India to target Taiwan for more substantial investment in the 1990s, followed by the establishment of "unofficial" relations, with unofficial representative offices established in each other's capitals in 1995. However, the scale of relations between Taiwan and India have remained minimal in both scale and intensity, and hardly demonstrate a successful application of the 'Look East Policy' or 'Act East Policy', as compared with India's relations with China, Japan and South Korea. Intriguingly, enough, some scholars argue that Taiwan remains 'off the radar' of India's Act East Policy.[2] However, as of early

2024, the question remains that, are there any concrete developments that reflect a shift away from these discouraging arguments or provide evidence of a growing relationship between India and Taiwan? An in-depth study is required to measure the development of relations between the two countries, particularly in the context of the ups and downs of India-China interactions since 1950 and more so in recent years.

Over the last three decades, Taiwan has invested an incredibly large amount in China and Vietnam drawn by of lower labour and land costs, among other factors, since the 1990s. India, as a free democracy with abundant supply of skilled labour and land, offers many essential advantages that China and Vietnam do not possess. The government and potential investors in Taiwan have long aspired for India to attract far more substantial investment from Taiwan, where it not been hindered by political constraints and mutual misunderstandings. An emerging trend of Taiwanese investment in India began to take shape around the beginning of the 21st century, when the cumulative FDI inflows from Taiwan to India were valued at USD 825.59 million from April 2000 to March 2023. As of July 2023, in terms of foreign exchange reserves, Taiwan ranks 6th with USD 564.83 billion, two places behind India's reserves of USD 603.87 billion, which ranks 4th among 194 countries worldwide.

Bilateral trade between India and Taiwan reached USD 7 billion in 2019, up from USD 2 billion in 2006, reflecting 2.5 times growth. This made India, Taiwan's 16th largest trade partner, 14th largest export destination, and 18th largest import source. The bilateral trade volume between India and Taiwan totalled USD 8.45 billion in 2022, representing an increase of 9.8 percent over the previous year. India's exports to Taiwan amounted to USD 3.14 billion, while Taiwan's exports to India stood at USD 5.31 billion.

In addition, technology enjoys a high priority for the Indian government. Making the Indian people more science-centric is regarded as one of the key elements for India's economic growth. Among the most attractive investment destinations for technology transactions, India ranks 3rd in the world. As of September 2020, India also ranked among the top 15 globally for indicators such as Information and Communication Technology (ICT), services exports, graduates in science and engineering, government online services and research and development (R&D)-intensive global companies.

Technological Strengths of Taiwan

Taiwan holds significant technological strengths and strategic importance, particularly in the realms of semiconductor manufacturing, electronics, and innovation. These aspects are crucial for India's aspirations in technology, economic growth, and global positioning.

- **Semiconductor Manufacturing**: Taiwan is a global leader in semiconductor manufacturing and is home to Taiwan Semiconductor Manufacturing Company (TSMC), one of the largest semiconductor foundries worldwide. TSMC's advanced fabrication technologies, including 5nm, 3nm and the upcoming 2nm processes, are critical for producing high-performance chips used in smartphones, computers, automotive electronics, and emerging technologies like artificial intelligence (AI) and Internet of Things (IoT). As of 2022, TSMC accounted for over 50 percent of the global semiconductor foundry market share and around 92 percent of the advanced process node market share (7nm and below).
- **Electronics and ICT Industry**: Taiwan boasts a robust electronics and ICT industry. Companies such as Foxconn, Asus, and Acer are prominent players in manufacturing consumer electronics, computer hardware, and networking equipment. Taiwan's expertise in hardware design, manufacturing, and assembly has made it a key hub for global electronics supply chains. Taiwan's electronics exports totalled around USD 178.71 billion in 2023, with a diverse range of products, including semiconductors, displays, smartphones, and computer peripherals.
- **Innovative and Research**: Taiwan invests heavily in R&D, fostering a culture of innovation. Institutions like the Industrial Technology Research Institute drive technological advancements in areas such as, semiconductors, green energy, biotechnology, AI, and robotics.

Taiwan Strategic Significance to India

Taiwan has been optimistic about its investments in India since the inauguration of Narendra Modi as Prime Minister in 2014, alongside India's 'Make in India' campaign and in synergy with the Taiwan's New Southbound Policy in 2016. To understand investors' operational situations, address challenges requiring immediate attention, and gather recommendations on strategies to attract more Taiwanese investment, India's Ministry of Commerce and Industry organised the first ever Roundtable meeting for Taiwanese investors in India on December 5, 2019, chaired by the Permanent Secretary. Years earlier, the India government had set up the Taiwan Plus Desk under 'Invest India' to offer one-stop service to promote, facilitate, and retain Taiwanese Investments in India. The Indian government recognises that countries like the US, South Korea, Japan, Taiwan and Singapore are keen to diversify their supply chains to India. Seizing this golden opportunity, Tamil Nadu, already a favoured investment destination, has taken pro-active steps by constituting a special Investment Promotion Task Force, under the Chairmanship of the Chief Secretary to attract investments. Andhra Pradesh, Karnataka, Puducherry and many other states are also implementing effective measures to attract Taiwanese investments. Between 2020 and 2023, Chief Ministers of southern states, one after another, held discussions with Taiwan's Director-General based in Chennai, Tamil Nadu.

- **Semiconductor Supply Chain**: Taiwan's prowess in semiconductor manufacturing holds immense strategic importance for India's technology sector. With India's ambitions to become a major player in semiconductor manufacturing, collaborations with Taiwanese companies and access to their advanced technologies can accelerate the development of India's semiconductor ecosystems.
- **Technology Partnerships**: Collaboration between Indian and Taiwanese companies can lead to technology transfer, joint R&D initiatives, and knowledge sharing. This can enhance India's capabilities in areas such as chip design, fabrication, and electronic manufacturing, supporting initiatives such as the 'Make in India' and 'Atmanirbhar Bharat' programs.

- **Global Competitiveness:** Leveraging Taiwan's technological strengths can enhance India's global competitiveness across various industries. Access to high-quality components, advanced manufacturing processes, and expertise in emerging technologies can empower Indian companies to compete effectively in international markets.
- **Strategic Alliances:** Strengthening ties with Taiwan can contribute to India's broader strategic alliances in the Indo-Pacific region. Taiwan's geopolitical significance, particularly in the context of the Taiwan Strait, aligns with India's interests in maintaining peace, stability, and freedom of navigation in the region. Building robust ties with Taiwan not only supports India's economic and technological ambitions but also advances broader strategic interests in the Indo-Pacific region.

Taiwan's technological strengths, especially in semiconductor manufacturing, electronics, and innovation, present significant opportunities for collaboration and strategic partnerships with India. By leveraging Taiwan's expertise, India can accelerate its technological growth, strengthen its industrial capabilities, and enhance its global competitiveness.

The Taiwanese side is increasingly energetic in facilitating India-bound investment. Fewer than 150 Taiwanese companies have invested more than USD 2.3 billion in India, creating over 100,000 job opportunities. Communication Technology India was held in Mumbai on November 24, 2020 as an online business networking event focussing on Smart City and IoT Solutions for the Asian Market. Had it not been for the COVID-19 pandemic, Taiwan Expo 2020 would have taken place from December 16-18, 2020, following annual events like the Smart City Summit and Taiwan Expo since 2017. Trade and investment promotion activities over the past two decades, held in both India and Taiwan have enhanced mutual understanding and appreciation of the strengths and potential that both countries possess. The Indian government and people are naturally sensitive to investment from China in certain key sectors owing to security and strategic concerns. However, such concerns do not pose significant obstacles with Taiwan. Most of the Taiwanese companies operating in India enjoy substantial economic and social benefits that result from the synergy of

India and Taiwanese entrepreneurship, indirectly fostering strong bonds of friendship between Taiwanese and Indian partners. As Madhav Das Nalapat aptly stated, "Taiwan is not a card to be played. It is an opportunity to be grasped."[3] There are clear signs of growing Taiwanese investment in India, facilitated by the supportive policies and the practical needs of Taiwanese companies seeking to resettle and expand their operations in India amid the US-China trade war. It is expected more blue-chip Taiwanese companies will establish operations in India, demonstrating that Taiwan should be not only be 'on the radar of India's Act East Policy', but also regarded as a natural business partner for India in the 21st century.

In the current strategic context, India's appointment of seasoned diplomat Gourangalal Das as the Director-General of the India-Taipei Association (ITA) coincided with Taiwan's appointment of Ambassador Baoshuan Ger as the Representative of the Taipei Economic and Cultural Centre in India (TECO) in mid-2020.Ambassador Chung-kwang Tien, Ger's predecessor, assumed the role of Deputy Minister in Taiwan's Ministry of Foreign Affairs after completing his seven year tenure in New Delhi. Three years later, the Indian government appointed Manharsinh L Yadav, the Director in the Prime Minister's Office, as the Director-General of the ITA. He assumed his new role in Taipei in August, 2023. It is generally believed that the emerging relations between India and Taiwan, based on the solid foundation laid by each Director-General of ITA and Representative of TECO, will continue to deepen and consolidate, expanding to cover wider areas of investment including ICT, trade, health, environment, and education.

The COVID-19 pandemic caused unexpected economic upheavals and supply constraints, prompting countries with manufacturing expertise to review their global supply chain deployment, which had become overly dependent on just a few countries. In this regard, India and Taiwan can play pivotal roles in advancing the ambitious initiative set forth by US president Joe Biden in February 2021, when he directed his administration to conduct year-long reviews of six sectors and a 100-day review of four product classes on which American companies are heavily dependent through imports. These include semiconductors and advanced packaging, critical minerals and materials, large-capacity batteries for vehicles and grid storage, and active pharmaceutical ingredients.[4] A report from the White House, published in February 2022 explicitly stated that US must reduce its dependence on China and other geopolitical competitors for essential products. The report also expresses support for a 'friend-shoring' approach "to offshore supply chains, focusing on building relationships with allies when conducting trade policy".[5] Taiwan and India are already engaged across these relevant sectors. At the same time, new opportunities are emerging for India and Taiwan to develop a much closer partnership, covering many fields, despite existing political constraints.

Section 3: Chapterisation

Chapter I: 'Introduction' elaborates on the basic background information regarding the relations between India and Taiwan, highlighting the emergence of India's international status and strategic objectives, along with Taiwan's technological strengths and its significance to India. This sets the stage for further discussion in the following chapters. The first part of Chapter II: 'Historical Ties between India and China' explores the relationship between India and China, which likely began millennia ago. The two ancient civilisations share a great deal of cultural heritage, particularly through Buddhism. Historical records indicate that interactions between India and China took place bilaterally, both over land and sea, via the so-called Silk Route. In the 1st Century AD proficient Buddhist scholar-monks were invited to China to spread Buddhism, followed by exchanges of scholar-monks travelling from China to India and from India to China. On the Indian side, thousands of Buddhist scholar-monks such as Kumarajiva (343-413) and Bodhidarma (483-540), made significant contributions to the development of Buddhism in China and East Asia. They were instrumental in translating and preaching Buddhist scriptures, leaving behind a remarkable collection in Chinese, which continues to be read today, reflecting the magnitude of their contribution over a thousand years later.

On the Chinese side, Faxian (342-424), Xuanzang (600-664), and Yijing (635-713) are the most well-known Chinese scholar-monks who travelled to India. They studied under Indian scholars in ancient languages and translated Buddhist scriptures into Chinese, both during their journeys back to China and later when entrusted by imperial courts to continue translating the hundreds of scriptures they had collected. Thanks to their efforts, and those of numerous scholar-monks who followed, Buddhism became localised and transformed, incorporating elements of Taoism and Confucianism. This transformation gave rise to Mahayana Buddhism with distinct Chinese characteristics. The second part of Chapter II examines the definitions and connections between Taiwan, officially known as the Republic of China and the historical concept of 'China' before 1949 when PRC came into being. The third part discusses major incidents during the period when the ROC held China's seat at the UN and the UNSC as one of the five Permanent Members from, 1945 to 1971, along with and its interactions with India during that time.

Chapter III: 'India and Taiwan Relations in a Bilateral Context' analyses how momentum was built up for bilateral relations between India and Taiwan against a backdrop of international circumstances conducive to a natural synergy of mutual understanding. More importantly, it examines how both sides engaged with each other, based on their respective perceptions of the other's value, signalling their stance to a looming common opponent, the PRC. India's 'One-China Policy' has had a persistent impact on India's relations with Taiwan. The bottom line of India's One-China Policy, since 1949, has created an invisible ceiling and frame for Taiwan. However, a significant upturn in India-Taiwan relations took place when Lee Teng-hui, Taiwan's first locally born President, initiated the 'Pragmatic Diplomacy' from 1988 to 2000, marking a shift away from of claiming to represent all of China. Friendly countries seized the opportunity to strengthen their relations with Taiwan without necessarily challenging China's One-China Policy.

After 1971, economic and political relations between India and Taiwan were lukewarm and detached, even though a clear strengthening trend followed the 1962 conflict between India and China. The grand design and vision of India's Look East Policy, and later the Act East Policy extended India's horizon, bringing Taiwan into greater focus. With the establishment of the unofficial Taipei Economic and Cultural Centre in New Delhi in 1995, and the simultaneous founding of the ITA in Taipei, the two sides succeeded in elevating their bilateral relations to historical heights, despite political constraints. The New Southbound Policy, introduced by President Tsai Ing-wen in 2016 prioritised India and 17 other countries as key destinations for Taiwanese investment out of China. Since the two terms of Chen Sui-bian's presidency, there has been a wide range of intermittent interactions that have resulted in substantial development in India-Taiwan relations.

On the education front, political implications, cultural infiltrations and interference in academic programmes under the guise of the Chinese Confucius Institutes have raised concerns and prompted reactions in many western countries. In contrast Taiwan Education Centres, which differ significantly from the Chinese Confucius Institutes in many aspects, have gained positive recognition and appreciation from partner universities in both India and western democracies. As of the end of 2023, there are 31 Taiwan Education Centres across India. A detailed comparison of the original grand design, missions, modus operandi, current effect, and feedback from India and the rest of the world regarding these two educational entities is presented for discussion.

There have been several cases of high-level exchange visits, including India's former President APJ Abdul Kalam's visit to Taipei in December 2010, marking the first ever instance of a former head of state of the Republic of India visiting the ROC in Taiwan since 1949. Both Ma Ying-jeou and Tsai Ing-wen also had stopped over in or visited India before assuming the presidency. Additionally, Parliamentary exchanges have also played an important role in fostering bilateral relations between India and Taiwan.

Although there are no formal diplomatic relations between India and Taiwan, both sides have signed a series of agreement and memoranda of understanding (MoU). Notably, these agreements were signed by Taiwan's Ambassador Chung-Kwang Tien of the Taipei Economic and Cultural Centre (TECC) in New Delhi and ITA Director General Sridharan Madhusudhanan, laying a solid foundation for closer India-Taiwan relations. These agreements and MOUs, include binding provisions that give the relevant authorities in both governments a 'legal' duty and the authority to implement them. They were signed by the Heads of Mission of the official representatives of the Republic of India and ROC on Taiwan respectively. Track 1.5 security dialogues also took place involving think tanks, military and civil officials from both sides during the DPP's tenure (2000-08), although these dialogues ceased when the KMT regained power in 2008. A significant milestone was the establishment of the TECC in Chennai in September 2012 to oversee Taiwan's interests in the five southern Indian states—Tamil Nadu, Andhra Pradesh, Telangana, Karnataka and Kerala—as well as Sri Lanka and the Maldives. In summer of 2023, both India and Taiwan announced their agreement to establish Taiwan's third office in Mumbai, signalling the need to address Taiwan's growing investment interests in western India. This development reflects the emerging trend of bilateral relations between the two countries, which have now reached a point where an additional office is necessary to manage Taiwan's regional interests effectively. There have also been conflicting territorial claims rooted in the ROC Constitution. Despite these complexities, the pragmatic need for strategic and security cooperation between India and Taiwan persist.

The government in Taiwan has quietly shifted away from strict adherence to the ROC Constitution to reflect the reality of the PRC's and ROC's respective jurisdictions over the past seventy years. Nonetheless, border and territorial disputes persist between India and the PRC, with the latter increasingly engaging in assertive military manoeuvres along the Himalayan borders. Some scholars and analysts have even argued for playing the Taiwan Card to confront the PRC. India's national sentiments against China, as well as Chinese brands, goods, and Apps grows stronger whenever the People's Liberation Army (PLA) causes casualties on the Indian side along the border. India and Taiwan also share common interests in South China Sea and the Indo-Pacific Strategy, as all Taiwanese westbound maritime routes pass through the South China Sea and the Indian Ocean. Maintaining freedom of navigation in these waters requires joint and vigorous efforts among like-minded countries. Another historical issue, Tibet, has at times posed a barrier to relations between India and ROC and continues to affect India-PRC relations. However, with the shift in the ROC constitution, Taiwan's territorial claims over Tibet are no longer an issue, paving the way for smoother bilateral relations between India and Taiwan.

Chapter IV: 'Taiwan and India: An Evaluation of Strengths and Potential' provides detailed insights into how Taiwan, as a hidden manufacturing powerhouse and investor, has long been underestimated in terms of its manufacturing competence and footprint, particularly in China, Southeast Asia, and increasingly in India. Evidence and data are presented to explain why Taiwan matters to India and vice versa. Taiwan's industrial capabilities are highly valued by the countries across the globe. Since the 1990s, Taiwan has been a leading manufacturer of electronic components. Notably, it has more iPhone component suppliers than any other country. Taiwan's total overseas investment amounts to hundreds of billions of US dollars, primarily directed towards Mainland China, ASEAN countries, India, and the rest of the world. This diversification strategy aims to mitigate manufacturing risk and reduce operational costs. As restructuring global supply chain becomes a sensitive issue among industrialised nations worldwide, Taiwan has consolidated its unique position through international collaborations, offering integrated and significant hardware manufacturing capabilities for ICT industries.

The Tesla supply chain also demonstrates a significant share of Taiwanese components. Over the years, Taiwan's strengths in supplying all major automakers have secured it an irreplaceable position in complementing Tesla's weakness. As one Taiwanese major manufacturer put it, "Taiwan's biggest weaknesses happen to be in areas where Tesla is strong". In an effort to avoid overreliance on China, specifically in the ICT and medical sectors, the US and Taiwan have reached an agreement to cooperate in restructuring the global supply chain and, more importantly, to make it more resilient. The purpose of the partnership is to encourage partners either to bring supply chains closer to home or build them in like-minded countries, such as India and ASEAN countries, to ensure that supply chains remain secure and free from political coercion by malicious regimes. The tremendous economic and industrial benefits that Taiwan has enjoyed can be attributed to its quasi-diplomatic model, which allows Taiwan to engage with other countries and develop bilateral and multilateral relations in their mutual interest, even without formal recognition. Several key points highlight India's strengths and potential for Taiwan's business and investment, aligning with the efforts of Invest India at the Union level, and Investment Promotion Organisations at the state level to attract inward investments from Taiwanese enterprises operating in China, Southeast Asia, and beyond. Essentially, India and Taiwan could take bold steps to engage on a highly anticipated issue from the Taiwanese side: the launch of Free Trade Agreement (FTA) negotiations. Sime scholars suggest that support is growing within the Indian government to formally begin negotiations on a trade deal with Taiwan, as both countries' relations with China deteriorate. Alternatively, both sides could explore an institutionalised framework to further integrate Taiwan's ICT manufacturing capabilities with India's Atmanirbhar Bharat policy goals.

Chapter V: 'Conclusion' summarises the emerging ties between India and Taiwan. Furthermore, Taiwan and India possess supplementary strategic and technological strengths, without national security concerns or border disputes. It is in the interest of both countries to further explore broader areas of collaboration in science and technology, including research and applications in AI, IoT, national defence, aerospace industries, medical health, and pharmaceutical development between governments and businesses, even within the constraints of diplomatic and political coherence. Coordination and collaboration in international organisations and mechanisms can be further strengthened through platforms such as the Raisina Dialogue, Quad, Exercise Malabar, RCEP, Indo-Pacific Initiative, COVID Vaccine research, World Health Assembly, UN Framework Convention on Climate Change, International Civil Aviation Organisation (ICAO), INTERPOL, and others. India supports Taiwan's meaningful participation in these frameworks by initiating bilateral mechanisms to elevate and enhance relations with Taiwan to a higher level. Taiwan has enhanced quasi-diplomatic engagement with the majority of countries worldwide under the umbrella of 'unofficial' relations. A wider scope of collaboration between India and Taiwan can still be explored, even within the framework of geopolitics and realpolitik. The final section presents policy recommendations, raising several creative and constructive points for the consideration by the authorities in both India and Taiwan. These recommendations aim to maximise benefits meaningful engagement, particularly in the context of the US-led restructuring of world supply chain for semiconductors, high-capacity batteries, pharmaceuticals, active pharmaceutical ingredients, rare earths, and more.

Section 4: Literature Review

The following books and publications are essential references that have contributed significantly to the writing of this book, particularly in articulating consistent viewpoints to present the author's understanding and analysis on India and Taiwan relations:

- Jagannath P. Panda, ed., *India and China in Asia: Between Equilibrium and Equations,* includes a contributor who echoes a statement made by Jagannath P. Panda in one of his 2016 publications asserting that "India-Taiwan relations are a lesser studied subject in the international relations academic discipline." The same contributor also concludes by arguing for India and Taiwan to perceive China threat and find ways to boost bilateral defence cooperation, particularly the security intelligence cooperation the PLA.[6]
- Joe Thomas Karackattu, *The Case for a Pragmatic India-Taiwan Partnership*, highlights the importance for India adopting a pragmatic approach towards Taiwan, He notes that while China holds comparative advantages in investing in large infrastructure projects, Taiwan's excels in small-and medium-sized enterprises, particularly in ICT and agriculture, including smart farming. Karackattu s recommends that India adopt a more flexible policy towards Taiwan, enabling Taiwan to access to India's vast and expanding market. This approach would Taiwan to re-orient its trade and investment goals and re-define its broader economic objectives in India by establishing closer partnership. He also argues that to ensure that the India-Taiwan relationship is a durable and long-lasting, objectives such as setting up manufacturing supply chains in India and cultivating a South Asia Silicon Valley should be actively pursued.
- B. R. Deepak, *India and China: Foreign Policy Approaches and Responses.* The author is a one of the most renowned experts in India on China-related issues, with long-term personal engagement with Chinese academic institutions following his university graduation. The book consists of six sections, featuring 65 articles covering various areas of

interest including 'Contemporary Issues', 'High-Level Visits', 'Border, Tibet, Nepal and Pakistan', 'The Pacific Conundrum', India-China and Africa', and 'Inside China'. The author compares the sharp differences between China and India following China's 'reform and open door' policy introduced in the late 1970s. He discusses and observes the reasons behind China's rise during his frequent visits to the country since 1996. He contends that the roots of discord between India and China can be traced back to the imperialist expansion in the Himalayas, which have regional and global dimensions. The author argues that three relationships—India-China, India-US and US-China—will define the century, with India striving to balance the interests of different stakeholders. Overtime, successive Indian governments have initiated policies conducive to creating a peaceful, stable and prosperous neighbourhood, while other policies have positioned India as a more active player in global institutions. One of the main forces driving global geo-economics, according to the author is China's 'One Belt One Road' (OBOR) strategy, supported by overcapacity, financial assistance, and technology. Meanwhile, India's globalisation initiatives including 'Make in India', 'Startup India', 'Digital India', and 'Smart City' projects have also significantly impacted its economic development. The author warns that, under the US Indo-Pacific grand strategy, if nations fail to adapt to each other, rising tensions and flashpoints may escalate into conflict zones. However, if they adapt well, the Asia-Pacific region could drive the world economy and contribute to world growth. He further argues that India's balancing and hedging strategies have kept it outside the Chinese OBOR initiative, partly due to the trust deficit between India and China. In addition, the US and Japan are influencing factors in India's decision not to join the Chinese initiative. The author echoes an argument made by Prof. Raja Mohan in September 2015, stating that "being nice to all is not an adequate strategy to cope with the historic power shift unfolding in Asia." India must clearly define the degree of its strategic autonomy is, and decide whether it will act as challenger, follower or contributor to the world order. The 65 articles in this book cover wide range of domestic, regional and global issues affecting India,

China and many other countries. The perspectives offered are very useful for academicians, policy formulators, researchers and students tin their analysis and formulations.[7]

- Rajiv Sikri, *Challenge and Strategy: Rethinking India's Foreign Policy*. The author a career diplomat aims to raise awareness of the challenges India faces in its foreign policy in the 21st century, encouraging an informed debate on policy options among young Indians, and global readers. The book emphasises trends over specific events, regions over individual countries and long-term factors over minor details. Sikri introduces some fresh based on his extensive experience in foreign affairs as an Indian diplomat. One notable chapter is Chapter 7, which touches on India's 'Look East' Policy includes a brief discussion on India's relations with Taiwan. Here Sikri critiques the limitations of India's 'One-China Policy'. While India, does not officially recognize Taiwan, both India and Taiwan established offices in each other's capitals to manage bilateral interests. India's interactions with Taiwan have generally been discreet, primarily at non-official or mid-level government levels. Despite this Taiwan has emerged as an important economic partner for India in East Asia and Taiwan, offering advanced technologies, substantial investment resources, and notable trade potential. The author pints out that only after 2006—presumably as a signal of India's displeasure with China with various political and military provocations by China—did India initiate more overt exchanges with Taiwanese political leaders. The author views this as a positive shift in India's Taiwan policy, suggesting that Taiwan could serve as a strategic platform observing China's activities. Nonetheless, the author also highlights the India to keep a close eye on the state of Taiwan-China relations, especially after the KMT came to power in the 2008 elections in Taiwan, as the KMT allegedly favours reunification with China and shares the Chinese government's stance on the border issues It is worth noting that this reflects a serious misunderstanding regarding the stance of any KMT-led Taiwanese government on the China and India border issue; however, it reflects India's hidden concerns. Furthermore, the author suggests that any closer Taiwan-China relations could allow China to redeploy many of its missiles and other military assets, currently targeted at Taiwan, to areas such as Tibet and Xinjiang. This redeployment could alter military balance and create security concerns for India. This viewpoint, to a certain degree demonstrates a pragmatic mindset within India with regard to China's ongoing threats and territory claims along the border with India. While this may appear theoretically valid, it underestimates China's capacity to manufacture and deploy its missiles against any neighbouring country as part of strategic build up. Even if Taiwan were to maintain cordial and peaceful relations with China, the latter's insistence on unification with Taiwan—and its determination to use force, if necessary—would remain unchanged. Therefore, it is misleading to imply that heightened tensions between China and Taiwan would serve India's interests in reducing the threat from China. On the contrary, India should enhance and upgrade its relations with Taiwan, and many other friendly countries as well, to develop more efficient ICT manufacturing capabilities for export, achieve its economic development goals, and to better secure India's key role in the Indo-Pacific Region.[8]

- Prashant Kumar Singh, *Transforming India-Taiwan Relations: New Perspectives*. The author argues that, while India does not recognise as a sovereign state, functional ties, cooperation and people-to-people relations could be developed as a separate category without attaching any diplomatic, political or strategic meanings. He proposes several pragmatic suggestions to enhancing India-Taiwan relations, asserting that closer engagement with Taiwan would lead India to have a more informed Taiwan policy. Taiwan's strategic location in the South and the East China Seas, and its unique geographical status also offer India valuable insights into the Asia-Pacific region. More importantly, Taiwan has expertise in critical areas such as the Chinese PLA, China-Japan tensions, and the dynamics of Sino-US relations. As both the US and Japan's support the One China Policy, their relations with Taiwan are limited, which as a result, makes Taiwan a neutral observer in regional politics. India could thus tap into Taiwan's consultative potential. As a thriving and industrialised economy, Taiwan is closely integrated with the international economy, standing among the world's leading trading countries. It is particularly noted for its global manufacturing capabilities in foundries integrated circuit packages, blank optical discs, mask Read-Only Memories, notebooks, tablets, Liquid Crystal Display monitors, motherboards, wireless local area network customer premises equipment, cable modems, and intelligent smart phones. Taiwan's high standards in agro-industries, including food-processing, precision machinery, business environment, research and development, innovation, and creativity are recognised worldwide. Taiwan also ranks highly in international rating by agencies like International Institute for Management Development, Business Environment Risk Intelligence and World Economic Forum. Furthermore, its higher education system ranks quite high. Ever since the New Southbound Policy was announced in 2016, India has become an important destination for Taiwan's manufacturing companies. Taiwanese FDI can contribute to India's manufacturing, infrastructure and other sectors. India and Taiwan can make a case for mutual benefit by being substantial complementary economies, as India's IT software and design advantages complement Taiwan's hardware manufacturing capabilities. This book addresses Taiwan as it pragmatically exists in the world today, without discussing its legal status. However, Taiwan remains an important factor in the East Asian security scenario and any formula that would downgrade Taiwan's international standing is unacceptable to all living in Taiwan. The author concludes by arguing that accelerated interaction and cooperation in functional areas between India and Taiwan would also contribute to increased mutual awareness. Whether Taiwan would eventually unify with China, or the status quo would persist, or some other form of cross-strait relations would emerge, is difficult to predict that at this moment. For India, to study and engage Taiwan is important irrespective of the scenarios.[9]

- Zorawar Daulet Singh, *Power & Diplomacy: India's Foreign Policies During the Cold War*. This book attempts to reconstruct the worldviews and strategies that underlay Indian geopolitics during first three decades of the Cold War. It compares the significant foreign policy shift between the Jawaharlal Nehru's peace-maker period and Indira Gandhi's security-seeker period, covering 1947-64, 1966-77 and 1980-84 respectively, by redefining some of the fundamental precepts on India's role in South and the Greater Asia. The author argues that there was a fundamental distinction between the interpretations of non-alignment in the Nehru and Indira Gandhi periods. He articulates that the focus of Nehru's foreign policy was on developing an expansive regional role, where India conceived an alternative bridging function for itself in the East-West competition in Asia, rather than exploiting the bipolar struggle for India's material advantage. Indian statecraft, through Nehru and Krishna V. K. Menon, during the Formosa (Taiwan) crisis of 1954-5 exemplified this quest to promote an 'Asian peace area' where the two principal great powers of PRC and US could limit their antagonism and learn to co-exist in the Western Pacific. The second Indochina crisis in 1965-6 illustrates Indira Gandhi's Asia policy marking the final displacement of Nehru's peacemaker role conception with an alternative security seeker role. The 1971 crisis in East Pakistan and the Sikkim crisis in 1975 are examples that highlight Indira Gandhi's ambitious geopolitical goals. In the author's opinion, Nehru's foreign policy leaned more towards the West than the East, favouring the UK in the early 1950s and shifting towards the Soviet Union by the mid-1960s. Nehru had focused on a wider conception of security where the Asian system rather than the sub-region was the main arena for order building. In comparison, Indira Gandhi asserted a more focussed approach within a narrower subcontinental realm. According to this book India's foreign policy has always been about choices rather than merely structural necessity. More specifically, India did not contemplate aligning its moral and material capacity solely with any single bloc. Nehru was reluctant to impose India's will on its periphery, while Indira Gandhi was more willing to do so in Southern Asia. Indian statecraft during the Cold War is a foundational element its strategic culture, and Indian security thinking and behaviour in the emerging multipolar world will likely carry forward aspects of this historical legacy. One critic challenges Indira Gandhi's leadership, arguing that the Simla Agreement, signed on July 2, 1972, was a disadvantageous peace deal with Pakistan following the 1971 war and that the subsequent Delhi Agreement failed to transform India's victory into a durable peace. After the war, India held over 15,000 sq km of Pakistan's territory and 93,000 its soldiers—nearly one-quarter of its army. However, India gave Pakistan everything it wants: the territory it lost to India in the war and the safe return of all its soldiers without anyone of them being held responsible for the genocidal campaign in what is now Bangladesh.[10]

- Juan Pablo Cardenal, Jacek Kucharczyk, Grigorij Meseznikov, Gabriela Paleschova, *Sharp Power: Rising Authoritarian Influence.* This book contains an introduction and five Chapters, of which the introduction is written by Christopher Walker and Jessica Ludwig; the first three Chapters were written by Juan Pablo Cardenal; Chapter 4 by Jacek Kucharczyk; and Chapter 5 by Grigorij Meseznikov and Gabriela Paleschova. The term 'power' has been used to describe all forms of influence that are not 'hard' in the sense of military force. The authors highlight Russia and China as the main countries at issue. The nature of these two countries' political systems invariably and fundamentally colours their efforts in educational and cultural initiatives, always accompanied by an authoritarian determination to monopolise ideas, suppress alternative narratives, and exploit partner institutions as shown in the case of China. Russia seems content to propagate the idea that its kleptocratic regime is a normal member of the international community, and that its actions and statements are no less valid than those of democracies. When speaking of the authoritarian regimes, their new forms of influence might be properly labelled as 'sharp power' in the sense that they pierce, penetrate, or perforate the information environments in the targeted countries. The term captures the malign and aggressive nature of the authoritarian initiatives, which starkly contrast with the benign attraction of soft power. The authors argue that the authoritarians' 'sharp power' efforts are typically difficult to detect because they benefit from a time lag, before the targeted democracies realise there is a problem. In addition to media and exchange-based activities, China has set up Confucius Institutes at local universities in the four countries examined: four in Peru, two in Argentina, five in Poland and two in Slovakia, while a sixth is set to open at Warsaw

University despite protests by students voicing concerns about academic freedom. Similar forms of Russian and Chinese sharp power influence are visible in a growing number of democracies around the world. The author recommends a few steps to address China and Russia's malign efforts to influence and manipulate democracies, namely:

- o Address the shortage of information on China and Russia.
- o Unmask authoritarian influence.
- o Inoculate democratic societies against malign authoritarian influence.
- o Reaffirm support for democratic values and ideals.
- o Reconceptualise 'soft power'.

It is fair to comment that the authors of this book did not compare 'sharp power' of Russia and China with the 'benign' attraction of 'public diplomacy' efforts that the US, Europe and other democracies have been implementing in the developing countries in recent decades. While the ultimate goals are similar, the approaches are comparable, and the beneficiaries differ. However, it is true that an increasing number of countries and universities highlight the hidden political agenda and voice their objection to 'sharp power'. The authors conclude that if the US and other powerful democracies do not rise to the challenge, they will be abdicating their leadership roles, abandoning their allies, and neglecting their own long-term security. If these autocratic regimes maintain their current momentum, the integrity of young democracies will be damaged, and this would deliver a devastating blow to the rules-based international order that has underpinned global security and prosperity.[11]

- Vijay Gokhale, *The Long Game: How the Chinese Negotiate with India*. Having served in Hong Kong, Taiwan and China and had been in charge of China affairs at Ministry of External Affairs (MEA), Government of India for nearly four decades, the author retired as the Foreign Secretary in 2020 and published this book in 2021. He highlights six key cases, in which he personally participated in at least four, to review how the Chinese negotiated with Indian counterparts. The six cases are namely:
- India's recognition of the PRC on December 30, 1949.

- The Agreement on Trade and Intercourse between Tibet and India of April 29, 1954.
- India's nuclear tests in 1998.
- The PRC's formal recognition of Sikkim as part of India on April 29, 2005.;
- The diplomatic negotiations between India and the PRC on the 123 Nuclear Deal in 2008,
- The listing of Masood Azhar as a terrorist in the UNSC 1267 Sanction List on May 1, 2019.

Using these six major cases, the author summarises the PRC's *modus operandi* in all the negotiations with Indian counterparts, which the Chinese dealt with the Indian counterparts, who were less experienced in the first two cases, and much more adept and well-prepared in the final four cases. He concludes with a chapter on 'Lessons for India' in which he advises future negotiators to know the adversary and study the details of earlier negotiations for better insights and clues. He emphasises the use of grand deception as a legitimate strategy of Chinese diplomacy, even when discussing mutual trust, noting that the Chinese are adept at buying time to strengthen negotiating position and to stall the other side against time constraints. Over the years, Indian diplomats have learnt how to handle the time pressure that the Chinese put on them and managed to achieve India's goals in negotiations with China. This is a very rare publication, especially authored by a former Indian Foreign Secretary, that specially addresses six of the most important cases between the PRC and India. In the author's opinion, India has somehow missed to garner certain benefits of national interest like Tibet and border issues, and in other cases India has done well to conclude them much more in the best interest of India.[12]

- *Taiwan and India Strategising the Relations,* edited by Alan Yao Yang and Sana Hashmi. It is a collection of 17 articles contributed by both Indian and Taiwanese scholars to examining the current state of the relations between Taiwan and India covering a wide range of domains and offering policy recommendations. While most articles reflect Indian perspectives, five articles, including a co-authored one, do present

Taiwanese viewpoints addressing topics such as political relations, post-pandemic cooperation, economic relations, and cultural exchanges. It is one of the most updated publications covering comprehensive issues between Taiwan and India.[13]

This book was first conceptualised in early 2016, a time when the relations between India and Taiwan were strengthening by all standards. The research then became the core content of the author's PhD thesis. Nearly all relevant books, articles, commentaries, news reports, and other forms of publications up to May 2024 were gathered and analysed, covering the period when the COVID-19 pandemic unexpectedly spread worldwide abruptly halting economic development plans and severely limiting international travel. This resulted in a negative impact on the mutually beneficial interactions between India and Taiwan, as it did for countries worldwide. Inevitably, the route of economic development, growth rate of the interaction, and investment projects under discussion between India and Taiwan may not be as optimistic as was foreseen years ago. To cope with the pandemic's negative impacts and to align with the Indian government's development plans, several new economic and investment policy guidelines and initiatives have been announced and implemented to improve infrastructure and streamline bureaucracy. As a result, potential investors worldwide are now more confident in making final decisions to expand their investments in India. Furthermore, the US administration in early 2021 enacted a series of key, far-reaching policy changes that are conducive not only the US domestic industrial and employment needs, but also to existing India-US relations and India's deeper involvement in the US-led Indo-Pacific strategy. Essentially, if US relations with India and Taiwan continue to evolve along the same path, with increased engagement in trade, investment, and regional security, substantial advancements in India Taiwan bilateral interactions are likely in the years ahead.

Limitations and challenges are inevitably encountered in the of research and writing process for this book. Diplomacy is delicate art of interaction between countries to secure national interests, where both policy directions and political will of the leadership playing a significant role. To gain deeper understanding of the policy-making process, primary sources—

such as declassified archives from the MEA of India and the Ministry of Foreign Affairs of ROC (now Taiwan)—are essential. Materials from the PRC are also inherently essential to understanding India Taiwan relations. However, access to these official archives is often restrictive, sensitive, or time-consuming. Therefore, secondary sources from publications, research papers, and articles play a complementary role by providing evidence for all arguments presented. The author's personal experiences and observations reflect a unique perspective on specific issues, which do not necessarily represent the official positions of his country's government, overseas missions or the institution he serves. Given the limitations imposed by the COVID-19 pandemic on international air travel, the book relies significantly on internet resources, partly due to the interruptions in international courier services, that affected the availability of books and journals. Furthermore, India's domestic, regional and global strategic priorities are far too complex to be fully explored within this book. Key actors, such as the US, EU, Russia, PRC, ASEAN, influence the bilateral relations between India and Taiwan to varying degrees. Meanwhile, new opportunities continue to arise stakeholders to seize. Narrowing down to a selective scope for a limited volume in this book proved challenging.

Notes

1. The martial law, which had been in effect since May 20, 1949 in Taiwan, were lifted by a Presidential order promulgated by President Chiang Ching-Kuo on July 15, 1987.
2. Pashant Kumar Singh, "Taiwan: A forgotten Frontier of India's 'Act East'?", in *India-Taiwan Relations in Asia and Beyond: The future,* ed., Jagannath P. Panda (New Delhi: Pentagon Press and IDSA, 2016), 25.
3. "Taiwan is an opportunity to be grasped: Madahav Nalapat", *The News 21*, Available online at https://thenews21.com/taiwan-is-an-opportunity-to-be-grasped-madhav-nalapat, accessed on October 13, 2020.
4. Jim Tankersley and Ana Swanson, "Amid Shortfalls, Biden Signs Executive Order to Bolster Critical Supply Chains", *New York Times,* at https://www.nytimes.com/2021/02/24/business/biden-supply-chain-executive-order.html, accessed on February 24, 2021.
5. *Executive Order on America's Supply Chains: A Year of Action and Progress*, The White House.

6. Jagannath P. Panda, ed., *India and China in Asia: Between Equilibrium and Equation* (London: Routledge, 2019).
7. B. R. Deepak, *India and China: Foreign Policy Approaches and Responses* (New Delhi: Viji Books India, 2016).
8. Rajiv Sikri, *Challenge and Strategy: Rethinking India's Foreign Policy* (New Delhi: Sage Publications, 2009).
9. Prashant Kumar Singh, *Transforming India-Taiwan Relations: New Perspectives, IDSA Monograph Series No. 35* (New Delhi: IDSA, 2014).
10. Zorawar Daulet Singh, *Power & Diplomacy: India's Foreign Policies During the Cold War*, (Oxford: Oxford University Press, 2019).
11. Juan Pablo Cardenal, Jacek Kucharczyk, Grigorij Meseznikov, Gabriela Paleschova, *Sharp Power: Rising Authoritarian Influence* (Washington D. C.: National Endowment for Democracy, December 2017).
12. Vijay Gokhale, *The Long Game: How the Chinese Negotiate with India* (Delhi: Penguin Random House India, July 2021).
13. *Taiwan and India Strategizing the Relations*, ed., Alan Yao Yang and Sana Hashmi, (Taipei: Taiwan-Asia Exchange Foundation, February 2022).

2

Historical Ties between India and China

Both neighbouring ancient civilisations of India and China claim that their historical origins date back over eight thousand or five thousand years respectively. Giver their geographical proximity, particularly Tibet and Western regions bordering India, there must have been some unrecorded early contact between them. These initial interactions were likely facilitated by camel convoys and other forms of travel, which enabled trade, communications and mutual understanding. This in turn extended to the imperial court in China. The cultural fusion that shaped the distinct identities of these two ancient civilisations has been a long and natural process.

It is generally believed that India and China began formal historical interactions as early as the 2nd century BC, primarily through trade along the ancient Silk Road routes. These interactions expanded significantly during the China's Han Dynasty and India's Maurya and Gupta Empires. However, it's important to note that no specific individuals or groups can be credited as the sole pioneers of these cross-cultural exchanges, as interactions were diverse and involved many actors over centuries. A combination of factors contributed to these early exchanges, including trade, religious missions, diplomatic relations, and intellectual engagement.

India–China interactions contributed to the cultural diffusion of Buddhism in China. This was a complex outcome of multi-ethnic collaborations among Chinese, Indian and other foreign monks, making Buddhism more acceptable within Chinese society.

Besides Buddhism, there are many other areas of interaction between India and China.[1]

Section 1: Early Interactions of the Two Ancient Civilisations

Records of the earliest links between India and China could date back more than two thousand years ago. The word 'Cina' appears a couple of times in the Indian epics *Mahabharata*, *Ramayana* and *Arthashastra*,, which is generally believed to have been composed in the 4th century BC, suggesting that India and China may have engaged in silk trade at that time. One of the most renowned Chinese diplomats of the Han Dynasty, Zhang Qian (張騫), according to the record of history (Shi Ji, 史記), embarked on his first diplomatic mission in 135 BC via the Silk Road to the Western Regions (西域) returning in 122 BC. During his travels, he heard of commodities such as cloth and bamboo, which allegedly originated from Sichuan, China. On his second trip, Zhang Qian instructed his deputy envoy to lead a small delegation to travel to India. In fact, the Emperor Wu of Han Dynasty had previously sent envoys on several occasions to explore the passage to India, but in vain. Emperors of Han Dynasty continued, in the 1st century BC, to yearly send seven to eight missions with over 100 persons each to the Western Regions.[2]

India is the birthplace of Buddhism, and as a result, India and China have shared a substantial common cultural background especially on Buddhism. In the 2nd century BC, there was also a sea route from Guangdong to Kanci (Kanchipuram in Tamil Nadu), with a recorded shipping schedule, according to the *Book of Han Dynasty* (*Han Shu*, 漢書) by Ban Gu (班固). Records show that Chinese gold and silk fabrics, as well as Indian gemstones, crystal and glassware, were among the main items for trade. In the 1st and 2nd centuries, the King of Kanci sent a rhinoceros to China, the King of Gandhara presented a white elephant, and the Kushan King offered lions to China. It is commonly believed that the Emperor Ming of Han (58-75 AD) had a dream of a 'golden Buddha', which had led him to dispatch emissaries to India, likely to the Western Regions, who returned with two prominent

Buddhist scholar-monks Kashyapa Matanga (迦葉摩騰) and Dharmaraksha. (竺法蘭) These monks are credited with translating the well-known *The Sutra of Forty-Two Chapters* (四十二章經). That may have marked the beginning of documented visits by Buddhist scholar monks from the Western Regions and eventually from India to China. The White Horse Monastery, the first Buddhist temple, in Luoyang was then built to accommodate these monks, enabling them translate Buddhist scriptures and to preach the dharma. The 1st wave of Indian scholar monks going to China lasted until 3rd century, followed by the 2nd wave from the 4th to 5th century, and the 3rd wave from the 5th to 6th century. With the propagation of Buddhism in China thousands of scholar monks visited the other country.[3] Most historical records reveal that India-China interactions were a two-way traffic, both on land and by sea route, the so-called 'Silk Route'. Indian proficient Buddhist scholar monks were invited to China in the 1st century to spread Buddhism, and afterwards thousands of scholar monks made their trips from China to India and from India to China alike.

On the Indian side, Kumarajiva (鳩摩羅什343-413, Eastern Jin Dynast) originally from the kingdom of Kucha in the Western Regions, was brought to China by force. Once there, he translated over 300 volumes of sutras from Sanskrit to Chinese, including the Diamond Sutra (金剛般若波羅蜜經), Amitabha Sutra (佛說阿彌陀經), Lotus Sutra (妙法蓮華經), and more, teaching over 3,000 followers in Chang'an (now Xi'an). Bodhidarma (達摩483-540, Southern Liang Dynasty) arrived in China in the 6th century, founding and is also credited with the establishment of the Shaolin Monastery and its martial arts. Others prominent figures include Vighna (維祇難years unknown, Three Kingdoms Period), Dharmamitra (356-442, Liu-Song Dynasty), Kalayasas (383-442, Liu-Song Dynasty), Buddhabhadra (佛陀跋陀羅359-429, Eastern Jin Dynasty), Gautama Samghadeva (瞿曇僧伽提婆Years unknown, Jin Dynasty), Dharmaksema (曇無懺385-433, Northern Liang Dynasty), Narendrayasas (那連提耶舍490-589, Sui Dynasty), Paramartha (真諦499-569, Southern Liang Dynasty), Jnanagupta (闍那崛多523-600, Sui Dynasty), Siksananda (652-710, Tang Dynasty, Chinese name: 實叉難陀), Pramiti (approx. 656-706, Tang Dynasty般刺密帝), Amoghavajra (不空705-774, Tang Dynasty),

Prajna (般若734-?, Tang Dynasty), Samghavarman (僧伽跋, years unknown, Song Dynasty), Samghabhuti (僧伽跋澄), Dhamanandi, Dhamayasas, Dharmaruci, Vimalaksa, and Buddhayaas. These scholars, while in China, dedicated themselves to translating and preaching Buddhist scriptures, leaving a remarkable collection in Chinese, which people can still read today to appreciate feel the magnitude and significance of their contributions.

Chinese Buddhist monks, meanwhile began to travel to the Western Regions to learn the dharma in the 3rd century, bringing back hundreds of Sanskrit sutras to China, which they translated and preached. Faxian (法顯343-424) of East Jin Dynasty, along with his fellow students, took central Asian route to India, where he visited holy places, studied dharma, and gathered and transcribed sutras during his journey from 399 to 412. He returned to China by sea, via Sri Lanka and Java, Indonesia. (For details, please refer Annexure 4) In 414, he completed writing his memoir, *A Record of Buddhist Kingdoms* (佛國記), which contains detailed accounts of the kingdoms he visited, as well as what he had seen and heard. Faxian's memoir provided geographical descriptions of places in India and Nepal related to the Buddha's life including his birthplace, his enlightenment, and where he, preached and reached Nirvana. These descriptions later enabled British and other explorers in the 19th Century to identify and locate these significant Buddhist sites, thanks to joint efforts by those working in India, Tibet, Nepal, Burma, and Ceylon. (For further details, please refer to Annexure 4.) Consequently, the term 'Buddhism' was coined in the West and the it was rediscovered after the Buddha's teachings were unknown outside Asia for nearly 2000 years.[4]

The Tang Dynasty, founded in 618, adopted an opening policy towards the outside world, allowing many Indians to travel to China for trade, residence and even official service. Xuanzang (玄奘600-664) and Yijing (義淨635-713) are the two most well-known scholar monks of Tang Dynasty. Both studied at Nalanda and became proficient in Sanskrit. Xuanzang's *Great Tang Records on the Western Regions* (大唐西域記) provides a detailed account of his India through from 629 to 645, serving as a valuable reference for the 'sahibs' in their pursuit of the exact locations of the Buddha's life. During his travels Xuanzang gathered and translated 657 Sanskrit Buddhist scriptures into Chinese. Yijin, after a 25 year journey to and from India via Srivijaya, Indonesia, returned to China in 695 bringing back some 400 Buddhist scriptures, which he subsequently translated them into Chinese. The *Account of Buddhism sent from the South Seas* (南海寄歸內法傳) and *Buddhist Monk's Pilgrimage of the Tang Dynasty* (大唐西域求法高僧傳) are among his best travel diaries. These works document his journey to India, it's the society, and the lifestyles of locals. (For details, please refer to Annexure 5) Both diaries serve as important reference sources for those seeking a deeper understanding about the development and the dharma of Buddhism.

In addition to Buddhism, some scholars argued that knowledge about ancient Indian calendar, astronomy, mathematics, logic, phonology, medicine, music, arts and industrial skills like sugar-making and wine-making were introduced by those Buddhist monks into Chinese daily life, thanks to the close interactions between India and China from Han Dynasty to Northern Song Dynasty, over a span of 1300 years.[5] The cultural interactions between India and China were naturally absorbed and became integral parts of Chinese civilisation. However, in the 11th century, with the Muslim invasion of India, Buddhism declined, leading to an interruption in the Chinese pilgrimages to India that had lasted for six centuries.

Section 2: Interactions Since 18th Century

Although interactions between India and China in terms of trade, medicine and political contacts continued sporadically alongside religious and cultural exchanges, it was not until the 18th century that overland and maritime contacts became more organised. This witnessed a booming cotton trade between Bombay and Guangzhou. In the 19th Century there was a surge of momentum in cotton yarn and opium trade between India and China, resulting in the so-called Opium War (1839-42) between the Qing Dynasty and Britain. In addition to the import-export trade, Indian diasporas conducted by in Chinese eastern port cities engaged in banking, real estate, manufacturing and share brokerage. A large number of Punjabi policemen and watchmen also served in Hong Kong and the foreign concessions in Shanghai, Guangzhou, Tianjin, Hankou, and other cities. For some time, they constituted half of the Indian diasporas in Eastern China.[6] As a result, the Chinese population often perceived Punjabi men with colourful turbans as representative of the Indian people, viewing them as loyal, brave and hardworking. Even Indian soldiers were reportedly involved in the Taiping Rebellion (1851-64) and the Boxer Rebellion (1899-1901) on both sides of the combating troops either by defection or being captured.[7] In 1893, Swami Vivekananda briefly visited China, specifically Hong Kong and Guangzhou, spending three days there.[8] The Nobel Prize laureate for literature, Rabindranath Tagore visited China three times from 1924 onwards, and decided to set up an institute for Chinese studies in the university he founded. The study of Indian civilisation began to be systematically taught in China the early 20th century. Prior to the end of World War II, schools and academies dedicated to teaching Indian and Chinese languages and culture were set up in both countries.

On the political front, Kang Youwei (康有為), a reformist leader in late Qing Dynasty, went into exile in Darjeeling in 1901 and toured around India for nearly 18 months. As nationalist and anti-imperialist campaigns took root in India and China, the Hindustani Ghadar Party was active in China from World War I until the 1930s. Dr Sun Yat-sen, the founding father of the Republic of China, expressed concern over India's freedom from the British colonial rule. He met with Indian students in China and Japan offering various forms of support. In the 1920s, Mahatma Gandhi and Jawaharlal Nehru became widely known in China for their struggle for an independent India. Jawaharlal Nehru frequently mentioned China in his speeches and letters about China, expressing his appreciation for its ancient civilisation, and he, along with other Indian National Congress leaders, worked to build links with the Chinese nationalists in early 20th century. In august 1939, Indian Prime Minister Jawaharlal Nehru made his first visit to China, describing his two-week stay as "memorable ones both personally for me and for the future relations of India and China." He gladly found that his desire for China and India to foster closer relations with each other was fully reciprocated by the leaders in China. He confessed that he returned to India as an even greater admirer of China and the Chinese people than he had been previously.[9]

Shortly before the fall of Hong Kong to Japan in December 1941, Britain, the US and the Netherlands became the allies with the ROC. As Japan's invasion of Burma in mid-January 1942 worsened the British situation in Malaya and Singapore, after concluding an alliance with Thailand a few days earlier. With the fact that Indochina was occupied by the Japanese forces, Chinese mainland, which was largely occupied by the Japanese, became encircled by the Japanese with the only opening left with India. When the worst-case scenario of Burma's complete occupation by the Japanese forces seemed imminent, India would be the only alternative supply route within the 'China-Burma-India' (CBI) Theatre of war. Tens of thousands of the ROC Expedition Force troops fought and lost their lives in Burma, with the remainder retreating to India, where they received further training at Ramgarh from 1943 to 1945 in preparation for fighting Japanese forces in Burma.[10] Over the span of three years and three months, the ROC Expedition Force missions in India and Burma, saw half of their 400,000 troops martyred, and were buried in the commemorative cemeteries in both countries, including eight Major Generals and two Lieutenant Generals lost in Burma alone. The Allied victories in Burma led to Japan's unconditional surrender in 1945, effectively preventing and invasion of India at the cost of 200,000 ROC troops and those from other allies.

When Japan advanced southwards in late 1941, the Indian Congress agreed to cooperate in the war effort to the extent of blockading aggressors, but not to the extent of aiding the British. Chiang Kai-shek and Madame Chiang visited India in February 1942, declaring that true international peace could not exist if either China or India, were denied freedom. Although their primary aim of the visit to persuade Indian nationalist leaders to participate in the war effort and to forestall the anti-British 'Quit India Movement', Mahatma Gandhi abandoned his approach of non-violence towards a possible Japanese invasion and explained to Chiang that the appeal to Britain to withdraw from India was not meant in any way to weaken India's defence capabilities or to embarrass China in its struggle against the Japanese Imperial Army.[11] After his visit to India, Chiang released a message to the Indian people on February 21, 1942, in which he stressed that he hoped that the Indian people would wholeheartedly join the allies and participate together in the struggle for survival for a free world until complete victory was achieved. He confidently believed that Great Britain would soon give Indian people real political power without demands from the people of India, and the people in India would believe that their participation in the war is not only a great help to the anti-aggression allies to secure victory, but also a turning-point in India's struggle for freedom.[12]

In order to mobilise further support from the US and at the invitation of the US Congress, Madame Chiang Soong Mei-ling was invited to address them on February 18, 1943 In her speech she highlighted that, with Congress having declared war against Japan, Germany, and Italy, it had achieved its immediate task. The then Representatives of the American people should further point the way to win the war, to help rebuild a world in which all people may live in harmony and peace."[13] Before this decisive move by the US, the ROC had been fighting alone against the Japanese invasion for five-and-a-half years.

Nehru saw that the visit of Chiang Kai-shek and his wife to India brought support for India's freedom struggle, helping to bring India out of her colonial rule increasing her awareness of the internationally concerned issues. Nehru witnessed the bonds between India and China got stronger, and so did the will to stand up with China and other nations against an invasion. Obviously there existed personal rapport between Nehru and Chiang Kai-shek, but their relationship was too complicated to handle. Chiang was the commander of Britain's major allies in World War II, while Nehru was a leader of India's struggle against British rule. During Chiang Kai-shek's visit in 1942, he aimed to win over the mind of Nehru and the Indian National Congress, which had refused to join in Britain's war effort or the Allied campaign. Chiang in the meantime worked hard to pressurise Britain to make substantial concessions for Indian independence. Chiang even communicated directly to the US President Franklin D. Roosevelt and to the American Ambassador in China and explained his views on India's critical political and military situation and the urgent need for Britain to resolve the political issue. He then instructed the Chinese Ambassador in London to represent his views to Prime Minister Winston Churchill as well.

On July 25, 1942, Chiang sent another urgent confidential message on the Indian situation to President Roosevelt urging that the US should advise both Britain and India to seek a reasonable and satisfactory solution. President Roosevelt forwarded this message via telegraph to Churchill seeking suggestions for an appropriate response. In his reply, Churchill stated that his British Government did not agree with Chiang's estimate of the situation that it was correct. He hoped that Chiang would be persuaded to cease activities aimed at aiding India and that Roosevelt should avoid exerting pressure on Britain. Subsequently, President Roosevelt notified Chiang of British negative position on India and advised Chiang and himself not to take the mediatory role Chiang had proposed to play.[14]

All in all, the friendship between Nehru and Chiang went beyond formality to reach a comfortable degree of personal warmth, which helped revive a series of organised cultural exchange between India and China. After the war India moved towards independence and China was stuck in a civil war leading to the Chinese Liberation Army's victory and Chiang Kai-shek's flight to Taiwan.[15] Nehru's concept of the India-China friendship was deeply embedded in his sense of history, culture and values. Although anti-imperial camaraderie was a significant element, his vision was essentially nationalist and defined in cultural terms. Thus, it would be wrong to attribute this vision to his socialist leanings or to a sense of being part of a socialistic fraternity along with China. Moreover, as is clear in his letters and speeches, he was impressed by the personalities of Chiang Kai-shek and Madame Chiang who were central to his vision of China. Hence, the Nehru government's shift in diplomatic recognition from the ROC to the PRC was not based on ideological belief but was simply an acknowledgement of the fact that the entire Chinese mainland was now occupied and governed separately under the new designation of the PRC. Furthermore, Nehru's distaste for Chiang Kai-shek in the 1950s was a late development and partly in response to the Cold War. Although Nehru considered Formosa (Taiwan) as China's historical territory and endorsed the PRC's claim of sovereignty, nevertheless, he accepted the 'distinct individuality' of Taiwan and supported autonomy for it.[16]

The Republic of China, as a member of the Allies, dispatched the Chinese Expedition Force of 100, 000 troops to Burma in early 1942 in an attempt to fight against and deter the invincible Japanese Imperial Army from entering India. Nearly two thirds of them tragically sacrificed their lives in the wilderness of Hukawang Valley, Northern Burma during their first expedition mission. Subsequently, the reinforcement troops were courageous enough to challenge the assault of the three times more powerful Japanese army of in April 1942, and in the end successfully rescued several times larger in number of the entrapped British soldiers at Yenangyaung and back to India.[17] The Battle of Yenangyaung in Burma was an incredible victory for General Sun Li-jen of the ROC and men of the 113th Regiment, New 38th Division of the ROC Expedition Force in Burma. They rescued the British First Burma Division from encirclement by the Imperial Japanese Army during World War II in the China-Burma-India Theatre, fighting against the numerically superior Japanese 33rd Division and achieving victory despite incurring serious casualties.

In recognition of General Sun's contribution for rescuing over seven thousand British troops and others besieged by the Japanese army, King George VI of Britain awarded him the Commander of the Order of British Empire (CBE) and the Companion of the Order of the Bath in 1943. The US also bestowed upon him an honour of the Officer of the Legion of Merit.

Section 3: What does 'China' Mean?

The term "China" generally refers to the Chinese mainland in a historical, geographical and cultural sense without distinctive political implication of any kind. The ethnic Chinese people traditionally believe their history dates back over 5,000 years. When it comes to be called a specific political entity, 'ait could refer to any dynasty across various periods in Chinese history, including the Xia Dynasty (c. 2070-1600 BC), Shang Dynasty (c. 1600-1050 BC), Zhou Dynasty (c. 1046-256 BC including the Spring and Autumn Period 770-476 BC and Waring States Period (475-221 BC), Qin Dynasty (221-206 BC) (The Qin dynasty marked the beginning of the Chinese Empire), Han Dynasty (206 BC-220 AD), Six Dynasties

Period (Three Kingdoms 220-265, Jin Dynasty 265-420, Northern and Southern Dynasties 386-589), Sui Dynasty (581-618), Tang Dynasty (618-906), Five Dynasties and Ten Kingdoms (907-960), Song Dynasty (960-1279), Yuan Dynasty (1279-1368), Ming Dynasty (1368-1644), Qing Dynasty (1644-1912), the Republic of China (1912-present) and then the PRC (1949-present). What is perplexing is the overlapping presence of the Republic of China (ROC) and the PRC in 1949 and the switch of diplomatic recognition from the former to the latter, when the defeated ROC government and troops relocated to Taiwan.

Academicians are always mindful whenever the term 'China' is used, especially after 1949, when the PRC was established on the Chinese mainland, while the ROC, which governed the legitimate government on the Chinese mainland from 1912, relocated to Taiwan with millions of officials, troops, huge quantity of gold reserve and the world-envying national treasury from the Forbidden City in Beijing. More importantly, the ROC government, led by Chiang Kai-shek, had fought against the formidable Japanese Imperial Army during the World War II which ended in 1945—more than four years before the PRC was established. The majority of those who sacrificed their lives in the battlegrounds fighting against the Japanese in China-India-Burma Theatre were ROC troops, except the New Fourth Army and the Eighth Route Army which were under the command of the Communist faction within the ROC army. When India sent a medical mission to Yan'an, Shan'xi Province, China, in 1938, it was actually at the request of a Communist general as a gesture of solidarity from India to China, as both countries were struggling for freedom. There are solid reasons for India and PRC to commemorate the anniversary of this medical mission and honour those who had devoted their expertise and even lives to serve and help the needy Chinese people during wartime.[18]

It is perplexing owing to the insistence of either of the two political entities to be the sole legitimate government of 'China'. This created a rather misleading impression among outsiders regarding Taiwan, as institutions and well-known companies established since the early 1950s used the word 'China' or 'Chinese' in their names, such as Academia Sinica, Central Bank of China, China Airlines, Chinese Petroleum Corporation,

Chinese Petrochemical Corporation, China Steel Corporation, China Shipbuilding Corporation, China External Trade Development Council, and the International Commercial Bank of China. Even the ROC embassies in diplomatic ally countries refer to themselves as 'Chinese Embassy' to underscore their claim of legitimacy as representing 'China'. The 'One China' principle has governed international recognition policies, preventing dual recognition of both ROC and PRC, as neither of them accepts the concept of duel recognition.

Based on pragmatic acknowledgement of international political reality, the majority of these confusing names were either gradually changed completely or modified by adding 'Taiwan' or its symbol to their designations for clearer identification purposes so that those names would be less confusing. However, many of them must keep their original designations for various reasons, such as, Academia Sinica and China Airlines. It is a historical fact that from 1945 to 1971, the ROC, governing mainland China until 1949 and later Taiwan, held the 'China' seat in the UN as one of the five permanent members of the Security Council, when it was recognised as the sole legitimate government of 'China' even though the PRC took control of the entire Chinese mainland after 1949. During the Cold War era, the ROC in Taiwan was often referred to as 'Free China' while the PRC was referred to as 'Communist China' or 'Red China', especially during the Cultural Revolution from 1966 to 1976 and following the 1989 Tiananmen Square massacre in on the Chinese mainland.

Ever since the consolidation of Taiwan's democracy under President Lee Ten-huithe preference among people in Taiwan to be identified as Taiwanese, rather than Chinese has strengthened. This sense of Taiwanese identity intensified under the DPP presidencies of Chen Sui-bian (2000-2008) and the current Tsai Ing-wen (2016-2024). Today, the term 'China' typically refers to the PRC in global usage, while "Taiwan" and "Taiwanese" have gradually become the most acceptable identity of ROC and its people. Evidence of this shift can be seen on Government's websites and on the ROC passports, where the word'Taiwan' is highlighted to reflect resolutions passed by the Legislative Yuan (Taiwan's Parliament) and to align with the preference of the majority of Taiwanese people.

Section 4: ROC and India in the UN

The ROC was one of the 50 Charter Members of the UN in October 1945 and held one of the five Permanent Members of the UNSC representing 'China' till October 25, 1971 when the PRC replaced the ROC through "UN General Assembly Resolution 2758 (XXVI). Restoration of the lawful rights of the PRC in the UN". This resolution states "Recognising that the representatives of the Government of the PRC are the only lawful representatives of China to the UN and that the PRC is one of the five permanent members of the Security Council ... and to recognise the representatives of its Government as the only legitimate representatives of China to the United nation, and to expel forthwith the representatives of Chiang Kai-shek from the place which they unlawfully occupy at the UN and in all the organisations related to it."[19] What has happened at the United Nations on that day is exactly the origin of the perplexing 'One China', 'Two Chinas', 'Communist China' and 'Free China' since then, especially during the Cold War and beyond. The United Nations General Assembly Resolution 2758 has been criticised as illegal by the ROC on Taiwan on the ground that, according to Article 6, the expulsion of a certain member requires the recommendation of the Security Council. And it can only take place if a nation "has persistently violated the principles contained in the present Charter."[20]

First, by any measure, the ROC's activities at the UN did not constitute 'persistently violated the Principles contained in the present Charter' by any standards and there was no Security Council recommendation for its expulsion after a 22-year-long debate between the two opposing camps at the annual UN General Assembly Plenary meetings. Second, claims of 'lawful rights' or the "restoration of the lawful rights" for the PR Clack foundation, as the PRC did not even exist at the time the UN was founded in 1945; Rather it was the ROC, which was one of the Charter members and was accorded the "lawful rights". On this specific issue one key question remains, if any of the PRC's "lawful rights" should be claimed to be restored, when exactly are the so-called "lawful rights" supposed to be transferred from the ROC to the PRC according to related international laws at that time? Apparently, there was little debate on the legal base and origin of the "lawful rights" for the PRC since it was mainly an issue of international politics. Third, simply because of the above defects, in the past two decades or so, the ROC government and people on many occasions attempted to challenge whether the UN General Assembly (UNGA) Resolution 2758 actually resolved Taiwan's representation in the UN, and a much more essential issue was that whether the Resolution 2758 categorically bars Taiwan from meaningfully participating in UN's Specialised Agencies as an observer.

Based on the UN archives, it seems that India never vocally supported the ROC status in the UN although both are Charter members. Since the ROC had been holding the China seat at the UNSC as one of the five permanent members from 1945 to 1971, it would be fair to say that the ROC consistently supported India's initiatives to become a member of the UNSC and India's stance on other major international issues, no less than fourteen times in total.[21] At least on two occasions that the ROC on Taiwan voted for India's membership to the UN Economic and Social Council despite the lukewarm attitude of the US and also for Vijaya Lakshmi Pandit to be the President of the UN General Assembly from 1953-54. India's interests before 1971 were generally supported by the ROC on Taiwan at the UN rather than by the PRC, which was not yet a member of the UN.

In his address to the UNGA in 1960, Prime Minister Jawaharlal Nehru referred to the issue of the proper representation of China in the UN by stressing that India has raised this issue for years before the UN for years because India felt that it was not proper for a great and powerful country to be unrepresented, given the urgent consequences for global issues, especially those concerning disarmament. Nehru further indicated that it was most extraordinary for some arguments to be raised to keep out China and "to give the seat meant for China to those who certainly do not represent China. Nehru also questioned why Mongolia remined excluded when so many countries are joining the UN"[22] What Nehru complained about was that the ROC's Permanent Representative, George Yeh, at the UN vetoed Mongolia's entry to the UN in 1955, which happened to be the only case in which the ROC Representative had ever cast a veto during its 26-year representation of China in the UN. It is contentious that the ROC argued Mongolia was a synecdoche of China that the ROC claimed to represent, therefore its representative could not possibly acknowledge Mongolia as a sovereign state even though the ROC had recognised Mongolia as a sovereign state in 1946.[23] However, the ROC withdrew recognition of Mongolia in 1953 and subsequently, it reaffirmed its recognition in early 2002 and then in September, 2002 establishing the Taipei Trade and Economic Representative Office at Ulan Batur.[24]

The ROC had another opposing front with India concerning Tibet for a similar reason as that of Mongolia, but the ROC had tried very hard to not make the Tibet issue to be even discussed at UN meetings. However, in 1960 the ROC's permanent representative made a statement on the tragic fate of the Tibetan people since 1959, when the Chinese Liberation Army invaded Tibet and killed Tibetan people stating, "The traditional Tibetan way of life has been uprooted. The right of the Tibetan people to religion has been forcibly violated and their right to exist as a distinct national or ethnical group has been denied. There has been mass killing of Buddhist monks and other leaders of Tibetan society."[25]

In the 1970 session of the United Nations General Assembly, the ROC's Premier Yen Chia-kan was invited to address the Assembly, the first time ever during the ROC's representation in the UN. He categorically rebutted that "Those who champion the cause of Peiping (PRC) have been in the habit of invoking the so-called principle of universality." He further stressed that "to admit a regime that glorifies war and violence, that has made subversion of established Governments its principal goal in foreign policy, is to negate the basic purposes of the Charter, thus undercutting the very foundation of the United Nations. Far from strengthening the UN, this a sure way of destroying it."[26]

The ROC's Permanent Representative Shu-Kai Chow delivered his parting address in 1971 before the UNGA's debate on the so-called 'question of Chinese representation'. He solemnly reminded the UN that there was no proof to imply that the Chinese Communist regime (PRC) was ready to give up its policy of world dominion. Chow insisted that the PRC went on to promote the violence of war, to use force to achieve its goals, to support armed insurrection in neighbouring countries and supply arms and ammunition to rebel troops in Southeast Asian countries like Thailand, Burma, Malaysia and Indonesia. He pointed out that the PRC continued to train, equip and finance guerillas world-wide. He finally remarked "Rhetoric and friendly gestures notwithstanding, there is no evidence that the regime now intends to pursue a course of action consistent with the UN Charter. Indeed, all signs point the other way."[27] The above statement might ring a bell to India, and many other countries alike, as Maoist's factions of guerillas have been active in many states ever since the PRC was established in 1949.

It has been a consistent position from the outset regarding India's support for PRC to replace ROC at the UN since 1950. India was a strong advocate for the PRC readmission to the UN and for it to take China's seat in the Security Council as a permanent member, which was then represented by the ROC on Taiwan. Jawaharlal Nehru referred to PRC in 1950 as "a Great Power, regardless of whether you like or dislike." He stressed that the existence of PRC was already a 'well-established fact' and that to continue to exclude the PRC from the Security Council was a 'unrealistic state of affair'. Nehru further commented in 1960 that it was absurd for the ROC to continue representing all of China at the UN. He argued that the entire balance of power had shifted both in the Far East and globally because of the new China. However, Nehru admitted that the PRC was dangerous in terms of its continuous tendency toward aggression with grievance.[28] Nehru's address to the 1960 UNGA was the only occasion that he dealt with the PRC representation issue against the ROC among his three addresses at the UNGA during his tenure of premiership and it indeed reflected his strong conviction of 'doing the right and proper thing', and 'it was not a question of liking or disliking'.[29]

Indira Gandhi addressed the UNGA in her capacity of India's Prime Minister in 1968 and 1970 and she conveyed no similar sentiments to those of her father, Jawaharlal Nehru, regarding championing the PRC's replacement of the ROC at the UN. Nehru's China policy bore the hope that India and China should be partners either in Asian or in the global arena. He believed that the prospects of this partnership would help resolve their bilateral issues, including the border disputes. However, that policy failed with the Chinesed invasion in the 1962 war. India's China policy under Indira Gandhi was essentially a form of cold war. India insisted that China should return

Indian territories which were lost in 1962. India was committed to building its economic and military power on its own and in the meantime with external help. Indira Gandhi chose to play the self-reliance card, pretty much the same as Modi's Atmanirbhar Bharat, and to close the economy except to US and international aid. Subsequently, India turned to the Soviet Union for building up India's military capabilities. The fundamental guiding thought was that India had to deal with China with strength.[30]

As PRC's Prime Minister Zhou Enlai acknowledged in 1971, if Resolution 2758 passed, "the status of Taiwan is not yet decided." The PRC knew this well; however, for pragmatic reasons it did not reject the resolution when it passed. Only after the PRC had taken the 'China' seat did it begin to leverage its position to promote the 'One China' stance on Taiwan at the UN level, and to rewrite Taiwan's status at the UN especially in the 1990s when Taiwan embarked on its democratisation process. The PRC internationalised its 'One China' Principle and revised the original intent of the resolution which was only to deal with the representation of 'China' at the UN and has nothing to do with the status of Taiwan where the government of the ROC is now based.[31]

As one critic indicated, '*Hindi-Chini bhai bhai* (Indian and Chinese are brothers)' and pushing China's case of a seat at the UN, while it was brutalising Tibet and preparing for war with India, was a manifestation of that pacifism and utopia ideals which we had adopted as state policy. He even argued that "India should take the lead in debunking Xi Jinping's 'One China' theory'. He further maintained that Taiwan is China's 'soft underbelly' and quietly India has been following China's orders to stay away from Taiwan.[32]

Whether India and China could manage to develop their friendly relations remains a volatile issue. As ITA's Director General Vijay Gokhale indicated in November 2004 that India did not regard China's rise as a threat. India's relations with China after 1962 were still a highly sensitive issue in its domestic politics. Chinese companies were not invited or allowed to work on airport and port construction, telecommunications, or even road projects due to concerns of helping a rival power build India's infrastructure might require strategic and security consideration. The main obstacles which existed between India and Taiwan were solely from India side. One case in point was that India initially hesitated in the very beginning to sign an agreement on avoidance of double taxation for Taiwanese investors simply because it believed that such an agreement would require parliamentary approval, which would imply an official status. The Indian government tried very hard not to make the opposition parties in the parliament to use that agreement to accuse the government of jeopardising hard-won friendly relations with China.[33] However, Taiwan's feelings about the real problems with India were not the same as what Indian officials said. The wind might blow in any other direction as China has repeatedly behaved in an assertive and provocative manner towards India since mid-2020.

Section 5: Summary Note

Friendship and interactions between India and China for over two thousand years laid a solid foundation for the people of these two ancient civilisations culturally, religiously, economically and socially. While specific individuals like Zhang Qian, Xuanzang, Kumarajiva, Bodhidarma and others are notable figures in the early history of India-China interactions, it is essential to recognise that these interactions were a collective effort involving merchants, diplomats, scholars, monks, artisans, and ordinary people from both civilisations. The pioneering of cross-cultural interactions between India and China was a dynamic and ongoing process that evolved over centuries, shaping the historical, cultural, and intellectual ties between these two ancient civilisations.

However, when it came to national interests and sovereignty issues, such as border and territorial disputes, one of the two neighbours would not hesitate to resort to military means even if they are as amiable and close as family members. Conflicts and casualties on either side have long-term consequences in their mutual perception and even psychologically. During World War II, the leadership of the ROC on the Chinese mainland wished to convince the leadership in India to support and join forces with the Britain as part of the Allies against the Japanese invasion, but in vain. The ROC had to fight the CBI Theatre of war jointly with other Allies and suffered tremendous casualties of tens of thousands of its troops and dozens of generals in Burma and India. Since the UN was established in 1945, the

ROC, as one of the founding members, had been holding the China seat in the Security Council until 1971 as one of the five permanent members.

According to the UN archives, the ROC, now on Taiwan, had always supported India in nearly all efforts in the UN except those about Tibet. However, India continued to advocate that the PRC should replace the ROC to take the China seat in the UN starting in 1950. The ROC left the UN and the China seat was taken by the PRC in 1971 by means of a UNGA Resolution 2758. This decision brought about the issue of 'One China', 'Two Chinas' and an ongoing debate and campaign both within and outside the UN, fuelled by the Taiwan side decades later. Due to the perplexing nature of the designation of 'China' at different times in history, the ROC on Taiwan gradually switched to highlight more of its Taiwan identity since the consolidation of democracy beginning in the late 1980s. The term 'China' is now exclusively used to refer to the PRC on the Chinese mainland, as more and more people in Taiwan tend to identify themselves as Taiwanese, with their country as the ROC on Taiwan.

At the time when the PRC's position on territory and sovereignty claims both in Arunachal Pradesh and Aksai Chin have evidently challenged India's national interest regarding territorial integrity and sovereignty rights, and in an emerging trend of Taiwanese investments in India's high-tech industries as a result of Taiwan relocating its manufacturing operations away from China to avoid economic, political and strategic repercussions, India now has the golden opportunities to engage with Taiwan more significantly and friendly beyond political constraints it had imposed on itself for decades. This shift allows India to navigate the 'One China' policy in a way that serves the best interest of both India and Taiwan.

Notes

1. Tansen Sen, "The Spread of Buddhism to China: A Re-examination of the Buddhist Interactions between Ancient India and China", *China Report* 48 (1-2) (July 2012): 11-27.
2. *Encyclopedia of India-China Cultural Contacts Vol. I*, Ministry of External Affairs, Republic of India (New Delhi: MaXposure Media Group, 2014), 3-4.
3. B R Deepa, *India and China: Foreign Policy Approaches and Responses* (New Delhi: Vij Books India, 2016), 56.

4. Charles Allen, *The Buddha and the Sahibs* (London: John Murray, 2003), 200-217, 256-279.
5. Master Dongchu, *Interaction of Buddhism between China and India* (中印佛教交通史), http://dongchu.dila.edu.tw/html/02/cwdc_03/cwdc_030374.html#d1e7703. (Chinese version).
6. *Encyclopedia of India-China Cultural Contacts Vol. 1*, Ministry of External Affairs, Republic of India (New Delhi: MaXposure Media Group, 2014), 9-13.
7. Madhavi Thampi, "Indian Soldiers, Policemen and Watchmen in China in the Nineteen and Early Twentieth Centuries", *China Report 35:4*, Nov. 1999, 417-8.
8. "Documentary highlights Swami Vivekananda's less known visit to China", *The Hindu*, https://www.thehindubusinessline.com/news/variety/documentary-highlights-swami-vivekanandas-less-known-visit-to-china/article32667578.ece, accessed on September 22, 2020.
9. Ramachandra Guha, "Jawaharlal Nehru and China: A Study in Failure?", Harvard-Yenching Institute Working Paper Series (Cambridge, MA: Harvard-Yenching Institute, 2011), 3. Available in https://www.harvard-yenching.org/wp-content/uploads/legacy_files/featurefiles/Ramachandra%20Guha_Jawaharlal%20Nehru%20and%20China.pdf.
10. K. C. Chan, "Britain's Reaction to Chiang Kai-shek's visit to India, February 1942", August 1975. *Encyclopedia of India-China Cultural Contacts, Vol. 1*, Ministry of External Affairs, Republic of India (New Delhi: MaXposure Media Group, 2014), 15, https://onlinelibrary.wiley.com/doi/abs/10.1111/j.1467-8497.1975.tb01141.x.
11. W. F. Van Eekelen, *Indian Foreign Policy and the Border Dispute with China* (The Hague: Martinus Nijhoff, 1964), 23.
12. http://www.ibiblio.org/pha/policy/1942/1942-02-21a.html.
13. Wu Ming-yen, "The Speech delivered by Madame Chiang Soong Mei-ling to the US House of Representatives in 1943", National Policy Foundation,. https://www.npf.org.tw/2/4398, accessed on June 30, 2008.
14. "Exchange of views between Generalissimo Chiang Kai-shek and President Roosevelt regarding situation in India", Foreign Relations of the United States: Diplomatic Papers, 1942, China. https://history.state.gov/historicaldocuments/frus1942China/comp17.
15. Avinash Mohan Saklani, "Nehru, Chiang Kai-shek, and the Second World War," in *India and China in the Colonial World,* ed. Madhavi Thampi (New York: Routledge, 2017), 167-183.
16. Prasant Kumar Singh, *Transforming India-Taiwan Relations: New Perspectives,* IDSA Monograph Series No. 35 (New Delhi: IDSA, April 2014), 27.
17. Chu Hung-yuan, *General Sun Li-jen's Political character demonstrated in the Battle of Yenangyaung,* in *China-India Relations in First Half of the Twentieth Century,*

ed. Hsieh Hsiao-chin and Fang Tien-sze, (Hsinchu, Taiwan: National Tsing Hua University Press, 2015), 129-165.

18. "An Indian doctor in China", Mumbai Mirror, March 6, 2020. https://mumbaimirror.indiatimes.com/opinion/city-columns/an-indian-doctor-in-china/articleshow/74502883.cms.
19. "2758 (XXVI). "Restoration of the lawful rights of the People's Republic of China in the United Nations", United Nations General Assembly. file:///Users/charles/Downloads/A_RES_2758(XXVI)-EN.pdf.
20. UN Charter Article 6: "A member of the United Nations who has persistently violated the Principles contained in the current Charter may be expelled from the Organization by the General Assembly upon the recommendation of the Security Council", https://legal.un.org/repertory/art6.shtml.
21. Fang Tien-sze, *An Assessment of Ambassador Luo Jialun's Mission to India: 1947-9*, in *China-India Relations in First Half of the Twentieth Century*, ed. Hsieh Hsiao-chin and Fang Tien-sze, (Hsinchu, Taiwan: National Tsing Hua University Press, 2015), 120. (in Chinese)
22. "882nd Plenary Meeting, United Nations General Assembly Fifteenth Session Official Records", United Nations, October 3, 1960. https://undocs.org/en/A/PV.882, accessed on February 20, 2021.
23. Keith Allan Clark II, "Republic of China's 1955 Veto of Mongolian Membership in the United Nations", *Journal of American-East Asian Relations Volume 25: Issue 3* (Unknown: Brill, September 3, 2018), 263-295. https://brill.com/view/journals/jaer/25/3/article-p263_263.xml.
24. "Mainland Policy and Work, 2002", Mainland Affairs Council, Republic of China (Taiwan). September 2, 2002. https://www.mac.gov.tw/en/News_Content.aspx?n=0D58AA484DB9A9B1&sms=35503662D9CE6DD9&s=5F761BAF31A2E3F4, accessed on April 24, 2021.
25. "892nd Plenary Meeting, United Nations General Assembly Fifteenth Session Official Records", United Nations, October 7, 1960. https://undocs.org/en/A/PV.892, accessed on February 20, 2021.
26. "1875th Plenary Meeting, United Nations General Assembly Twenty-Fifth Session Official Records", United Nations, October 20, 1970. http://undocs.org/en/A/PV.1875, accessed on February 20, 2021.
27. "1959th Plenary Meeting, United Nations General Assembly Twenty-Sixth Session Official Records", United Nations, October 8, 1971. http://undocs.org/en/A/PV.1959, accessed on February 20, 2021.
28. Nabarun Roy, "Why did Nehru want the People's Republic of China in the United Nations?", The Diplomat, April 7, 2018. https://thediplomat.com/2018/04/why-did-nehru-want-the-peoples-republic-of-china-in-the-united-nations/, accessed on February 20, 2021.

29. Supra, note 22.
30. Kanti Bajpai, "Back to the future: India's China policy has come full circle since Indira Gandhi", The Times of India, October 30, 2020. https://timesofindia.indiatimes.com/blogs/toi-edit-page/back-to-the-future-indias-china-policy-has-come-full-circle-since-indira-gandhi/.
31. Jessica Drun and Bonnie S. Glaser, "The Distortion of UN Resolution 2758 and Limits on Taiwan's Access to the United Nations", The German Marshall Fund of the United States, https://www.gmfus.org/news/distortion-un-resolution-2758-and-limits-taiwans-access-united-nations, accessed on March 24, 2022.
32. Mayank Singh, "Hindi-Chini bhai bhai is history, and a poor one at that", The Times of India,. https://timesofindia.indiatimes.com/blogs/voices/hindi-chini-bhai-bhai-is-history-and-a-poor-at-that/, accessed on March 15, 2019.
33. "B. Singapore 3294, Public Library of US Diplomacy", WikiLeaks. https://wikileaks.org/plusd/cables/04TAIPEI3845_a.html, accessed on April 11, 2020.

3

India and Taiwan Relations in a Bilateral Context

> *"India must begin economic and technological engagements with Taiwan, besides supporting it politically."*
>
> –Arvind Gupta

India got independence from the UK on August 15, 1947, followed by the nation's adoption of the Constitution of India on January 26, 1950, which replaced the Dominion of India. Nearly a month earlier on December 30, 1949, the Indian government declared the ROC Ambassador based in New Delhi as persona non-grata. The ROC Ambassador was asked to leave India when India derecognised his country. On the following day, the government of India offered its recognition to the PRC.[1] On April 1, 1950, India established diplomatic relations with the PRC, which made India one of the first nations to adopt the 'One-China Principle' to recognise the PRC, together with Burma and Pakistan. India made it clear that 'Taiwan is an inalienable part of China'.[2] Although the 'One-China Principle' was not officially coined at that time, the Chinese Communists did make it mandatory for any country wishing to establish diplomatic relations with the PRC to withdraw all recognition from the ROC. It was either full recognition of the PRC or nothing at all. More specifically, the PRC made India recognise it as the sole, legitimate government, which means the PRC does not allow two Chinas to legally exist at the same time. Thus, India was asked to 'make a clean break' with the ROC so as to unconditionally refuse any kind of support and assistance to the ROC, and then to make it into an official declaration, as a proof of India's not being an American camp-follower.[3] Essentially, the prerequisites of Indian model for establishing diplomatic relations with the PRC were conceived and developed later as the 'One China Principle'—a model for other countries to follow.

71 years later, India's former Foreign Secretary Vijay Gokhale commented on the recognition by the Government of India of the PRC in December 1949, opining that "the lapses on India's part—the absence of wider political consultations within the Indian leadership, the overlooking of its national interest in its anxiety over the timing, and the erroneous assumption that the act of officially recognising the People's Republic of China was tantamount to the automatic establishment of formal diplomatic relations—led the Government of India to see the act of recognition as its only objective. In the process, India unilaterally gave up some crucial negotiating."[4] The current border disputes between India and PRC could have been avoided if proper negotiations had been conducted.

Ever since this diplomatic switch the bilateral ties between India and the ROC on Taiwan ceased to exist. Furthermore, as India joined the non-aligned movement and Taiwan aligned with the US grouping during the Cold War era, the prospect of informal contacts between India and Taiwan was not possible. According to UN General Assembly Resolution 2758, the PRC began representing China at the UN from November 15, 1971, and its delegates were seated at the UN Security Council meeting held on November 23, 1971. As a result, the ROC on Taiwan was deprived of the legitimate right it had earned to represent China since the inception of the UN, alongside 50 other Charter members in 1945.

Section 1: India's "One-China Policy" and its Impact on Relations with Taiwan

In the span of 1950 to 1995, there were very few interactions between India and the ROC on Taiwan. Despite the 1962 Sino-Indo War and the PRC's 'covert and overt' military assistance to Pakistan, India maintained the 'One-China Policy'—a policy of non-recognition of the ROC on Taiwan—that resulted in almost no contact at all with Taiwan.

Throughout the Cold War years, even low-level Taiwan officials were not issued visas to visit India due to the constraints of the latter's self-imposed 'One-China Policy'.

Did Taiwan, as many had believed, cease to be a matter of interest for India after 1950? In fact, during the Korean War between 1950-1953, India had suggested to the US "that a declaration about Formosa (Taiwan) would ease the situation"; it had also suggested to the PRC that "any injudicious or provocative step would be dangerous and should therefore be avoided, although India knew well that its influence was limited and its role as a peacemaker was challenging. The First Taiwan Strait Crisis (1954-55) set the stage for India to regard it as a responsibility to advocate for peace at a time, when the conflict risked escalating into a global issue. India, acting as a intermediary, conveyed the PRC's position to the US that the PRC "was not interested in fighting with them over Taiwan", and that its immediate concerns were focussed solely on the offshore islands. This offshore-islands-for-cease-fire idea proposal by India, which was encouraged by the UK, was ultimately rejected by the PRC without India's knowledge. The growing distrust between the US and India was deepened and the US was biased about India's neutrality and sincerity when the UK took India's help to serve its own purposes. India's intervention with the PRC was no longer required when the UK established its own channel to the PRC, and the PRC chose the UK channel to approach the US which led to the de-escalation of tension in the Taiwan Strait. Although India had no role to play in the final act of the First Taiwan Strait Crisis, India was from the very beginning actively involved in diplomatic efforts because of its geopolitical interests.[5]

It was Narasimha Rao's Government from 1991 to 1996 which reoriented India's foreign policy towards Taiwan in response to India's domestic and foreign challenges, providing an opening for improved relations between the two countries after more than four decades of India's indifference to Taiwan. More precisely, it was Prime Minister Rao's personal initiative to think about a possible way of setting up an office in Taiwan after his visit to China in 1994. During Rao's tenure as the Prime Minister, India had to work out effective measures to deal with one of its worst economic crises domestically. At the same time, India's long-term ally, the Soviet Union, ceased providing financial and defence support, compelling India to adapt to a completely different international order externally. As a strategic and deliberate move, a very high-powered unofficial delegation visited Taiwan, led by Inder Kumar Gujral (later Prime Minister 1997-1998) and RN Malhotra (former Governor, Reserve Bank of India), A P Venkateswaran (former Foreign Secretary) and Economist Charan Wadhwa. After their visit, a report with recommendations was prepared to encourage the establishment of an office in Taiwan in order to attract Taiwanese investment to India. Vinod C. Khanna was the first Director-General of the de facto Indian Mission in Taiwan, the ITA, where he set up the office and served a two-year tenure in Taipei from 1995 to 1997. His pioneering efforts laid the foundation to expand India's interests in Taiwan and 'to steer clear of political issues and concentrate on attracting Taiwanese investment, promoting bilateral trade and encouraging tourism to India'. However, his conundrum was how to ensure an optimal middle path–maintaining a productive relationship with Taiwan government without giving it any 'diplomatic' implication whatsoever.

It is understandable that Khanna's highest priority in Taiwan was 'to attract Taiwanese investments' in addition to trade, commerce and tourism. It was during his tenure that the two countries began working on agreements relating to avoidance of double taxation and investment protection with the challenge, with the challenge of finding appropriate wording that did not imply any form of recognition for the ROC—a goal that the Taiwanese counterpart constantly endeavoured to achieve. In order to function properly, Khanna had to deal with the Taiwan's Ministry of Foreign Affairs, especially the Director-General of the East Asian and the Pacific Department P.Y. Teng who a few months later assumed the post of the first Representative of the TECC in New Delhi.[6]

The opening of the representative offices of India and Taiwan in 1995, although with completely different agendas at the time, marked a landmark breakthrough, ushering in a new chapter in India-Taiwan bilateral relations both unofficially and even officially. Despite the challenges Khanna faced in fostering mutually beneficial relations between the two countries, he managed to arrange a low-profile visit by Commerce Secretary, Tejinder Khanna avoiding publicity and thus preventing protests from the PRC. This effort laid a foundation not only for the India-Taiwan economic relationship but also for collaboration in cultural, think tank, and scientific fields. From the outset the representatives from India and Taiwan began to walk a tightrope in each other's capital aiming to achieve their long-term objectives, while avoiding full political engagement due to India's 'One-China Policy' constraints. It is fair to say that all subsequent Director-Generals of the ITA in Taipei, following Vinod C. Khanna and the Representatives of TECC in New Delhi after P.Y. Teng, have consistently strived to fulfill their missions, advancing their national interests within these political limitations. (For details, refer Annexure 6)

To facilitate investment, the "Agreement between the TECC in New Delhi and the ITA in Taipei on the Promotion and Protection on Investment" was signed in 2002. This agreement represented a pragmatic manoeuvre with both sides carefully navigating the 'One-China Policy' to secure prior approval from India's Cabinet without raising concerns from the PRC. Vijay Gokhale, Director-General of ITA in Taipei from 2004 to 2007, shared his insights on the reasons of India-Taiwan closer ties, emphasising "The relatively undeveloped state of relations between Taiwan and India was largely due to India's complicated and sensitive ties with the PRC. And it was not until 1991 after the end of the Cold War and India's financial crisis that economic pragmatism began to play a more important role in India's foreign policy." He further clarified that economic factors, such as the potential for trade and investment, were the primary motivations reasons for India's shift from a no-contact policy with Taiwan. Moreover, he pointed out that "Taiwan dreams of parlaying closer economic, political, and educational ties with India into an economic and even strategic counterweight to China's regional dominance." However, he underscored that "India seeks Taiwan investment along with manufacturing and commercial expertise but rejects the idea of forming any sort of counterweight to China as pure fantasy." He opined that both sides' overly optimistic expectations to promote bilateral economic relations had encountered frictions and restrictions from the Indian side, but insisted that educational, scientific and technical exchanges were fruitful.[7] Great challenges remained as one of the countries sought to avoid any political implications that could displease the PRC, while both worked diligently to remove the structural obstacles that were hampering their closer relations in every field.

In a hearing of the Parliamentary Committee on External Affairs, Foreign Secretary Vijay Gokhale reiterated India's baseline policy on Taiwan He submitted to the Committee on February 22, 2018, stating "India does not accord any diplomatic recognition to Taiwan. India recognises only the People's Republic of China as the legitimate government of China. However, India's economic and commercial links as well as people to people contacts with Taiwan have expanded in recent years." He further elaborated, "This is a policy the Government of India established on December 30, 1949. On the same day, The Government of India declared the Ambassador of the so-called Republic of China resident in New Delhi, Lo Chia-Lun, as persona non-grata. That was an irretrievable step taken by derecognising that entity and asking its envoy to leave the country. The following day, the then government formally recognised the PRC."[8] Foreign Secretary Vijay Gokhale stressed that "all successive Government have adopted this policy" and "whether in terms of trade or in terms of people-to-people exchanges, there has been progress in our contacts with Taiwan within the policy parameters that the Government of India has laid down." Nonetheless, he reminded the Committee that "we have to also be aware that this is an issue which is highly sensitive for China and for our larger relationship with China, which is our neighbour and a country with which we have to build a long-term relationship."[9]

Regarding the relations between India and Taiwan, India's Parliamentary Committee on External Affairs expressed its stance on Taiwan issue as part of the Recommendation No. 3 after the report by the MEA on August 25, 2018. The Committee noted that "India does not accord any diplomatic recognition to Taiwan despite the flourishing nature of exchanges between the countries, such as in the fields of people to people contacts, trade and personal exchanges. The MEA has argued that it does not want to upend this policy of the Government of India in deference to China's sensitivity on the matter." The Committee further highlighted that "It comes as a matter of concern to the Committee that even when India is overly cautious about China's sensibilities while dealing the Taiwan and Tibet, China does not exhibit the same deference while dealing with India's sovereignty concerns, be it in the case of Arunachal Pradesh or that of the China-Pakistan Economic Corridor (CPEC) in Pakistan Occupied Kashmir (PoK).... It is difficult for the Committee to be content with India's continuing with its conventionally deferential foreign policy towards China." The Committee further expressed its position on the issue that "dealing with a country like China essentially requires a flexible approach. The Committee strongly feel that the Government should contemplate using all options including its relations with Taiwan, as part of such an approach."[10] However, there have been calls for closer engagement with Taiwan reflecting a clear sign of Indian public anger and frustration in dealing with China in recent years, in particular in 2020.

From the perspective of the ROC government on Taiwan, the so-called 'China hands' in the Government of India, especially within the MEA, are the key policymakers who determine the direction and the degree of engagement in India's relations with Taiwan. Naturally, they are entitled to formulate all policy towards a specific issues, areas, regions, countries or organisations in the best interests of India. The diplomats from the ROC on Taiwan working in India are well aware of whom they need to interact with and understand how these 'China hands' perceive Taiwan's ambitions to further their political agenda through deeper economic engagement.

The ongoing border standoff between India and China in the second half of 2020 increased Indian public antagonism towards China. Editorials in prominent Indian national newspapers and articles conveyed strong recommendations for a pragmatic shift in India's policy concerning Taiwan, suggesting support for Taiwan's pursuit of observer status at World Health Assembly (WHA) and proposing adjustments to India's 'One-China Policy' to enhance its relations with Taiwan. Numerous Indian scholars and thank tanks echoed similar sentiments, advocating for more serious engagement with Taiwan and for a stronger role for Taiwan in India's Indo-Pacific strategic framework or in brief, for India to consider the 'Taiwan card'. Whether India's MEA of India will adapt to those pragmatic advice remains a big question. Nonetheless Taiwan's identity and National Day gained significant visibility in Indian media. The PRC embassy in New

Delhi responded by issuing an open letter on October 7, 2020, to all the media houses in India and reminding them not to 'recognise' Taiwan either by celebrating or marking 'National Day of Taiwan' which falls on October 10. In the open letter the PRC Embassy further demanded, "We hope Indian media can stick to Indian government's position on Taiwan question and do not violate the One-China principle." The PRC Embassy went on arguing "In particular, Taiwan shall not be referred to as a 'country (nation)' or 'Republic of China' or the leader of China's Taiwan region as 'President', so as not to send the wrong signals to the general public." In response on the following day, the Spokesperson of the MEA of India reminded the Chinese that "There is a free media in India that reports on issues that they see fit."[11]

Indian general public were surprisingly reminded by an embassy of a neighbouring authoritarian country, where there is no freedom of the press, that Indian media should adhere to the government's position on Taiwan avoid violating the 'One-China principle'. It is equally absurd to be congratulated by the PRC government on the result of a general election in a democratic country like India without mentioning 'democratic election', 'democracy' or 'people's voice' simply because there is no democratic election in China at all under its one-party-ruled political system.[12]

Another incident occurred in early July, 2018 when Taiwan strongly protested Air India's decision to change its designation to 'Chinese Taipei' on its website. Responding to a question raised, India's MEA stated that Air India's decision to change the destination of Taiwan into Chinese Taipei is "entirely consistent with international norms and our own position on Taiwan since 1949."[13] It reflected a situation where significant obstacles persist within the MEA under the self-imposed 'One-China Policy'. The term "Chinese Taipei" was actually a creation by the PRC to forcing Taiwan to accept it in order to participate in the International Olympic Committee in 1981 and the subsequent Olympic Games. Especially its official form of Chinese translation is "中華台北", rather than the PRC's intentional misuse of "中國台北" which it often uses to refer to the Taiwan team in its television broadcasts and news reports.

Nevertheless, as many observers have pointed out, since 2010, there has been no joint statement between the leaders of India and China reaffirming

India's commitment to the 'One-China' principle. Some argue this could be due to India's dissatisfaction with China's undertakings in Kashmir. One former Indian deputy national security advisor, Arvind Gupta, proposed that India should take a more dynamic approach outside the "One-China" commitment and that there must be required reciprocity in all relations between China and India.[14] He further argued that "India must begin economic and technological engagements with Taiwan, besides supporting it politically.[15] Essentially these remarks reflects an alternative attitude toward India's position of the 'One-China' principle, allowing Taiwan some space and flexibility in promoting mutually beneficial relations in the future, as well as serving as a bargaining chip to counter the PRC's assertive and dominant position on India's territorial concerns.

On April 2, 2021, a train carrying 490 passengers collided with a fallen truck in eastern Taiwan and derailed in a tunnel, killing over 50 people and injuring dozens. India's MEA spokesperson Arindam Bagchi tweeted, "We are deeply saddened by the loss of so many lives in the railway accident in Taiwan. Our deepest condolences to the families and our prayers for the early recovery of the injured."[16] This immediate humanitarian gesture may be the first occasion on which the Indian government officially expressed its condolences to the families of the victims in a train accident in Taiwan, following the India-Taipei Association's message of condolences in Taipei on April 2. Over 600 Heads of State, Heads of Governments, Foreign Ministries and dignitaries from over 80 countries and international organisations within a day in the aftermath of the accident have expressed condolences and sympathies.[17] Chinese Communist Party (CCP) Secretary-General Xi Jinping is among them as well.[18] As the Ministry of Foreign Affairs, Republic of China (Taiwan) confirmed in a press release on April 5, 2021, there were over 780 Heads of State, Heads of Governments, Foreign Ministries and dignitaries from over 94 countries and international organisations globally have done so.[19] Furthermore, there were 846 Heads of State, Heads of Governments, Foreign Ministries and dignitaries from over 97 countries and international organisations across the globe who have expressed condolences and sympathies via various channels, according to the Ministry of Foreign Affairs on April 6, 2021.[20] To democratic people around the world, this gesture clearly indicates that politics has no role in humanitarian concern and empathy for the loss of lives in a tragedy. However, to the 'wolf warriors' of the PRC, politics permeate every aspect of life.

Business relations between India and Taiwan have been expanding over the past two decades, although India has maintained a low profile on political contacts with Taiwan. In early July 2023, Taiwan announced plans to open a third office in Mumbai to deepen exchanges and cooperation in western India. When asked to comment, the India's External Affairs Ministry Spokesman, Arindam Bagchi, said on July 6, 2023 that India's foreign policy on Taiwan is clear and consistent and the government 'facilitates and promotes interactions with Taiwan in areas of trade, tourism, culture, education and other such people-to-people contacts and exchanges."[21] It appeared that the Indian government has downplayed down the political implication of agreeing to the establishment of a third Taiwanese government office in India, especially in Mumbai. This proposal has been reportedly raised by Taiwan side for years but not received a positive response from the Indian side. However, with increasing Taiwanese investment targeting the western and northwestern part of India, the setting up of a TECC office in Mumbai has become more and more essential for Taiwan. This new office will provide immediate assistance and services to nearby Taiwanese companies and factories and facilitate bilateral interactions that were previous taken care of by the TECC office in New Delhi.

India has not sent official congratulatory messages to Taiwan, unlike the US, EU and its member states, Japan, South Korea, Australia, Singapore, The Philippines, and others, in the wake of the Taiwan's presidential election on January 13, 2024., The India's MEA Spokesperson Randhir Jaiswal said on January 18, 2024 that India "has taken note of the recent development" in Taiwan and commented that "India has strong and growing people to people ties, culture, education, trade and investment links with Taiwan". The Government of India facilitates these exchanges an looks forward to continuing them for shared prosperity and development."[22] Compared to the congratulatory messages sent by the governments, international organisations and parliamentarians from more than 80 countries world-wide within the first week after Taiwan's presidential election, India's lukewarm and somewhat disappointing response can be interpreted as a goodwill gesture, maintaining its long-standing foreign policy towards Taiwan without introducing sensitive political implications that might worsen its relations with the PRC. As one prominent scholar commented, "the democratic ideological glue is missing in India's cautious response to Taiwan's elections."[23]

Section 2: India's Look East, Act East and Taiwan's New Southbound Policy

India's Look East Policy opened the gateway to engage the Southeast Asia. The Act East Policy, as an extension, was launched to intensify economic, strategic and diplomatic relations with countries in East Asia. Taiwan's New Southbound Policy, covering 18 countries, was initiated to encourage Taiwanese investors to explore the golden opportunity and potential that India is offers to the world. With governments' favourable policy guidelines in place, India and Taiwan can engage each other with much clearer objectives in mind, which, years later, have proven to be mutually beneficial.

The Look East Policy

India's Look East Policy was launched in 1991 by the Government of India led by Prime Minister Narasimha Rao. It was a timely initiative just after the end of the Cold War when most Asian countries were conducting a major shift in their economic and strategic policies to address negative regional challenges of economic and security challenges. In India's case, the Look East Policy aimed to foster political, economic, and security co-operation with Southeast Asian countries. After the Cold War, India planned to act as a counterweight to China in Southeast Asia. When Prime Minister Rao_initiated the Look East Policy, he had three objectives clearly in mind: revitalising political contacts with the ASEAN countries, to enhancing economic interactions with them in trade, investment, science and technology, and tourism, and establishing strategic and defence links, with some nations. In early 1990s, India adopted economic reforms, marking a significant shift in its development strategy. India joined ASEAN as a sectoral partner in 1992 and then became a full partner with it in 1994. Today, India is an active member of the ASEAN Regional Forum, the East Asian Summit and the ASEAN Defence Ministers Meeting Plus. Currently, in addition to annual summit-level meetings with ASEAN, India is actively participating in other 30 sectoral dialogue mechanisms and seven Ministerial-level meetings.[24] Furthermore, India re-designed a multi-dimensional foreign policy to foster closer economic and strategic ties with the US, notably enhancing relations in 2008, when the bilateral relations steadily strengthened.

The Look East Policy has contributed to strengthening India's political, economic and cultural ties with the Southeast Asian and the Pacific countries. It also ensured that India plays an important part in the regional economic and security mechanisms.[25] India's bilateral ties with Taiwan, Japan and South Korea have been substantially strengthened over common values on democracy, human rights and strategic interests. They have been India's major sources of Foreign Direct Investment ever since.[26] During Vinod C. Khanna's tenure of ITA's Director-General in Taipei from 1995-1997, the India government began to ease visa restrictions on Taiwanese passport holders, a friendly and timely move that facilitated \much closer ties between the two countries.

The Look East Policy provided a golden opportunity for India and Taiwan to explore possibilities of enhancing collaboration in mutual interest, within the constraint of the India's "One-China Policy". It also offered an opportune moment for both sides to think about something meaningful and doable outside the box. The ensuing two decades witnessed a series of modest economic and diplomatic achievements starting from exchange of visits and then the visible establishment of India-Taipei Association (ITA), India's "unofficial" representative office in Taipei in 1995. Unsurprisingly, the government of the ROC on Taiwan would not miss out this best timing to nudge an inch further for the Indian side to allow Taiwan a more sensible presence in India. Through a series of tactic and quiet negotiation between the ROC Ministry of Foreign Affairs and the India's MEA and finally concluded an acquiescence by exchange of letter, without signing some form of formal document, for Taiwan to set up the Taipei Economic and Cultural

Centre in New Delhi only a few months later than the establishment of India's ITA in Taipei. For practical needs the two representative offices, no matter how "unofficial" they thought they are, would have to deal with the Ministry of Foreign Affairs in Taipei or the MEA in New Delhi for certificate, tax refund, other arrangements and negotiations, etc. The two representative offices were authorised to handle consular affairs on behalf of their respective government.

Meanwhile Taiwan was undergoing a period of democratic transformation after President Lee Teng-hui assumed the presidency by means of an indirect election system in 1988, and subsequently through a direct election from 1996 until 2000. In early June, 1995, President Lee departed for on a short "private" visit to the US. During this visit, he championed for the 'Republic of China' and the 'Republic of China on Taiwan' fifteen times in his speech at his alma mater, Cornell University in Ithaca, New York on June 9, 1995. This visit was seen as a bold symbol of a Taiwanese president setting foot on the American soil after suffering decades of international isolation. The PRC promptly published more than five articles to criticise President Lee during his US trip for challenging the 'One-China' Policy.

The PRC continued by launching tests of six missiles targeting at an area of 60 km north of Taiwan from July 21 to July 26, 1995. The missile tests included four short range and two intermediate range missiles, all mobile and nuclear-capable. The missiles were launched after PRC's invective denunciation of President Lee Teng-hui's 'private' visit to his alma mater, Cornell University. At the same time, the Chinese PLA mobilised forces and moved fighter aircrafts to the coast of Fujian Province, which resulted in a sharp drop in Taiwan's local currency value.[27] All these actions were part of a constituted effort to coerce to the not to vote for Lee in the coming presidential election, but in vain.

On March 23, 1996, the Taiwanese voters overwhelmingly elected Lee Teng-hui as their first directly elected President in Taiwan's history. Vinod C. Khanna Director-General of the ITA in Taipei happened to witness the entire historical incidents and global reactions in Taiwan. It was President Lee who announced the 'Pragmatic Diplomacy' aimed at establishing substantial relations with like-minded countries, and initiated the Southbound Policy, which encouraged Taiwanese companies to relocate their investments to Southeast Asian countries, such as Indonesia, Vietnam, Thailand, the Philippines, rather than to China. That was the beginning when some far-sighted Taiwanese companies began showing interest in India as a viable investment alternative for their sustainable global operations. Many of them finally started their manufacturing bases in Gujarat, Delhi, Tamil Nadu, Andhra Pradesh and Karnataka.

When India opened its 'unofficial' representative office in Taiwan in 1995, the bilateral trade volume was only USD 700 million. By 2003, this bilateral trade volume had doubled to USD 1.4 billion. Despite this growth, Taiwan's exports to India still accounted for only 0.6 percent of its total exports and Taiwan's imports from India were less than 0.6 percent of the total imports. Taiwan's total cumulative investment in India up to 2002 was only about USD 110 million compared to USD 1.1 billion Taiwan investment in the Philippines, USD 4.3 billion in Singapore. One of the obvious reasons for this discrepancy was the political will of the governments concerned, influenced significantly by their adherence to the 'One-China Policy', which they all claimed to uphold. In April 2002 a Taiwan airline launched direct flights between Delhi and Taipei, providing a further boost to investment, trade relations and mutual understanding between India and Taiwan. Direct links for both goods and passengers from both countries now save both time and costs.

The Act East Policy

India's Minister of External Affairs, Sushma Swaraj, said in Hanoi in August 2014 to 15 Indian Heads of Mission in Southeast and East Asia and directed them to 'Act East' and not just 'Look East'. She stressed India needs an Act East Policy which should replace India's twenty-year-old Look East Policy.[28] According to Reconnecting Asia, Centre for Strategic and International Studies, Taiwan is within the geographic scope of Act East Policy which covers 11 countries including India, Taiwan and nine ASEAN members except Thailand.[29] India's Prime Minister Narendra Modi made his remarks at the East Asia Summit in Naypyitaw, Myanmar on November 13, 2014 in which he specified that since his entering office six months ago, his government 'had moved with a great sense of priority and speed' to turn India's 'Look East Policy' into 'Act East Policy'.[30]

After Inder Kumar Gujral, Narendra Modi was the second Prime Minister to have visited Taiwan before assuming office and without any government position at the time of the visit. Modi was the General Secretary of the BJP at the time he visited Taiwan in 1999. He then was elected the Chief Minister of Gujarat (2001-2014).[31] It is generally believed that during Modi's tenure as the Chief Minister of Gujarat, Taiwan established very close contact with him personally and the state of Gujarat. Taiwan's China Steel Corporation (CSC) set up a branch in Gujarat in October 2011, with hot commissioning initiated in September, 2014. And official operations commencing in May 2015. CSC subsequently announced an additional investment of USD 178 million to build a new plant to produce electrical steel in Gujarat, marking the second largest investment in India from Taiwan at the time. China Synthetic Rubber Co. also announced an investment of USD 330 million for a new factory in Andhra Pradesh.[32] Through the joint efforts of India and Taiwan, trade, investment, and tourism between the two have increased greatly over the past few years. Bilateral trade in 2018 reached USD 750 million, six times the volume in 2000. This increasing trend in bilateral became even more pronounced after the COVID-19 pandemic, with trade volume between India and Taiwan reaching USD 8.45 billion in 2022.

The New Southbound Policy

Taiwan's President Tsai Ing-wen launched the New Southbound Policy before assuming the presidency in 2016, aiming to enhancing relations with 10 ASEAN countries, six South Asian countries, Australia, and New Zealand. (For details, please refer Annexure 7) It is Taiwan's people-centric and diverse regional strategy that actively seeks to expand and deepen economic and other areas of collaboration with these 18 Indo-Pacific countries, and to strengthen friendship with them. President Tsai has highlighted Southeast Asia and India as significant focus points for her New Southbound Policy, with goals and ideals of that closely align with those outlined in the ASEAN Outlook on the Indo-Pacific and

India's Act East Policy. Tsai firmly believed that by working together, these initiatives can achieve mutual benefits, fostering complementary, economic, and social successes.

India's FDI policy was amended in April 2020, requiring all investments, irrespective of the sectoral cap, from countries sharing a land border with India, including China, to obtain prior government approval. And the prior approval is also needed even when the investment is made indirectly from these countries. The Indian government's FDI policy review was conducted to curb 'opportunistic takeovers/acquisitions of Indian companies due to the current COVID-19 pandemic'. Since India treats Taiwanese investments separately from those of Chinese, they have been subject to security clearance. The recent policy changes do not cover FDI from Taiwan and therefore are excluded from the changes.[33] Meanwhile, the state government of Tamil Nadu established a special Investment Promotion Task Force for attracting Investments under the Chairmanship of Chief Secretary with, among others, Taiwan External Trade Development Council (TAITRA) as a member. This Task Force is committed to taking pro-active steps to attract investments from countries such as the US, South Korea, Japan, Taiwan, and Singapore against the background that the economic upheavals and supply constraints caused by the COVID-19 have prompted those countries to rethink their existing supply chains which are likely to diversify by establishing supply chains originating in India.[34] Since the first three months of 2021, the Chief Ministers of Tamil Nadu, Andhra Pradesh and Karnataka, and even Puducherry have adopted more proactive approaches to attract Taiwanese investments by introducing their advantages for foreign investors. This is a promising sign of synergy between the two countries, aimed at making the most of initiatives like India's 'Make in India', 'Digital India' 'Smart City', 'Skill India' and 'Atmanirbhar Bharat'.

Up to the end of 2020, according to Taiwan's official figure of the accumulated investment from Taiwan to India reached over USD 941 million.[35] The total number of Taiwanese companies was less than 150 in 2020, according to official data from both countries. These figures are apparently underestimated, as many companies mobilised investment capital from outside Taiwan, meaning their origin may not be accounted for under

Taiwan. Moreover, the employment generated and the economic turnover these companies contribute extending far beyond what the official statistics reflect.

Section 3: Mutually Beneficial Interactions

Since the establishment of the ITA in Taipei and the TECC in New Delhi in 1995, followed by the TECC in Chennai in 2012 and the preparatory work for the TECC in Mumbai, the relations between India and Taiwan have embarked on an steady enhancement, extending beyond economic and investment engagements primarily from Taiwan to India. Areas such as language training, higher education, science and technology, health, culture, and non-governmental organisations (NGOs) activities are witnessing mutually beneficial growth. Sridharan Madhusudhanan, Director-General of ITA in Taiwan from 2016 to 2020 observed three positive trends in India-Taiwan relations: logical strengthening, organic expansion and new possibilities. He further elaborated, "In almost all the fields of engagement, from infrastructure projects to electronics, from automobile tyres to sports shoes, from technical textile to food products, from academic exchanges to cultural interactions, we see continued growth with increased momentum". The number of Indian students in Taiwan has increased threefold over the past couple of years, while people in both countries are also exploring new possibilities for cooperation in areas such as start-ups and renewable energy.[36] In order to help nurture Indian talents, Taiwan offered Taiwan Scholarships, Huayu Enrichment Scholarships to 79 students pursuing Masters or Doctoral degrees or dedicated to Mandarin Chinese language training in Taiwan in 2019. In 2020, 2021 and 2022, the total numbers of these two scholarships increased to 84 (45+39), 117 (45+72) and 114 (48+66),besides many others provided by the International Cooperation and Development Fund (Taiwan ICDF) and individual Taiwanese universities.[37] Furthermore, for scholars interested in research on subjects related to India and Taiwan, Indo-Pacific, regional and security issues, dozens of Taiwan Fellowships are available, covering research, accommodation and living cost for a period of up to one year each. The government of the ROC on Taiwan firmly believe educational and academic exchange of talent and expertise are bilaterally beneficial and the most feasible ways if the two country wish to deepen mutual understanding and collaboration in all possible fields.

In 2020, Taiwan's image received a much-needed boost among Asian countries, specifically India as Taiwan donated 1 million surgical masks and hundreds oxygen generators at the most critical time in 2020 and 2021. Taiwan's effective response to COVID-19 pandemic facilitated its international outreach, and in 2020 presented Taiwan with golden opportunities to further engage other Asian countries. The pandemic cruelly taught the world a lesson that international cooperation should extend beyond the traditional domains of security, trade and political constraints. It is also essential for Taiwan to engage India and other 17 destination countries by enhancing cooperation in health under the framework of the New Southbound Policy.

India is one of the frontrunners in developing COVID-19 vaccines, with its storing capabilities in mass production and research in biochemistry and vaccines. When the PRC exerted pressure on Taiwan's diplomatic allies in Latin America to switch diplomatic recognition to the PRC in exchange for vaccine donations, India stepped in to agree to provide Paraguay with 200,000 COVAXIN vaccines in two batches starting from March 2021 to alleviate its dire shortage of vaccines. No matter what the official interpretations may highlight from either India or Taiwan, India has donated at least 680,000 doses to Taiwan's diplomatic allies, including those to Paraguay.[38] undoubtedly, India has earned a lasting reputation for helping those in need at the most challenging times of the global pandemic.

India has long been the research and manufacturing hub for nearly all kinds of vaccines, maintaining high standards of quality and reasonably affordable costs. Countries across the globe have benefited from India's expertise which not only saves lives, but also improves life expectancies world-side. Many argue that Taiwan should engage more extensively with India in vaccine development and clinical trials to ensure a credible and required stages in the development of new vaccines.

Based on fundamental commitment to democratic values in its political governance, Taiwan has stood as a frontline state for over seven decades, consistently resisting the PRC's authoritarian sharp power and frequent military coercion. As long as Taiwan remains a free and democratic country, it offers a stark contrast to the authoritarian models, demonstrating a more hopeful form of governance, for China and other Indo-Pacific countries to follow. Taiwan is determined to persist in democracy, security, prosperity, and "warm power" acting as a beacon of hope for the region. Further, Taiwan values a free, fair, just, and open society, valuing freedom, democracy, rule of law, diversity, and tolerance. More essentially, Taiwanese have chosen to fight for what they believe in, and they are ready to open arms to whoever is willing to join them for common goals.[39] On India's 75th Independence Day, Taiwan's foreign Minister Joseph Wu pointed it out specifically that "India and Taiwan are great democratic partners holding authoritarianism at bay".[40] The extent to which India and Taiwan can foster closer relations in areas of mutual concern without China's interference in India's foreign policy depends heavily on India's national interests to be secured along its borders with China and Pakistan. Therefore, Track 2 security dialogues between Taiwan and India have been conducted over the past twenty years, aiming to explore and expand the potential of bilateral relations and to guarantee mutual understanding in the execution of their respective foreign policies.

Section 4: Taiwan Education Centres vis-à-vis Chinese Confucius Institutes

Taiwan Education Centres

Taiwan and China are supposedly the two best providers of Mandarin Chinese language programs for India and the rest of the world, though their respective policy guidelines and methodologies behind the infrastructure differ in one essential core nature—with or without the influence of Chinese Communist ideology. As a democratic country which has inherited the traditional forms of Chinese culture without ideological imposition, Taiwan began to set up Taiwan Education Centres in 2007 to offer Mandarin Chinese language courses and proficiency tests based on Taiwan's policy of teaching Mandarin Chinese as a second foreign language overseas. China, on the other hand, started to establish

Confucius Institutes in 2004 as non-profit public institutions to promote Chinese language and culture in foreign countries, the first one being in Seoul, South Korea, followed by one in Maryland, USA which closed in 2020. An obvious irony is that the Confucius Institute does not teach Confucianism—that the PRC aimed to destroy during the Cultural Revolution from 1966 to 1976.

Taiwan and China have followed the footsteps of Western countries in promoting Mandarin Chinese language courses overseas, aiming to equip the students with different levels of proficiency. India is inherently the biggest talent pool and a huge market, and hence Mandarin Chinese language training in India has become a blue ocean for both Taiwan and China to advance Mandarin Chinese language and culture, provided that ideology and border disputes did not come to the surface.

Taiwan's Ministry of Education entrusted the Foundation for International Cooperation in Higher Education of Taiwan (FICHET) with the responsibility of operating Taiwan Education Centres internationally. Under FICHET's guidance, there are six Taiwan Education Centres (country level) based in the capitals or major cities of Japan, Mongolia, Thailand, the Philippines, Indonesia, and India, overseeing country-wide operations.

Taiwan signed an MOU with Amity University Haryana on February 26, 2021,[41] which marked the setting up 19 Taiwan Education Centres on India's university campuses, based on a university-to-university basis and Mandarin Chinese Programs on a Ministry-to-university basis. Altogether there are more than two dozen of Mandarin Chinese teachers from Taiwan in service in India for the time being and each and every one of them receives a yearly, renewable visa.[42] As a result of mutual efforts, the number of the Taiwan Education Centres in India increased to 31 at the end of 2023 with institutions like Presidency University in Bengaluru, Karpagam Academy of Higher Education in Coimbatore, the IIT Gandhinagar and many other education institutions have signed MOUs. In mid-March 2024, the number of Taiwan Education Centre in India increased to 32 following an MOU was signed with Rajagiri Colleges of Social Sciences and Rajagiri Business School. However, owing to the high demand for mutually beneficial establishment of Taiwan Education Centre in India, it can be expected that more MOUs will be inked as long as Taiwan has the capacity of supplying enough high-quality Mandarin teachers in the years to come.

Teachers from Taiwan are professionally trained and authorised to teach Mandarin Chinese language courses and conduct proficiency test at different levels as a second foreign language. Throughout the various interactions, the Mandarin Chinese teachers have the privilege of selecting most talented and interested students, if the latter so wish, to pursue higher education degrees in Taiwan in the long run, or to refer them to talent hunting companies which are in great need to recruit employees with Mandarin Chinese language capability.[43]

Over the years, the Mandarin Chinese teachers from Taiwan have taught over 6,000 students at partnered Indian universities. They have actively participated in local education fairs, representing Taiwanese universities, and have meticulously planned Taiwan Higher Education expositions. Meanwhile, they organise seminars, or forums to foster research cooperation and academic exchange between Taiwan and the host country. The 1st India-Taiwan Bilateral Forum on Mandarin Chinese Course Materials for Indian Learners took place in Jawaharlal Nehru University (JNU), New Delhi in March 2017 to exchange views and ideas on the teaching materials. The Second Forum was held at Amity University, Noida in May, 2018.[44] The Third Forum was conducted online in JNU in October 2021 due to the COVID-19 pandemic. And the Fourth Forum was held in a hybrid manner in Taiwan from September 30 to October 1, 2022.[45]

Taiwan' capability in providing high-quality Mandarin Chinese trainings at different levels, based on university campuses, has garnered recognition and appreciation from Indian counterparts and students who have attended the classes. It is anticipated that the number of Taiwan Education Centres in India could reasonably increase to 40 or 50 in the years to due to high demand.

Confucius Institutes

China's Office of Chinese Language Council International (Hanban), affiliated with China's Ministry of Education was set up to oversee the operations of Confucius Institutes abroad. In 2020, Hanban rebranded itself as the Centre for Language Education and Cooperation. Its Constitution stipulates that the Confucius Institutes "shall not contravene concerning the laws and regulations of China". As of the end of October 2020, the Hanban website lists three Confucius Institutes in India, namely, University of Mumbai, Vellore Institute of Technology, and Lovely Professional University. Additionally there are three Confucius Classrooms at the School of Chinese Language Kolkata, Bharathiar University, and KR Mangalam University. Chinese teachers from China are granted a one-month, non-renewable visa by the Indian government.

There have been reports raising concerns about the 'Sharp Power' that exerted by Confucius Institutes in recent years. Research by the Australian Strategic Policy Institute (ASPI) indicated that the Confucius Institutes are closely controlled by the United Front Work Department of the CCP, with a former chief of this department serving as chair of the Confucius Institute's headquarters in Beijing. A 2019 study by University College Dublin recorded a noticeable shift in the tone of local media reports in favour of the PRC following the establishment of a Confucius Institute. In 2017, the US National Association of Scholars questioned the transparency of Confucius Institutes' contracts, a selective knowledge of Chinese history, avoiding contents related to human rights abuses in China. The American Association of University Professors raised a red flag in 2014 that Confucius Institutes promote the PRC's political goals and undermine the independence and integrity of academic institutions. Some well-established academic publications were influenced not to mention Taiwan, Tibet or Xinjiang.[46]

Due to significant concerns over Chinese academic and cultural influence on campuses, numerous colleges and universities within the US have decided to end cooperation with and close Confucius Institutes in their institutions. Similarly, universities in Germany, India, Denmark, the Netherlands, Belgium, France, Sweden, and Australia took similar steps, demanding greater transparency, exposing interference in academic activities or even shutting down Confucius Institutes.

Sharing concerns that the PRC government's action could pose risks to research, and threaten academic freedom, the US government announced that Confucius Institutes offer biased Chinese language and cultural education as part of "Beijing's multifaceted propaganda efforts". It emphasised that "The PRC government partially funds these programs, under guidance from the CCP's United Front Work Department." Therefore, in August 2020, the US Department of State designated the Confucius Institute US Centre 'as a foreign mission of the People's Republic of China'.[47] While Chinese statistics indicate that there are 81 Confucius Institutes and 13 Confucius Classrooms across the US by October 2020, US statistics indicated there were 75 Confucius Institutes, with 65 active on US university campuses as of mid-August 2020. In addition, nearly 500 Confucius Classrooms were based on K-12 campuses, often affiliated with university-based Confucius Institutes. As part of the US grand strategy to counter China's sharp power, both President Donald Trump and Secretary of State Michael Pompeo announced that all Confucius Institutes in the US would close by the end of 2020. There were 103 Confucius Institutes in the US in 2017, but its number dropped to 18 in April 2022, including four universities having indicated that they plan to close their Confucius Institutes and one is under review.[48] Following the precedence of Sweden and Denmark, Finland's University of Helsinki terminated its contract with Confucius Institute in June 2022, claiming to choose its own teachers and employ them on its own and to have its "Chinese language instruction to be research-based".[49]

In the aftermath of the Galwan Valley clash with China in June, 2020, India imposed a ban on dozens of Chinese apps as anti-Chinese sentiments reached historical highs. In addition, in July 2020, India's Ministry of Education sent out a letter to a few institutions asking for information about the activities arranged by their Confucius institutes and Chinese language training centres. This letter drew people's attention to the Chinese Confucius Institute program, a key pillar of PRC's global influence campaign, placing the future of the future of India-China educational cooperation in question. The Indian government had long monitored the Confucius Institute arrangement, exercising stringent visa restrictions on PRC Chinese teachers, though no prior steps had been taken to oversee the operations. In August 2020, the India's MEA explained that the government was following 2009 guidelines to require Indian institutions entering into agreements with foreign institutions to seek MEA's approval.[50] Apparently this guideline should also include Taiwan Education Centres; however, there have been no negative impacts on them so far, as Taiwanese teachers are highly professional and have no involvement in ideological infiltration.

Faced with this backlash, China rebranded the program by renaming Hanban as the Centre for Language Education and Cooperation in late 2020, implying that Confucius Institute brand may be phased out. However, most of the 550 Confucius Institutes and over 1,000 Confucius Classrooms around the world are still functioning as usual, even with different names. Those in Pakistan (5+2), Nepal (2+2), Sri Lanka (2+2), Bangladesh (2+1) and Myanmar (0+3) are intact.[51] India has decided to review three Confucius Institutes and three Confucius Classrooms and, more significantly, to remove Mandarin Chinese from the list of foreign languages permitted be to taught in schools under the new National Education Policy. The PRC had sharply reacted and asked India to "treat Confucius Institutes and China-India higher education cooperation in an objective and fair manner, avoid politicising normal cooperation, and maintain healthy and stable development of China-India people-to-people and cultural exchanges."[52]

Up to September 2023, only 136 Confucius Institutes world-wide have been closed, including five in Canada, 110 in the US, two in Australia, four in France and Sweden, two in Belgium, one in Spain, Denmark, Netherlands, Switzerland and Finland respectively.[53] In the wake of the British House of Commons spy scandal, which involves a British researcher with links to Members of Parliament and access to highly sensitive information, in early September 2023, the British Education Minister Gillian Keegan reportedly has agreed to shut down the 30 Confucius Institutes and 150 Confucius Classrooms "on condition that the teachers are replaced by staff from Taiwan".[54]

Compared to the PRC's Confucius Institutes, the Taiwan Education Centres operate smoothly in India and the rest of the world alike, with some programs conducted online during COVID-19 pandemic to facilitate the Mandarin Chinese language training. India's long-term goal remains to nurture experts proficient in Mandarin Chinese for academic, strategic, or commercial purposes. Taiwan, as a democratic country that upholds human rights and the rule of law without border disputes or strategic conflicts with India, is well positioned to engage India in deeper collaboration in Mandarin Chinese courses. Sources reveal some form of foundation has been laid in confidence with Taiwan to train officers with strategic expertise. Taiwan has the capabilities to work more closely with India in Mandarin Chinese language training. It can also assist India in enhancing expertise in intelligence gathering and analysis. As one journalist noted, an added advantage of learning Mandarin through Taiwan Education Centres is that instructions are provided in traditional Chinese characters, rather than the PRC's simplified form. The traditional script is better for learning Mandarin as it allows the learner to grasp the origin of characters as well as character-word associations. Additionally, learning about Chinese culture through Taiwan is better and convenient, as much of Chinese cultural heritage was lost during the Cultural Revolution. But many of those cultural traditions and relics have been preserved in Taiwan. Moreover, with Taiwan Education Centres there are no worries about ideological propaganda, soft power infiltration or espionage. Both India and Taiwan are democratic countries that respect open academic cultures. Strategically, Taiwan holds unparalleled knowledge of because of historical reasons. Therefore, it makes sense to collaborate with Taiwan to know more about what's happening in China.[55]

Median Indian media outlet published an editorial arguing that "Taiwan is looking to actively engage Southeast and South Asian nations like India...there are multiple areas where India and Taiwan can collaborate from smart cities and farm technogies to semiconductors, renewable energy and even Mandarin Learning—Taiwan Education Centres can easily substitute for China's problematic Confucius Institutes." The editorial further emphasised that "with the troop disengagement process in eastern Ladakh stalled, Beijing clearly doesn't respect 'One India'. There is no reason, then, for India to overly sensitive about China's territorial claims...it may be time for New Delhi and Taipei to elevate their relationship and forge their own fraternity as well."[56] It will not be surprising that the PRC's 'wolf warriors,' immediately launched a sarcastic attack on India's free press, only to demonstrate to the world the PRC's authoritarian nature and disrespect for India's freedom of the press. By any standard, such action constitutes blunt interference in India's 'internal affairs'.

Section 5: High Level Exchange of Visits

As the interactions between two countries grew closer and closer starting from mid-1990s, high level visits naturally became possible. First, former Indian Defence Minister George Fernandes, in his private capacity, attended a trilateral conference jointly hosted by India, Japan and Taiwan in 2004. India then hosted separate Taiwanese delegations of parliamentarians and party officials for dialogues with their counterparts in Delhi in 2005 and 2006. In 2007, Ma Ying-jeou, Chairman of Taiwan's KMT party paid a private visit to India and delivered a speech at the Indian Council on World Affairs. In December 2010, India's former President A.P.J. Abdul Kalam visited Taiwan on a cultural tour, marking the first ever instance of a former head of state of the Republic of India visiting the ROC in Taiwan since 1949. Additionally, Taiwanese dignitaries such as the Education Minister, Planning and Development Minister, Deputy Minister of Foreign Affairs, Deputy Defence Minister and Vice Minister of Economic Affairs reportedly visited India in 2011. In the same year former Chairperson of the Taiwan's Democratic Progressive Party (DPP), Tsai Ing-wen also paid a visit to Delhi and former Vice President Annette Lu visited India in January 2012. Then in separate visits in 2012 and 2014, former Taiwanese President Ma Ying-jeou and Former Vice President Wu Den-yih transited in Mumbai and Delhi airports respectively.[57]

Groups of Parliamentarians from both sides have occasionally exchanged visits, provided that Chinese retaliation and reaction remained manageable. The Taiwan-India Parliamentary Friendship Association in Taiwan was established in 2016, with around 70 members, including 43 parliamentarians. Delegations from the Association visited India in 2014 and 2017, and additional visits were planned but could not be realised during the COVID-19 pandemic. The establishment of the India-Taiwan Parliamentary Friendship Forum in December 2016 marked a milestone in the emerging relations between India and Taiwan. The Forum was revived in 2020 to facilitate intensive dialogue among parliamentarians from the two democracies after the interruption caused by the COVID-19 pandemic.

A Minister Without Portfolio, a Deputy Minister of Economic Affairs attended the Vibrant Gujarat Summit in 2015. In 2017, the mayor of Taipei

City, Vice Minister of Economic Affairs, the Deputy Minister of Health and Welfare, and the Deputy Minister of Education from Taiwan visited India in 2017. Mr James Huang, Chairman of the (TAITRA) visited India and inaugurated the 'Smart Asia 2017' Exposition in Bangalore in late 2017. Since then, he has made no fewer than six visits to India to promote trade, investment and collaborations. In subsequent years, a few Expos focused on India were conducted in various formats to cope with COVID restrictions. Notably, the Taiwan Expo in India 2023 was scheduled to take place in Mumbai on October 5 to 7, 2023 to promote bilateral trade in Smart City, Smart Manufacturing, Smart Agriculture, Smart Life, Smart Medical, and other areas.

After the COVID-19 pandemic, at least one Foreign Minister, one Deputy Minister of Economic Affairs and one Deputy Minister of Science made either unannounced or official visits to India in 2022. In 2023 one Deputy Minister of Education also visited India to further promote higher education collaboration between the two countries. In September 2023, the President of Taiwan's Control Yuan, Chen Chu, participated as an observer in the Conference of National Human Rights Institutions of Asia Pacific in New Delhi.

Some Union Secretaries Principal Secretaries at the state level from India visited Taiwan to attend bilateral or multilateral meetings on science and technology, education, trade promotion fairs, and smart city forums. In May 2020, two BJP Parliamentarians from India virtually participated in the inauguration ceremony of Taiwan's President Tsai Ing-wen. In their joint message they remarked "both India and Taiwan are democratic countries, bonded by shared values of freedom, democracy and respect for human rights. Over the past years, India and Taiwan have enhanced bilateral relations enormously in wide-ranging areas, especially trade, investment and people to people exchanges".[58]

Pragmatic interactions between India's MEA and Taiwan's Ministry of Foreign Affairs have been ongoing for two decades or so. Regular bilateral meetings at Joint Secretary—Director-General level occur as needed to enhance coordination and communication on foreign policy matters, though higher level personal interactions still lack momentum due to political constraints on the Indian side. Taiwan, however, has consistently shown willingness to engage with India on issues of mutual concern. The visit of three retired Indian Armed forces Chiefs—Air Chief Marshal RKS Bhaduria, General Manoj Naravane and Admiral Karambir Singh—to attend the Kaetagalan Forum 2023 Indo-Pacific Security Dialogue in Taipei in August 2023 marks a significant milestone in the substantial relations between India and Taiwan. This was the first instance of such a high-level visit since India broke diplomatic ties with the ROC on Taiwan in 1949, even following the establishment of ITA and TECC in 1995.

Section 6: Agreements and MOUs

Since the establishment of ITA in Taiwan and TECC in New Delhi in 1995, Taiwan has shown strong interest in enhancing economic and political relations with India by signing various agreements to promote bilateral investment and trade. However, India's priorities were more limited focussing primarily on attracting Taiwanese investment in India. Politically, Taiwan faced limited opportunities for substantial progress without India's proactive friendship and goodwill. In 2001, six years after the ITA and TECC were established India and Taiwan inked an MOU on Civil Aviation, in 2001 and a Taiwanese airlines began direct flights between Delhi and Taipei in 2002. The two countries signed the Agreement on the Promotion and Protection on Investment in 2002, followed by an MOU on Science and Technology Cooperation in 2007. A consensus on degree-recognition in higher education was reached in 2010, and both sides agreed to further ease visa rules and requirements on a mutually beneficial basis. In 2011, the Double Taxation Avoidance Agreement, and the Agreement on Mutual Assistance in Customs Matters were inked. That same year an MOU was signed to set up a joint working group for a feasibility study on an Economic Cooperation Agreement. The Agreement on Temporary Admission for Goods was signed in 2013. In 2015, an MOU on cooperation in Micro, Small and Medium Enterprises (MSME) was signed in 2015, followed by the MOU on Agricultural Cooperation, and the Air Services Agreement signed in 2016. IN 2017, an MOU on Industrial Collaboration was established. In 2018, the Mutual

Recognition of the Respective Authorised Economic Operator Program and the Bilateral Investment Agreement were signed. An MOU on Higher Education Cooperation followed in 2019. IN 2021, the two sides inked the Arrangements Governing the Mutual Recognition of Organic Equivalence. Subsequent agreements in 2022 included the MOU on Cooperation of Intellectual Property Rights, the Agreement on Standards and Conformity Assessment, and the MOU on Cooperation of Tradition Medicine. Most recently on February 16, 2024, India and Taiwan signed an MOU on Labor Force Cooperation to better utilise human capital and facilitate employment(For details, please refer Annexure 8)

While the ITA and TECC have signed numerous documents that constitute various forms of agreements between the two countries, these accomplishments are largely attributable to the hard work of the twelve Director-Generals of the ITA in Taiwan beginning with Vinod C. Khanna, and the seven Representatives of the TECC in New Delhi starting with P. Y. Teng. Notably, more than half of the substantial Agreements and MOUs were signed between 2016 and 2020 by Sridharan Madhusudhanan on the Indian side, and between 2013 and 2020 by Chung-kwang Tien on the Taiwanese side. This clearly indicates that warmth and momentum were building steadily enabling both sides to have concluded some of the key agreements and MOUs as long as the political situations permitted and the need for closer economic collaboration became pressing.

Why did India and Taiwan favour to sign more MOUs than Agreements? According to the UN, "The MOU is often used to denote a less formal international instrument than a typical treaty or international agreement. It often sets out operational arrangements under a framework international agreement. It is also used for the regulation of technical or detailed matters. An MOU typically consists of a single instrument and is entered into among States and/or international organisations." It is a convenient instrument and usually does not need to get cabinet and parliamentary approval in a democratic country. It could be binding or non-binding dependent upon the actual intention of the signatories.[59] In the case of India-Taiwan relations, parliamentary approval implies diplomatic recognition of each other's sovereignty and that is against India's long self-imposed "One-China Policy".

However, screening from the above-mentioned long history of the interactions between India and Taiwan, there are already at least five agreements signed by India and Taiwan governments in the name of the ITA in Taiwan and TECC in New Delhi respectively. Notably, an agreement is 'a form of treaty which is a generic term embracing all instruments binding under international law, regardless of their formal designation, concluded between two or more international juridical persons'. The Vienna Convention 1969 defines a treaty as "an international agreement concluded between States in written form and governed by international law, whether embodied in a single instrument or in two or more related instruments and whatever its particular designation" (article 2 [1] [a]). Therefore, 'conventions, agreements, protocols and exchange of letters or notes may all constitute treaties. Treaties may be concluded between: States, International organisations with treaty-making capacity and States, or International organisations with treaty-making capacity. The application of the term treaty, in the generic sense, signifies that the parties intend to create rights and obligations enforceable under international law'.[60] A case in point was Indian Cabinet approved the Bilateral Investment Agreement in October 2018 and the media covered this piece of news widely.[61]

Now the real issues arise: Did those agreements pragmatically recognise Taiwan's sovereignty? Do they create any political complications in the relations between the PRC and India because they infringe upon India's promise to follow the 'One-China Policy'? India could categorically deny the two questions, but Taiwan might agree to disagree. Simply because the two countries finally came to terms with each other's practical needs and entered into so many agreements and MOUs with an aim to promoting bilateral commercial and investment interest, these initiatives have led to a significant increase from USD 1.2 billion in 2000 to USD 5.9 billion in 2014. Foxconn in Taiwan, one of the largest hardware manufacturers worldwide, announced in August, 2015 an investment of USD 5 billion in India, following in the foot steps of other well-known Taiwanese manufacturers'.

Gourangalal Das, the ITA Director General from July 2020 to August 2023, stressed that 'bilateral investments, people-to-people exchanges, and technical cooperation' are the three key areas on which his office will work hard to promote India-Taiwan relations. Taiwanese investors can find great opportunities for sustained growth in India. They can also share their world-renowned manufacturing skills and know-how with Indian partners to facilitate India's technical transformation in a short time. Das argued there is much room for collaborations in higher education and tourism in terms of people-to-people interaction. Although 3000 Indian students are pursuing Master's and PhD degrees in Taiwan, they constitute only a tiny portion of the three-quarter million Indian students pursuing higher education all over the world. Similarly, while 10000 tourists annually travel rom Taiwan to visit India, this number represents a very small portion of the 16 million outbound trips annually by Taiwan tourists. Das also indicated "Taiwan's advancements in functional and technical fields, ranging from agriculture to smart cities, industrial automation, science parks and ICT manufacturing, in addition to Taiwan's position in global supply chains." In 2020, India with a population of nearly 1.4 billion is Taiwan's 17th largest trading partner, and Taiwan is India's 31st. Thus, the ITA's focus is on expanding trade and investments with Taiwan before a bilateral trade agreement between India and Taiwan becomes possible.[62]

Section 7: Territorial Claims, Strategic and Security Issues

The world's longest disputed border of 3,488 km exists between India and China, the two nuclear-armed Asian powers with a population of nearly 1.4 billion each. Although both countries claim vast lots on each other's territory along the Himalayan frontier, no bullet was fired for nearly 50 years until the Galwan Valley incident in June, 2020. The PRC currently claims 90,000 sq km of territory in India's Arunachal Pradesh state, while India claims 38,000 sq km of land currently under Chinese control, which includes Aksai Chin plateau near the Ladakh region.

During Xi Jinping's visit to New Delhi in September 2014, Indian Prime Minister Narendra Modi reportedly discussed the border disputes and urged his guest to propose a solution. Since Modi became Prime Minister in 2014 up until the 2020 standoff, he and Xi Jinping have met no less than 18 times, officially or unofficially. To everybody's surprise, India and China encountered a 73-day standoff in Doklam in 2017. China has since reinforced and maintained its military presence in the Tibetan Plateau and has been increasing its pressure on Nepal, Sri Lanka, Maldives, Pakistan and Myanmar. Bit by bit, China is challenging India's influence in the Indian Ocean Region (IOR).

Territorial disputes are often related to a treaty law and the same issue may involve multiple dimensions. Diplomatic channels and mechanisms are often open for successive treaties or protocols. It is argued that "effective control and the principle of historic rights are sine qua non to fill the gaps in law that a treaty may not have adequately addressed or to guide the related parties where a treaty is absent at all." Therefore, 'one party's subjective interpretation and insistence in certain principles may clash with globally accepted standards'.[63] The border disputes between India and the PRC on Tibet actually fit in this situation as it rolled out in 2020.

However, the PRC has never based its territorial claim on international law or norms in its border disputes with neighbouring countries. Instead, it has presented one-sided historical statements to help legitimise its claims to territories long held by others. The PRC does not recognise the international value and principle in handling border disputes. As one scholar rightly pointed out, the PRC's principles can always be bent, and if it cannot be bent, it creates another principle for negotiation.[64] A case in point is the PRC's settlement of its border dispute with Myanmar in 1960 along the McMahon Line as the de facto border based on the watershed principle. However, the PRC did not follow this precedent it made with Myanmar by recognising the McMahon Line in dealing with India. In addition to occupying Aksai Chin in India's western sector, the PRC expanded its claims in 2006 to include Arunachal Pradesh in northeastern India as 'South Tibet', a territory about three times the size of Taiwan, as a bargaining chip to force India to accept its occupation of Aksai Chin.

Border and Territorial Disputes between India and "China"

The territorial claims, especially the border disputes, between India and 'China' may date back to the Simla Convention in 1914, signed by the representatives of British India and Tibet, who agreed to a de facto border known as the McMahon Line. However, this agreement was always contentious to the ROC government, which just came into being in 1912, and 'China' was not yet a unified country in 1914 when the Simla Convention was signed without the participation of the ROC government. More essentially, the ROC government genuinely believed that Tibet was within its jurisdiction, regardless the relationship between "China" and Tibet. Consequently, the ROC government never recognised the legitimacy of the Simla Convention. In turn, the PRC government since 1949 has rejected the Convention for exactly the same reason as the ROC. Furthermore, India's retired Foreign Secretary, Vijay Gokhale, mentioned in one of his newly published books that the Dalai Lama's government in Lhasa had addressed a letter in October 1947 to India's Prime Minister Jawaharlal Nehru 'seeking the return of all indisputable Tibetan territories gradually included into India, which included parts of modern-day Arunachal Pradesh, Ladakh, Darjeeling, Sikkim and Bhutan'.[65]

There is much to be learnt from past lessons. When Zhou Enlai first visited India in 1954 for 3 days and had five long sessions with Nehru without mentioning Tibet or the border problem. Later when Zhou visited Indian again in 1960 with an unexpected offer of a 'workable solution' to the border dispute. He presented a 'package deal' for a possible final resolution, proposing that the PRC would accept India's control over Arunachal Pradesh in exchange for the India's recognition of the PRC's control over Aksai Chin to be recognised by India. This in essence meant the PRC's de facto recognition of India's jurisdiction up to the McMahon Line, but Nehru categorically rejected the offer from Zhou.[66] However, the PRC militarily captured Aksai Chin throughout the 1950s and during the 1962 war, at the end of which, the PRC announced its withdrawal to its claimed 'Line of Actual Control (LAC)'.[67] Chinese troops withdrew to the McMahon Line in Arunachal Pradesh but still continued to hold military control over Aksai Chin ever since.[68] Notably, the size of Aksai Chin is 38,850 sq km, bigger than Taiwan's size of 36,000 sq km.

The confrontational incidents taking place along the Indo-China border since 2018, not to mention earlier episodes, reflect a crucial reality:, from India's perspective, it is Chinese troops who have provoked conflicts by either constructing roads and structures on, or trespassing into, the land claimed by India. Typically, the Chinese version of events would be simply opposite or contradictory to the India's. The Chinese tendency to distort of the incidents and the casualties India suffered in any unfortunate encounters naturally antagonises Indian feelings, further fuelled by the cold-blooded statements from the PRC Embassy's 'wolf warrior' diplomats'. The latter half of 2020 witnessed a re-emergence of wide-spread anti-Chinese sentiments which became so strong that both the government and people of India took measures to boycott Chinese products, mobile apps and business contracts, etc. The PRC's 'wolf warrior' diplomacy backfires not only in India, but also in many European countries like UK, Italy, Czech Republic, etc.[69]

Chinese and Indian Foreign ministers Wang Yi and S Jaishankar commented in public on the future relations between the two countries on March 7, 2021. Wang Yi remarked, "The boundary dispute, an issue left from history, is not the whole story of the China-India relationship. It is important that the two sides manage the dispute properly and at the same time, expand and enhance cooperation to create enabling conditions for the settlement of the issue". Immediately Jaishankar solemnly replied, "When a relationship is doing well, we would respond positively. So, if you extend your hand, I'm going to extend my hand too. But if you point a gun at me, I'll point a gun at you. I mean that's reasonable, that's logical."[70] Again when Wang Yi held talks with the Indian Ambassador Pradeep Kumar Rawat in June 2022, Wang reiterated that "common interests between China and India far outweigh the differences" and called on India and China to "work in the same direction to maintain the warming momentum in China-India relations and bring them back to the track of stable and sound development at an early date."[71]

Looking ahead, the PRC will likely continue to exert muscle on the border dispute with India while still extracting economic benefits from the relationship. In response, India will cooperate economically with the PRC in a more limited manner while continuing to contest the Chinese designs along the LAC. Both sides should avoid military conflict along the border, as neither side would concede defeat to face their people domestically. Facing the PRC's coercion occasionally, India shall narrow the gap in comprehensive national power, particularly in respect to economic self-reliance and by deploying additional troops permanently along the LAC to show it abides by the Agreement on The Maintenance of Peace along The LAC on The India-China Border, signed between India and the PRC in September, 1993.[72] As the armies of the two countries began disengagement of troops in eastern Ladakh, whether 'Hindi-Chini Bhai-Bhai' has been revived and survived the virtual 14th BRICS Summit in June, 2022, as Prime Minister Narendra Modi emphasised that "as BRICS members we should understand security concerns of each other and provide mutual support in designation of terrorists and this sensitive issue should not be politicised." He also highlighted "India's focus on a free, open, inclusive, and rules-based maritime space" and "respect for sovereignty and territorial integrity of all nations from the IOR to Pacific Ocean".[73]

How does the PRC view the border disputes and the illegitimate occupation of Indian territories? In his speech on the 100th anniversary of the CCP, Chinese President Xi Jinping reiterated 'Peace, concord, and harmony are ideas the Chinese nation has pursued and carried forward for more than 5000 years. The Chinese nation does not carry aggressive or hegemonic traits in its genes".[74] When addressing the French Institute of International Relations on August 30, 2021, Chinese Foreign Minister Wang Yi touted, "Some people say that China's revival is to change or even conquer the world. This is ignorance of Chinese history and Chinese civilisation. There has never been a gene of aggression in the blood of the Chinese nation."[75] In commenting the bout of tensions along the LAC on September 1, 2020, in rebuttal of India's statement a day earlier that India had pre-empted China's provocative military movement to change the status quo along the LAC on the southern bank of the Pangong Lake, Chinese Foreign Ministry's Spokesperson Hua Chunying said, "Seventy-odd years since the founding of new China, China never provoked any war or conflict and never occupied an inch of other country's territory. China border troops always strictly abide the LAC and never crossed the line."[76]

In brief, the PRC implies that it has neither provoked the war with Vietnam in 1979 nor occupied an inch of India's territories, such as Aksai Chin and Arunachal Pradesh in 1962, let alone engaged in unilateral trespassing actions that resulted in the standoffs in Pangong Lake and

Galwan Valley in the past couple of years. Additionally, throughout its 5000-year history, PRC's leadership and senior officials genuinely believe that Chinese nation has never occupied territories belonging to other countries asserting that it "does not carry aggressive or hegemonic traits in its genes". However, historical records clearly indicate that the areas of China's 14 Dynasties vary from 2.10 million sq km to 22.67 million sq km, and to the current PRC's 9.70 million sq km.[77] Even the territorial area of each respective dynasty fluctuated due to wars and international factors, as documented in the well-acknowledged history textbooks both in China and abroad. It would be fair to say that territories do not expand considerably through natural causes without war and conquest, however, to oversimplify the historical expansion of the 'Chinese nation' likely by force, as lacking 'traits in its genes' for the only purpose of cementing the peaceful image of the 'Chinese nation'. No matter how evident the counter-truth may be, and how genuinely the majority of the people on the Chinese mainland believe it, individuals in India, Tibet, Xinjiang, Mongolia, even Vietnam may have a lot to comment on these arguments.

As Vijay Gokhale indicated, India's "public trust in China has been deeply damaged and is unlikely to recover for some time. Indians believe that China took advantage of the pandemic to bully India. Ways to rebuild public trust need to be identified." He further concluded that India and China "are standing at a crossroads, it might be the final chance to take the path to coexistence of cooperation and competition".[78]

Section 8: South China Sea and Indo-Pacific Strategy

On the issue of the South China Sea, Taiwan's President Tsai Ing-wen in 2016 clarified the Taiwan government's official stance, stating that "The South China Sea Islands are part of the territory of the Republic of China. That the ROC is entitled to all rights over the South China Sea Islands and their relevant waters in accordance with international law and the law of the sea is beyond dispute". She acknowledged that the South China Sea issues are highly complex, overlapping claims from several countries, which undoubtedly encompass the political and economic interests of the claimants and impact regional security and diplomatic relations. President

Tsai reaffirmed that "The ROC government will continue to engage in cooperative consultations with each of the States.... It will not renounce its sovereignty or legal rights."[79]

The largest island of the Spratly Islands in South China Sea, Taiping Island, is part of ROC territory and has been under the ROC's actual control since 1946. Over the past decade the PRC has become more and more assertive in 'reclaiming' the 'historic waters' laying claim to almost the 1.3 million sq mile area as its sovereign territory by through its notorious 'nine-dash line', also referred to as the 'U-shaped line'. The line encompasses the South China Sea. China has since been building military facilities on artificial islets in the South China Sea, disregarding the international laws and the overlapping claims of Brunei, Malaysia, the Philippines, Taiwan, and Vietnam. Essentially, the origin of the nine-dash line came from a map published in 1936 by the ROC government based in Nanjing.[80] And more importantly, the original map is still kept by the ROC government in Taiwan.

Both the ROC and the PRC maintain that their jurisdiction over the South China Sea is consistent and continuous, and dates back no later than the Ming and Qing dynasties. In 1947, a map issued by the ROC government, then on the Chinese mainland, then based on the Chinese mainland, issued a map clearly depicting an 11-dash line, or the U-shape line, covering the entire South China Sea and the islands within it.[81] And that was exactly the official origin of the PRC's claims. The ROC's official stance on the South China Sea is that, at the end of World War II, the nations possessing territory around the South China Sea at the time, as well as the allied countries, never raised any objections to the ROC sovereignty claim or to military personnel it dispatched to enforce control over the islands. It is the ROC's belief that "due to their long-term inaction and tacit recognition of the ROC's jurisdiction over the islands, the countries are now bound under the doctrine of estoppel in international law; that is, they are prevented from now asserting the country to that which they have tacitly recognised."[82]

Taiwan's position on the South China Sea disputes has been firm and clear: they should be settled peacefully in accordance with international law and the law of the sea, including the UN Convention on the Law of the Sea (UNCLOS); Taiwan should be invited to participate in any international mechanisms aimed at resolving disputes; all the states concerned are obligated to maintain freedom of navigation and overflight in the South China Sea; and all the disputes should be resolved by setting aside differences in respective claims and promoting joint development of resources. The ROC supports negotiations to be conducted on the basis of equality and is willing to work out solutions with other states concerned to promote peace and stability in the region.[83]

On July 12, 2016, a historic and binding ruling on the PRC's claims against the Philippines in the South China Sea was issued by an independent arbitral tribunal established under the UNCLOS. The arbitral tribunal ruled, among other things, that the PRC's claims to ;historic rights' within the entirety of the U-shaped, '9-dash line' shown on its maps of the South China Sea are "mostly incompatible" with UNCLOS. UNCLOS is clear on such issues, stating that "the entitlements in the sea have to be with areas measured from land". The tribunal also ruled that "none of the Spratly Islands, nor an isolated reef known as Scarborough Shoal, are capable of supporting human habitation in their natural state". In other words, none of those islands or reefs in the South China Sea are entitled to an exclusive economic zone around them. The PRC's response immediately after the ruling was to dismiss it as "nothing more than a piece of waste paper".[84]

The government of the ROC on Taiwan also issued a statement and claimed, "We absolutely will not accept the tribunal decision, and we maintain that the ruling is not legally binding on the ROC". However similar, the responses from both sides of the Taiwan Strait, some scholars argue that there have been unnoticed changes in Taiwan's maritime legislation and rhetoric in the past few years, which they interpreted as "Taiwan no longer advocates historic rights in the South China Sea and is willing to abide by international law and UNCLOS in its sovereignty and sovereign rights claims".[85]

The PRC not only has claimed almost the entire South China Sea as its sovereign territory, but also has been increasing presence in the IOR, with its growing assertive activities posing serious challenges to India's leadership, security and strategic interests in the region. To counter the PRC's emerging influence, India has to take a new approach to deal with issues in the region.

Over the years, the PRC has been rather proactive, unrestrained by democratic institutions in its dealings with other countries in the world. What India could do at this juncture is to move swiftly to engage like-minded countries more vigorously in the IOR before the PRC's footprints spread all over it to undermine India's traditional leading role.[86] Many experts and scholars argue that India does have wider stakes in the South China Sea as nearly 55 percent of India's trade with the Indo-Pacific region passes through these waters. To keep the trade route safe, secure and uphold regional stability and freedom of navigation is in India's interest. A stable maritime order and open sea lanes matters India's economic prosperity and that of the region.[87]

India, in July, 2020 publicly stated that the South China Sea is a 'part of global commons' and it staunchly supports for upholding the 'freedom of navigation and overflight in these international waterways', an assertion similar to the US rejection to the PRC's maritime claim in the region.[88]

The Indo-Pacific Strategy requires India's active involvement as a key player, especially in the Quad in recent years. Quad, short for the Quadrilateral Security Dialogue, is an informal strategic forum comprising Australia, Japan, India and the US, initially proposed by Japan's Prime Minister Shinzo Abe in August 2007. However, the forum ceased to exist following the withdrawal of Australia in February 2018. At the 2017 ASEAN Summit, the four leaders agreed to revive the forum, and India, Japan and the US continued to hold the Exercise Malabar through 2019, after which Australia joined at the invitation of India in 2020.

India's perspective on the 'Indo-Pacific' holds significant importance. In his speech at the Shangri-La Dialogue in June, 2018, India's Prime Minister Narendra Modi emphasised that, in the Indian vision, "India's own engagement in the Indo-Pacific Region —from the shores of Africa to that of the Americas—will be inclusive". Modi further elaborated stating "India will engage with the world in peace, with respect, through dialogue and absolute commitment to international law." He highlighted the significance of 'unity in diversity', which he describes as "the foundation of India's civilisational ethos—of pluralism, co-existence, open-ness and dialogue". He claimed, "the ideals of democracy that define India as a nation also shape the way it engages the world". He further laid out a key component of India's Indo-

Pacific policy that is inclusive but not targeting China. This definition is far away from the US version of Indo-Pacific Strategy.[89]

The Quad foreign ministers held a meeting on the sidelines of the UNGA session in New York in September 2019. Subsequently, they met in person in Tokyo in October 2020 and virtually in February 2021. A landmark development was Australia's participation the India-Japan-US Exercise Malabar in November 2020 after a gap of 13 years. Australia's being invited by India to these exercises carried symbolic weight, as the Quadwas widely believed to be a grouping to counter the threats posed by an intransigent China.[90] As far as this issue is concerned, India's Foreign Minister S Jaishankar on many occasions gave pointers to what he thinks the Indo-Pacific and the Quad are about. In his opinion, the 'rebalance' of global geopolitics is already under way and India is stepping out for the first time in its history. In addition, all the participating states are 'independent minded nations' with 'different mindsets' and 'convergences'.[91]

In late January 2021, the Indian Navy participated in an anti-submarine military exercise with the Quad countries and Canada in Guam. The Exercise Sea Dragon 2021, conducted nearly two months after the conclusion of Exercise Malabar involving the Quad countries, focused on anti-submarine drills, including in-flight training ranging from tracking simulated targets to tracing a nuclear submarine. Participants in this exercise include the US Navy, the Royal Australian Air Force, Canadian Air Force, Indian Navy, and Japan Maritime Self-Defence Force.[92]

A historic virtual Quad summit took place on March 12, 2021 and a joint statement "The Spirit of the Quad" was released in which the leaders of Australia, India, Japan and the US "pledged to strengthen their cooperation on the defining challenges of time", and, among other commitments, "to promote a free, open rules-based order, rooted international law to advance security and prosperity and counter threats to both in the Indo-Pacific and beyond." Their determination was to 'support the rule of law, freedom of navigation and overflight, peaceful resolution of disputes, democratic values, and territorial integrity'. The Quad leaders agreed to prioritise international law in the maritime domain, particularly as stipulated in the UNCLOS, and to facilitate maritime security collaboration, "to meet challenges to the rules-based maritime order in the East and South China Seas." The statement also emphasised the "urgent need to restore Myanmar democracy and the priority of strengthening democratic resilience."[93]

Strategically speaking, India and Taiwan share the common interest in blocking the PRC from making the South China Sea its exclusive maritime zone. India has long-standing territorial disputes with the PRC, and more recently, the PRC has boldly increased assertive activities on Indian territories. For over seven decades, the PRC has reiterated its threat to unify Taiwan by force if necessary. To uphold an open and inclusive Indo-Pacific, India should take more effective measures to ensure freedom of navigation in the South China Sea, through which 50 percent of its trade takes place, according to a report by the CSIS. However, one more updated research revealed that as of 2019-20, only about 18 percent of India's trade went through the South China Sea.[94] (For more details, refer Annexure 9) One possible measure would be to join hands with Taiwan and other stakeholders in the South China Sea, and to further consolidate Taiwan's status as an independent state through mechanisms such as the Quad and other bilateral frameworks. More efforts should also be made to coordinate joint development projects in the South China Sea with other stakeholders, including Taiwan. While some analysts argue that India should resist any expansion of the Quad, it would be more feasible at least expand the Quad Plus mechanism, based on subjects, to maximise the expertise to be pooled into the grouping.

The PRC's Maritime Traffic Safety Law, which came into force on September 1, 2021, required "all foreign vessels entering Chinese territorial waters to notify maritime authorities, among other stipulations. Earlier in February 2021, the PRC also passed a new Coast Guard Law authorising its Coast Guard to use force against foreign vessels allegedly infringing on its sovereignty. Both legislations obviously infringe upon UNCLOS provisions regarding the right of innocent passage, which does not require permission from the government of the coastal state. They also violate UNCLOS due to the PRC's inflated definitions of the baselines for its territorial sea and exclusive economic zone, thereby infringing upon the rights of foreign vessels to navigate those waters as allowed by international law. Some argue that the PRC wants to be an "order-maker" by resetting "the order that has been in place for decades "and "to establish a legal basis to justify physical confrontation on the seas".[95]

In the Chair's Statement of the G7 Foreign and Development Ministers' Meeting in mid-December 2021, it was clearly stated that "On China, we discussed ... issues and challenges ... the situation in Hong Kong and Xinjiang, in the East and South China Seas and the importance of peace and stability across the Taiwan Strait". The Ministers also 'strongly reaffirmed the commitments and position set out in the G7 Foreign and Development Ministers' communiqué from 5 May and the G7 Leaders' communiqué from 12 June'.[96] Notably, in the G7 Ministers' communiqué in May, the Ministers expressed that they "remain seriously concerned about the situation in and around the East and South China Seas". They also 'underscore the importance of peace and stability across the Taiwan Strait and encourage the peaceful resolution of cross-Strait issues'.[97] While in the G7 Leaders' communiqué in June, the leaders "reiterated the importance of maintaining a free and open Indo Pacific, which was inclusive and based on the rule of law." Furthermore, they "underscored the importance of peace and stability across the Taiwan Strait and encouraged the peaceful resolution of cross-Strait issues".[98]

In January 2022, the Department of State of the United States published its latest study titled "People's Republic of China: Maritime Claims in the South China Sea", as part of its series *Limits in the Seas*, despite the USA not being one of the signatories of the 1982 UNCLOS. It concludes, firstly, by indicating firstly that "the PRC's claims to sovereignty over maritime features (in the South China Sea) that do not meet the international law definition of an 'island' and fall entirely beyond lawful territorial seas are inconsistent with international law and not recognised by the United States and other States". Secondly, the study maintains that the PRC's arguments for establishing baselines enclosing the Paracel Islands and other 'island groups' in the South China Sea are also inconsistent with international law, as they do not meet the geographic criteria for straight baselines reflected in Article 7 of the Convention"" Thirdly, the study rejects the PRC's claims to maritime zones based on its arguments concerning 'Nanhai Zhudao' (Islands in the South China Sea), stating that its assertion of internal waters, territorial sea, exclusive economic zone, or continental shelf by treating the island groups in the South China Sea 'as a whole' is not permitted by international law. Lastly, the study asserts that the PRC's claim to 'historic rights in the South China Sea' is 'inconsistent with international law to the extent it exceeds the PRC's possible maritime entitlement' provided by the Convention. Notably, 'the PRC's historic rights claim has been protested by the United States and many other States and rejected by the tribunal in *The South China Sea Arbitration*'."[99]

India has deeply invested in ASEAN because of its Act East policy and Indo-Pacific vision and it is 'convinced that the progress and prosperity of this region is best served by staunch adherence to a rules-based order'. India's External Affairs Minister S Jaishankar stressed at a joint press conference in the Philippines that "UNCLOS 1982 is particularly important in that regard as the constitution of the seas. All parties must adhere to it in its entirety, both in letter and in spirit". He then firmly reiterated "India's support to the Philippines for upholding its national sovereignty."[100]

India has been more and more outspoken on the South China Sea issue and is exploring new areas of cooperation, including defence and security with the Philippines.

Tibet

Pursuant to Article 4 of the Constitution of the ROC, the territory of the Republic of China according to its existing national boundaries shall not be altered except by resolution of the National Assembly.[101] The ROC has traditionally regarded Tibet and Mongolia its inherent territory. Consequently, the ROC government on Taiwan has long viewed itself as the sole legitimate representative of "China", and its position on border issue with Tibet was exactly the same as that of the PRC before the Sino-Indian war on October 20, 1962. Regarding the McMahon Line—a demarcation line between the Northeast region of India and Tibet proposed by British colonial administrator Sir Henry McMahon at the 1914 Simla Convention and signed by British and Tibetan representatives—it is the recognised boundary between China and India, although its legal status has been disputed by the current PRC and the ROC governments for nearly six decades. Subsequently, in November 1962, The Ministry of Foreign Affairs of the ROC on Taiwan in a statement emphasised that "the so-called McMahon Line was a unilateral proposal defining the border of China and India when the latter was under the British Rule". Subsequently, in November 1962, the Ministry dispatched a telegram in November, 1962 to all overseas missions with instructions on a unified position regarding the McMahon Line outlining three key points: to refrain from criticising India's or Jawaharlal Nehru's remarks; not to voluntarily discuss the issue of the McMahon Line, but if asked, to explain Taiwan's consistent position of not recognising; and not to approach India's embassies in foreign countries voluntarily, but if approached by them, respond with a friendly gesture and receive them courteously without suggesting any immediate desire to resume diplomatic relations with India. The other three points relate to the anti-communism ideology and a clear tactic of blaming only the PRC, instead of India. The ROC's Foreign Minister personally drafted an explanatory note for dispatch, to coin the Sino-Indian war in 1962 as 'a struggle between International Communism and Indian Nationalism. Chinese people should not be against Indian people; the border issues between China and India will be naturally and reasonably resolved when the Chinese Mainland is recovered by the ROC'.[102]

In the 1990s, the ROC Government announced a landmark policy stating that Taiwan's de facto jurisdiction covers only Taiwan, Penghu, Kinmen, Matsu and other nearby islands at present, which have not been ruled by the PRC since 1949, so that both entities have to deal with each other not via their Ministry of Foreign Affairs, but via special semi-official organisations entrusted by the ROC's Mainland Affairs Council and the PRC's Taiwan Affairs Office. At the end of 2017, the ROC government decided to abolish the Mongolian and Tibetan Affairs Commission, ending its existence for nearly 90 years since 1928. This move symbolised another significant step towards de-emphasising the Chinese ideology that considers Mongolia and Tibet as part of the ROC's territory. Following this people-to-people interaction and religious exchanges occurred without political misconception between Tibet and Taiwan. The Director-General of the Taipei Economic and Cultural Centre in Chennai was invited to a Tibetan cultural performance in Chennai as a gesture of appreciation for the Indian government's support in accommodating the Dalai Lama and tens of thousands of Tibetans who fled the PRC's invasion in 1959. The Dalai Lama visited Taiwan in 1997, 2001 and 2009, during the presidencies of Lee Teng-hui, Chen Shui-bian and Ma Ying-jeou, marking substantial developments between Tibet and Taiwan over decades of misunderstanding of the role that the Mongolian and Tibetan Affairs Commission in Taiwan government had played. The Dalai Lama, in a birthday message via video link to supporters in Taiwan in July 2020, said he was willing to visit Taiwan again as the political circumstances evolve, saying "Whatever happens I'll remain with you in spirit". In response, the Spokesperson of Taiwan's Ministry of Foreign Affairs remarked, "We will, in accordance with the principle of mutual respect and at a time of convenience for both sides, welcome the Dalai Lama to come to Taiwan again to propagate Buddhist teachings."[103] The planned trip for the Dalai Lama to Taiwan will be possible only if the political conditions across the Taiwan Strait and the COVID-19 pandemic restrictions permit. The stance of the Indian government's and the PRC's reaction and pressure will be two crucial factors in deciding the feasibility of the visit. However, the Dalai Lama said on November 10, 2021 that "he prefers to stay in India since relations between Taiwan and mainland China are 'quite delicate'; and "he has no particular plans to meet China's president Xi Jinping."[104] However, the Dalai Lama pointed out that "the true repository of China's culture and traditions" and the PRC is now "too politicised". He also opined that "Chinese culture, including Buddhism, mainland Chinese brothers and sisters can learn a lot from Taiwanese brothers and sisters".[105]

Taiwanese society is familiar with Tibetan Buddhism and the religious interactions between Tibetan and Taiwanese have been frequent and friendly. In March, 2021, a group of Tibetans and Taiwanese gathered in Taipei to commemorate the 62nd anniversary of the March 10, 1959 Tibetan rebellion against the PRC's rule, followed by a military crackdown in Tibet that eventually forced the Dalai Lama and numerous Tibetans to flee to India.[106] To continue facilitating the bilateral relations between Tibet and Taiwan, the Central Tibetan Administration appointed Kelsang Gyaltsen Bawa as the new Representative to Taiwan in late 2020, and he took charge as the new Representative of Office of Tibet in Taipei on April 22, 2021.[107]

Prime Minister Jawaharlal Nehru wrote to V K Krishna Menon in August,1950 regarding the issue of Tibet stating "it is true that we recognise Chinese suzerainty but at the same time we recognise Tibetan autonomy and the two went together so far as we were concerned. "In his letter dated September 2, 1950, he further indicated that he had repeatedly advised the India's Ambassador to the PRC, K M Panikkar, to caution the PRC government that "it would be most unfortunate if they indulged in any warlike operation either against Formosa (Taiwan) or Tibet." Nehru also reaffirmed India's position on Tibet many times in his letters and telegrams to Ambassador Panikkar in October 1950 emphasising that a "Chinese invasion of Tibet would be deplorable and...not in the interest of China or of peace. Until Chinese Government halt progress of their forces and give assurance for peaceful negotiations we cannot help in the matter any further".[108] Nehru stressed the need for the PRC to resort to military action to overrun Tibet seemed to be 'very remote', and he believed that 'any such action is bound to create a great deal of prejudice against China', and 'it will put an end to our efforts to bring her to the United Nations. It will give a tremendous handle to her enemies, and Korea and Formosa (Taiwan) will be affected'. Nehru further made it clear that if unfortunately, there is a war on a large scale in Tibet, "it will be our earnest endeavour to keep out of it." And he thought "Burma and Indonesia are likely to do the same".[109]

Vijay Gokhale identified 'Tibet as the central point in India-China relations'. He analysed that Jawaharlal Nehru believed India's "principal objective was to develop a friendship with China because India and China would be the two emerging powers to shape a post-World War Asia.... But the Chinese never saw it that way". And in Gokhale's opinion, Nehru's vision was 'wishful thinking', a 'romantic' view of China and a 'blinkered approach' at a time 'India lacked diplomatic experience, and diplomatic systems were not fully developed."[110]

On July 6, 2021, India's Prime Minister Narendra Modi on a phone call greeted the Dalai Lama on his 86th birthday. In the meantime, Taiwan's President Tsai Ing-wen, in a Twitter post, wished the Dalai Lama 'a very happy 86th birthday' and thanked him for "teaching us the importance of coming together to help one another through this pandemic".[111] Many other dignitaries such as Ambassadors, Union Ministers and Chief Ministers in India also greeted the Tibetan spiritual leader on his birthday.

On July 21, 2021, the PRC's President Xi Jinping visited Tibet for three days, travelling to areas very close to Arunachal Pradesh. According to the PRC's official media, his visit was intended to mark the 70th anniversary of 'the peaceful liberation of Tibet'. The unilateral argument of the 'peaceful liberation of Tibet' by the PRC refers to the Seventeenth Point Agreement signed on May 23, 1951, which has been rejected by the Dalai Lama on the ground that Tibet was forced to sign it at that time, and the PRC violated its commitments subsequently. It resulted in his exodus to India in 1959.[112]

The PRC sent in 40 thousand of its PLA troops to Tibet in 1950, capturing the border town of Chamdo with over 5,000 Tibetans 'killed, wounded of captured'. The PRC warned that the alternative to signing the Seventeenth Point Agreement would be an 'immediate military operation in the remaining parts of Tibet'. Consequently, Tibet signed the agreement under the threat of force or duress from the PRC, which could render it invalid according to international law. The argument for the PRC to interpret its invasion of Tibet as 'peaceful liberation' is based on a 1974 UN resolution in which an aggression is defined as 'the use of armed force by a State against the sovereignty, territorial integrity or political independence of another State'. More specifically, the PRC once said, "the battle created the conditions for the peaceful liberation of Tibet".[113] By this definition, the PRC could not have invaded Tibet since it did not consider Tibet to be another state.[114] Likewise, this theory may apply to the case with Taiwan simply because the PRC never considers Taiwan to be another state. Therefore, PRC's so-called 'peaceful reunification', touted for decades, with Taiwan, may mean invasion by force as defined by the rest of the world. By the same token, the future battle to occupy Taiwan 'may create the condition for the peaceful reunification of Taiwan'. Taiwan should not underestimate the causal effect in the PRC's articulation and formulation of its own version of the international law.

Furthermore, Xi's visit to Tibet in late July 2021 'signals China's opening of another front to India in the eastern sector' because it coincides with the existing armed stalemate on the Indian borders in the western Aksai Chin-

Ladakh regions and the tweet by Prime Minister Narendra Modi on greeting the Dalai Lama on his birthday in early July, as one scholar analysed.[115] India should not overlook the purpose and implication of Xi's visit to Tibet, particularly so close to Arunachal Pradesh, which the PRC refers to as 'South Tibet'. Following China's initial release of standardised Chinese names of six places in Arunachal Pradesh in 2017, China renamed 15 more places in Arunachal Pradesh at the end of 2021, asserting that southern Tibet "has been China's inherent territories...the competent authorities in China... have published the names for the relevant area. These are matters that is within China's sovereignty". India's MEA spokesperson, rebutted this renaming of places in Arunachal Pradesh, stating, that "Arunachal Pradesh has always been, and will always be an integral part of India. Assigning invented names to places in Arunachal Pradesh does not alter this fact".[116] However, the PRC continued to release its standardised names of 11 places in Arunachal Pradesh in April 2023 and an additional list of 30 new names in March 2024. The PRC's last announcement of the new names of places in Arunachal Pradesh came in the wake of India's Prime Minister Narendra Modi inauguration of the Sela Tunnel in early March 2024, which invited the PRC's opposition, followed by a statement from the US side that "The United States recognises Arunachal Pradesh as Indian territory and we strongly oppose any unilateral attempts to advance territorial claims by incursions or encroachments, military or civilian, across the LAC." As expected, the PRC slammed the US for interfering in its border dispute with India.[117]

On January 12, 2022, India and China held the 14th round of Corps-Commander level talks with an aim to resolve the issues of disengagement along the LAC in Eastern Ladakh. No matter how many hours each round of talks lasts, they all end in a stalemate and the 'constructive suggestions' made by the Indian Army were neither agreeable to the Chinese side nor it could provide any 'forward-looking' proposals. No concrete outcome was visible on the disengagement process in the remaining friction points.[118] On March 11, 2022, the 15th round of Corps-Commander level talks between India and China was held for 13 hours in which "India pressed for early disengagement of troops in remaining friction points, including resolution of pending issues in Depsang Bulge and Demchok".[119] Subsequently on May 31, 2022, India and China agreed to 'continue the discussions through diplomatic and military channels to resolve the remaining issues along the LAC at the earliest so as to create conditions for restoration of normalcy in bilateral relations'. They further agreed to convene the 16th round of senior military commanders at an early date to achieve the objective of complete disengagement from all friction points along the LAC in the western sector in accordance with the existing bilateral agreements and protocols.[120]

To the surprise of many observers, India's MEA published a Joint Press Release on July 18, 2022 regarding the 16th Round of India-China Corps Commander Level Meeting, which took place on July 17, 2022. The release stated that the "two sides continued discussions for the resolution of the relevant issues along the LAC in the Western Sector in a constructive and forward-looking manner, emphasising they had "a frank and in-depth exchange of views." The two sides also reaffirmed that "the resolution if remaining issues would help in restoration of peace and tranquillity along the LAC in the Western Sector and enable progress in bilateral relations." They agreed 'to maintain the security and stability on the ground in the western Sector' and 'to stay in close contact and maintain dialogue through military and diplomatic channels and work out a mutually acceptable resolution of the remaining issues at the earliest'.[121] The meeting reportedly lasted for 12 hours, and little was achieved except "exchange of views" as discussions continued with the goal of reaching 'a mutually acceptable resolution' of the remaining issues 'at the earliest'. In essence, the primary outcome India could claim from the 16 rounds of talks with China is the 'restoration of peace and tranquillity', rather than reversing any Chinese gains on disputed borders. As expected, no breakthrough occurred in the 17th round military talks on December 20, 2022. The 18th round of military talks between India and China took place on April 23, 2023, yielding no substantial outcomes, while the 19th round was held on August 13-14, 2023, focussed on building confidence with each other and avoiding clashes between the troops of both sides through strict adherence to border protocols and sharing of patrol information. The 20th round of military talks took place on October 9-10,

2023, followed on by the 21st round held on February 19, 2024 with no clear forward movement.

The India-China high-level military talks could continue indefinitely, as China has the advantage of remaining in the unjustifiably occupied Indian territories, while India's options are limited to pushing for another round of negotiations before any major international event, excercising strategic patience or, at worse, adopting a stance if 'strategic passivity'. India's core interests are unlikely to be respected by China, which persistently underscores its own core interest as 'red lines' in Tibet and Taiwan, forcing India and the rest of the world to respect and follow its expectations.

The PRC's negotiation tactics is to keep conducting the so-called 'negotiation' on issues over Indian territories that the Chinese illegitimately occupies, knowing it already holds these areas and will not yield an inch of it to India, let alone consider a complete withdrawal. The only proposal China might offer is an exchange of Aksai Chin for Arunachal Pradesh. However, the core issue remains that both territories inherently belong to India and an aggressive China will continue to occupy vast areas of Indian land under any scenario. As some military and strategic experts argue that the PRC "has no interest in resolving the border dispute with India", an expansion in India's economy and military capability would convince the PRC's leadership to view India as not just "an inward-looking democracy that has yet to focus on economic growth and military prowess."[122]

Regarding the PRC's negotiation tactics, Vijay Gokhale summed up his 20-some-year experience in dealing with the PRC, describing it as a 'flawed' explaining that the PRC is "now looking at becoming the dominant global power. Any potential competitors are to be scared away." He reiterated that "either both sides respect previous agreements, or we are prepared to respond to any provocation". According to Gokhale, one of the three lessons for India when negotiating with the PRC is India is to "presume the Chinese negotiate to deceive".[123] Essentially, the issue of Tibet are handled by two countries with completely different mindsets. The PRC has been playing with time to procrastinate the negotiations, invoking historical friendly relations, such as *Hindi-Chini bhai bhai*, to diffuse heated discussion on core issues, and to divert from taking concrete steps to honour signed agreements, simply because the Chinese troops are in fact on Indian soil, not the other way around. It is likely that more rounds of negotiation at different levels will be required to make even a little progress, because the PRC controls the tone, set the rules, and frames issues within 'red lines' to manage India and other concerned countries. The PRC knows clearly that it holds the key to the final settlement of the border issues, which it has intentionally and illegitimately occupied from India. Chinese policy makers know it well how India eagerly wishes to resolve these issues, especially given that India has to deploy more than 200,000 troops along the border with China, in addition to the 600,000 troops deployed along the border with Pakistan. More solid proofs indicates that China has also accelerated settlement-building along its disputed border with Bhutan. Reuters reported that through satellite image analysis China has built, some under construction, 'more than 200 structures, including two-storey buildings in six locations'.[124] Bhutan has been negotiating with China for several decades to settle disputes along their 477-kilometer border without substantial results. In addition to Bhutan's territorial integrity, there are security implications for India as well, because India has always been and still is Bhutan's key ally and economic partner. How is India going to effectively assist Bhutan with its border disputes with China remains to be seen?

Additionally, a Nepalese government report allegedly accuses China of encroaching into the district of Humla in north-west Nepal, according to a BBC News report in early February 2022. The recent Chinese trespassing in Nepal could be in breach of a series of treaties that China and Nepal signed in early 1960s. To guarantee security in that area, the report recommended Nepalese security forces be stationed there and both countries 'should reactivate a dormant mechanism set up to resolve these kinds of border issues'. Traditionally, tens of thousands of Tibetans on the other side of the region have fled to escape China's repression, many residing in Nepal, others made way to India and elsewhere.[125]

India should recognise the precious experience and expertise Taiwan has developed and acquired from its long-standing struggle against the provocative and assertive PRC. Historically, India has not hesitated to approach and engage Taiwan through thinktanks or even via semi-official channels, though official engagement is still limited to certain working levels. It is essential for India to carefully weigh the pros and cons ensuring its national interest are upheld without offending the PRC or stepping out of the red lines that PRC has set for India with regard to interactions with Taiwan. The key issue now is to determine where India's red lines are. Will the PRC follow India's insistence in those red lines and behave as a friendly neighbour?

Summary Notes

India's self-imposed 'One-China Policy' has long hampered relations with the ROC on Taiwan, though gradual progress and substantial developments have occurred over the past two decades or so, thanks to India's Look East Policy and Act East Policies and Taiwan's New Southbound Policy. These policies have led to mutually beneficial interactions, gaining greater momentum and bringing about substantial results. Both ITA and TECC Heads of Missions have worked diligently to lay a foundation for progress, signing more than a dozen agreements and MOUs that facilitate smoother collaboration in trade, investment, education, science and technology, culture, and people-to-people interactions, in addition to making possible some unnoticed high-level exchange of visits, especially India's foreign policy towards Taiwan has transformed "from benign neglect to pragmatism."[126]

Beyond the Quad, with Australia, India, Japan and the US actively participating, India also has been one of the key players in the BRICS and the Shanghai Cooperation Organisation, in which China plays a dominant role. Reports suggest that India had agreed to collaborate with China on space cooperation, including the integration of two Indian satellites into a Chinese-designed virtual constellation for data-sharing. Furthermore, India benefits from receiving nearly one-quarter of the loans approved by the Asian Infrastructure Investment Bank based in China under the SCO.[127]

On a more alarming note, China was India's primary trading partner, with an annual trade deficit of more than USD 60 billion in China's favour and there would be no abatement if India did not launch it ambitious

"Atmanirbhar Bharat" initiative in 2020. However, India's trade deficit with China hit a record US$77 billion from April 2021 to March 2022. India's veteran experts on Chinese affairs within the MEA understand how to balance India's delicate relations with China, which would be too costly to jeopardise, if India were to show sympathy and support for Taiwan in response to China's unjustifiable bullying and threats Therefore, the India's current stance of acquiescence remains the only viable approach, resulting from its acceptance of the 'One-China' principle as asserted by the PRC. However observers have already sensed a change of India's position on its 'One-China Policy' since 2010.

China no doubt is India's primary strategic challenger involving border disputes and territory claims. Taiwan, in fact, played a role in some of the border and territorial issues between India and China earlier than the PRC did not only before 1949, but also in the 21st century, owing to historical and constitutional connections. Nowadays, Taiwan still maintains control over the Pratas Islands and Taiping Island, the largest island in the Spratly Islands in the South China Sea. Taiwan is obviously one of the key stakeholders in the South China Sea, and therefore, should be invited to participate in any multilateral negotiations or meetings in relation to the South China Sea, where around 55 percent of India's maritime trade passes through. More essentially, India plays a key and symbolic role in the Quad, and by extension in the Indo-Pacific Strategy. How Taiwan could be accommodated in the Quad Plus mechanism would be meaningful and worth India's support, given Taiwan's strategic position in the middle of the first island chain to defend the assertive 'peaceful rise of China'. If included, Taiwan could play a crucial role in this endeavour. Furthermore, Taiwan has a better understanding of the PRC's traditional Communist ideology, strategic depth and military capabilities because of its close geographic location, linguistic and cultural ties with China. A closer relationship with Taiwan will help India understand the PRC's hidden strategic agenda, tactics and propaganda.

Taiwan has transformed entirely into a full-fledged democracy beginning in the 1990s, and adjusted stipulations in its Constitution to acknowledge that its current de facto jurisdiction covers only Taiwan, Penghu, Kinmen, Matsu and surrounding islands. Taiwan's relations with Tibet have become smoother after Taiwan removed the Mongolian and Tibetan Commission from the central government structure.

Surely, Taiwan has proved its capabilities to play a critical role in the success of the Indian government's 'Make in India', 'Digital India', 'Smart City', 'Skill India', 'Atmanirbhar Bharat' initiatives and 'Viksit Bharat' vision. Some scholars argue that one major obstacle hampering close ties between India and Taiwan is India's adherence to the 'One-China Policy'. However this should not deter India from enhancing close economic and other forms of ties with Taiwan, just as the PRC is expanding its involvement with Islamabad in Pakistan-occupied Kashmir (PoK). India should take bold initiatives to engage with Taiwan, as doing so aligns with India's long-term interests and demonstrates to the PRC that India can independently its assert to determine the nature of its relations with Taiwan.

Notes

1. "Sino-India Relations Including Doklam, Border situation and Cooperation in International Organizations", Twenty Second Report to the Committee on External Affairs (2017-18)(Sixteenth Lok Sabha) by the Ministry of External Affairs, presented to Honourable Speaker on September 4, 2018. http://164.100.47.193/lsscommittee/External%20Affairs/16_External_Affairs_22.pdf.
2. Dipanjan Roy Chaudhury, "Rethink India's one-China Policy", Economic Times, July 3, 2020. https://economictimes.indiatimes.com/news/defence/rethink-indias-one-china-policy/articleshow/76762670.cms.
3. Vijay Gokhale, *The Long Game: How the Chinese Negotiate with India.* (Gurugram: Penguin Random House India, 2021), 8-10.
4. Peter Gordon, *The Long Game: How the Chinese Negotiate with India*' by Vijay Gokhale", Asian Review of Books, July 12, 2021. https://asianreviewofbooks.com/content/the-long-game-how-the-chinese-negotiate-with-india-by-vijay-gokhale/.
5. Vijay Gokhale, *What Should India Do Before the Next Taiwan Strait Crisis*?, Carnegie India, April 17, 2023. https://carnegieindia.org/2023/04/17/what-should-india-do-before-next-taiwan-strait-crisis-pub-89515.
6. Vinod C. Khanna, "The India-Taipei Association: A Mission Extraordinaire", *Indian Foreign Affairs Journal Vol. 5, No, 2* (April-June 2010): 240-251.
7. "Public Library of US Policy", WikiLeaks. Accessed April 11, 2020. https://wikileaks.org/plusd/cables/04TAIPEI3845_a.html.
8. Supra, note 1.
9. Ibid.

10. Ibid.
11. Kallol Bhattacherjee, "Indian media is free, says in MEA response to Chinese Embassy's note to press on Taiwan", The Hindu, October 8, 2020. https://www.thehindu.com/news/national/indian-mea-response-to-chinese-embassyus-notye-to-press-on-taiwan/article32806814.ece.
12. "Election results 2019: Xi Jinping, Putin, Netanyahu congratulate Narendra Modi", *The Hindu*, May 23, 2019, https://www.thehindu.com/elections/lok-sabha-2019/election-results-2019-reactions-foreign-international-leaders-narendra-modi-bjp/article27218189.ece.
13. Jayanth Jacob, "Air India's decision consistent with international norms, India's position on Taiwan: MEA", *Hindustan Times,* July 6, 2018, https://www.hindustantimes.com/india-news/air-india-s-decision-consistent-with-international-norms-india-s-position-on-taiwan-mea/story-x6jr4PV2zX5ded0S9WPdGO.html.
14. Jassie Hsi Cheng, "The Taiwan-India 'Milk Tea Alliance'", *The Diplomat, October 20, 2020,* https://thediplomat.com/2020/10/the-taiwan-india-milk-tea-alliance.
15. Dipanjan Roy Chaudhury, "India's one China policy may not be permanent future amid Beijing's aggression", *The Economic Times,* June 13, 2020, https://economictimes.indiatimes.com/news/defence/indias-one-chona-policy-may-not-be-permanent-feature-amid-beijings-aggression/articleshow/76351486.cms.
16. Shrishti Goel, "Taiwan train Accident Leaves Over 50 Dead; MEA Expresses Condolence to Kin of Victims", *Republic*, April 3, 2021, https://www.republicworld.com/india-news/general-news/taiwan-train-accident-leaves-over-50-dead-mea-expresses-condolence-to-kin-of-victims.html.
17. "MOFA expresses appreciation to over 600 dignitaries and friends from 80 countries and International Organizations who have extended condolences and sympathies to the Taiwan Rail accident", *Press Release No. 048, Ministry of Foreign Affairs, Republic of China (Taiwan)*, April 3, 2021, https://www.mofa.gov.tw/News_Content.aspx?n=95&sms=73&s=95618.
18. Shan Jie, "Mainland pays tribute to victims of train crash in Taiwan island; netizens, experts calling for accountability", *Global Times,* April 3, 2021, https://www.globaltimes.cn/page/202104/1220166.shtml.
19. "MOFA expresses appreciation to 780 dignitaries and friends from 94 countries and International Organizations who have extended condolences and sympathies to the Taiwan Rail accident", *Press Release No. 052, Ministry of Foreign Affairs, Republic of China (Taiwan),* April 3, 2021, https://www.mofa.gov.tw/News_Content.aspx?n=95&sms=73&s=95624.
20. "MOFA expresses appreciation to 846 dignitaries and friends from 97 countries and International Organizations who have extended condolences and sympathies to the Taiwan Rail accident", *Press Release No. 055, Ministry of Foreign Affairs, Republic*

of China (Taiwan), April 3, 2021, https://www.mofa.gov.tw/News_Content.aspx?n=95&sms=73&s=95630.

21. "India facilitates, promotes interactions with Taiwan: MEA on Taipei Economic and Cultural Centre in Mumbai", *ANI*, July 6, 2023, https://theprint.in/world/india-facilitates-promotes-interactions-with-taiwan-mea-on-taipei-economic-and-cultural-centre-in-mumbai/1657791/.
22. Divya A, "Looking forward to continuing people to people exchanges with Taiwan: India", *The Indian Express*, January 19, 2024, https://indianexpress.com/article/india/looking-forward-to-continuing-people-to-people-exchanges-with-taiwan-india-9116255/.
23. Srikanth Kondapalli, "Taiwan election results — good for India, bad for China", *The Indian Express*, January 16, 2024, https://indianexpress.com/article/opinion/columns/taiwan-election-results-good-india-bad-china-9111841/.
24. K. V. Kesavan, "India's 'Act East' policy and regional cooperation", *Raisina Debate, Observer Research Foundation*, February 14, 2020, https://www.orfonline.org/expert-speak/indias-act-east%20policy-and-regional-cooperation-61375/.
25. Rejaul Laskar, "Promoting National Interest Through Diplomacy", *Extraordinary and Plenipotentiary Diplomatist* 1 (9) (December 2013): 59-60.
26. Walter Ladwig, "Delhi's Pacific Ambition: Naval Power, 'Look East,' and India's Emerging Role in the Asia-Pacific," *Asian Security*, Vol. 5, No. 2 (June 2009): 98-101.
27. "Taiwan Strait", *Global Security*. July 21, 1995 to March 23, 1996, https://www.globalsecurity.org/military/ops/taiwan_strait.htm.
28. "Sushma Swaraj tells Indian envoys to Act East and not just Look East", *The Economic Times*, August 26, 2014, https://economictimes.indiatimes.com/news/politics-and-nation/sushma-swaraj-tells-indian-envoys-to-act-east-and-not-just-look-east/articleshow/40907671.cms.
29. "Act East", *Reconnecting Asia, CSIS*, https://reconnectingasia.csis.org/database/initiatives/act-east/b17b6a1c-5c17-40f0-a2ec-c6a8ce802ab9/.
30. "English rendering of PM's remarks at the East Asia Summit, Nay Pyi Taw", *PMINDIA, Government of India*, November 13, 2014, accessed on March 23, 2021. https://www.pmindia.gov.in/en/news_updates/english-rendering-of-pms-remarks-at-the-east-asia-summit-nay-pyi-taw/.
31. Prashant Kumar Singh, "India-Taiwan Ties: Can They Overcome Structural Challenge?", *Eurasia Border Review Vol 9, No. 1* (2018 Fall): 1-28. https://src-h.slav.hokudai.ac.jp/puvlictn/eurasia_border_review/Vol91/V9N1_01-Prashant.pdf.
32. T. E. Raja Simhan, "China Steel Corp to invest $178 m in new plant in Gujarat", *The Hindu*, August 25, 2011, https://www.thehindubusinessline.com/companies/China-Steel-Corp-to-invest-178-m-in-new-plant-in-Gujarat/article20327566.ece.

33. Kirtika Suneja and Deepshjikha Sikarwar, "New FDI rules not for Taiwan inflows", *The Economic Times,* April 30, 2020, https://economictimes.indiatimes.com/news/economy/policy/new-fdi-rules-not-for-taiwan-inflows/articleshow/75479443.cms.
34. Constitution of a special Investment Promotion Task Force under the Chairmanship of Chief Secretary to attract Investors-Orders-Issued, G.O. (Ms) No.123, Industries (MIB.1) Department, Tamil Nadu, India, April 29, 2020.
35. https://www.moeaic.gov.tw/chinese/news_bsAb.jsp.
36. Yun-yu Chen, "Sridharan: India-Taiwan relations expand to fill the gap of industrial supply chains", *CNA,* January 22, 2020, https://www.cna.com.tw/news/aipl/202001220320.aspx. (in Chinese)
37. Lin Hsing-chien, "Indian tribal students awarded Taiwan Huayu Enrichment Scholarships for the first time", *Central News Agency,* July 29, 2022, https://www.cna.com.tw/news/aopl/202207290153.aspx. (In Chinese)
38. Shannon Tiezzi, "How Are Taiwan's Diplomatic Allies Faring in the Great Vaccine Race?", *The Diplomat,* July 9, 2021, https://thediplomat.com/2021/07/how-are-taiwans-diplomatic-allies-faring-in-the-great-vaccine-race/.
39. Szu-chien Hsu, Remarks at CSIS on June 10, 2019. https://www.csis.org/analysis/dr-szu-chien-hsu-deputy-minister-foreign-affairs-republic-china-taiwan-remarks.
40. Keoni Everington, "Indians in Taiwan celebrate 75 years of Indian independence", *Taiwan News, August 16, 2021,*" https://www.taiwannews.com.tw/en/news/4270886.
41. "MoU signing between Taipei Economic and Cultural Center in India and Amity University Haryana", *Amity University,* February 26, 2021, https://www.amity.edu/gurugram/events/10948/mou-signing-between-taipei-economic-and-cultural-centre-in-india-and-amity-university-haryana.
42. "Taiwan India Relations", *Taipei Economic and Cultural Center in India,* accessed on August 16, 2021. https://www.roc-taiwan.org/in_en/post/39.html.
43. "Taiwan Education Center—Introduction and Structure", *Foundation for International Cooperation in Higher Education of Taiwan,* https://www.fichet.org.tw/en/what-we-do/taiwan-education-centers/.
44. "The First India–Taiwan Bilateral Forum on Mandarin Chinese Course Materials for Indian Learners held in Jawaharlal Nehru University (JNU), New Delhi", *Ministry of Education, Republic of China (Taiwan),* March 10, 2017, https://english.moe.gov.tw/cp-13-17102-0013B-1.html.
45. "The Fourth India-Taiwan Bilateral Forum on Mandarin Chinese Teaching Materials for Indian Learners", *Taiwan Education Center,* https://www.tecindianthu.tw/edcontent_d.php?lang=tw&tb=7&cid=5&id=1000.
46. "Confucius Institute U.S. Center' Designation as a Foreign Mission", *Office of the Spokesperson, U.S. Department of State,* August 13, 2020, https://2017-2021.state.gov/confucius-institute-u-s-center-designation-as-a-foreign-mission/index.html.
47. Ibid.

48. Thomas Lum and Hannah Fisher, "Confucius Institutes in the United States: Selected Issues", Congressional Research Service, May 20, 2022. https://crsreports.congress.gov/proiduct/pdf/lF/lF11180.
49. "Helsinki University closes China-funded Confucius Institute", *Yle News, June 18, 2022*, https://yle.fi/news/3-12500430.
50. Ananth Krishnan, "The Hindu explains: What are Confucius Institutes and why are they under the scanner in India", August 9, 2020. https://www.thehindu.com/news/national/the-hindu-explains-what-are-confucius-institutes-and-why-are-they-under-the-scanner-in-india/article32306693.ece.
51. Introduction, Hanban, August 9, 2020. http://english.hanban.org/node_7880.htm.
52. Anirban Bhaumik, "Once probed for spying, China's Confucius Institutes now among models for India to learn lessons on soft power projections", *Deccan Herald,* August 14, 2023, https://www.deccanherald.com/india/learn-soft-power-lessons-from-confucius-inst-parliamentary-panel-tells-mea-2646355.
53. "Cutting Ties with Confucius Institutes", *In the Name of Confucius*, https://inthenameofconfuciusmovie.com/cutting-ties-with-confucius-institutes/.
54. Glen Owen, "Chinese teachers in British classrooms are to be replaced by recruits from Taiwan after Commons spy scandal", *Daily Mail*, September 16, 2023, https://www.dailymail.co.uk/news/article-12526631/Chinese-teachers-British-classrooms-replaced-recruits-Taiwan-Commons-spy-scandal.html.
55. **Rudroneel Ghosh**, "Chinese Learning: If Confucius Institutes are a problem, Taiwan Education Centres can fill the void", *The Times of India*, August 6, 2020, https://timesofindia.indiatimes.com/blogs/talkingturkey/chinese-learning-if-confucius-institutes-are-a-problem-taiwan-education-centres-in-india-can-fill-the-void/.
56. "Taiwan message: New Delhi-Taipei cooperation is both mutually beneficial and a pointed signal to China", *The Times of India*, April 4, 2021, https://timesofindia.indiatimes.com/blogs/toi-editorials/taiwan-message-new-delhi-taipei-cooperation-is-both-mutually-beneficial-and-a-pointed -signal-to-china/.
57. "Where is India on the One China Policy?", *The Diplomat. March 6, 2017*, https://thediplomat.com/2017/03/where-is-india-on-the-one-china-policy/.
58. Ananth Krishnan, "BJP MPs praise Taiwan as 'democratic country as President Tsai Ing-wen begins new term', *The Hindu*, May 20, 2020, https://www.thehindu.com/news/national/bjp-mps-praise-taiwan-as-democratic-country-as-president-tsai-ing-wen-begins-new-term/article31635242.ece.
59. "Treaties Handbook", Treaty Section of the Office of Legal Affairs, United Nations, 71-72, accessed on February 25, 2021. https://treaties.un.org/doc/source/publications/THB/English.pdf.
60. Ibid., 68.

61. "Cabinet okays India-Taiwan investment pact", *Business Standard*, October 24, 2018, https://www.business-standard.com/article/news-ians/cabinet-okays-india-taiwan-investment-pact-118102400924_1.html.
62. "Top Indian envoy discusses priority areas of cooperation with Taiwan", Focus Taiwan, January 9, 2021. https://focustaiwan.tw/politics/202101090002.
63. Utkarsh Pandey, "The India-China Border Question: An Analysis of International Law and State Practices," *ORF Occasional Paper No. 290* (New Delhi: Observer Research Foundation, December 2020).
64. Brahma Chellaney, "Beijing's bendable principles", *Japan Times*, June 2, 2015, https://www.japantimes.co.jp/opinion/2015/06/02/commentary/world-commentary/beijings-bendable-principles/.
65. Pia Krishnankutty, "India should presume that China negotiates to deceive, says former foreign secretary Vijay Gokhale", *The Print*, July 19, 2021, https://theprint.in/india/india-should-presume-that-china-negotiates-to-deceive-says-former-foreign-secretary-vijay-gokhale/698750/.
66. "Explained: The offer that Zhou made, and Nehru rejected...the lessons from it", *The Indian Express*, June 19, 2020, https://indianexpress.com/article/explained/india-china-border-dispute-jawaharlal-nehru-zhou-enlai-6466231/.
67. "Sino-Indian War", Wikipedia, accessed on April 6, 2021. https://en.wikipedia.org/wiki/Sino-Indian_War.
68. Prabhash K. Dutta, "How China captured Aksai Chin", *India Today*, June 22, 2020, https://www.indiatoday.in/india/story/how-china-captured-aksai-chin-1691562-2020-06-22.
69. Steven Lee Myers, "China's Aggressive Diplomacy Weakens Xi Jinping's Global Standing", *New York Times*, April 17, 2020, https://www.nytimes.com/2020/04/17/world/asia/coronavirus-china-xi-jinping.html; Ben Westcott and Steven Jiang, "China is embracing a new brand of foreign policy. Here is what wolf warrior diplomacy means", *CNN*, May 29, 2020, https://edition.cnn.com/2020/05/28/asia/china-wolf-warrior-diplomacy-intl-hnk/index.html.
70. H. S. Panag, "LAC disengagement done. India, China can now return to old love-hate routine", *The Print*, March 18, 2021, https://theprint.in/opinion/lac-disengagement-done-india-china-can-now-return-to-old-love-hate-routine/623812/.
71. "Put India-China border issue in appropriate place: Wang Yi", *The Hindu*, June 23, 2022, https://www.thehindu.com/news/international/ahead-of-brics-meet-chinas-foreign-minister-meets-indian-envoy/article6556887.exe.
72. "Agreement On The Maintenance Of Peace Along The Line Of Actual Control In The India-China Border", *The Stimson Center*, September 7, 1993, accessed on April 4, 2021. https://web.archive.org/web/20150924110627/http://www.stimson.org/research-pages/agreement-on-the-maintenance-of-peace-along-the-line-of-actual-control-in-the-india-china-border/.

73. "PM participates in the 14th BRICS Summit", *Prime Minister's Office, Government of India*, June 24, 2022, https://pib.gov.in/PressReleaselframePage.aspx?PRID=1836853.
74. "Full text of Xi Jinping's speech on the CCP's 100th anniversary", *Nikkei Asia*, July 1, 2021, https://asia.nikkei.com/Politics/Full-text-of-Xi-Jinping-s-speech-on-the-CCP-s-100th-anniversary.
75. "Wang Yi Delivers a Speech at the French Institute of International Relations", *Ministry of Foreign Affairs, the People's Republic of China*, August 30, 2020, https://www.fmprc.gov.cn/mfa_eng/zxxx_662805/t1811319.shtml.
76. Sutirtho Patranobis, "China in 70 years has not occupied an inch of foreign land: Beijing", *Hindustan Times*, September 1, 2020, https://www.hindustantimes.com/world-news/china-in-70-years-has-not-occupied-an-inch-of-foreign-land-beijing/story-eVxbF0U7ZL8GZPVZmqt9xI.html.
77. "What are the areas of China's 14 Dynasties: the smallest is 5 times larger than Japan, and the largest is 87 times larger than that of Japan" (in Chinese). Accessed on July 6, 2021. https://www.sohu.com/a/343624093_679063; "Largest countries in the World 2021", World Population Review. Accessed on July 7, 2021. https://worldpopulationreview.com/country-rankings/largest-countries-in-the-world.
78. Vijay Gokhale, *The Road from Galwan: The Future of India-China Relations* (New Delhi: Carnegie India, 2021), 23. https://carnegieendowment.org/files/Gokhale_Galwan.pdf.
79. Vijay Gokhale, *The Road from Galwan: The Future of India-China Relations* (New Delhi: Carnegie India, 2021), 23. https://carnegieendowment.org/files/Gokhale_Galwan.pdf.
80. 's Claims in the South China Sea", The Diplomat, June 28, 2019. https://thediplomat.com/2019/06/rethinking-taiwan's-claims-in-the-south-china-sea/.
81. "Peace in the South China Sea, National Territory Secure Forever: Position Paper on ROC South China Sea Policy", *Ministry of Foreign Affairs, ROC Taiwan*, 2016, 9-16, https://en.mofa.gov.tw/Upload/WebArchive/1989/Position%20Paper%20on%20ROC%20South%20China%20Sea%20Policy%20(illustrated%20pamphlet%20PDF).pdf.
82. Ibid., 17.
83. Ibid., 27.
84. Bill Hayton, "Two Years On, South China Sea Ruling Remains a Battleground for the Rules-Based Order", *The Royal Institute of International Affairs, July 11, 2018*, Accessed on April 12, 2021. https://www.chathamhouse.org/2018/07/two-years-south-china-sea-ruling-remains-battleground-rules-based-order.
85. Tin-Hui Lin, "Taiwan's Policy Evolution after the South China Sea Arbitration", *The National Bureau of Asian Research*, March 22, 2018, Accessed on April 12, 2021.

https://www.nbr.org/publication/taiwan-policy-evolution-after-the-south-china-sea-arbitration/.

86. Gopal Suri, *China's Expanding Military Maritime Footprints in the Indian Ocean Region (IOR): India's Response* (New Delhi :Vivekananda International Foundation, 2017), 110-111.

87. Harsh V. Pant, "The strategic signal of an Indian presence in the South China Sea", *Observer Research Foundation*, September 2, 2021, https://www.orfonbline.org/research/strategic-signal-indian-presence-south-china-sea/.

88. "India reiterates its stand, says South China Sea a part of global commons", *Business Standard*, July 16, 2020, https://www.business-standard.com/article/current-affairs/india-reiterates-its-stand-says-south-china-sea-a-part-of-global-commons-120071601917_1.html.

89. "Prime Minister's Keynote Address at Shargri La Dialogue (June 01, 2018)", *Ministry of External Affairs, Government of India*, June 1, 2018, https://www.mea.gov.in/Speeches-Statements.htm?dtl/29943/Prime+Ministers+Keynote+Address+at+Shangri+La+Dialogue+June+01+2018.

90. Abhijnan Rej, "In 'Historic' Summit Quad Commits to Meeting Key Indo-Pacific Challenges", *The Diplomat*, March 13, 2021, https://thediplomat.com/2021/03/in-historic-summit-quad-commits-to-meeting-key-indo-pacific-challenges/.

91. Indrani Bagchi, "India should take the lead in the Quad", *The Times of India*, October 18, 2020, https://timesofindia.indiatimes.com/blogs/Globespotting/india-should-take-the-lead-in-the-quad/.

92. Amrita Nayak Dutta, "With P8I aircraft, Navy takes part in Quad anti-submarine warfare exercise in Guam", *The Print*, January 22, 2021, https://theprint.in/defence/navy-takes-part-in-quad-anti-submarine-warfare-exercise-with-p8i-aircraft/590430/.

93. "Quad Leaders' Joint Statement: 'The Spirit of the Quad'", *White House, USA*, March 12, 2021, https://www.whitehouse.gov/briefing-room/statements-release/2021/03/12/quad-leaders-joint-statement-the spirit-of-the-quad/.

94. Manoj Joshi, "How Beijing's New Maritime Rules in the South China Sea Will Affect India and Others", *Observer Research Foundation*, September 6, 2021, https://www.orfonline/research/how/beijings-new-maritime-rules-in-the-south-china-sea-will-affect-india-and-others/.

95. Nguyen Thanh Trung and Le Ngoc Khanh Ngan, "Cidifying Waters and Reshaping Orders: China's Strategy for Dominating the South China Sea", *Center for Strategic and International Studies*, September 27, 2021, https://amti.csis.org/codifying-waters-and-reshaping-orders-chinas-strategy-for-dominating-the-south-china-sea/.

96. "G7 United Kingdom 2021 Chair's Statement", *Foreign, Commonwealth and Development Office, the United Kingdom*, December 12, 2021, https://assets.publishing.service.gov.uk/government/uploads/system/uploads/attachment_data/file/1040131/

G7_Foreign_and_Development_Ministers_Meeting_December_2021_-_Chair_s_Statement.pdf.

97. "G7 Foreign and Development Ministers' Meeting Communiqué", *Foreign, Commonwealth and Development Office, the United Kingdom*, May 5, 2021, https://assets.publishing.service.gov.uk/government/uploads/system/uploads/attachment_data/file/983631/G7-foreign-and-development-ministers-meeting-communique-london-5-may-2021.pdf.
98. "Carbis Bay G7 Summit Communiqué: Our Shared Agenda for global Action to Build Back Better", *Foreign, Commonwealth and Development Office, the United Kingdom*, June 12, 2021, https://www.consilium.europa.eu/media/50361/carbis-bay-g7-summit-communique.pdf.
99. "People's Republic of China: Maritime Claims in the South China Sea, Limits in the Seas No. 150, Department of State, the United States of America", *January 2022*, https://www.state.gov/wp-content/uploads/2022/01/LIS150-SCS.pdf.
100. "Remarks by EAM, Dr. S. Jaishankar at the Joint Press conference with Foreign Minister of Philippines", *Ministry of External Affairs, Government of India*, March 26, 2024, https://www.mea.gov.in/Speeches-Statements.htm?dtl/37745/Remarks+by+EAM+Dr+S+Jaishankar+at+the+Joint+Press+conference+with+Foreign+Minister+of+Philippines.
101. "Constitution of the Republic of China (Taiwan)", *Ministry of Justice of the Republic of China (Taiwan)*. January 1, 1947, Accessed on March 20, 2021. https://law.moj.gov.tw/ENG/LawClass/LawAll.aspx?pcode=A0000001.
102. Mu-min Chen, "Decoding secret diplomatic archives of Taiwan and India: Interactions between Taiwan and India post 1962 Sino-Indian war", *The Reporter, June 6, 2020* https://www.twreporter.org/a/opinion-sino-indian-war-taiwan-secret-diplomatic-archives. (In Chinese)
103. "Dalai Lama is welcome to visit Taiwan", *The Hindu, July 6, 2021*, https://www.thehindu.com/news/international/dalai-lama-is-welcome-to-visit-taiwan/article32006648.ece.
104. Joydeep Bose, "Dalai Lama was asked if he wants to visit Taiwan. Here's his answer", *Hindustan Times*, November 10, 2021, https://www.hindustantimes.com/world-news/dalai-lama-was-asked-if-he-wants-to-visit-taiwan-here-s-his-answer-101636521624751.html.
105. Antoni Slodkowski and Elaine Lies, "Dalai Lama: China's leaders 'don't understand variety of cultures'", *Reuters*, November 10, 2021, https://www.reuters.com/world/china/dalai-lama-says-prefers-india-since-taiwan-china-relations-delicate-2021-11-10/.
106. "Rally held in Taipei to commemorate Tibet National Uprising Day", *Focus Taiwan. March 7, 2021*, https://focustaiwan.tw/politics/202103070009.

107. "Kelsang Gyaltsen Bawa takes charge as new Representative of Office of Tibet, Taiwan", *Central Tibetan Administration*, April 22, 2021, https://tibet.net/kelsang-gyaltsen-bawa-takes-charge-as-new-representative-of-office-of-tibet-taiwan/
108. Jawaharlal Nehru, "Cable to K. M. Panikkar", *Selected Works of Jawaharlal Nehru Second Series Vol. 15*, October 1950-February 1951, Part 2 (New Delhi: Jawaharlal Nehru Memorial Fund, 1993), 438. https://nehruselectedworks.com/pdfviewer.php?style=UI_Zine_Material.xml&subfolder=&doc=s2v15p2.pdf|10|592#page=472.
109. Ibid., 432, 440, 442.
110. Supra, note 78.
111. Shishir Gupta, "Taiwan President follows PM Modi, wishes Dalai Lama on his 86th birthday", *Hindustan Times*, July 6, 2021, https://www.hindustantimes.com/india-news/taiwan-president-follows-pm-modi-wishes-dalai-lama-on-his-86th-birthday-101625588047651.html; Wen, Kuei-hsiang, "The President wishes the Dalai Lama on his 86th birthday, thanking him for sharing wisdom of facing the pandemic" (in Chinese), *Central News Agency*, July 6, 2021, https://www.cna.com.tw/news/aipl/202107060175.aspx.
112. Ananth Krishnan, "Xi Jinping visits Tibet border region, first by Chinese leader in years", *The Hindu*, July 23, 2021, https://www.thehindu.com/news/international/xi-jinping-visits-tibet-border-region-first-by-chinese-leader-in-years/article35481755.ece.
113. "Full Text: Tibet Since 1951: Liberation, Development and Prosperity", *Xinhuanet*, May 21, 2021, http://www.xinhuanet.com/english/2021-05/21/c_139959978.htm.
114. William Echols, "Whitewash: China Calls Invasion of Tibet 'Peaceful Liberation'", *Poligraph. Info*, May 25, 2021, https://www.polygraph.info/a/fact-check-china-tibet-1951-liberation/31273424.html.
115. Srikanth Kondapalli, "Xi's Tibet visit: Bad Signal for India?", *Rediff.com*, July 24, 2021, https://www.rediff.com/news/column/srikanth-kondapalli-is-xi-jinping-tibet-visit-bad-signal-for-india/20210724.htm.
116. "China says Arunachal Pradesh 'inherent part' of its territories", *Business Standard*, December 31, 2021, https://www.business-standard.com/article/international/china-says-arunachal-pradesh-inherent-part-of-its-territory-121123100627_1.html.
117. Shreyashi Sanyal, "China slams the U.S. for interfering in Arunachal Pradesh border dispute with India", *CNBC*, March 22, 2024, https://www.cnbc.com/2024/03/21/us-rejects-chinas-claim-to-arunachal-pradesh-says-it-is-a-part-of-india.html.
118. "India, China hold 12th military-level talks, agree to resolve border dispute expeditiously", *Zee News*, August 2, 2021, https://zeenews.india.com/india/india-china-hold-12th-military-level-talks-agree-to-resolve-border-dispute-expeditiously-2381277.html. "Ladakh standoff: India, China 14th round of military

talks lasted for 13 hours", Livemint, January 13, 2022. https://www.livemint.com/news/india/ladakh-standoff-india-china-14th-round-of-military-talks-lasted-for-13-hours-11642041819914.html.

119. Nanjeet Negi, "India pushes for resolution in eastern Ladakh in 15th round talks with China", *India Today*, March 12, 2022, https://www.indiatoday.in/india/story/india-pushes-resolution-friction-points-china-15th-round-corps-commander-talks-1924473-2022-03-12.
120. Rezaul H. Laskar and Sutirtho Patranobis, "India, China diplomats discuss Ladakh faceoff, 16th round of military talks next", *Hindustan Times*, May 31, 2022, https://www.hindustantimes.com/india-news/india-china-diplomats-discuss-ladakh-faceoff-16th-round-military-talks-next-101654011609131.html.
121. "Joint Press Release of the 16th Round of India-China Corps Commander Level Meeting", *Ministry of External Affairs, Government of India*, July 18, 2022, https://www.mea.gov.in/press-releases.htm?dtl/35496/Joint+Press+Release+of+the+16th+Round+of+IndiaChina+Corps+Commander+Level+Meeting.
122. Husain Haqqani and Aparna Pande, "India needs to find a sweet spot between ignoring and provoking China", *The Print*, July 11, 2021, https://theprint.in/india-needs-to-find-a-sweet-spot-between-ignoring-and-provoking-china/694077/.
123. Supra, note 78.
124. Devjyot Ghoshal and Anand Katakam, "China Steps up construction along disputed Bhutan border, satellite images show", *Reuters*, January 13, 2022, https:// www.reuters.com/world/china/china-steps-up-construction-along-disputed-bhutan-border-satellite-images-show-2022-01-12/.
125. Michael Bristow, "China Encroaching along Nepal Border—Report", BBC News, February 9, 2022. https://www.bbc.com/news/world-asia-60288007.
126. D. P. Tripathi and B. R. Deepak, ed., *India and Taiwan: From Benign Neglect to Pragmatism*, (New Delhi: VIJ Books, 2016).
127. Sushant Singh, "India's China Policy Is Confused", *Foreign Policy*, June 14, 2022, https://foreignpolicy.com/2022/06/14/india-china-policy-ladakh-border-clash-quad-modi/.

4

Taiwan and India: An Evaluation of Strengths and Potential

"Taiwan is not a pariah state in any definition of the phrase.... Taiwanese people deserve great admiration for their many superb achievements...... Taiwan.... is a unique international entity though one without precedent in world history."

–Ranjit Gupta

India's economic interaction with Taiwan has gained much more momentum in the past two decades, narked by several key bilateral agreements and MOUs signed by the Director Generals of the ITA in Taipei and the Representatives of the TECC in New Delhi. These agreements cover areas such as agriculture, investments, heritage railways, civil aviation, double taxation avoidance, industrial cooperation, small and medium enterprises, and customs, among others. FDI inflow from Taiwan to India has increased nearly ten times between 2018 and 2019. The bilateral trade volume between India and Taiwan has risen from USD 0.94 billion in 1995, USD 1.2 billion in 2000, to USD 2.72 billion in 2006, USD 7.56 billion in 2011, and USD 5.80 billion in 2019. Even under the shadow of COVID-19 pandemic, the India-Taiwan bilateral trade reached USD 4.80 billion in 2020, USD 7.70 billion in 2021 and USD 8.45 billion in 2022. The landmark Double Taxation Avoidance Agreement and the Customs Cooperation Agreement signed in 2011 laid a solid foundation for strengthening trade and investment relations between the two countries. More significantly, the signing of the Bilateral Investment Agreement (BIA) in 2018 helps not only to promote inward investment flow to India, but also to ensure protection of Taiwanese investments in India according to international standards, in addition to the safety and rights of Taiwanese investors.[1]

India and Taiwan are considered 'natural partners' as there are no border issues, significant trade imbalances maritime disputes, or terror-related problems between them.[2] How India and Taiwan can complement each other's strengths—by combining Taiwan's expertise in hardware manufacturing, R&D and management with India's abundant human resource with high-quality scientific and technological talent—has long been rooted in the strategic thinking of experts from both countries.

Section 1: Taiwan's Industrial Capabilities and Overseas Investment

Taiwan's industrial foundation was established with assistance from the US through economic and military aid after the Korean War broke out in June 1950. By June 1965, the US had provided Taiwan with USD 1.5 billion economic aid and USD 3.1 billion military aid. In President John F. Kennedy's annual report of the Foreign Assistance Program for Fiscal Year 1962, published in August 1963, he noted, "Taiwan is making rapid economic progress. In 1961, agricultural production increased about 7 percent manufacturing output about 13 percent and gross national product about 7.5 percent in constant prices. In the last half of the fiscal 1962, exports were up about 30 percent over the same period last year. Manufacturing wages rose by about 20 percent while cost of living index rose about 7 percent in 1961, producing a substantial net gain in living standards."[3] Given the fact that the ROC government just relocated to Taiwan after the defeat by the PRC on the mainland in 1949, Taiwan faced severe inflation and its economic infrastructure was inadequate to sustain financial stability, particularly with the urgent need for its defensive build-ups for imminent attack by the PLA. President Kennedy further emphasised "if not owing to the massive US military and economic assistance, such progress in Taiwan would not have been possible. In actual terms, the development in Taiwan then depended extremely heavily on capital from foreign countries. The US economic aid of over USD 1 billion accounted for about 43 percent of gross investment during the decade and represented nearly 90 percent of the external capital flow and donations. US military aid freed local resources from the otherwise intolerably heavier defence expenditure."[4]

The US aid in total USD 4.6 billion between 1950 and 1965 was utilised to develop Taiwan's light industries, infrastructure, agriculture, education and health, etc. Additional forms of loan and counterpart fund mechanisms, also contributed significantly, helping to stabilise Taiwan's economic, financial, military, social and political situations in face of the PRC's threat of invasion.

Taiwan was among the Four Asian Tigers or Dragons, together with Hong Kong, Singapore, and South Korea, which were characterised as one of the fast-growing economies in the past four decades before the 1990s, especially for its export volumes and industrialisation. South Korea's GDP in 1960 was almost at the same level as Sudan's and Taiwan's was just nearly on par with that of Zaire.[5] However, Taiwan's GDP growth rate, which stood at 3.11 percent in 2020 outpaced the PRC's 2.3 percent despite the global coronavirus pandemic.[6] Taiwan's GDP growth rate was 6.45% in 2021 with its GDP Per Capita exceeded USD 30,000 for the first time in history. The primary Taiwan was to be able to maintain relatively high economic growth was its successful early-stage to prevent the spread of the COVID-19 virus.

With a relatively small population of 23.5 million on an area of 36,000 sq km, the ROC on Taiwan managed to hold foreign exchange reserves of USD 543.33 billion as of the end of February 2021,[7] ranking the 6th in the world, while India was the 4th, with Russia in between.[8] Taiwan had the 4th largest foreign exchange reserves of USD 570.595 billion at the end of December 2023 only after China, Japan and Switzerland. India's reserves at USD 549.7 billion took 5th place.[9]

According to the World Digital Competitiveness Ranking 2020 by the International Institute for Management Development (IMD), Taiwan ranked 11th out of 63 major countries and economies worldwide. Furthermore, Taiwan stood out as the 3rd among 29 economies with a population of over 20 million and it ranked 11th among 34 developed economies with a GDP per capita over USD 20,000. Taiwan has been ranked among the top 3 in the world in seven criteria. In three of these, 'agility of companies' 'mobile broadband subscribers' and "IT and media stock market capitalisation'—Taiwan ranked No 1 globally. In three others—'Total R&D personnel per capita', 'opportunities and threats' and 'smartphone possession', Taiwan ranked 2nd; and in the last one, 'higher education achievement ', Taiwan ranked 3rd.[10] In IMD's 2023 World Digital Competitiveness Ranking, which assessed 64 major countries and economies worldwide, Taiwan advanced to 9th place, moving forward two places from its 2022 ranking. Notably, Taiwan leads in five key indicators worldwide: 'total R&D personnel per capita", 'IT and media stock market capitalisation', 'mobile broadband subscribers', 'agility of companies' and 'use of big data and analytics'. Additionally, Taiwan secured the 3rd place in: 'higher education achievement" and 'total expenditure on R&D (in percentage)'. Again and again the annual IMD assessment underscores Taiwan's digital prowess in R&D capacity, IT, internet access availability, higher education, and corporate performance.[11]

Taiwan has been a well-known inter communication technology (ICT) manufacturing hub globally. With over seven decades of industrial development, it has established a strong ICT industry base, boasting semiconductor manufacturing clusters and advanced production capabilities that few countries can match. Taiwan's technological and manufacturing advantages have enabled it to rapidly nurture numerous outstanding companies that offer advanced ICT-related products and services based on the original design manufacturer (ODM) model to the suppliers in the US and other major markets. Collectively, Taiwan's entire manufacturing industry in Taiwan has established strong supply chains with US suppliers, making possible for their products to be exported to countries in Southeast Asia and beyond. In recent years, Taiwanese government has identified cloud and mobile computing as the most promising ICT software and service industries to develop in the near future, with cybersecurity of ICT products as one of the major concerns.[12]

Taiwan has much to offer as an important stakeholder and a valuable partner in combating the unprecedented COVID-19 pandemic crisis now savaging the world. The Taiwanese government has donated 54 million surgical masks and other medical equipment valued over USD 70 million to more than 80 countries in need. Since the end of 2019, Taiwan has proactively shared information, expertise and experience on pandemic control with government officials, experts, and scholars worldwide. Taiwan has organised COVID-19-related forums under the Global Cooperation and Training Framework (GCTF) program sponsored activities and participated in Asia-Pacific Economic Cooperation's (APEC's) High-Level Meeting on health and the economy. By February 2021, Taiwan had held over 140 virtual bilateral and multilateral conferences and meetings with participants from over 60 countries.

On the investment front, Mr. Sridharan Madhusudhanan, the Director General of the India-Taipei Association from 2016 to 2020, acknowledged that direct investment from Taiwan to India increased tenfold in 2018. In his opinion, several Taiwanese companies, such as Foxconn, Delta Electronics Co., Wistron Corp. and Century Development Corporation (CDC), are already reaping benefits from their investments in India and are operating successfully with promising prospects. CDC, a Taiwan-based joint venture that develops industrial parks in worldwide is building a Taiwan Technology and Innovation Park in Bengaluru, Karnataka, which is the first industrial cluster designed and built for Taiwanese businesses in India. Upon completion, this park is expected to attract further Taiwanese investments to India. To enhance India's investment framework for Taiwanese investors, India and Taiwan updated a bilateral investment agreement in December 2018. More significantly, they also jointly established an investment facilitation office in New Delhi exclusively for Taiwanese businesses, called 'Taiwan Plus'. Mr. Gourangaral Das, the ITA's Director General who succeeded Mr. Sridharan Madhusudhanan, continued to promote India's efforts to attract Taiwanese investment to India in his three-year tenure from 2020-2023.

In terms of language training and higher education, Taiwan had set up only 14 Taiwan Education Centres in Indian universities and other educational institutions as of 2020 to promote Mandarin Chinese language. By then, these centres have trained over 6,000 students, and awarded scholarships to Indian students to study for degree programs or for language training in Taiwan. The All-India Council for Technical Education (AICTE) has also established collaborations with Taiwan to facilitate wide range of academic interactions between India and Taiwan. As India is a well-known hub of talented students, these exchange programs and scholarships, help to strengthen the an academic relationship between India and Taiwan, which in the long run, will help boost the bilateral economic and socio-cultural relations. According to statistics in 2018, there were 2,398 Indian students in Taiwan, with 1202 studying for bachelor's, master's and doctoral degree programs, and 1196 enrolled in student exchange programs and Mandarin Chinese language programs. By 2019, these numbers rose to 2783, with 1362 in degree programs and 1421 in language and exchange programs, while in 2020 their numbers dropped to 2239, 1373 and 866 due to travel limitations caused by COVID-19 pandemic.[13] As a result of the joint efforts by the stakeholders from both Taiwan and India, there are already 24 Taiwan Education Centres (TECs) all over India at the end of 2021.[14] In September, 2023 there were 29 TECs based in the universities across India and in total over12,000 students having attended Mandarin classes at these TECs. In the meantime, more than 3000 Indian students are currently studying in Taiwan for Mandarin and degree programs. The number of TECs increased to 32 in March 2024 and is expected to grow further in the years to come, as the demand for high-quality Mandarin Chinese instruction is substantial across different states all over India. Taiwan is widely recognised to be the best provider of Mandarin Chinese teaching without the slightest ideological or strategic concern.

To foster friendship between India and Taiwan and to promote Taiwanese products and services, the first Taiwan Expo in India was held in 2018, reportedly attracting over more than 18,000 visitors looking for business opportunities and successfully showcasing Taiwan's diverse strengths across sectors. The second edition of Taiwan Expo was held in May 2019 in New Delhi, focussing on six areas of Taiwanese expertise, namely, smart cities, smart health care, Taiwanese lifestyle, Taiwanese agriculture, Taiwan green tech and education, culture and tourism. This event also featured business-matching and industrial seminars to introduce Taiwan's high quality products and services, aiming to foster closer cooperation and promote more exchanges between Taiwan and India. Amid the COVID-19 pandemic, the third Taiwan Expo in Mumbai was held online in mid-December 2020. Despite challenging circumstances, partners in both India and Taiwan continue to organise various trade and investment promotion activities in the two countries.

The Taiwan Expo India 2021 was launched in Taipei on October 27, 2021, in a hybrid format, combining physical and online forms. TAITRA's Chairman, James Huang hosted the event from, while Invest India's Managing Director and CEO, Deepak Bagla represented India. Also joining online were Taiwan's Representative to India, Baushuan Ger, and India's Director-General of ITA, Gourangalal Das, among others. Theme Pavilions were set up to showcase products of Taiwanese excellence, E-Mobility, 'Fashion + Function' by Taiwan Textiles, Taipei International Electronics Show and artificial intelligence of things (AIoT) Taiwan and several exhibit areas of anti-COVID-19, healthy lifestyle, education and business service, foods and agricultural technology, ICT and electronics and so on. Over 900 one-on-one business matching meetings were conducted.[15]

Themed around the concept of 'Together Towards Tomorrow', the Taiwan Expo India 2022 took place in Mumbai on September 28, 2022, for three days featuring 52 of the latest products from 26 iconic brands across four themed pavilions in the physical exhibition, along with 100 exhibitors in a virtual pavilion under categories of smart manufacturing, ICT, smart city, transportation, healthcare, lifestyle, beauty and skincare, and smart agriculture. Over 500 Indian businesses attended the Expo and more than 500 registrations for business-to-business online meetings. The Taiwan Expo India 2023 followed on October 5-7 in Mumbai, themed 'Explore Taiwan in India' to showcase quality Taiwanese brands to the Indian market. The six themes in seven pavilions included smart manufacturing, smart city, smart medical, smart agriculture, smart lifestyle and electric vehicles.

As an island country relying heavily on trade and investment, Taiwan's trade volume in 2020 was USD 631.77 billion, which made Taiwan the 17th largest trading country in the world. Exports and imports have reached USD 345.28 billion and USD 286.49 billion respectively in 2020,[16] making Taiwan the 15th largest exporting country and 18th for import.[17] Taiwan's trade volume in 2021 increased to USD 827.9 billion making Taiwan the 16th

largest trading country worldwide, with exports and imports reaching USD 446.4 billion and USD 381.5 billion ranking 16th and 17th respectively.[18] Taiwan's performance in export and import in 2022 outshined previous years, reaching USD 479 billion and USD 428 billion respectively both ranking 17th globally with a total trade volume of USD 907. The trade volume between India and Taiwan in 2022 reached a record high of USD 8.45 billion. From 1952 to 2020, Taiwan's inflow investment amount accumulated to USD 187.275 billion and outflow investment totalled USD 157.497 billion from 1952 to 2020.[19] Taiwan's investment to India has accumulated to USD 4.0 billion in 2022. (For details, please refer Annexures 10 and 11)

Pegatron Corp, Apple's second largest contract manufacturer and an iPhone assembler in Taiwan, has been approved in January 2021 by the Taiwan government to invest US$140 million in India.[20] Foxconn Technology Group announced in July 2020 plans to expand its plant in Tamil Nadu by investing USD 1 billion and adding 6,000 jobs to its existing 20,000. Wistron Corp, a Taiwanese original equipment manufacturer (OEM), disclosed in May 2020 its plan to invest USD 165 million to increase production capacity in Bengaluru. Maxxis Group, a major Taiwanese tyre manufacturer, announced in March, 2020 an investment of USD 400 million in Gujarat as part of its expansion plan.[21] Although there was no substantial announcement during the COVID-19 pandemic in 2021 and 2022, significant investment announcements to India have since been made, as more and more Taiwanese investors are seek a much better destination like India while seriously moving out of China owing to geopolitical and economic considerations.

Taiwan's Gogoro and India's Belrise Industries established in January 2023 a Strategic Energy Partnership in Maharashtra to build a USD 2.5 billion battery swapping infrastructure. Foxconn received approval from the Karnataka government in March 2023 for a further investment of USD 968 million, creating 5,000 jobs and was allocated land for constructing phone manufacturing facilities. Foxconn's also began building its new facilities in Hyderabad in March 2023. Additionally, Pou Chen Group, the world's largest manufacturer of casual and athletic footwear for leading brands, committed in April 2023 to invest USD 280 million over the next 12 years, creating 20,000 jobs in Tamil Nadu. Furthermore, in September 2023 Foxconn

Technology Group reportedly collaborated with ST Micro-electronics NV to submit a joint bid for constructing a semiconductor manufacturing plant in India, following a failed attempt of teaming with Vedanta Resources Ltd.

Section 2: Taiwan's Position in Global Supply Chain

Over the past seven decades, Taiwan has developed a few unique industrial strengths in export-oriented manufacturing, which have contributed to its continued economic growth and prosperity. Taiwan has nurtured a high-tech, sophisticated business culture with the help of a hardworking and disciplined workforce, essential for necessary for the successful operation of various industries. Moreover, Taiwan has maintained a relatively stable internal political situation, and it has cautiously handled the cross-Strait relations with the PRC to avoid escalation beyond manageable levels. Taiwan's critical role in global supply chain has recently gained attention particularly in international media, due to its significant contribution to the supply of high-level semiconductor chips.

Since 2020, the US has placed greater emphasis on revitalising its domestic manufacturing industry and reaffirmed its commitment to taking the lead in mastering advanced technologies and innovations, including AI, 5G biotechnology, and advanced materials. Taiwan a reliable partner in the global supply chain, T has long played a major role in global manufacturing industry. It has an internationally competitive advantage in the high-end manufacturing capabilities, and more obviously in recent years, Taiwan has been acknowledged as one of the key manufacturers of semiconductors dominating the global supply for high-level semi-conductor chips. When there is a global shortage of chips, Taiwan should take this opportunity to advance the complementary characteristics of the industrial and scientific research capabilities of Taiwan and the US and to promote a much closer bilateral industrial strategic collaboration.[22]

The world's largest contract chipmaker, Taiwan Semiconductor Manufacturing Co. Ltd. (TSMC), is headquartered in Taiwan, and reportedly holds over half of the global market share in contract chip-making. Microchips are essential components in computers, smartphones, game consoles and electric vehicles. Today, countries in the world now appreciate the fact that the Industry 4.0 technologies such as—5G smartphones, autonomous vehicles, AI, and high-performance computers—rely heavily on chips that TSMC manufactures. This reliance has raised concerns in the US and other democratic countries about what would happen should Taiwan someday be taken over by the PRC. To ease the US concerns and worries, TSMC has agreed to build a fabrication plant in Arizona for its advanced 5-nanometer process, currently under construction. However, by the time it starts production in 2024, the 5-nanometer technology will no longer be cutting-edge, as TSMC has already developed its 3-nanometer process in Taiwan, with production reportedly beginning in early 2021. Apple is the first customer for the 3-nanometer process, with many others ready to purchase them. It has been reported that, given the US companies' and military heavy dependence on TSMC's products, it is only natural for the US to be concerned about the security of its microelectronics and supply chains. Many other industrialised countries also share the same concerns. Consequently, in early February 2021, the US and Taiwan held their first bilateral economic dialogue under the Biden administration. Among other issues, representatives discussed Taiwan's role in global supply chains and the possible solutions to the severe shortage of high-end chips for the automotive industry in both the US and Europe. After the dialogue, the US claimed that these developments are consistent with the its version of the 'One-China Policy', as it is flexible enough to enable the US to adapt to new conditions and opportunities.

TSMC is the most well-known, but not the only major semiconductor manufacturing company in Taiwan. Other key manufacturers include Advanced Semiconductor Engineering Technology, Acer UnipacOptronics, MediaTek, LITE-ON Technology, United Microelectronics (UMC), Nanya Technology, Silicon ware Precision Industries, EDOM Technology, Sino-American Silicon Products, and MediaTek. Collectively, these companies have positioned Taiwan as a leader in the global semiconductor industry. Additionally, Taiwan is competitive in other high-tech industries as well, such as computer hardware components, software, AI, electric vehicle batteries and charging stations, sensors and many more ICT key components. To harvest the advantages, Google, Amazon and Microsoft have all announced new plans to invest in Taiwan recently.[23] Tesla has been working with Taiwanese suppliers for years with regards to reduction gears, lithium ion batteries, high-speed IT, and light modules with "the flexibility and capacity for innovation of Taiwanese suppliers, which have enabled them not only to win but to far outpace their rivals."[24]

Since January 2021, TSMC has reported record profits each month and announced plans to further invest USD 28 billion in 2021 to develop new chips and expand plant capacity in Taiwan, Japan and the US. So, what is Taiwan's crucial role in the world economy? Earlier in 2021, companies like Toyota and Volkswagen had to slow down or halt certain production lines due to a dire shortage of chips essential for every vehicle. Many auto manufacturers and concerned governments have directly or indirectly urged the Taiwanese government and chipmakers,, to increase chip production to ease the car manufacturing logjam. TSMC was the first company to adopt the independent chip foundry model focusing solely on manufacturing chips based on purchasers' designs. Additionally, a few other Taiwanese semiconductor companies are specialise in specific stages of the chip manufacturing process. This unique industry structure has enabled Taiwan to build up unique advanced expertise in chip manufacturing. The Taiwanese government also made consistent policy support available in funding and tax benefits. Several science and industrial parks have been built all over Taiwan by the government to provide integrated ecosystem for a leading semiconductor industry in the world.[25]

The global semiconductor market grew by 6.8 percent in 2020 reaching USD 440.4 billion. It was valued at USD 607.4 billion in 2023 and is expected to expand to USD 1,028.8 billion by 2030. Taiwan's semiconductor industry encompasses a wide range of expertise, including integrated circuits manufacturing, design, and packaging. It has efficient OEM wafer manufacturing capabilities and complete supply chain. Consequently, they have enabled Taiwan to excel from other competitors and to dominate the global supply chains.[26]

TSMC and other smaller Taiwanese companies control over two-thirds of the global market for contract manufacturing in advanced microchips. Together they enable semiconductor designs by leading brands to become fully functional physical chips. In brief, Taiwan's chip-making companies are global leaders in cutting-edge chip technology, with manufacturing capabilities that are indispensable for the nearly all consumer electronics to advanced fighter jets, missiles, and more. An often-overlooked fact is that Taiwan controls 30 percent of the global market in chip packaging and testing—the final and most critical stage of semiconductor manufacturing. Additionally, Taiwan holds nearly 30 percent of the world's supply of printed circuit boards, on which chips are mounted.

Technologically, Taiwan could be one of the most successful societies on Earth given the fact that Taiwan has none of the natural resources needed for its industrial development. It is a flourishing democracy, governed by rule of law. Taiwan holds regularly free and fair elections, and it is firmly committed to protecting the political and human rights of all its citizens. It also boasts a free society and competitive media environment that allows freedom of expression and speech, and it endorses and respects religious diversity. More significantly, Taiwan is a responsible international stakeholder, committed to good causes course based on the rule of law, and it does not create troubles for any neighbouring country. It also has a population of 23.5 million, larger than most UN member states.[27]

To face the challenges of international competition, the ROC government on Taiwan has pledged to develop six core strategic industries in the years ahead. The first is on information and digital industries. Taiwan is committed to leveraging its strengths in semiconductor manufacturing and ICT industries to secure a pivotal role in global supply chains, and to establishing itself as a major innovation base for the development of next generation technologies, including IoT and AI. Second, Taiwan has begun to develop a cybersecurity industry that integrates with 5G, digital transformation, and its national security requirements. Taiwan will continue to enhance cybersecurity systems and an integral industrial chain that can protect it from cyberattack and earn the trust of like-minded countries. Third, Taiwan is committed to creating highly advanced biotech and medical technology industries that are well integrated into the international biomedical system. From the outset of the COVID-19 pandemic, Taiwan has proven that they are capable of working out advanced technologies to produce reagents, new drugs and vaccines, and these technologies will get the utmost support from the government and transform Taiwan into one of the key contributors in the global battle against the COVID-19. Fourth, Taiwan is developing its national defence and strategic industries integrated with both military and civilian capabilities, which can be further advanced into the aviation and space industries. Fifth, Taiwan will mobilise all resources and technologies to accelerate green energy development and renewable energy industries so that Taiwan can achieve its ambitious goal of generating one-fifth of its overall capacity from green sources by 2025. Sixth, the government will establish and consolidate strategic stockpile industries to ensure critical supplies, maintain essential industrial chains within Taiwan and sustain the vital items such as face masks, medical supplies, energy, and food. Lastly, Taiwan has to develop a diverse talent pool by bringing in the world's top technical, R&D, and management human resource to enhance its competitiveness. Looking to the future, through education and training, Taiwan must cultivate many more bilingual and digital talents for its industries to overcome the global challenges. In the years to come, Taiwan's economy will be elevated to a new level with the completion of all the above-mentioned efforts.[28] In the journey of achieving the goals, India certainly is an inalienable partner for Taiwan.

To jointly nurture electronics design and manufacturing, expertise especially in semiconductors, India's Tata Electronics Private Limited entered into an MoU with Shanmugha Arts, Science, Technology & Research Academy (SASTRA) University in collaboration with Asia University and Yuan Ze University in Taiwan in June, 2021. Together they launched a two-year Master of Technology degree program in August, 2021. This degree program focuses on very large-scale integration design with first year on SASTRA University campus and second year in Taiwan's Asia University or Yuan Ze University including a six-month industry internship in the most advanced semiconductor manufacturing industry. It is regarded as a timely collaboration in developing India's talent and deep domain expertise to be industry-ready.[29] Sri Ramaswamy Memorial Institute of Science and Technology and Taiwan's National Chung Cheng University opened the Taiwan-India Living Lab on big data analytics on September 8, 2022, with a focus on smart healthcare.

India has a growing demand for semiconductors, to be used in industries ranging from cell phones to cars, with the market value to increase from the current level of USD 2 billion to the tune of USD 100 billion by 2025. To cope with this burgeoning demand for the chips, the Indian Union cabinet approved a budget of USD 10 billion in mid-December, 2021 as part of a production incentive scheme aimed at developing a local semiconductor and display manufacturing ecosystem. Another commitment of USD 30 billion was also announced to make India a global hub for electronics manufacturing, focusing on 'semiconductors as the foundation block'. Furthermore, India and Taiwan have reportedly held talks with competent manufacturers like Taiwan's TSMC and UMC for setting up a semiconductor hub in India. TSMC has set up a 5 nm fabrication plant with a cost of USD 12 billion in Arizona in the US which is generally believed to start production in 2024.[30] It also announced to build a USD 7 billion factory in southern Japan in November 2021 with production beginning by the end of 2024 to supply essential chips to Japan's electronic device makers and auto companies. In the meantime, TSMC announced that it would invest USD 2.8 billion in China to ramp up the production of semiconductors used in automobiles. It will install new production lines at an existing plant in Nanjing, which are slated to begin mass-production in 2023 to meet the growing demand for 28-Nanometer automotive chips. More importantly, TSMC's 3 nm process plant in Taiwan has started production in 2021. Following similar announcements by Samsung and Intel, the Taiwanese chipmaking titan made an announcement in mid-June 2022 that it will begin production of ultra-advanced 2 nm chips by 2025 based on 'nanosheet transistor architecture' to deliver significant improvements in performance and power efficiency.[31] To boost the resilient capabilities of the chips supply chain, some European countries have been soliciting TSMC to set up a chip fabrication plant. In August 2023, it was announced that a joint venture will be established with Bosch, Infineon, and NXP in Dresden, Germany under the framework of the European Chips Act.

India is the second largest mobile phone manufacturer in the world and is eager to establish itself as a global hub for semiconductor research and manufacturing in which Indian talented scientists and engineers already play crucial roles globally. On March 13, 2024, Prime Minister Narendra Modi laid the foundation stone for three semiconductor projects, with a budget of over USD 15.2 billion,, The most significant of these projects is the joint venture between Tata Electronics and Taiwan's Powerchip Semiconductor Manufacturing Corporation, (PSMC), to build the first 12-inch wafer fab in Dholera, Gujarat and create 20,000 job opportunities in the future. It will 'achieve the goal of Made in India in order to meet the needs of its international customers as well as the need of India's rapidly growing domestic market and to enhance the resilience of global supply chain'.[32]

Section 3: Taiwan's Model of Quasi-diplomatic Relations

The ROC on Taiwan has faced significant challenges in establishing external relations with countries lacking formal diplomatic ties since 1949 due to political constraints imposed by their 'One-China Policy' or the.One-China Principle'. In 1949 alone, the number of the ROC's diplomatic allies dropped from 52 to 38. However, when the PRC participated in the Korean War in 1952 and faced isolation from the international community, the number of the ROC's diplomatic allies increased to 70 by 1969, the highest to date. After the ROC lost the China seat in the UN, its diplomatic allies for the second time drastically decreased to 22 in 1978 when the US formally severed ties with Taiwan. A shift occurred when President Lee Teng-hui launched an offensive 'Pragmatic Diplomacy' from 1989 till 2000, increasing the number of the ROC's diplomatic allies to 30. During President Chen Shui-bian's tenure from 2000 to 2008 with the initiatives of 'Public Diplomacy', the number again decreased to 23. The number of its diplomatic allies dropped to 22 during President Ma Ying-jeou's tenure from 2008 to 1016 under his 'Viable Diplomacy'. Since President Tsai Ing-wen began her tenure in 1996 with 'Steadfast Diplomacy', the ROC's diplomatic allies have further decreased to 15 by March 2021. Following the severance of diplomatic ties between Taiwan and Nicaragua in December 2021 and Honduras in March 2023, Taiwan's remaining 13 diplomatic allies include the Holy See in Europe, four countries in the Pacific, seven in Latin America and the Caribbean, and one in Africa.

On the international organisation front, the Republic of China (Taiwan) had the great privilege of becoming the selected site when the Central American Bank for Economic Integration when it established its first Country Office outside of Central America on July 6, 2021.[33] The ROC (Taiwan) also enjoys full membership in 45 Intergovernmental Organisations (IGOs), participate as an observer or in other entities in 27 IGOs, multilateral mechanisms and their subsidiaries. Additionally, Taiwan is represented by individuals or group delegations in 3204 International Nongovernmental Organisations (INGOs). Taiwan government-operated official development agency, the TaiwanICDF, conducts 72-83 cooperation projects in 33 countries across the globe with its 21 technical, investment and trade service missions and in collaboration with INGOs or NGOs.

Since Taiwan's economy has been export-oriented for decades, promoting its economic and trade interests in foreign countries has always been the top priority of Taiwan's foreign policy. However, facing a general trend of adversity in international arena since the 1950s, the ROC on Taiwan had to re-establish its contacts with countries with which it had severed diplomatic ties. Taiwan's Ministry of Foreign Affairs could be the only case in the world, often needing to gain access to a foreign country even in private capacity, given the political constraints by the host countries, to advance its national interests. To take the UK as an example, it was not until 1963 did Taiwan set up the Free Chinese Centre, which changed to the current name Taipei Representative Office in the UK in 1992. The ROC on Taiwan's Embassy and Consulate-Generals in the US all changed to a new designation as the Coordination Council for North American Affairs (CCNAA) Office in Washington DC and offices in 12 cities all over the country in March 1979, while the US counterpart American Institute in Taiwan set up its main office in Taipei and a branch office in Kaohsiung. The CCNAA then was changed to the Taiwan Council for US Affairs in June 2019, but all offices in the US still use the Taipei Economic and Cultural Representative Office and Taipei Economic and Cultural Office formats. Japan is another case in point that the relations between Japan and Taiwan started from the Association of East Asian Relations after the severance of diplomatic relations in December 1972 and changed to Taiwan-Japan Relations Association in May, 2017.[34]

Based on the agreement signed by the two countries, Taiwan's Representative Office in Tokyo and five other branch offices in Japan, and Japan's office in Taipei and branch office in Kaohsiung continued to function accordingly. The Republic of Korea severed diplomatic ties with the ROC on Taiwan in August 1992. The Taipei Mission in Korea was set up in Seoul in January 1994 while the Korean Mission in Taipei was established in November 1993.

Relations with other countries vary significantly depending on the economic prospects, bilateral political dynamics between leaders and support from the host country's Parliament. Therefore, the designations of Taiwan's offices in those countries without diplomatic ties also vary, ranging from completely non-official to quasi-diplomatic or para diplomatic as bilateral relations have evolved over the past few decades. Taiwan's quasi-diplomatic activities are somewhat specific due to the existence of the consular function, which in essence resemble traditional diplomacy, but short of a completely diplomatic character.[35]

The ROC on Taiwan has 111 overseas missions in more than 70 countries as of January 15, 2024, including the Permanent Mission of the Separate Customs Territory of Taiwan, Penghu, Kinmen and Matsu to the WTO. Altogether, there are 12 Embassies and two Consulates-General, and 21 different designations of Taiwan's overseas missions all over the world depending on what have been agreed upon at the time of setting up the office in a specific country. Among them, five offices carry the designation of the Taipei Economic and Cultural Representative Office, 42 Taipei Economic and Cultural Offices, 18 Taipei Representative Offices, three Taipei Economic and Cultural Centres, three Taipei Missions, two Taipei Economic and Trade Offices, three Taipei Trade Offices, one Taipei Commercial Representative Office, one Taipei Trade and Economic Representative Office, one Taipei Economic and Cultural Mission, one Commercial Office of Taipei, two Taipei Liaison Offices, one Taiwan Representative Office, one Taiwanese Representative Office, two Délégation Culturelle et Économique de Taipei, and one Representative Office in Moscow for the Taipei-Moscow Economic and Cultural Coordination Commission, etc.[36]

All 12 diplomatic allies have their Embassies in Taiwan, alongside 57 foreign missions from 48 countries including the EU. Likewise, all foreign missions of Taiwan also carry a garden variety of designation if the respective sending state deems appropriate. They range from 'European Economic and Trade Office', "American Institute in Taiwan, Taipei Office', 'Japan-Taiwan Exchange Association, Taipei Office', 'Korean Mission in Taipei', 'Australian Office', 'New Zealand Commerce and Industry Office', 'British Office', 'German Institute Taipe"', 'French Office in Taipei', 'Canadian Trade Office in Taipei', 'The Trade Council of Denmark, Taipei"' 'The Swedish Trade and Invest Council', 'Indonesia Economic and Trade Office to Taipei', 'Vietnam Economic and Cultural Office in Taipei', 'Manila Economic and Cultural Office', 'Singapore Trade Office in Taipei', 'Thailand Trade and Economic Office', 'Malaysian Friendship and Trade Centre, Taipei', 'Brunei Darussalam Trade and Tourism Office in Taipei', 'Ulaanbaatar Trade and Economic Representative Office in Taipei', 'Representative Office in Taipei for the Moscow-Taipei Coordination Commission on Economic and Cultural Cooperation', 'Saudi Arabian Trade Office', 'Nigeria Trade Office in Taiwan, ROC', 'Liaison Office of South Africa', 'The Republic of Somaliland Representative Office in Taiwan', 'Mexican Trade Services Documentation and Cultural Office', 'Commercial Office of Brazil to Taipei', 'Argentina Trade and Cultural Office', and 'Chilean Trade Office'. Only the Embassies' vehicles are entitled to use CD plates (使in Chinese), others are only entitled to plates for foreign missions (外in Chinese), which were issued by the Protocol Department, Ministry of Foreign Affairs of the ROC on Taiwan.

India's case took much longer after India cut diplomatic ties with the ROC in late 1949. The India-Taipei Association (ITA) was established in 1995 and the TECC, New Delhi was set up a few months later in the same year. Subsequently, the TECC, Chennai was established in mid-2012. And Taiwan announced its plan to open the TECC, Mumbai later in 2023 or early 2024, the third office in India. All these offices provide consular services, including visa, passport and authentication of documents, etc. Except for the first couple of the Director-Generals of the ITA in Taipei, who were not career diplomats, all successors were career diplomats. Meanwhile the Representatives and Director-Generals of the TECC both in New Delhi and Chennai have consistently been career diplomats from the very beginning.

Since 1949, Taiwan's unique diplomatic environment has fostered the development of its own quasi-diplomatic practices marked by resilience and perseverance, to establish and strengthen relations with its counterparts. The political will of the administration and the support from the receiving state's parliament are crucial for smooth interactions between the two countries. Relations improve as trade volume and investment grow, influencing the designations and status of Taiwan's Missions abroad.

In case of diplomatic allies, the appointment process and communication patterns between Taiwan and the sending and receiving states are conducted entirely in accordance with the provisions of the Vienna Convention on Diplomatic Relations 1961 and the Vienna Convention on Consular Relations 1963. Nonetheless, in the case of non-diplomatic countries, there are some forms of agreement before the government of the ROC on Taiwan announces the appointment of its Ambassador or Representative-designate to a specific state, even though they do not present credentials to the Head of the State or the Minister of Foreign Affairs. Usually, Taiwan's mission and its head do not have the right to fly the national flag and emblem on the premises of the mission, including the residence of the head of the mission and on his means of transport. However, as far as the pragmatic function of the mission is concerned, it is almost the same as a full-fledged embassy like others. In some cases, Taiwan's head of mission is invited to participate in the activities of the Diplomatic Corps and the Consular Corps, perhaps out of courtesy or at the invitation of friendly and active members.

In practice, there are various forms of courtesy calls made by the newly arrived designate upon the Deputy Minister of Foreign Affairs or the Director-General of the receiving State responsible for the region. Formal communication may occur in the form of Note Verbale, or an official letter from the mission. Through bilateral arrangements, nearly all Taiwanese diplomatic personnel enjoy certain privileges and immunities, including, in some cases, exemptions from taxation, federal and state service charges, etc. For instance in the US, Taiwan's staff across all 13 offices are granted a specially designated vehicle plate exclusively for Taiwan under a bilateral agreement. In some receiving states, Taiwan's diplomats are issued special diplomatic ID cards, distinct from those provided to diplomats from countries with formal diplomatic relations, depending upon the flexibility of the receiving State.

In India for instance, the designations of the TECC in New Delhi and Chennai are listed under a specific category on the Diplomatic List, at least for certain periods. Official business meetings can take place preferred by India's MEA counterparts. Similarly in the UK it is not unusual for meetings, briefings and debriefings to be held at the Foreign and Commonwealth Office, now known as the Foreign, Commonwealth and Development Office. Essentially, it is the prerogative of the receiving State to decide what kind of privileges and immunities should be accorded to the diplomats from Taiwan, and what kind of formality they should follow to conduct their interactions with the Taiwanese counterparts. Any dictation and demand from a third party should be deemed inappropriate as an interference with the sovereignty of the receiving State. Notably, the bilateral relations between Taiwan and the receiving State are ever evolving, depending upon the substantial national interests and the international political environment that concern the two countries.

Taiwan's quasi-diplomatic relations with the majority of countries worldwide are not only unique, but also exemplary, for its size of 36,000 sq KM, and its 23.5 million population to be accommodated. Despite all the political constraints and geopolitical considerations, Taiwan is recognised as a bona fide member of the international community. Before and during the COVID-19 pandemic, Taiwan's passport holders enjoyed Visa-free, Visa on arrival, or E-Visa access to at least 171 countries and regions s, including EU, US, UK, India, Japan, and Korea.[37] According to the Henley Passport Index, Taiwan stands 32nd on Q1 2021 Global Ranking, while Japan was the No. 1.[38] The Henley Passport Index Q1 2022 Global Ranking gives Japan and Singapore No. 1 status, while Taiwan retains the same status at 32nd with 145 destination countries granting visa-free or landing visa treatment to its passport holders.[39] Taiwan is 34th in the Henley Passport Index, Q3 2023 Global Ranking while Singapore stands at No 1. Taiwanese passports are welcome by almost all the countries besides its 12 diplomatic allies, one should ponder whether the popularity of Taiwan's passports will be like that of Japan's if Taiwan maintains diplomatic relations with the majority of countries across the globe.

In recognition of the imminent need for bilateral interactions, India has eased unnecessary restrictions on Taiwan's passport over the years since 1995. Before India's lockdown during COVID-19 pandemic, Taiwan's passport was applicable to e-Visa or Visa-on-Arrival for tourist and business purposes. In 2023 when India resumed issuance of e-Tourist Visa, e-Business Visa, e-Medical Visa and Visa on Arrival to Taiwanese passport holders, all those who must travel to India praised the convenience of this time-saving arrangement which definitely is conducive to enhancing the tourism, trade and investment relations between the two countries.

On the Taiwan side, starting from mid-2019, India is on the list of six new Southbound Policy destination countries whose citizens are eligible to apply online for an ROC (Taiwan) Travel Authorisation Certificate if certain basic requirements are met. This initiative aims to boost the visit of Indian tourists and businessmen to Taiwan, in response to India's further easing of visa requirements for Taiwanese, while the PRC nationals remain under stricter scrutiny and more restrictions when applying for Indian visa. As people in diplomatic circles generally believe, visa services are at least a symbol of sovereignty exercised by a state in its overseas missions. What the Indian government does with regard to visa issuance to Taiwanese passport holders is similar to the measures undertaken by other sovereign States all over the world, distinct from those of the PRC's. In pragmatic sense, there is a clear demarcation between the identity of Taiwan and that of the PRC, and by extension, their respective citizens. Even when the PRC's Ministry of Foreign Affairs announced "Sanctions on Relevant EU Entities and Personnel" on March 22, 2021, it clearly stated that it would sanction ten individuals and four entities on the EU side. The individuals concerned and their families were prohibited from entering the mainland, Hong Kong and Macao of China. They and companies and institutions associated with them were restricted from doing business with China."[40] The PRC government simply reiterated the fact that it does not have jurisdiction over Taiwan; therefore, it practically cannot prohibit anybody in democratic States from entering Taiwan.

However, the PRC's 'wolf warrior' diplomats overseas thought they are in a position to dictate to certain host states not to do anything that makes them unhappy to see as to writing threatening letters or to commenting on Twitter with inappropriate and undiplomatic wordings. There was a shocking case in March 2021 in France where the PRC Ambassador was summoned by the French Foreign Minister over the former's 'unacceptable' insults and attempts at intimidation against French elected officials and researchers for their planned visit to Taiwan or opinions about Xinjiang. The French Minister firmly expressed "We defend those who embody freedom of speech and democracy. Always and everywhere."[41]

The Indian populace will instantly recall an incident that took place in early October 2020, when the PRC Embassy in New Delhi sent an email letter advising the journalists in India to follow their government's 'One-China' principle after newspapers carried advertisements for Taiwan's National Day. The PRC Embassy hoped that "Indian media can stick to Indian government's position on Taiwan question and do not violate the 'one-China' principle." The email continued by stating "In particular, Taiwan shall not be referred to as a 'country (nation)' or 'Republic of China' or the leader of China's Taiwan region as 'President'..."[42] One day later, the Indian MEA spokesperson clearly conveyed the government's position by saying, "There is a free media in India, that reports on issues that they see fit."[43] As a result, the National Day of the ROC on Taiwan which falls on October 10 became well-known and much discussed in India's. Many people openly chose to side with Taiwan for the first time in the past seventy years. More symbolically, India's public opinion expressed much stronger support for closer bilateral relations between India and Taiwan, even for playing the 'Taiwan Card' against the PRC, and for Indian government to review its self-imposed 'One-China Policy', unless the PRC reciprocates with a 'One-India Policy'.

Ranjit Gupta, the Director-General of India-Taipei Association from 2000-2003, argued that "Taiwan is not a pariah state in any definition of the phrase ... Taiwanese people deserve great admiration for their many superb achievements. Though China terms it a renegade province, Taiwan is very considerably beyond that; it is a unique international entity though one without precedent in world history." He further articulated that the challenge is "to transcend conventional approaches to interaction with Taiwan in the context of its 'unique' status."[44] Most countries world-wide including India, but excluding the PRC, are making the best of Taiwan's 'unique' quasi-diplomatic model to enhance their relations in areas such as trade, investment, strategic, human rights, climate change, and public health.

Besides Taiwan's two offices in India, and the third in Mumbai in the pipeline, and India's one office in Taiwan, eight member states of the ASEAN have set up representative offices in Taiwan to promote bilateral trade, investment, and people-to-people relations, with the exception of Cambodia and Laos. Although international politics have created political constraints and diplomatic interactions between Taiwan and these countries, economic and investment benefits can still be achieved through pragmatic arrangements without provoking outcry and hindrance from the third parties. (For details, please refer Annexure 12)

Following the establishment of the Taiwan's representative office in Somaliland in August 2020, Somaliland also set up its representative office in Taiwan in September 2020. Further to its announcing of a donation of 20,000 doses of COVID-19 vaccine to Taiwan in late June 2021, Lithuania, on July 1, 2021 announced its plans to establish representative offices in Taiwan and several other Asian countries, with a view to reach out to the Indo-Pacific region for its export markets, and to avoid being over-reliant on China.[45] In return, the ROC government announced on July 20, 2021 that it has decided to establish the Taiwanese Representative Office in Lithuania very soon.[46] To counter this development, which it viewed contrary to its interests, the PRC recalled its ambassador to Lithuania and demanded that the latter recall its ambassador to the PRC on August 10, 2021. Lithuania's foreign ministry responded by saying that while it regretted the PRC's decision to recall its ambassador and respected the principle of 'one China', Lithuania was "determined to pursue mutually beneficial ties with Taiwan."[47] The Economic Minister of Lithuanian government revealed that the country's representative office in Taiwan was scheduled to open in early 2022. While the Taiwanese Representative Office in Lithuania would be ready to function at the end of 2021, according to Taiwan's National Development Minister, during his delegation's visit in Lithuania in late October 2021.[48]

The PRC's hostility towards Lithuania has gone beyond the its physical borders. As a show of solidarity, EU Commission President Ursula von der Leyen and Council President Charles Michel said that the PRC's reaction to Lithuania's announcement of the opening of representative offices in and from Taiwan, calling them 'unjustified' and 'disproportionate'. They jointly vowed to 'push back' against "threats, political pressure and coercive measures' directed at EU member states by the PRC. They argued that Lithuania's decision does not constitute a breach of the EU's "One-China Policy", asserting that the EU and its member states have a right to further develop relations and cooperation with Taiwan.[49]

After an informal meeting at the UN Framework Convention on Climate Change Conference of the Parties (COP26) in Glasgow in early November 2021, the President of Lithuania, Gitanas Nauseda, stated that US President Joe Biden had pledged to support the mutual establishment of representative offices in Taiwan and Lithuania and expressed his concerns on the situation in the Taiwan Strait.[50] Furthermore, the leader of the first-ever official European Parliament's 13-member delegation to Taiwan, Raphaël Glucksmann, conveyed a clear message in early November, 2021 that Taiwan is the 'most vivid, enlightening democracy in the Indo-Pacific region' and 'a treasure that all democrats around the world should cherish and protect'. He further pointed out that Taiwan is not alone and Europe is standing with Taiwan 'in the defence of freedom and rule of law'. The purpose of the delegation's visit to Taiwan was to 'earn about its capacity to build a strong democracy while confronting a high level of threats from China' as "Europe is also facing large scale actions orchestrated by an authoritarian regime to weaken its democracy."[51]

As planned, the Taiwanese Representative Office in Lithuania was officially opened in Vilnius on November 18, 2021, despite the PRC recalling its ambassador from Vilnius and expelling the Lithuanian ambassador from Beijing, as well as imposing more retaliatory sanctions, such as the suspension of direct freight train services to Lithuania. Subsequently, on November 21, 2021, the PRC government announced to downgrade its diplomatic relations with Lithuania to Chargé d'Affaires level and urged Lithuania to 'correct its mistakes immediately'. In response, the Lithuania government expressed 'regret' over the PRC's decision and reaffirmed its 'One-China Policy', and at the same time, it has the right to expand cooperation with Taiwan including Taiwan to establish 'non-diplomatic representation' in the country based on 'economic interests'.[52] On June 15, 2022, Lithuania's vice minister of economic and innovation said the trade office would be opened in Taiwan in September to further strengthen bilateral and economic relations. This move came despite the coercive taken by the PRC to halt exports of all Lithuanian products, which has seriously impacted some business sectors in Lithuania.[53] Despite all the political pressure economic boycotts from the PRC, Lithuania designated its first Representative and announced that its Representative Office in Taiwan was scheduled to open in mid-September, 2022.

Since the diplomatic rift shows no sign of abatement between Lithuania and the PRC, and between more and more EU member states and the PRC, this situation will give more room for Taiwan, Lithuania, and other EU members to further enhance their substantial relationship. One thing for sure is that the PRC's bullying approach in oppressing and coercing democratic countries in Europe would not bring about any consequences in PRC's favour. Some observers even speculated there is a likelihood that PRC may be bold enough to sever diplomatic ties with Lithuania. The utmost to observe at this stage is whether the PRC will deliver Xi Jinping's pledge that "China will never seek hegemony nor take advantage of its size to coerce smaller countries".[54]

The international community has shown high degree of friendship and goodwill to Taiwan in its time of need amid the prevalence of COVID-19 since 2021. To demonstrate this cycle of kindness, Slovakia on July 16, 2021 pledged to donate 10,000 doses of Astra Zeneca (AZ) COVID-19 vaccine to Taiwan.[55] However, when the vaccines arrived on September 26, 2021, the actual number of doses donated were actually 160,000.[56] The Czech Republic on August 27, 2021 donated 30,000 doses of Moderna COVID-19 vaccine to Taiwan as a "concrete help to a country that has already helped us several times."[57] Lithuania donated two batches of AstraZeneca vaccine,

20,000 and 235,900 respectively, on July 31 and October 7, 2021. Poland donated 400,000 doses of the AstraZeneca vaccine which arrived in Taiwan on September 5, 2021, making Poland the third-largest vaccine donor, only after 4.204 million doses from Japan and the US donation of 4 million doses.

The Commission and the High Representative of the Union for Foreign Affairs and Security Policy of the EU, on September 16, 2021, released a Joint Communication to the European Parliament and the Council: 'The EU strategy for cooperation in the Indo-Pacific' In this document it was specified that the Indo-Pacific region is 'home to three-fifths of the world's population, produces 60 per cent of global GDP"; the Indo-Pacific and Europe together 'account for over 70 percent of the global trade in goods and services, and over 60 percent of FDI flows'. The document also expressed concerns over 'the display of force and increasing tensions in the South and East China Sea and in the Taiwan Strait' that 'may have a direct impact on European security and prosperity'; and on the issue of resilient and diversified value chains, the document pledges that the EU will work with its Indo-Pacific partners to reinforce value chains with Japan, South Korea, and Taiwan for semiconductors. More significantly, the EU commits that it will "pursue its deep trade and investment relations with partners with whom it does not have trade and investment agreements, such as Taiwan".[58]

Another milestone report was passed by 580 votes in favour and 26 against with 66 abstentions on October 21, 2021, by the European Parliament on enhancing EU-Taiwan relations. Taiwan was hailed in the report as a "key EU partner and democratic ally in the Indo-Pacific," one that contributes to maintaining a rule-based order amid an intensifying rivalry between the China's continued military coercion and disinformation campaign. The report also urges the EU to do more to address these tensions, to protect Taiwan's democracy, and Taiwan's status as an important EU partner. It further calls on the EU to launch an impact assessment, public consultation, and scoping exercise for an EU-Taiwan BIA. Additionally, it calls for the name change of the European Economic and Trade Office in Taiwan into "EU Office in Taiwan", among other measures.[59] In total, the European Parliament has adopted 13 resolutions demonstrating support for Taiwan democracy with the most significant one being the one passed in October 2021.

Again, on March 9, 2022, the European Parliament adopted a resolution on foreign interference in all democratic processes in the EU by 552 in favour and 81 against, and 60 abstentions. The resolution indicates a need for global, multilateral cooperation and support among like-minded partners in dealing with foreign malicious interference. It highlights that other democracies such as Australia and Taiwan have developed advanced skills and strategies to combat this issue., Taiwan is known to stand at the forefront of the fight against information manipulation, mainly from China. It emphasises that the success of the Taiwanese system is founded on cooperation among all branches of the government, as well as with independent NGOs specialised in fact-checking and media literacy, and with social media platforms, such as Facebook, It also stresses the promotion of media literacy for all generations, debunking disinformation, and the curbing the spread of manipulative messages. Additionally, the INGE Special Committee went on a three-day official mission to Taiwan to discuss disinformation and foreign electoral intervention. Essentially, the EU 'sees Taiwan as an important partner in boosting the production of semiconductors within the EU'.[60]

In addition, a motion supporting Taiwan's meaningful participation in Interpol was passed in the Netherlands' House of Representative by a vote of 149 to 0 with one absentee.[61] A trend of stronger attention and support for Taiwan's security and freedom is from the US, Europe, Japan, Canada, Australia, and South Korea.

The 2020 Tokyo Olympics, which concluded on August 8, 2021, incidentally highlighted the absurdity of Team Taiwan's designation as Chinese Taipei, to participate in the Olympic Games, a humiliating agreement dating back to 1981. Athletes from Team Taiwan won two gold medals, four silver medals and six bronze medals; However, it was not Taiwan's national anthem that was played at the medal-awarding ceremony, but its national flag anthem. Moreover, what was hoisted was not the Taiwan's National Flag, but, it's the flag of its Olympic Committee. At the opening ceremony, Team Taiwan was introduced as 'Taiwan' by the NHK anchor-women, which invited wide attention and discussion among media across the globe about why Team Taiwan's designation in the Olympic

Games is 'Chinese Taipei' instead of 'Taiwan'. As a result, media in some countries just used 'Taiwan' to replace its misleading Olympic designation.[62] As CNN commented, "Chinese Taipei is a name that appears on no maps. It's a legal fiction." It continued to opine that an International Olympic Committee compromised fifty years ago "to the so-called one China policy that comes with a ban on the use of Taiwan's flag in any Olympic capacity" which meant "this island nation of 23 million, with its own democratically elected government, has been effectively erased." CNN concluded by indicating that "buying into this particular lie of Chinese Taipei, it will leave the international community impotent to forcefully object if or when there's violence in the South China Sea."[63]

The 'Chinese Taipei' issue did not arouse many reports or discussions in the Indian media because it has long been accustomed to using this term to describe Taiwan in the Olympic Games and, by extension in many other international organisations. Indian people know it well, and so do the media houses. One very rare instance is a piece of report by India Today in which it contains detailed examples that some of Japan's and Taiwan's victorious Olympic athletes have been subjected to a storm of online abuse from Chinese citizens".[64]

The acronym 'ROC' has long been used to indicate "the Republic of China"—which is Taiwan's official name in its Constitution. The 'ROC' appeared in the 2020 Tokyo Olympics and created some ripples because it actually represents 'Russian Olympic Committee' which inadvertently made the Guardian use Taiwan's National Flag on the first day to identify its country.[65]

Over the years, Taiwan's quasi-diplomatic model with pragmatic approaches to avoid political implications has become a daily norm for Taiwan's survival and contribution to building bilateral relations with a few dozen of the 181 of the 193 member states of the UN that do not maintain diplomatic ties with Taiwan. Even the PRC cannot and will not object to these engagements if the relations with Taiwan are essentially based on economic and investment needs, unless the designations of the Taiwan's representative offices in the host countries contain 'Taiwan' or "'Republic of China'.

Taiwan's model of developing and maintaining quasi-diplomatic relations across the globe has received ever stronger support in the past four years, especially after the Russian invasion of Ukraine in February 2022. Although Taiwan's access to international organisations is still facing a ruthless blockade from the PRC by means of the so-called 'One-China Principle' the PRC had framed its diplomatic allies to follow as a red line for their own versions of 'One-China Policy' when they attempt to establish closer pragmatic relations with Taiwan. However, the trend to change the unilateral dominance by the PRC of a country's independent foreign policy has gained momentum over the years. Many more members of the democratic community, including India, are willing to speak out their strategic necessity to develop closer economic and even political ties with Taiwan, despite the risks of retaliatory reactions from the PRC. One scholar argues that the PRC "has set the discourse in its ties with India and Taiwan. That must change. Letting China decide the course of India's foreign policy while overlooking Taiwan has not proven to be a beneficial strategy."[66] The point is how closely both India and Taiwan can develop their bilateral relations based on the mutually beneficial model of engagement from which they have managed to bypass the official nature in the past two-and-half decades.

Section 4: India's Strengths and Potential for Taiwan

India is the largest democracy in the world and has innumerable economic strengths that no other country can compare. Human resource is India's No. 1 strength. There are 19 million students enrolled in high schools annually and 10 million students are enrolled in undergraduate degree courses across India. Among the over 9 million college graduates, 2.1 million graduates and 0.3 million post-graduates left from non-engineering colleges. While about 2.5 to 3 percent of them get employed in other fields or continue to pursue higher degree in other countries, the rest choose to work for the IT industry. To meet the market demand in India and across the globe, more and more high school graduates will continue to pursue undergraduate programs, making more skilled workers at all levels to be available to the IT industry. India has the strength and potential for Taiwan, Japan, South Korea, Singapore, China, and the US in this regard. 'By 2025, one-fifth of the world's working age population will be Indian'. And 'India will by 2035 overtake China as the world's most populous country", according to the Australian government.[67]

India also has the largest pool of English-speaking professionals on software and hardware which became one of the most attractive talent pools that Taiwan is looking to work with. A large number of high-quality science and engineering graduates are trained every year thanks to the Indian education system's emphasis on mathematics and science. Proficiencies in quantitative and scientific concepts with good command over the English language have produced a talent pool that enables India to meet the international demand for IT design and manufacturing. Indian software engineers and high-level managers have established their world-wide credentials for strong technical and managerial skills, as well as their eagerness to accommodate clients to support the service industry. Already India is one of the best outsourced countries owing to its easy access to specialised engineering talent, particularly in the areas related to telecommunications and computer science.

Essential to the success of industries is the policy support initiated by the Government of India, such as 'Make in India', 'Digital India', and 'Skill India'. Prime Minister Narendra Modi, in his Independence Day address in August 2020, championed the call for 'Atmanirbhar Bharat' and called upon Indian companies to play a big role in the global supply chain. For convenient reason, at least for a decade India has been so heavily dependent on China for mobile phones, electronic goods, and pharmaceuticals, that a massive trade deficit was created annually in China's favour. Modi stressed that self-reliance did not merely refer to decreasing the import demands from China; rather it is about our skills, our human resources, our creativity and with that we need to touch new heights...to strengthen skill development for a self-reliant India, for improving our competency".[68] There are five pillars of 'Atmanirbhar Bharat'—Economy, Infrastructure, System, Vibrant Demography and Demand—in which a special economic and comprehensive package of INR 20 lakh crores was reserved for this initiative. That budget alone is equivalent to 10 percent of India's GDP.[69]

India has the 2nd largest telephone market, and the 3rd largest scientific and technical manpower in the world. In terms of the number of digital consumers, India is also the one of the 3rd largest global economies, estimated to reach 900 million internet subscribers by 2025 when 100 percent FDI is supposed to be through the Automatic Route.[70] Several sectors in Taiwan's industries are critical for India's next phase of technological evolution, such as electronics, semi-conductors, and 5G where Taiwan's manufacturing capabilities are not only at the cutting edge, but also continuously in R&D. Most importantly, Taiwan's public health system is supposed to be one of the most advanced globally, and so in the middle or in the wake of the COVID-19 pandemic, India can also work with Taiwan and learn from each other's experiences.[71] India's first indigenous COVID-19 vaccine, COVAXIN, developed by Bharat Biotech in collaboration with the Indian Council of Medical Research (ICMR) and National Institute of Virology (NIV), has successfully gained emergency use authorisation (EUA) from India and many other countries. COVAXIN conducted its large-scale Phase 3 efficacy trial in India in October 2020 and its results indicated high efficacy in preventing COVID-19 after the second dose. According to an analysis from the National Institute of Virology, it indicates that the vaccine-induced antibodies from COVAXIN vaccination can effectively neutralise the UK variant strains and other heterologous strains. Mongolia, Myanmar, Sri Lanka, Philippines, Bahrain, Oman, Maldives and Mauritius are some of the countries which have received supplies through government to government route by India. [72] As an astonishing achievement made by Bharat Biotech again, India's first nasal COVID-19 vaccine INCOVACC has gained emergency use authorisation from the Government of India in early September 2022 and has become the world's first intranasal COVID-19 vaccine.[73]

India's strengths and potential can also be testified from the Australian perspective. It has been revealed "by 2030 there will be over 850 million internet users in India. By 2035 India's five largest cities will have economies of comparable size to middle income countries today". It further stated that India is so big and diverse with a robust democracy and a vocal media, that any new policy offer will only mean compromises, delays, and therefore will be less than ideal. Australia predicted that India would surpass China as the world's most populous country by 2035. And India's domestic market may make it the world's 3rd largest economy by 2035, following China and the US. As a matter of fact, India is the 3rd largest economy if measured by purchasing power parity. As the largest democracy in the world, by any standard India is an essential and powerful partner for any democracy to invite to participate in regional institutions in the Indo-Pacific.

In 2019, India overtook the UK and France to become the 5th largest economy with a GDP size of USD 2.94 trillion. And before the COVID-19 pandemic, India was the fastest growing economy in the world. Strategically speaking, five states in India—Maharashtra, Gujarat, Karnataka, Tamil Nadu, and Telangana—altogether produce 70 percent of India's exports.[74] There are more states in India that are suitable candidates for Taiwan and other interested countries to enhance relations in trade, investment, higher education, health, cultural, and tourism. These include Andhra Pradesh, West Bengal, Punjab, Delhi and Uttar Pradesh, depending on which sectors are to be focused. As the largest democracy in the world, India has the potential to replicate the market that China has offered to any potential investor, though in different ways.

Prime Minister Narendra Modi's 'Make in India' drive has helped to turn India into the world's second-biggest mobile manufacturer after China. Modi's government believes it is time for chip companies to set up their operations in India. Governments across the globe are soliciting inward investment and subsidising chip manufacturing plants as shortages delay the auto and electronics industries and expose how badly the world depends on Taiwan's chip supplies. Now that the Indian government has offered more than USD 1 billion as a cash incentive to each semiconductor company that constructs manufacturing plants in India. This is part of its commitment to building up its own smartphone assembly industry and securing its electronics supply chain. The government guarantees to be a buyer and will announce mandates for private companies to purchase Indian made chips. This is a wise and pragmatic move for India to establish reliable suppliers for its own industries, aiming to cut over-dependence on China, especially after the border skirmishes in 2020. The Indian government made clear that locally made chips will be designated as 'trusted sources' and can be used in sensitive products like CCTV cameras and 5G equipment, etc.[75]

To reap the substantial benefit from the policy support for smartphone assembly industry, Taiwan's Wistron, an iPhone manufacture, had been reportedly partnering with India's Optiemus Electronics to jointly manufacture or assemble smartphones and laptops, with the latter's investment of over USD 200 million to expand its manufacturing capabilities in the next three to five years. Revenues of USD 5.13 billion were expected to yield an employment of 11,000 workers which would be created over five years for Optiemus.[76] Another leading iPhone manufacturer Foxconn had announced its plan to joint venture with India's Vedanta to manufacture semiconductors with an initial investment of USD 120 million. Although these two cases of collaboration failed in 2023, new forms of joint ventures have been formulated soon later making their new Indian counterparts dominant in these partnerships. Many other Taiwan's qualified partners are also exploring new opportunities of partnership in India, such as Power Semiconductor Manufacturing Corporation already engaging with Tata Electronics to build India's first 12-inch fab in Gujarat.

To Taiwan, India offers a ready consumer market and talent pool for several emerging industries. The consumer market in India has reached a scale of USD 1.5 trillion and is expected to grow to USD 6 trillion by the year 2030. India is believed to become the third-largest consumer market in the world in the next decade. What India needs to do at this moment is to look for new markets and to engage with reliable partners if India wishes to elevate the standards of the present market conditions and policy guidelines.[77] Based on the optimistic prospect, the World Bank had estimated India's GDP growth to be in the range of 7.5 percent to 12.5 percent during Financial Year (FY) 2021-22, depending on the success of its vaccination campaign to contain the COVID-19 pandemic.[78] However, despite significant global challenges, India's GDP growth in FY 2022-23 was at 7.2 percent making it one of the fastest-growing major economies in the world, according the World Bank, which further forecasts India's GDP growth for FY 2023-24 to be at 6.3 percent due to challenging external conditions and waning pent-up demand.

In the midst of COVID-19 pandemic, not a single country, developed or developing alike, emerged intact in 2020. Without resorting to a single day lockdown, Taiwan remarkably had among the lowest number of COVID-19 cases in the world, with only 1030 cases by the end of March2021. With a new wave of the pandemic taking place in India in April 2021, stricter anti-pandemic measures and faster vaccination process were to be implemented in addition to mobilising global or regional assistance to cope with the COVID-19 crisis. To address the sudden surge of the confirmed cases—reaching 14576 from May 11 to August 7, 2021, Taiwan raised the nationwide COVID-19 alert to Level 2 on May 11, then Level 3 on May 19, before lowering it Level 2 again on July 27. Data from August 8 and 9 showed just 7 and 8 confirmed cases respectively, demonstrating the effectiveness of Taiwan's preventive measures amid the vaccine rollout.[79] With the global spread of BA.4 and BA.5 variants all over the world, Taiwan reported 30,000 to 40,000 daily cases in September 2022, enforcing three-days quarantine followed by four days of self-initiated epidemic prevention to effectively contain the COVID-19 pandemic. Taiwan's quarantine policy has since eased, opening up to international travellers, as the daily confirmed cases fell to 10,000 in the second half of 2022.

For India, Taiwan could serve as a role model for countering the COVID-19 pandemic, especially in the initial earlier stages, and for jointly implementing the 'Make in India' and 'Atmanirbhar Bharat' initiatives in more viable ways. More precisely, India could identify Taiwan as a key priority partner over the coming decade to build affordable and sustainable public health coverage. With participation from Taiwan's and other stakeholders, India will be able to strengthen its highly strategic R&D capabilities in science and technology and to ensure that India's local factories are deeply embedded in the global supply chain. As the entire world faces a semiconductor chip shortage in the automotive sector, Taiwan's position and value in the global supply chain for key products outshines those of other competitors. Trade volume in goods between the Taiwan and the US has increased three times since 2000 to USD 150 billion in 2020.[80] As far as foreign relations are concerned, and given India's traditional non-alignment position, the extent to which India can balance its leverage role in dealing with the democratic camp led by the US, alongside other key players like Russia, China, and ASEAN will decide how closely Taiwan can deepen industrial and investment collaboration with India, as this involves sensitive strategic considerations beyond purely technical and market issues.

Section 5: Summary Note

Compared to India's advantages in all aspects, Taiwan seems to be a relatively minor player in the global arena. However, while Japan, South Korea, and Singapore, are focusing on industries and investments on sectors of their expertise to explore potential opportunities in India. China in the meantime has launched its ambitious global "OBOR" initiative, which physically, strategically encroaches upon India, conflicting with India's national security interests and territorial integrity. China's threat and belligerent image worsen in India by ongoing border disputes, territorial claims, and a significant trade deficit in China's favour over the years. Indian public perception about Chinese products and the provocative remarks of its "wolf warrior" diplomats in India, has led to China being viewed as a less trusted and unreliable partner as India seeks to attract FDI in strategic sectors.

Taiwan is globally recognised as a highly reliable manufacturing partner in strategic sectors, including semiconductors and other products with key industrial significance. India has launched ambitious self-reliant initiatives supported by clear and firm government policies. The next imperative will be to identify the most qualified and trustworthy partners with whom India can establish full-scale local manufacturing collaboration, such as ICT (including mobile phones and semiconductors), 5G, electric vehicles, agriculture, education, health, environmental protection, software development, start-ups, cyber security, Smart City, and more. Taiwan is should be among the top priority countries to join forces with India. Taking semiconductor manufacturing for example, the Indian government decided in early 2021 to offer more than USD 1 billion in cash incentives to each semiconductor company that builds manufacturing factories in India, so that India can boost its own smartphone assembly industry and strengthen its electronics supply chain.[81] Indian government has announced new policy guidelines and measures on 'Make in India', 'Atmanirbhar Bharat' and PLI schemes which are essential to achieving these goals with the capital and technical inputs by the world-renowned high-tech partners like Taiwan. India should take it as a top priority 'to ensure availability of basic infrastructure such as lots of pure water and undisturbed electricity supplies'[82] because semiconductor manufacturing consumes tens of billions of US dollars not only for the initial investment, but also as the follow-up financial investment to make it viable and technologically advanced.

In this regard, Taiwan could be the first suitable candidate, given that some Taiwanese companies are already manufacturing smartphones for most popular brands in India, securing the supply chain for high-end smartphones is both a strategic must and one a policy objective as it aims to enter the semiconductor manufacturing sector. Further to partnering with Wistron, Foxconn, and PSMC, India needs to attract more chip manufacturing companies such as TSMC, UMC or any other viable Taiwanese manufacturer over the next couple of years. India's vision of 'Viksit Bharat 2047', the government's roadmap to making India a completely developed nation by 2047, requires accelerating the consolidation of manufacturing capabilities to become a leading producer and exporter of both semiconductor and the high-level smartphones in a matter of years. The first priority is a strong political and prompt action at the highest levels of Indian government, and Taiwan is well prepared for closer collaboration with India.

Notes

1. "Taiwan Plus, Invest India", *Ministry of Commerce and Industry, Government of India,* https://www.investindia.gov.in/country/taiwan-plus.
2. Aprameya Rao, "India, Taiwan natural partners: Envoy Tien", *Deccan Chronicle,* October 25, 2019, https://www.deccanchronicle.com/business/in-other-news/251019/india-taiwan-natural-partners-envoy-tien.html.
3. The President's Annual Report of the Foreign Assistance Program of the United States for Fiscal year 1962, (Washington, D. C.: Govt. Printing Office, August 28, 1963), 20.
4. David W. Chang, "U.S. Aid and Economic Progress in Taiwan." *Asian Survey* 5, no. 3 (1965): 152. https://jstor.org/stable/2642405.

5. Paul Morris. "Asia's Four Little Tigers: A Comparison of the Role of Education in Their Development." *Comparative Education* 32, no. 1 (1996): 95-109. http://www.jstor.org/stable/3099602.
6. C. Textor, "GDP growth rate in Taiwan 2010-2021", *Statista, February 22, 2021.* https://www.statista.com/statistics/328535/gross-domestic-product-gdp-annual-growth-rate-in-taiwan/.
7. "Foreign Exchange Reserves as of the End of February 2021", *Central Bank of the Republic of China (Taiwan),* March 5, 2021, https://www.cbc.gov.tw/en/cp-448-132390-947a7-2.html.
8. "List of countries by foreign-exchange reserves", *Wikipedia.* Accessed on March 29, 2021, https://en.wikipedia.org/wiki/List_of_countries_by_foreign-exchange_reserves.
9. Su Ssu-yun, Chang Ai and Frances Huang, "Taiwan's forex reserves hit new high at end of 2023", *Focus Taiwan*, January 6, 2024. https://focustaiwan.tw/business/202401060008.
10. "Taiwan jumps to 11th in IMD World Digital Competitiveness Ranking 2020-Achieves maximum performance", *National Development Council, Republic of China (Taiwan),* https://www.ndc.gov.tw/en/nc_8455_34453.
11. "2023 IMD World Digital Competitiveness: Taiwan Has Advanced to the 9th Position Globally, With the Leading Position in Five Key Indicators Worldwide", *Ministry of Digital Affairs, Republic of China (Taiwan),* https://moda.gov.tw/en/press/press-releases/9089.
12. "Taiwan-Country Commercial Guide: Information and Telecommunications Technology", *International Trade Administration of USA*, September 25, 2020, https://www.trade.gov/country-commercial-guides/taiwan-information-and-telecommunications-technology.
13. Shruti Niraj, "AICTE and Taiwan join hands to push academic collaboration between the two countries", *The Times of India*, April 30, 2019, https://timesofindia.indiatimes.com/home/education/news/aicte-and-taiwan-join-hands-to-push-academic-collaboration-between-the-two-countries/articleshow/69114396.cms. "The New Southbound Talent Development Program", *Ministry of Education, the Republic of China (Taiwan)*, Accessed on December 29, 2021. https://www.edunsbp.moe.gov.tw/overview_students_en1011.html.
14. "India's 24th Taiwan Education Centre – TEC comes up in Bengaluru", *Asian Community News*, December 28, 2021, https://www.asianommunitynews.com/indias-24th-taiwan-education-centre-tec-comes-up-in-bengaluru/.
15. Lin Sing-chien, "Grand opening of Taiwan Expo India 2021 to strengthen industrial linkage in COVID-19 pandemic", *Central News Agency*, October 27, 2021. https://www.cna.com.tw/news/afe/202110270176.aspx. (In Chinese)

16. Wu Chia-jung and Elizabeth Hsu, "Taiwan records historical high in exports in 2020", *Focus Taiwan*, January 8, 2021, https://focustaiwan.tw/business/202101080019
17. Wu Chia-jung and Frances Huang, "Taiwan becomes world's No. 15 largest exporter", *Focus Taiwan*, April 3, 2021, https://focustaiwan.tw/business/202104030010
18. "Taiwan world's 16th largest trading economy in 2021: MOF", *Focus Taiwan*, April 15, 2022, https://focustaiwan.tw/business/202204150008.
19. "Statistics of the Investment Commission December 2020", *Ministry of Economic Affairs, Republic of China (Taiwan)*, https://www.moeaic.gov.tw/english/index.jsp.
20. "Taiwan approves $140 million Pegatron investment in India", *World News, WION News*, published on January 29, 2021, YouTube video, 01:55, https://www.youtube.com/watch?v=6_4yA-yv2f0.
21. "Recent Investment", *Taiwan Plus, Invest India*, accessed on April 26, 2021. https://www.investindia.gov.in/country/taiwan-plus
22. "The global economy is picking up slowly, Taiwan's four major manufacturing industries are all growing", *Market Prospects*, January 13, 2021, https://www.market-prospects.com/articles/taiwan-major-manufacturing-industries-are-all-growing.
23. James Lee, "Supply chains critical to Taiwan's security", *East Asia Forum*, March 10, 2021, https://www.eastasiaforum.org/2021/03/10/geoeconomics-and-the-security-of-taiwan/.
24. Kuo-chen Lu, "Taiwan's Tesla Boom, and Looking for More", *Commonwealth, August 27, 2020*, accessed on March 30, 2021. https://english.cw.com.tw/article/article.action?id=2787.
25. Mary Hui, "Semiconductors helped make Taiwan Asia's top-performing economy in 2020", *Yahoo News*, February 3, 2021, https://finance.yahoo.com/news/semiconductors-helped-taiwasn-asia-top-080043575.
26. "Taiwan's semiconductor industry sets new output milestone in 2020", *Focus Taiwan*, February 22, 2021, https://focustaiwan.tw/business/202102220012.
27. Robert D. Blackwill and Philip Zelikow, *The United States, China, and Taiwan: A Strategy to Prevent War, Council Special Report No. 90 (New York: Council on Foreign Relations*, February 2021), https://cdn.cfr.org/sites/default/files/report_pdf/csr90_1.pdf.
28. "Inaugural address of ROC 15th-term President Tsai Ing-wen", *Office of the President, Republic of China (Taiwan)*, May 20, 2020, https://english.president.gov.tw/News/6004.
29. Sindhu Hariharan, "Tata Electronics and SASTRA University to foster talent in electronics design and manufacturing", *The Times of India*, June 29, 2021, https://timesofindia.indiatimes.com/home/education/news/tata-electronics-and-sastra-university-to-foster-talent-in-electronics-design-and-manufacturing/articleshow/83848516.cms;"Asia University and Yuan Ze University assist nurturing

India's semiconductor talent", *Central News Agency, August 19, 2021*, https://www.cna.com.tw/news.ait/202108190246.aspx. (In Chinese)

30. Rezaul H. Laskar, "India, Taiwan start talks on free trade agreement", *Hindustan Times*, December 16, 2021, https://www.hindustantimes.com/world-news/india-taiwan-start-talks-on-free-trade-agreement-101639673988033.
31. Cheng Ting-fang, Lauly Li and Kim Jaewon, "TSMC says it will make ultra-advanced 2nm chips by 2025", *Nikkei Asia*, June 17, 2022, https://asia.nikkei.com/Business/Tech/Semiconductors/TSMC-says-it-will-make-ultra-advanced-2nm-chips-by-2025.
32. "Tata Joins hands with PSMC to build India's first 12-inch fab", *TSMC*, February 29, 2024, https://www.powerchip.com/en-global/insights/press-releases/content/20240229.
33. Wu Chia-jung, Pan Tzu-yu and Frances Huang, "American development bank opens first office in Asia in Taiwan", *Focus Taiwan*, July 6, 2021, https://focustaiwan.tw/business/202107060011.
34. "財団法人交流協会と亜東関係協会との間の在外事務所相互設置に関する取り決め", 政策研究大學院大學 (National Graduate Institute for Policy Studies). https://worldjpn.grips.ac.jp/documents/texts/JPCH/19721226.O1J.html. (In Japanese)
35. Erik Pajtinka, "Between Diplomacy and Paradiplomacy: Taiwan's Foreign Relations in Current Practice", *Journal of Nationalism, Memory & Language Politics,* Volume 11: Issue 1 (April 2017). https://sciendo.com/article/10.1515/jnmlp-2017-0003.
36. "Links to Embassies and Missions", *Ministry of Foreign Affairs, Republic of China (Taiwan)*, https://en.mofa.gov.tw/OverseasOfficeLink.aspx?n=1573&sms=957; "Taiwan, Nauru end diplomatic relations", *Focus Taiwan*, January 15, 2024. https://focustaiwan.tw/politics/202401150008.
37. "Visa-Exempt, Landing Visa and e-Visa for Taiwan Passport Holder", Bureau of Consular Affairs, Ministry of Foreign Affairs, Republic of China (Taiwan). https://www.boca.gov.tw/cp-37-220-9f130-1.html. (In Chinese)
38. "Henley Passport Index: Q1 2021 Global Ranking". January 5, 2021. Accessed March 26, 2021. https://www.henleypassportindex.com/assets/2021/Q1/henley_passport_index_2021_Q1_infographic_global_ranking_201209_1.pdf.
39. "Henley Passport Index: Q1 2022 Global Ranking". January 11, 2022. https://cdn.henleyglobal.com/storage/app/media/hpi/henley_passport_index_2022_q1_infographic_global_ranking_211221_1.pdf.
40. https://fmprc.gov.cn/mfa_eng/xwfw_665399/s2510_665401/t1863106.shtml.
41. John Irish, "France summons Chinese envoy over 'unacceptable' insults", Reuters, March 23, 2021. https://www.reuters.com/article/us-france-china-idUSKBN2BF1MU.; "Wolf Warriors and a crazed hyena French researcher not intimidated after clash with China Envoy", France 24, March 23, 2021. https://

www.france24.com/en/europe/20210323-wolf-warriors-and-a-crazed-hyena-french-researcher-not-intimidated-after-clash-with-china-envoy.

42. Sanjeev Miglani, "China tells Indian media not to call Taiwan a country, Taiwan says 'get lost'", *Reuters*, October 8, 2020, accessed on March 25, 2021. https://www.reuters.com/article/india-china-taiwan-idUSKBN26T1LE.
43. Kallol Bhattacherjee, "Indian media is free, says in MEA response to Chinese Embassy's note to press on Taiwan", *The Hindu*, October 8, 2020, https://www.thehindu.com/news/national/indian-media-is-free-says-in-mea-response-to-chinese-embassys-note-to-press-on-taiwan/article32806814.ece.
44. Anita Sharma and Sreemati Chakrabarti, *Taiwan Today (*Delhi: Anthem Press 2010), xxv-xxvi.
45. Chung Yu-chen and Emerson Lim, "MOFA welcomes Lithuania's plan to set up trade office in Taiwan", *Central New Agency*, July 2, 2021, https://focustaiwan.tw/politics/202107020018.
46. "Taiwan is to establish 'The Taiwanese Representative Office in Lithuania' opening new page for cooperation and communication", *Ministry of Foreign Affairs, the Republic of China (Taiwan)*, July 20, 2021, https://www.mofa.gov.tw/News_Content.aspx?n=73&s=96170. (In Chinese)
47. Christian Shepherd, Katherin Hille and Richard Milne, "China recalls ambassador to Lithuania over Taiwan office", *Financial Times, August 10, 2021*, https://www.ft.com/content/a8d2b571-0b8e-4c9c-858b-f1b56aec1af4.
48. Chen Yun-yu and Frances Huang, "Lithuania set to open representative office in Taiwan in early 2022", *Focus Taiwan*, October 27, 2021, https://focustaiwan.tw/business/202110270021; Chen Yun-yu, "Lithuanian economic minister: representative office in Taiwan is set to open in early 2022", *Central News Agency*, October 27, 2021, https://www.cna.com.tw/news/firstnews/202110270301.aspx. (In Chinese)
49. Tang Pei-chun and Teng Pei-ju, "As Lithuania faces China intimidation, EU leaders vow to push back", *Focus Taiwan*, October 29, 2021, https://focustaiwan.tw/politics/202110290008.
50. Kelvin Chen, "US president supports closer Taiwan-Lithuania relations", *Taiwan News*, November 4, 2021, https://www.taiwannews.com.tw/en/news/4334717.
51. Joseph Yeh, "Europe is standing with Taiwan in defending freedom: EP delegation", *Focus Taiwan*, November 4, 2021, https://focustaiwan.tw/politics/202111040006.
52. Chai Sze-chia and Joseph Yeh, "China has no right to interfere with Taiwan-Lithuania exchanges: MAC", *Focus Taiwan*, November 21, 2021, https://focustaiwan/cross-strait/202111210013.
53. Joseph Yeh, "Lithuania looks to open trade office in Taiwan in September", *Focus Taiwan*, June 15, 2022, https://focustaiwan.tw/politics/202206150023.

54. Gabriel Crossley, Rozanna Latiff and Martin Petty, "Xi tells Southeast Asian leaders China does not seek 'hegemony'", *Reuters*, November 22, 2021, https://www.reuters.com/world/china/xi-says-china-will-never-seek-hegemony-summet-with-asean-2021-11-22/.
55. Chung Yu-chen, Lin Yu-li, Tang Pei-chun and Lee Hsin-Yin, "Taiwan thanks Slovakia for pledging COVID-19 vaccine donation", *Focus Taiwan,* July 16, 2021, https://focustaiwan.tw/politiocs/202107160008.
56. Wu Jui-chi, Yu Kai-hsiang, Sophia Yeh and James Lo, "Slovakia-donated COVID-19 vaccines arrive in Taiwan", *Focus Taiwan,* September 26, 2021, https://focustaiwan.tw/society/202109260003.
57. Li Yu-li, Chung Yu-chen and Elizabeth Hsu, "Czech Republic pledges vaccines to Taiwan", *Focus Taiwan, July 27, 2021*, https://focustaiwan.tw/politics/202107270008.
58. "Joint Communication to the European Parliament and the Council: The EU strategy for cooperation in the Indo-Pacific", *European Commission and High Representative of the Union for Foreign Affairs and Security Policy of the European Union*, September 16, 2021, https://eeas.europa.eu/sites/default/files/jointcommunication_2021_24_1_en.pdf.
59. "Joint Communication to the European Parliament and the Council: The EU strategy for cooperation in the Indo-Pacific", *European Commission and High Representative of the Union for Foreign Affairs and Security Policy of the European Union,*
60. September 16, 2021, https://eeas.europa.eu/sites/default/files/jointcommunication_2021_24_1_en.pdf.ropa.eu/oeil/popups/ficheprocedure.do?lang=en&reference=2020/2268(INI)"2020/2268(INI))", *European Parliament,* March 9, 2022, https://www.europarl.europa.eu/doceo/document/TA-9-2022-0064_EN.html.
61. Tang Pei-chun and Teng Pei-ju, "Dutch parliament passes motion backing Taiwan's participation in Interpol", *Focus Taiwan,* November 24, 2021, http://focustaiwan.tw/politics/202111240006.
62. Shannon Tiezzi, "Taiwan – Sorry, 'Chinese Taipei' – Is Having a Fantastic Olympics", *The Diplomat,* August 5, 2021, https://thediplomat.com/2021/08/taiwan-sorry-chinese-taipei-is-having-a-fantastic-olympics/.
63. *New Day,* anchored by John Berman and John Avlon, aired August 6, 2021 on CNN. http://edition.cnn.com/TRANSCRIPTS/2108/06/nday.02.html.
64. Saikiran Kannan, "Tokyo 2020: China's social media trolls take aim at Taiwan and Japan's Olympic athletes", *India Today,* August 5, 2021, https://www.indiatoday.in/sports/tokyo-olympics/story/tokyo-2020-china-s-social-media-trolls-take-aim-at-taiwan-and-japan-s-olympic-athletes-1837376-2021-08-05.
65. "Russia using ROC to participate in the Olympics misled UK's The Guardian to think it is Taiwan", *Central News Agency,* July 2, 2021, https://www.cna.com.tw/news/aspt/202107240252.aspx. (In Chinese)

66. Sana Hashmi, "India-Taiwan Ties: A Case for Stronger Partnership", *Asie. Visions, Ifri, No 125*, November 2021, https://www.ifri.org/sites/default/files/india-taiwan_ties_since_the-1920s_a_classic_case_of_friendliness_mutual_neglect_and_redefining_ties.pdf.
67. *An India Economic Strategy to 2035.* Department of Foreign Affairs and Trade, Government of Australia, 2018. https://www.dfat.gov.au/geo/india/ies/overview.html.
68. "PM Modi pushes for self-reliant India with 'Make for World' call," *The Times of India*, August 16, 2020, https://timesofindia.indiatimes.com/india/pm-modi-pushes-for-self-reliant-india-with-make-for-world-call/articleshow/77568558.cms.
69. "Atmanirbhar Bharat Abhiyaan", *Invest India, Ministry of Commerce and Industry, Government of India*, accessed on March 31, 2021. https://cdnbbsr.s3waas.gov.in/s3850af92f8d9903e7a0559a98ecc857/uploads/2020/05/2020051717.pdf.
70. "Electronic Systems", *Taiwan Plus, Invest India, Ministry of Commerce and Industry, Government of India*, accessed on March 30, 2021, https://www.investindia.gov.in/country/taiwan-plus.
71. Harsh V. Pant and Premesha Saha, "The Taiwan Question in Indian Foreign Policy", *Raisina Debates, Observer Research Foundation*, May 16, 2020, https://www.orfonline.org/expert-speak/taiwan-question-indian-foreign-policy-66249/.
72. "COVAXIN – India's First Indigenous COVID-19 Vaccine", Bharat Biotech. Accessed on March 31, 2021. https://www.bharatbiotech.com/covaxin.html.
73. Swati Bharadwaj, "India's 1st nasal Covid vaccine gets approval", The Times of India, September 7, 2022. https://timesofindia.indiatimes.com/city/hyderabad/indias-first-nasal-covid-vaccine-gets-approval/articleshow/94037891.cms.
74. "Economic Survey 2018: 5 states show the way with 70% of exports, enjoy higher standard of living", *The Indian Express*, January 30, 2018, https://indianexpress.com/article/business/economy/economic-survey-five-states-show-the-way-with-70-of-exports-enjoy-higher-standard-of-living-union-budget-5044319/.
75. Sankalp Phartiyal and Aditi Shah, "Exclusive: A billion for every chip-maker who 'makes in India,' sources say", *Reuters*, March 31, 2021, https://www.reuters.com/article/india-semiconductor/exclusive-a-billion-for-every-chip-maker-who-makes-in-india-sources-say-idUSKBN2BN12H.
76. Sankalp Phartiyal, "Wistron partners with India's Optiemus in boost for electronics manufacturing". *Reuters*, August 24, 2021, https://www.reuters.com/business/wistron-partners-with-indias-optiemus-boost-electronics-manufacturing-2021-08-24/.
77. Niranjan Hiranandani, "Advantage India", *The Hindu*, October 8, 2020, https://www.thehindubusinessline.com/opinion/advantage-india-during-covid-scenario/article32785099.ece.
78. "India's GDP growth estimated to be in range of 7.5-12.5%: World Bank", *The Hindu*, March 31, 2021, https://www.thehindubusinessline.com/news/national/

india-gdp-growth-estimated-to-be-in-range-of-725-125-says-world-bank/article34203804.ece.

79. Evelyn Kao, "Taiwan reports eight new COVID-19 cases, four deaths", *Focus Taiwan*, August 9, 2021, https://focustaiwan.tw/society/202108090008.
80. Rahul Jacob, "Why India needs to look east at Taiwan", *Mint*, March 18, 2021, https://www.livemint.com/tehnology/tech-news/why-india-needs-to-look-east-at-taiwan-11615996534314.html.
81. Sankalp Phaitiyal and Aditi Shah, "Exclusive: A billion for every chip-maker who 'makes in India,' sources say", *Reuters*, March 31, 2021, https://www.reuters.com/article/india-semiconductor-idUSKBN2BN12H
82. Danish Khan, "India must ensure basic infra to woo chip makers: NXP", *The Economic Times*, May 27, 2021, https://economictimes.indiatimes.com/industry/cons-products/electronics/india-must-ensure-basic-infra-to-woo-chip-makers-nxp/articleshow/82984540.cms.

5
Conclusion

"We have substantial technology and economic and commercial relations with Taiwan and certainly Taiwan has a reputation when it comes to electronics and of course, more recently with semiconductors. So, there has been an upswing in the levels of cooperation..."

— Subrahmanyam Jaishankar

The Republic of China on Taiwan is a democratic nation of 23.5 million peace-loving and hard-working people living on a mountainous island smaller than the Aksai Chin. Since its government's relocation to Taiwan from the mainland in 1949, Taiwan's resilient existence and startling performance in ICT industries over the past 75 years have outshone many competitors, despite the constant military threat and coercion from the PRC. Since 2000, Taiwan has witnessed three peaceful transfers of power between its two major political parties, with the same party being elected in 2024, demonstrating its 'vibrant and competitive democratic system'. Taiwan has been rated as 'Free' for the 26th consecutive year by Freedom House, ranking 7th in the world and remaining 2nd freest in Asia after Japan in the Freedom in the World 2024.[1] In addition, Taiwan retained its ranking of 1st in Asia and 10th globally among the 167 countries and territories in the Democracy Index 2023 released by Economist Intelligence Unit, with an overall score of 8.92 out of 10.[2] The country's free and fair elections, strong institutions, and respect for civil liberties contribute to its political stability and governance effectiveness, supported by its strong anti-corruption measures, transparent governance practices, and rule-of-law framework.

In terms of technological advancements, Taiwan's semiconductor industry accounted for over 70 percent of the global market share and 92 percent of advanced chips production in 2023. TSMC, the world's largest contract chipmaker, reported record revenues of over USD 64 billion in 2023, highlighting Taiwan's dominance in semiconductor manufacturing. Taiwan's ICT exports reached USD 142 billion in 2023, with products such as smartphones, laptops, and networking equipment contributing significantly to global markets. Additionally, Taiwan's biotechnology sector has seen steady growth, with the Taiwan Biotechnology Industry Organisation reporting a 12 percent increase in biotech exports in 2023, reaching USD 4.5 billion. The country's healthcare system, highly rated by the World Health Organisation (WHO) for its efficiency and universal coverage, is a testament to its strengths in this sector. In terms of trade and economic performance, Taiwan's total exports in 2023 amounted to USD 426 billion, with electronics, machinery, chemicals, and textiles being the top export categories. The country's export-oriented economy continues to drive economic growth and stability. Taiwan's FDI inflows reached USD 18.7 billion in 2023, with key sectors including technology, manufacturing, and services. Taiwan's investment environment and incentives attract foreign investors seeking innovation and market access.

Taiwan has been actively engaging in regional forums such as the APEC and many others. It also has been in close contact with existing members of the Comprehensive and Progressive Agreement for Trans-Pacific Partnership with an aim of getting membership in the coming years. As a full-fledged democracy posing no threat of any country, Taiwan's contributions to regional security, economic cooperation, and cultural exchanges are recognised by partner countries and international organisations. On Indo-pacific strategies, Taiwan has established security partnerships with like-minded countries, including the US, Japan, Australia, and India. Collaborative efforts focus on maritime security, cybersecurity, and defence cooperation in the Indo-Pacific region.

India is the most populous democracy in the world, occupying a land area about one third of the size of China. With a population of 1.43 billion, India not only the dominant power in South Asia and one of the key players in the Non-Aligned Movement but also an indispensable member of all international organisations and groupings. India's presence in any of them carries heavy-weight significance, often influencing the balance of power.

'Viksit Bharat' or 'Developed India' is the current government's ambitious roadmap to transforming India into a developed nation with an economic scale of USD 30 trillion by 2047, marking 100 years since independence, with a projected population of 1.65 billion. Its core vision is to foster inclusive economic participation among all citizens.[3] India's policy framework includes long-term development plans and strategies, such as the National Development Agenda, focusing on sustainable economic growth, job creation, poverty alleviation, and inclusive development. Policies emphasise infrastructure investments in transportation, energy, digital connectivity, urban development, and rural infrastructure to support economic activities and improve living standards. Initiatives like Make in India, Start-up India, and Atmanirbhar Bharat promote industrial growth, innovation, entrepreneurship, and technology adoption across sectors, fostering a competitive and resilient economy.

Policies also focus on digital infrastructure development, e-governance, digital literacy, digital payments, broadband connectivity, cybersecurity, and digital inclusion to drive digital transformation and innovation across sectors. Strategies promote adoption and development of emerging technologies such as AI, IoT, blockchain, 5G, biotechnology, and space technology to enhance productivity, competitiveness, and technological capabilities. Additional policies regarding promotion of international trade, investment, economic diplomacy, regional cooperation, and participation in global initiatives, forums, and trade agreements leverage international opportunities and enhance India's global stature. Bilateral and multilateral partnerships, strategic alliances, and diplomatic engagements with key countries and organisations are significantly highlighted to support India's foreign policy objectives, security interests, and global influence. In addition policies focus on strengthening national security capabilities, defence modernisation, border security, counterterrorism, cybersecurity, maritime security, and strategic deterrence to safeguard India's sovereignty and territorial integrity.

India's economy is one of the fastest growing in the world, with a GDP growth rate of 8.4 percent in 2021-2022, followed by a robust 7.6 percent growth rate in 2023-2024 over and above 7% growth rate in 2022-2023.[4] India's diverse economy encompasses agriculture, manufacturing, services, and technology sectors. India is a key player in global trade, with exports of goods and services reaching USD 765.6 billion in 2023. The government's focus on trade diversification and ease of doing business has attracted foreign investment across sectors. India's Act East Policy and Indo-Pacific Vision emphasise enhanced engagement with countries in the Indo-Pacific region, promoting economic cooperation, maritime security, and strategic partnerships. India is also the key member of the Quad along with the US, Japan, and Australia, focusing on regional stability and security. Bilateral relationships with countries like Japan, Australia, ASEAN nations, and Taiwan strengthen India's Indo-Pacific presence and strategic influence.

Compared with India, Taiwan does not seem geopolitically significant, especially over the past seven decades. However, the forefathers of the majority of Taiwanese people, who once lived on the Chinese mainland, shared historical interactions with India in religious, cultural, and commercial realms although the current mainland residents are under the rule of the Communist PRC. The phrase '*Hindi Chini bhai bhai*' before 1949 symbolised India's brotherly relationship with the ROC and its predecessors in Chinese history, unrelated to the PRC, or Communist China during the Cold War era. The ROC government was based on the Chinese mainland from 1911 to 1949, and until 1971 the ROC, as a founding member of the UN, held China's permanent seat in the UNSC since the UN's inception in 1945. According to UN archives the ROC supported India's initiatives, with the exception of issues related to Tibet due to constitutional constraints In fact the ROC consistently supported India's bid for UNSC membership and supported India's stance on other major international issues, no less than fourteen times before 1971. The ROC, now based in Taiwan, is positioned as a potential competitor to India; rather Taiwan is supposed by all means to be a natural partner for India, sharing common values in democracy, the rule of law and the commitment to peace and stability across the Taiwan Strait and the Indo-Pacific.

Relations between India and Taiwan came to nearly a halt after India switched diplomatic recognition from the ROC to the PRC at the end of 1949 when the ROC government relocated to Taiwan. Regardless of the sensitive and complex nature of India's evolving interactions with the PRC, history has presented India with opportunities to re-engage with Taiwan, fostering mutually beneficial relations almost from scratch since early 1990s. This period marked the beginning of efforts by both India and Taiwan began to explore the viability of establishing and strengthening substantial economic and investment relations, despite the constraints of India's 'One-China Policy'.

India and PRC are neighbours sharing a border of over 4,000 km. However, when issues of border disputes, territorial disputes, and sovereignty arise, the PRC has not hesitated to resort to military means, despite its claims of being as amiable and close as family members with India. Consequently, conflicts and casualties on both sides have led to long-term consequences in mutual perceptions, fostering a sense of hostility, as territorial and sovereignty issues are the most sensitive matters between the two sides. This tension is compounded by India's significant annual with the PRC, particularly the USD 85.09 billion deficit in FY2023-24. To the discontent of the Indian people, India's sensitivities and interests in territorial disputes in Arunachal Pradesh, Aksai Chin, and Jammu and Kashmir have long been ignored by the PRC, while China has consistently demanded that India respect its own sensitivity and interests regarding Tibet, Xinjiang, and Taiwan. Indian scholars and media have noticed that the Government of India has refrained from reiterating or mentioning its 'One-China Policy' since 2008, despite requests by the PRC to do so.

Section 1: Summary of India-Taiwan Emerging Ties

The friendship and mutual understanding between the peoples of the two ancient civilisations, India and 'China' have existed for over two thousand years, spanning religious, cultural, economic or social realms. Cultural exchanges between India and China could date back to centuries ago, even conceptual and linguistic exchanges could have existed in 1500-1000 BC between China's Shang and Zhou dynasties and India's ancient Vedic civilisation.[5]

During World War II, Chiang Kai-shek of the ROC, then based on the Chinese mainland, attempted to convince India's leadership in India to support Britain as part of the Allies against the Japanese invasion, but in vain. Without substantial support from India to defend against the Japanese Imperial Army's advance to India via Burma, the ROC expeditionary troops were compelled to fight the CBI Theatre of war alongside other Western Allies, suffering tremendous casualties, including the loss of tens of thousands of its troops and more than a dozen of generals. Following the establishment of the UN in 1945, the ROC held the "China" seat as one of the five permanent members of the Security Council until 1971. Although India continued to advocate in 1950 for the PRC to replace the ROC in occupying the 'China' seat in the UN,, the ROC on Taiwan, continued to support India's initiatives and endeavours within the UN.

The ROC on Taiwan left the UN in 1971 and the 'China' seat was subsequently taken by the PRC. Due to the perplexing nature of the designation of 'China' at different times in history, the ROC on Taiwan gradually began to emphasis its Taiwan identity, particularly with the consolidation of democracy from the late 1980s. In international arena, the term 'China' is now almost exclusively used to refer to the PRC on the Chinese mainland. Meanwhile an increasing number of people in Taiwan identify themselves as Taiwanese and their country as the ROC on Taiwan, the ROC (Taiwan), or simply Taiwan.

Section 2: Mutually Beneficial Economic and Technological Partnership

Vijay Gokhale, the ITA Director General from 2003 to 2007, once commented that Taiwan officials were "living in fantasy" with their inflated expectations that India-Taiwan relations could serve as a counterweight to China's influence. He explained that "India had no interest in relations with Taiwan outside of the economic sphere". and that India repeatedly declined Taiwan's attempts for its Vice Minister of Foreign Affairs to visit India, even to promote what Taiwan viewed as mutually beneficial interests. Gokhale revealed that India had also flatly rejected many times, Taiwan's inquiries about the possibility of signing a by saying that it was 'simply not going to happen', and 'far beyond the realm of the possible'. After the Cold War ended in 1991, India encountered a financial crisis, leading its foreign policy to adopt a more economically approach. This was the backdrop against which India and Taiwan had the opportunity to improve their relations. According to Vijay Gokhale, the 'economic factors such as the potential for trade and investment were the only reasons, India finally ended its no-contact policy with Taiwan'.

When India set up its unofficial ITA office in Taiwan in 1995, their bilateral trade volume was only USD 0.94 billion,[6] which increased to USD 1.2 billion in 2000, USD 1.4 billion by 2003, USD 2.72 billion in 2006, USD D 5.80 billion in 2019, USD 4.80 billion in 2020 and USD 7.70 billion in 2021 even under the shadow of COVID-19 pandemic. The recovery trend continued, with total bilateral trade volume reaching USD 8.45 billion in 2022, the highest in history, making India the 14th largest buyer of Taiwanese goods and the 17th largest supplier. However, trade volume in 2023 slightly dropped to USD 8.23 billion, making India the 16th largest trading partner.

As the relations between the two countries significantly improved in the next twenty years, the overall bilateral ties between India and Taiwan in 2023 have far surpassed what Gokhale and his successors could have envisaged. In his response to a question about India's relations with Taiwan at Wilton Park on November 15, 2023, India's Minister of External Affairs, Dr Subrahmanyam Jaishankar, stated, "We have substantial technology and economic and commercial relations with Taiwan and certainly Taiwan has a reputation when it comes to electronics and of course, more recently with semiconductors. So, there has been an upswing in the levels of cooperation..."[7] This brief statement encapsulates the nature and current status of the emerging ties between India and Taiwan, and more notably, represents the first ever open and candid remarks by an Indian External Minister expressing both personal and official views on Taiwan. The People of Taiwan have welcomed this unexpected friendly gesture, fully aware that

India has no intention to create any political implications contrary to its persistent foreign policy.

On April 29, 2024, during an interactive session on Northeast India's Integration on, Dr Subrahmanyam Jaishankar, mentioned the Japan and Southeast Asia are indeed important to India, and added "Taiwan is another important player...a partner of India's first semiconductor foundry...Taiwan recently signed an agreement of mobility with India..."[8] India and Taiwan share economic synergies, with potential for collaboration in technology, trade, and investment. India's large consumer market and growing economy offer Taiwanese businesses opportunities for expansion and diversification.

Both India and Taiwan excel in technology sectors such as semiconductors, ICT, and biotechnology. Collaborative efforts in research, innovation, and technology transfer could benefit both countries and contribute to global advancements. India's strategic position in the Indo-Pacific region and its democratic values align with Taiwan's interests in regional security, economic integration, and democratic partnerships. Enhanced cooperation between India and Taiwan could bolster regional stability and prosperity, and there is a growing appreciation of this opportunity among people of both countries.

India's self-imposed 'One-China Policy' to maintain smooth diplomatic relations with its neighbour, the PRC, is deeply rooted in India's far-reaching geopolitical and strategic considerations. At the same time, this policy has somewhat hampered India's relations with the ROC on Taiwan, given the slow progress and development in the past three decades.. Nevertheless, India's Look East Policy, Act East Policy and Taiwan's New Southbound Policy, have provided a new impetus, fostering mutually beneficial interactions and delivering tangible outcomes in a wide range of areas in unofficial and pragmatic channels. It should be acknowledged that all the heads of missions at ITA in Taipei and TECC in New Delhi have done their utmost to lay a solid foundation and advance progress, over 20 agreements and MOUs have been signed to facilitate smoother and deeper collaboration in trade, investment, education, science and technology, culture, and migrant workers, among other areas, and to enable some discrete high-level bilateral exchanges. As a result, India's foreign policy towards Taiwan, according to some scholars, has transformed 'from benign neglect to pragmatism'.[9]

Taiwan fully understands that the glass ceiling placed by the India continues to hinder constructive engagement. In spite of all the difficulties, the public and private sectors in Taiwan are working diligently to help their Indian counterparts appreciate the mutual benefits and potential that both sides can achieve together.

Many key manufacturing companies from Taiwan have announced plans to partner with local Indian companies and to expand their manufacturing plants with substantial amount of investment in the next couple of years. By the end of 2020, accumulated investment in India had exceeded USD 941 million, with quite a few major investment plans in the pipeline. Taiwan's new investment in India before June 2022 include Pegatron, which received approved by the Taiwan government to invest USD 140 million in India. Foxconn has already promised an investment of USD 20 billion, out of which USD 5 billion will be invested in Maharashtra and USD 1 billion in Tamil Nadu. Wistron has announced a plan to invest USD 165 million to increase production capacity in Bengaluru. Maxxis, which has already invested USD 60 million to set up a factory in Gujarat, has further disclosed plans to invest USD 400 million in its expansion plan there.

In June 2022, Taiwan Plus reported that Taiwanese companies had invested more than USD 2.3 billion in India, creating over 100,000 job opportunities. It was also emphasised that Foxconn alone has invested USD 500 million and created significant employment of 30,000 jobs. Fengtay Industry Co. in Tamil Nadu, with over 30,000 employees, is the single largest foreign employer in the entire India. Apache located in Andhra Pradesh also employs around 10,000 people.

Taiwan's longstanding manufacturers of leading global brands are uniquely placed to benefit from India's manufacturing policies, like Make in India and Production-Linked Initiatives (PLI) covering mobile phones and PCs, telecom products, semiconductors, and green technology to auto components and e-vehicles. Taiwan's strategic role in global supply chains makes it a desired partner for India's goal of *Atmanirbhar Bharat* (self-reliant India). In August 2021, Wistron signed an agreement with Optiemus electronics to manufacture mobile devices in addition to IT hardware and telecom products as part of the USD 200 million investment deal struck by the two companies in 2018 for a five-year period. Foxconn also announced its joint-venture with India's Vedanta to manufacture semiconductors with a total investment of USD 19.5 billion. In late June 2022, on the same day of the BRICS virtual summit meeting, when Foxconn's Chairman was personally received by Prime Minister Narendra Modi in New Delhi, who welcomed Foxconn's expansion in India, especially to enter the semiconductor business with Vedanta group in Gujarat.[10] Unfortunately, Foxconn withdrew a few months later. Subsequently in January 2024, Foxconn announced a partnership with HCL Group to set up an outsourced assembly and testing unit to expand its iPhone manufacturing capabilities in India in a deal worth USD 1.6 billion. Additionally, Tata Electronics also finalised a deal to take over 100% stake in Wistron India, based in Karnataka to become the first Indian company to manufacture iPhones. Furthermore, Tata and Pegatron are reportedly in partnership talks for iPhone assembly in Tamil Nadu as of February 2024. In late February 2024, the Indian government approved three proposals to set up chip-manufacturing plants, including one by Tata Sons and Taiwan's PSMC to build a 12-inch fab and create more than 20,000 local jobs opportunities in Gujarat. On March 13, 2024, Prime Minister Narendra Modi addressed 'India's Techade: Chips for Viksit Bharat' event laying the foundation stone for three semiconductor facilities in Gujarat and Assam which he described "will play a key role in making India a semiconductor hub". And he noted in his address "the virtual presence of semiconductor industry players from Taiwan".[11] It refers exactly to the Tata Sons and PSMC fab. Apple also announced its goal of manufacturing a quarter of all its iPhones in India by 2025, while D 63 billion by 2026. This ambitious vision is well supported by partnering with the world-leading Taiwanese iPhone and semiconductor manufacturing companies.

Taiwan's Ministry of Education established 32 Taiwan Education Centres at India's universities in April 2024, a significant increase from not a single one in 1995 and only 14 in 2018. Higher educational institutions in India and Taiwan have concluded over 250 MOUs for their exchange and research programmes. More than 3000 Indian students are pursuing postgraduate degrees in Science, Technology, Engineering, and Mathematics (STEM) disciplines in Taiwan, with over 1000 of them studying for doctoral degrees. Additionally, nearly 30 high schools and primary schools in India have signed sisterhood MOUs with counterparts in Taiwan. In the field of science and technology, nearly 100 joint research projects have been successfully implemented since 2007. With the successful development of Taiwan's New Southbound Policy, the prospect for a much closer collaboration relationship appears promising, depending upon the pragmatic policy guidelines from both sides.

The ROC on Taiwan, in fact, did play a role in some the border and territorial issues between India and 'China' not only before 1949, but also in the 21st century, owing to historical and constitutional connections. Up to the present, the ROC on Taiwan, as one of the claimants of the South China Sea, still maintains actual control over the Pratas Islands and Taiping Island, the largest island in the Spratly Islands in the South China Sea. Taiwan is obviously one of the stakeholders in the South China Sea and should be invited to participate in any multilateral negotiations or meetings in relation to the South China Sea, through which reportedly more than 50 percent of India's trade passes. While India engages with other stakeholders like the US, the PRC, Vietnam, Indonesia, Malaysia and Brunei to ensure freedom of navigation in the South China Sea, Taiwan is often absent from these discussions due to political considerations. More essentially, India plays both a key and symbolic role in the Quad mechanism, extending to the Quad-Plus and the Indo-Pacific Strategy. This has prompted some to consider how exactly Taiwan could be further involved in the Quad-Plus Dialogue and other regional and multilateral mechanisms in which India plays a leading role. As Taiwan's unique position in the global supply chains have been more and more recognised by countries world-wide, it presents an opportunity that may merit India's support, given Taiwan's strategic location in the middle of the first island chain, to defend the assertive 'peaceful rise of China'. Any effort by India to include Taiwan, even as an observer, in any regional security mechanisms would be extremely crucial.

Taiwan has transformed entirely into a full-fledged democracy since the 1990s, and has amended its Constitution to acknowledge that its current de facto jurisdiction covers only Taiwan, Penghu, Kinmen, Matsu and surrounding islands. Taiwan's relations with Tibet have become smoother since Taiwan removed the Mongolian and Tibetan Commission from the central government structure. Activities in support of Tibetan culture and human rights are freely held in Taiwan, and both the government and people of Taiwan would welcome a visit from the Dalai Lama, anytime he wishes to make the trip, though this is going to be a testing point for both the PRC and India.

From 1950 to 1965, Taiwan received a total of USD 1.5 billion as US economic aid f alongside support from Japan, Saudi Arabia, the World Bank and other international organisations under the UN system. Diligent efforts and proper policy guidelines in utilising the foreign aid has successfully developed a sound foundation and capabilities in ICT manufacturing for export as well as improvements in infrastructure, education, public health and agriculture, and more. Taiwan has since become one of the substantial investors in the Chinese mainland, Vietnam, and other Southeast Asian countries in the past few decades, positioning it to play a critical role in the success of the current Indian government's 'Make in India', 'Digital India', 'Smart City', 'Skill India', 'Atmanirbhar Bharat' and 'Viksit Bharat' initiatives. Some scholars and media argue that one major obstacle that hampers closer ties between India and Taiwan is India's stance on the 'One-China Policy'; however, this should not refrain India from forging closer security and economic ties with Taiwan since the PRC has been assisting and supporting Islamabad in Pakistan-occupied Kashmir and occupying India's territories in the northwest. One recommendation is that India should actively seek closer ties with Taiwan and assert its right to decide what kind of relations it wishes to have with Taiwan without worrying too much about India's relations with the PRC.

There are only about 300 Taiwanese companies operating in India in 2024, compared to over 100,000 in China. Surprisingly, there are over 1.5 million Taiwanese nationals working in China, while there are less than 1,000 Taiwanese citizens living in India. In addition, there are around 66,000 Taiwanese in Vietnam, which has always been a popular investment destination for Taiwanese companies. People argue that for Taiwanese individuals living and working in India is much more difficult than in China or Vietnam for Taiwanese because of inherent cultural and bureaucratic differences. As the Chairperson of a leading Taiwanese construction company, which has been operating in India since 2005, commented on the difficulties in operating in India, she said, "If you can survive in India, you will be able to survive anywhere, even on the Moon."[12] It can be regarded as an overstatement, but it certainly reflected the constant frustration and difficulties that her company had encountered over the years in India. It takes both political will and infrastructure to boost India's ease of doing business and industrial capabilities This aligns with India's ambitious 'Atmanirbhar Bharat' and 'Viksit Bharat' initiatives, supported by a clear and firm policy support package from the government.

In his 75th Independence Day address, Prime Minister Narendra Modi announced his government aims to invest USD 1.35 trillion in infrastructure to boost India's economic growth and create job opportunities for millions of Indian youth.[13] The infrastructure program, 'Gati Shakti', will 'help local manufacturers turn globally competitive and also develop possibilities of new future economic zones in the country'.[14] This commitment, reiterated by Prime Minister Modi will be warmly welcomed by all foreign investors, especially those from Taiwan, who for so many years have urged the Indian government, both at the Union and State levels, to elevate quality of infrastructure, especially when India's economic output dropped by a record 7.3 percent amid the rampage of the second wave of COVID-19 pandemic. India's total vaccination doses reached 554,730,609 on August 17, 2021,[15] and by June 16, 2022, 1.96 billion doses had been administered, covering 73.5 percent of the entire population with 65.3 percent (901 million) completely vaccinated and 8.2 percent (112 million) partially vaccinated. Up to early September 2022, the total vaccination doses exceeded 2.13 billion, with 67 percent of India's population completely vaccinated.[16] That is an incredible achievement for a country of India's size. As the pandemic comes under control, it will be time to accelerate India's economic development in full gear. In addition to India's indigenous COVAXIN, the Bharat Biotech's first nasal COVID-19 vaccine iNCOVACC has gained emergency use authorisation from the Government of India in early September 2022 and becoming the world's first intranasal COVID-19 vaccine. Taiwan has much to learn from India's biotechnological industry and should seek to establish more comprehensive collaboration with India's viable partners.

Taiwan has been proactive in hosting trade promotion activities in both India and Taiwan in the past years, even during the COVID-19 pandemic. The Taiwan Expo 2021 took place online from October 27 to29 focusing on six categories: anti-COVOD-19, education and business service, foods and agricultural technology, furniture and household items, healthy lifestyle, ICT and electromechanics. From September 28to30, 2022 the Taiwan Expo 2022 India was held as a multimodal event designed to focus on six themes: Smart City, Smart Manufacturing, Smart Transportation, Smart Healthcare, Smart Living, And Smart Agriculture. To bridge Taiwan Excellence with investment opportunities in India's promising industries and vast market, Taiwan's TAITRA, in collaboration with Indian counterparts, has accumulated precious experience and identified appropriate patterns, paving the way for greater mutual benefits and confidence in the years to come.

The next imperative step for India's industrial development will be to identify the most qualified and trustworthy partners with whom India can establish full-scale collaborations for local manufacturing, such as ICT, including semiconductor, smart mobile phones, 5G, electric vehicles, agriculture, education, health, environmental protection, software development, start-ups, cyber security, Smart Cities and more. In all these areas, Taiwan should undoubtedly be among India's top priorities if India so wishes and is ready to put economic interests ahead of political constraints that have deterred India from engaging with Taiwan for decades.

While Japan, South Korea and Singapore are all focused on specific industries and investments of their respective expertise to explore opportunities in India, Taiwan, which is smaller size and population and with no diplomatic ties with India, may appear to be a relatively minor player. This may be true from the perspective of some bureaucrats in the government of India. However, the PRC has launched its ambitious global "OBOR" initiative which have turned out to be a debt trap for many countries and encroaches on India's strategic interest, conflicting with India's national security and territorial integrity. China's threatening posture and belligerent image have worsened with the ongoing border disputes and territorial claims reported widely in both domestic and international media, alongside India's substantial trade deficits in China's favour over the years. Indian public perception about Chinese products, coupled with provocative remarks from its 'wolf warrior' diplomats in India, making the PRC a less trusted and unreliable partner as India seeks FDI in strategic sectors. In contrast, Taiwan has been globally recognised as a much more reliable manufacturing partner for strategic semiconductors and many other products of industrial significance at a time when the US and other key industrialised countries are taking immediate measures to realign the global supply chain to mitigate Chinese dominance in key industries. It would be in India's long-term interest that India is committed to embrace the democratic values to uphold a 'free and open' Indo-Pacific with an aim to attract more FDI from the US, Japan, South Korea, Singapore and Taiwan in post COVID-19 pandemic.

As a result of the Indian government's incentives and relatively affordable labour costs, Taiwan's investments are mainly focused on ICT products, electronic engineering, footwear, construction, optics, petrochemicals, machinery, auto parts, and services. Currently, the largest sector is smartphone assembly. All Taiwan's major Apple suppliers—Foxconn, Rising Star, Wistron, and Pegatron—have relocated to India, attracted by various incentives offered by the Indian government. Some of them also had or still have close collaboration with Chinese mobile phone manufacturers, such as Oppo, Realme, Xiaomi, Vivo, etc. In India, Taiwan's Foxconn is the largest single investor, reportedly with USD 1 billion invested to date and further investment pledged. Beyond ICT,, Taiwan's China Steel Gujarat is the largest State-Owned Enterprise investor in India. Both Foxconn and China Steel have identified India as one of the most promising manufacturing hubs.

Taiwan's New Southbound Policy initiated in 2016, aimed to look beyond China and foster closer engagement with South and Southeast Asian countries, Australia and New Zealand. For certain obvious reasons, it has not yet resulted in as much investment in India as expected. Over the last ten years, based on official statistics, Taiwanese businessmen have invested over USD 30 billion in Vietnam, around USD 18 billion in Indonesia, but only about USD 1 billion in India. While these three figures are by far underestimated, they do offer a clear reference for India to gear up and attract more Taiwanese investment. To alter this unfavourable situation, India needs to present a comprehensive set of new policies to make it attractive for Taiwanese businesses to invest. India has announced a few ambitious initiatives, such as 'Atmanirbhar Bharat' and 'Viksit Bharat'. More significantly, a FTA between India and Taiwan would be a crucial step towards becoming closer to trade and investment partners with strategic significance. Although India's Manmohan Singh government was once very keen to approach Taiwan for FTA negotiation, Taiwan's Ma Ying-jeou government was then reportedly reluctant to engage with India at that time lest it should impact Cross-Strait relations by pronouncing that "now is not the time to engage in official talks on the signing of a FTA with India".[17]

If the momentum for negotiating an FTA waned in March 2011 due to political consideration from Taiwanese side, the Tsai Ing-wen government has since 2016 taken a markedly different approach on the FTA issue with India. The opportunity to resume the much-needed FTA talks with India has reemerged, should India still wish to conclude such an agreement as it had considered more than a decade ago. Such an FTA would help remove tariff barriers, enhance India's production competitiveness, and increase profitability. Unfortunately it is not in the radar of the Indian government yet. Some scholars argue that the lack of political will in Indian government and the limited engagement with Taiwan are among the main reasons for India's hesitance about signing an FTA with Taiwan, combined with the unnecessary concerns about the PRC's possible reactions. India's strong infrastructure and rule-based industrial practices are crucial in attracting substantial foreign investments. In the short term, how to increase the bilateral trade volume should be put on top priority for the two governments to work out so that more substantial investments from Taiwan to India may follow.[18] Ultimately it is entirely up to the India's government to decide whether the time is right to re-engage with Taiwan on the negotiation for a long-awaited FTA between the two complementary economies.

Over the years, Taiwanese manufacturers have collaborated extensively in India working alongside Indian, US, Japanese, South Korean and Chinese partners in assembling smart mobile phones. Given that Taiwanese semiconductor manufacturers produce more than 70 percent of the world's output of chips, they are strong candidates to invest in India. Taiwanese companies, like TSMC and Foxconn, have announced plans to set up new plants in the US, Japan, China, and Germany to secure strategic interests and realign global supply chains in partnership with the US, Japanese and Chinese technology companies. Many of these new plants are either under construction or nearing completion. To secure the supply chain for high-level smartphones is both a strategic must and an optimal entry point for India to advance into the semiconductor manufacturing sector. Foxconn and Vedanta signed an MOU with the State government of Gujarat in September, 2022 to set up a USD 20 billion semiconductor and display unit which is supposed to be one major progress accelerating India's semiconductor manufacturing ambitions.[19] However, this joint venture plan failed in mid-2023 and both parties have expressed their next move to line up with other potential partners. Reportedly, Foxconn has applied to the Indian authorities in December 2023 for approval of its new plan of setting up semiconductor manufacturing facilities in India, likely in partnership with STMicroelectronics. Meanwhile the US Micron Technology Inc. has been approved by the Indian Government to set up semiconductor plant in June 2023 and has been under construction since then.[20] If India can partner with Taiwan's TSMC, Foxconn or UMC, or any other viable manufacturer from Taiwan to set up sophisticated levels of semiconductor manufacturing facilities, India will surely become the next most important manufacturer and exporter of semiconductors and high-level smartphones in a matter of a decade or so. Tata Electronics has acquired a 100 percent equity stake in Wistron India which makes them the first Indian company to make Apple iPhones. The Wistron plant is located in the outskirt of Bengaluru.[21]

People in high-tech circles recognise that assembling smart phones and manufacturing semiconductors involve vastly different levels of technology. One essential reason behind TSMC's efficiency and profitability is its strategy to manufacture all high-end products in Taiwan. In fact, TSMC's main factories in Taiwan are geographically so close that its technical staff can provide mutual support when necessary within two hours, besides benefitting from a complete local supply chain. It has been acknowledged that the production cost in the US will be about 8 to 10 percent costlier than in Taiwan. Therefore, for TSMC to divert its manufacturing operations across the globe is not cost-effective at all. Despite the extra cost and possible opposition from local trade union, TSMC announced a USD 100 billion investment over three years in early April, 2021 to build a fab in the US after its authorities officially offered to subsidise and abridge the cost gap. However, the manufacturing facilities are still under construction as of mid-2024. In late April 2021, TSMC announced a USD 2.8 billion in China and the new plant is slated to begin mass-production in 2023 to ramp up the production of semiconductor to meet the growing demand for 28nm chips used in automobiles.[22] In Japan, TSMC's investment focuses on technology; construction was completed and the Japan Advanced Semiconductor Manufacturing, Inc. (JASM) in Kumamoto Prefecture, held its opening ceremony on February 24, 2024. An expansion plan underscores the the strong bond and mutual confidence between Taiwan and Japan..

Although has not been a priority for TSMC, the supply chain disruption caused by the US-China trade war and economic impacts of Russian invasion of Ukraine, have made it becomes imperative for Europe to strengthen its partnership with TSMC and establish an advanced semiconductor manufacturing facility in Europe. In August 2023, TSMC announced that it would invest up to 3.499 billion euros (USD 3.641 billion) and hold a 70 percent stake in a joint venture with Bosch, Infineon Technologies and NXP Semiconductors o build a semiconductor fab in Dresden, Germany. It is planned to break ground in the second half of 2024 with mass production scheduled to commence in 2027. The 12nm, 16nm, 22nm and 28nm processes will be applied 'to produce chips for automotive electronics and specialty industrial devices'.[23]

In Europe, traditional geopolitical advantages have increasingly led to a dependency on importing computer chips of certain specifications. European chipmaking companies have dominated the global market for automotive chips and other applications, but have long prioritised chip design over manufacturing Some of Europe's largest chipmaking companies still operate fabrication factories, but have avoided significant investments to increase production capacity, choosing instead to outsource portions of their orders other foundries like TSMC. Consequently, Europe's chip manufacturing capacity lags a few generations behind the advanced processes of technology of TSMC in Taiwan and Samsung in South Korea. The challenge is exactly like a scenario that one European company faced. It is currently specialised in 22nm, but 'going from 22 to 2nm is like jumping to the top of the Taipei 101 skyscraper "if you fail, you crash". In the US, TSMC's commitment is relatively modest with a USD 12 billion investment in an Arizona facility, expected to run on 5nm process, a technology which no doubt is cutting-edge at present, but when TSMC starts mass production in 2024 it will be left behind the 3nm and 2nm facilities, its own company is building in Taiwan, which was reportedly to have made trial run in early 2021.[24] And it is widely reported that the TSMC's 3nm facility in Taiwan is slated to start mass production in the second half of 2022,[25] and TSMC actually did and the company has announced plans to start 2nm mass production in 2025.

TSMC has announced plans to build a third fab at TSMC Arizona, raising its total investment in the US to more than USD 65 billion. This marks the largest FDI in Arizona's history, and the largest greenfield FDI project in U.S. history. With the third fab, TSMC Arizona, will create about 6,000 jobs, over 20,000 accumulated unique construction jobs, as well as tens of thousands of indirect supplier jobs. TSMC Arizona will play a vital role in the US government's goal of onshoring semiconductor manufacturing to strengthen national economic competitiveness. According to its official sources, "TSMC Arizona's first fab will operate its leading-edge semiconductor process technology (N4 process), commencing production in the first half of 2025. The second fab will utilise its leading edge N3 and N2 process technology and be operational in 2028. The recently announced third fab will manufacture chips using 2nm or even more advanced process technology, with production starting by the end of the decade."[26]

Practically speaking, investment in semiconductor manufacturing must be sustainable for investors, as it requires ongoing funding rather than a one-time commitment. Experts estimate that reaching 3nm technology will initially cost at least USD 15 billion, with another USD 2 billion needed two years later, and after that, another USD 20 billion is needed to maintain the competitive edge. This cycle makes semi-conductor investment massive and ongoing to stay at the forefront of technology. Indian policymakers and entrepreneurs understand that constant investment in research and development is the key to success in semi-conductor manufacturing—a principle that allowed TSMC to dominate the global market. Reportedly, Global Foundries in the US, UMC in Taiwan and many other manufacturers abandoned their ambitions to compete at the most advanced levels due to prohibitively high investments required. From technical perspective, most of the chips used in automobiles can be produced with 28-65 nm nodes. In recent years, the US has acquired a secure defence supply chain specific to its needs, which is supposed to be one of the main reasons for TSMC's commitment to invest in the US. Technology is essentially key to weapons development and production. Sophisticated chips are essential to equip the processors powering supercomputers to control missile trajectory models. Missiles also need the heat-resistant chips to ensure precise functioning. The significance of semiconductors for defence cannot be understated with the rise of Unmanned Aerial Vehicle systems developed by many countries world-wide.[27]

In May 2020, Indian Prime Minister Narendra Modi first announced his blueprint for making India self-reliant, Modi focused on five pillars, which are economy, infrastructure, technology-driven governing system, vibrant demography and supply chain.[28] He then said in early May 2022 that "Atmanirbhar Bharat is our path as well as our resolve."[29] On the occasion of India's 76th Independence Day, Prime Minister Modi addressed the nation and pledged for a developed India by 2047, emphasising the significance and the immediate effect of 'Atmanirbhar Bharat' so far. He touted, "Through PLI schemes, we are becoming a manufacturing powerhouse of the world. People are coming to India to 'Make In India'. Prime Minister Modi further reminded the nation that India's 'techade' is finally here. With 5G and chip manufacturing, we are bringing revolution through Digital India to grassroots", elaborating how the digital movement with production of semiconductors, 5G and optical fibre enhances India's strength in education, health and change in common man's lives.[30] India is going to become the next ICT manufacturing hub with the much-needed investments from all over the world, including those from Taiwan.

On the regional security aspect, in a joint statement issued after the US-Japan summit in mid-April 2021, US President Joe Biden and Japanese Prime Minister Yoshihide Suga "underscore the importance of peace and stability across the Taiwan Strait and encouraged the peaceful resolution of cross-Strait issues." It was the first time since 1969 that the US and Japan issued a statement that mentions Taiwan, and besides, the US and Japan 'recognised the importance of candid conversation with China', reiterating their intention to share concerns directly, and acknowledged the need to work with China on areas of common interest. Biden said in a joint press conference after the meeting, "We are committed to working together to take on the challenges from China and on issues like the East China Sea, the South China Sea, as well as North Korea, to ensure a future of a free and open Indo-Pacific."[31] On January 20, 2022, Taiwan's Air Force Commander Hsiung Hou-chi was invited to participate in a virtual regional air force meeting attended by the air force chiefs from twelve Indo-Pacific countries hosted by Indian Air Force to discuss "challenges of distributed logistics and agile combat employment while operating from austere locations".[32] This may have been the first instance of a high-ranking Taiwanese air force commander joining and being publicly recognised in such a regional meeting. Following the visit of Nancy Pelosi, the Speaker of the House of Representatives of the USA, and her delegation to Taiwan on August 2 and3, 2022, Chinese PLA shot eleven ballistic missiles that landed in the environ of Taiwan's territorial waters on August 3, 2022. The entailing naval and air exercises along the Taiwan Strait with dozens of sorties of PLA's aircraft and vessels crossing the median line of the Strait on a daily basis constituted a series of unilateral, malicious, intentional and provocative military actions to coerce, intimidate and showcase to Taiwan, Japan, the US and the rest of the world that China can at will escalate military threats, change the status quo of the Taiwan Strait, de-stabilise the peace and stability, and disrupt the freedom of navigation in the Taiwan Strait. The international community reacted strongly in condemning China and expressed support for democratic Taiwan, with joint statements from G7 Foreign Ministers and the ASEAN Foreign Ministers' meeting.

How did India respond to the situation? Following the line of India's consistent policy, the External Affairs Minister of India, S Jaishankar, reiterated "India's support for ASEAN unity and centrality in a free, open, inclusive and rules-based Indo-Pacific" in the ASEAN-India foreign Ministers' Meeting and other related meetings held on August 3 to5, 2022 in Phnom Penh, Cambodia. While the Secretary of State of the US and Foreign Ministers of Australia and Japan made a statement after their trilateral strategic dialogue on August 5, 2022 not only expressing "their commitment to deepening the trilateral partnership among the three countries", but also highlighting their "commitment to freedom, rule of law, human rights, sovereignty and territorial integrity, peaceful settlement of disputes without resorting to threat or use of force, and freedom of navigation and overflight." They also reaffirmed "their commitment to maintaining peace and stability across the Taiwan Strait", expressed "their concern about the PRC's recent actions that gravely affect international peace and stability, including the use of large-scale military exercises", and condemned the PRC's launch of ballistic missiles, five of which landed in Japan's exclusive economic zones, raising tension and destabilising the region.[33]

In their joint statement, The US, Japan and Australia urged China to put an immediate halt to its military exercises, while the EU stressed that the status quo across the Taiwan Strait should not be changed unilaterally by force. In the aftermath, British Foreign Secretary Liz Truss summoned China's ambassador to explain his government's recent actions towards the self-ruled democracy—Taiwan by means of "increasingly aggressive behaviour and rhetoric which threatens peace and stability in the region". She urged Beijing to resolve any differences 'by peaceful means'.[34] Within a few days, 79 Members of Parliament and the European Parliament from 28 European countries and Canada issued a joint statement expressing their concern over China's military intimidation against Taiwan escalating tension and changing the status quo in the Taiwan Strait. Many more countries, except India, followed suit in expressing their concerns and sentiments over Chinese coercive and provocative activities. Despite calls from Indian media and scholars for the government to some form of support for Taiwan, or at least an to organise and official delegation to visit

Taiwan as a show of solidarity and support, India kept silent for more than ten days. People in Taiwan, India and the rest of the world wondered when and how India—a key player in the Indo-Pacific region and the worlds' most populous democracy – would respond to the crisis across the Taiwan Strait, as tensions could have direct or indirect impact on India's economy and overall interests as well.

India has understandable reasons for not immediately joining the other three Quad members in expressing the same sentiments regarding the PRC's launch of ballistic missiles which landed in the waters surrounding Taiwan and Japan's exclusive economic zones. Such a stance would mean a drastic shift of India's foreign policy from traditional non-alignment position and it could be viewed as contrary to India's national interests amid its pending border disputes with the PRC and its lack of diplomatic ties with Taiwan. While the US, Australia and Japan would have wished to have India on board, it remains clear that no one can force India to do anything against its political will and national interests.

In a press conference on August 12, 2022, Arindam Bagchi, the spokesperson of India's MEA, while answering questions put to him, expressed India's position on the crisis across the Taiwan Strait, "Like many other countries, India too is concerned at recent developments." He further stated, "We urge the exercise of restraint, avoidance of unilateral actions to change status quo, de-escalation of tensions and efforts to maintain peace and stability in the region." And on the issues of India's 'One-China Policy', his brisk answer was, "Relevant policies are well known and consistent, and don't require reiteration."[35] India provided a well-deliberated and balanced response to the press without mentioning 'Taiwan', 'China', 'missiles', 'military drills' or 'One-China Policy'. However, India's first ever response to China's highly provocative military coercions should be was likely welcome by Taiwan, Japan, the US and other like-minded countries. As many observers anticipated, India's response was displeasing to China, when it claimed to have garnered support from more than one hundred countries to reiterate their observance of the Chinese defined 'One-China Principle'. But China failed to force India to do so. To reflect India's consistent foreign policy, in the Joint Statement of the Second India-Japan 2+2 Foreign and Defence Ministerial Meeting held in Tokyo on

September 8, 2022 attended by Minister of External Affairs, S. Jaishankar, and Minister of Defence, Rajnath Singh on behalf of India, it is reaffirmed that "their commitment to a rules-based global order that respects sovereignty and territorial integrity of nations", and emphasised "the need for all countries to seek peaceful resolution of disputes in accordance with international law without resorting to threat or use of force or any attempt to unilaterally change the status quo".[36]

Another US Congressional delegation visited Taiwan, 12 days after Nancy Pelosi's visit, prompting China to announce a new round of live-fire military exercises near Taiwan. Without being intimidated by Chinese military coercions, one Japanese Parliamentary delegation visited Taiwan from August 22-24, 2022, followed by other US Congressional delegations, State Governors, Japanese, British, Canadian, French, German and the European Parliamentary as well as thinktanks later in the year. Therefore, many more delegations from other democratic countries will certainly follow suit to visit Taiwan, though China will not back off from her ferocious provocation and it has announced to continue conducting military drills around Taiwan ever after as those parliamentarian delegations to Taiwan were seen by China as explicit support for Taiwan's independence. The side elevating tensions across the Taiwan Strait is evident: it must be the side firing ballistic missiles and conducting military exercises targeting Taiwan and coercing other countries from visiting Taiwan. On a daily basis, the PLA's aircraft and naval vessels cross Taiwan Strait median line to alter the status quo and disrupt peace and stability. In an interview with Indian journalists from eight media outlets, ABP Network, BBC News India, CNN-News18, News Nation, The Time Groups, The Week, TV9 and Zee Media Corporation, in Taipei on August 24, 2022, Taiwan's Minister of Foreign Affairs, Jaushieh Joseph Wu, expressed appreciation for India's MEA for the concern it voiced over China's drills undermining the Taiwan Strait's status quo. He further argued that Taiwan and India should work together to curb authoritarian expansion.[37] At that time, there was hope that Indian parliamentarians would be able to organise an unofficial delegation and make a trip to Taiwan just to show Indian people's support for Taiwan's democracy and the peace and stability across the Taiwan Strait. However, this expectation remained unfulfilled. In response to a statement by the Chinese Embassy in Colombo, Sri Lanka regarding a Chinese military ship docking at Hambantota port, the High Commission of India in Sri Lanka on August 29, 2022 accused China of 'militarisation of the Taiwan Strait', which could be the first time the Indian government has used the descriptor.[38] Since the PLA has committed to continuous military drills across the Taiwan Strait and its daily crossings of the median line as the 'new normal', India has responded with a restrained approach. This measure aims to avoid escalating hostilities further, which could not be conducive to resolving its border disputes with China While many democratic countries did send heavy-weight delegations to congratulate the inauguration of the Taiwan's 16th President and Vice President, India was represented by its ITA Director General Manharsinh Laxmanbhai Yadav.

In the wake of India's Lok Sabha polls, Taiwan's President, Lai Chingh-te, sincerely congratulated Prime Minister Narendra Modi on his election victory on June 5, 2024, and expressed his expectations on "enhancing the fast-growing Taiwan-India partnership, expanding our collaboration on trade, technology and other sectors to contribute to peace and prosperity in the Indi-Pacific". An immediate response from Prime Minister Modi followed saying "Thank you @ChingteLai for your warm message. I look forward to closer ties as we work towards mutually beneficial economic and technological partnership". Subsequently, the PRC protested by saying that there is "no such thing as 'president' of the Taiwan region", and "it opposes all official interactions between Taiwan and countries having diplomatic relations with China." More absurdly, PRC emphasised that India "is supposed to recognise, be alarmed about and resist the Taiwan authorities' political calculations".[39] The US Department of State Spokesperson Matthew Miller, in responding a question put to him, answered by saying "Such congratulatory messages are the normal course of diplomatic business".[40] As Brahma Chellaney commented, "With the PRC stepping up its coercive pressures on Taiwan, India has a stake in Taiwan's autonomous status and in its defence. So, 'closer ties' must extend beyond economic realm."[41] With an aim to promote 'closer ties' of "mutually beneficial economic and technological partnership" between India and Taiwan, the issues then are how far India is willing to step forward to help stabilise the situation across the Taiwan Strait, to counter China's aggressive military exercises in the region, how strong India would like to make it stance and in what ways India will contribute its heavy-weight input to morally support Taiwan's choice of democratic way of life.

India and the US successfully conducted the 18th edition of an annual joint military exercise Yudh Abhyas in Auli, Uttarakhand state, focusing on high-altitude warfare training in mid-October 2022 to 'improve interoperability and improve our respective capabilities to address a range of regional security challenges'. The location of this exercise is only 95 km from the disputed border near the LAC with China. Both India and China still maintain a large troop presence in the border region pending meetings to further ease the tensions and lower the risk of potential miscalculation and unexpected clashes.[42] China immediately expressed its objection to 'any third party to meddle in the China-India border issue in any form' and India was requested to abide by the important consensus reached by the two leaders and the relevant agreements. India had stated that both countries 'should stick to agreements', which has yet to happen. In response, India further rebutted by saying, "The India-US exercises are something completely different, and I don't know what colour has been given that it is targeting there or violating existing agreements."[43] Likewise, India took part in a military exercise with Russia in early September 2022, despite the US expressing concerns about it. India has its own independent foreign policy and conducts military exercises in different groupings to protect its own national interests. As an encouraging development, Indian and Chinese troops began a small scale disengagement from Gogra-Hotsprings in Ladakh on September 8, 2022, paving the way for a harmonious Shanghai Cooperation Organisation Summit meeting a week later in Uzbekistan. However, Prime Minister Narendra Modi did not have official dialogue with Chinese Xi Jinping for certain undisclosed reasons, very likely having something to do with pending border issues. As Arindam Bagchi, the India's Official Spokesperson of the MEA, clearly expressed, "I don't think India is a country you pressure and hope to get results...and I think India's position stems from our own beliefs and our interests of what we need to do."[44] China can only hope to resume harmonious diplomatic relations with India when it finally takes substantial steps to resolve the border disputes with India.

The 19th Exercise Yudh Abhyas was conducted from late September to early October 2023, in Fort Wainwright, Alaska in which the two Armies practiced a series of tactical drills to enhance interoperability in conducting UN peacekeeping operations.

In late 2021, the US initiated a semiconductor working group known as the Chip 4 Alliance. The first meeting of the senior officials from the US, South Korea, Japan, and Taiwan took place virtually on February 16, 2023, after its preliminary meeting in September 2022 that only involved working-level officials from the four governments. It is presumably a strong stance to formulate and consolidate major chip-making countries to counter the more and more aggressive and assertive China. It follows the passing of the CHIPS and Science Act of 2022 by the US Congress in July 2022 and the signing of an Executive Order by President Joe Biden to implement it on August 25, 2022. The new Act 'includes safeguards to ensure that recipients of Federal funds from these programs cannot build advanced semiconductor production facilities in countries that present a national security concern', and allocates a total of USD 54.2 billion in total appropriations for CHIPS and Public Wireless Supply Chain Innovation to ensure the goal of promoting domestic competitiveness.[45] It aims to "lower the costs of goods, create high paying manufacturing jobs around the country, and ensure we make more critical technologies at home".[46] Furthermore, the US government took another move to counter China high-tech potential by announcing a ban on exporting advanced electronic design automation (EDA) software to China on August 12, 2022, which will result in development difficulties to Chinese IC design. It is generally believed that India stands to benefit from this export ban to China if India implements its 'Atmanirbhar Bharat' initiative on chip-making with like-minded countries.

India and the US signed an MOU in March 2023 to boost coordination of their chip-industry incentives plans, with the US expressing its desire to 'see India achieve its aspirations to play a larger role' in the global chips supply chain. It will be a major step forward in highlighting India's geopolitical importance to the US and its allies at the time the US policymakers are collaborating with its allies, especially in the grouping of Quad, to contain China's assertiveness.[47] On November 27, 2023, India's Minister for Electronics and IT, Ashwini Vaishnaw, proudly claimed that "99.2 percent mobile phones used in India are domestically manufactured, a significant transformation from a decade ago when 98 percent were imported... That is the success of the 'Make in India' programme of Prime Minister Modi".[48] It takes India's firm political will, timely policy goals, detailed and effective incentives to the success of 'Make in India'. Taiwan has the golden opportunity to play an essential part in fulfilling India's digital ambition, but it is by no means purely an issue of enhancing India's industrial capability. It involves a much wider consideration—the restructuring of global supply chain and how India is placed in it.

India and Taiwan are two of the word's major foreign exchange reserves holders, with global ranking No. 5 and No. 6 respectively in 2023 with India one notch higher. The emerging ties between India and Taiwan have been an encouraging signal for both countries; however, what have been achieved in the past two and a half decades are merely a very small portion of the potential for cooperation and joint development without conflict of interest in sovereignty or border dispute. It is really about time that the authorities concerned in India and Taiwan overcame political constraints that have hindered engagement to establish optimised collaboration economically, technologically, and even politically and strategically by leveraging strengths that both countries possess.

Section 3: Mechanisms to be Developed Amid and Post COVID-19 Pandemic

India plays a key role in many global and regional organisations and initiatives, supported by contributions that align with the interests of other like-minded countries. Due to the PRC's opposition to Taiwan's participation in international or regional forums or mechanisms, especially within UN Conventions, Taiwan has long been excluded from such international gatherings. This is despite Taiwan's impressive economic achievements and investment capabilities in countries without diplomatic ties for decades. Southeast Asian countries are a prime example since 1990s and even more so after 1996 when Taiwan launched the New Southbound Policy, in which India became one the most significant destinations and has attracted so much attention from Taiwan's potential investors. who wished to relocate out of China to avoid the negative economic and political impacts of US-China trade war, shortage of electricity supply, lockdown due to COVID-19 pandemic, increasing hostility and strategic conflicts on many key issues, including the restructuring of global supply chain.

In addition to the economic complementarity that India and Taiwan inherently possess in nature, there are certainly several mechanisms in which India plays host or takes a leading role, allowing India to lend support to Taiwan in the latter's democratic existence and industrial excellence. This support would align with the common values of freedom of speech, and a rule-based democracy in collaboration with other democracies, without infringing India's foreign policy goals or national interests. By doing so, India also gets the necessary support and investment from Taiwan and other major industrialised countries in achieving India's short-term and long-term development goals within a short time. How to de-hyphenate India-China-Taiwan relations[49] in a subtle and determined way is the key to the enhancement of India and Taiwan relations in all aspects.

Raisina Dialogue

Raisina Dialogue is an annual, multilateral and geopolitical conference held in New Delhi which is organised by the MEA of the government of India along with the Observer Research Foundation (ORF). To host the Raisina Dialogue annually reflects on India's vital role in the IOR and its ambition to jointly build a stable regional and world order, together with other countries across the globe.[50] The Raisina Dialogue is designed to be a free forum in which heads of state, heads of government, cabinet ministers, local government officials, executives from major private sector, NGOs as well as members of the media and academia gather together and present their views for discussion on certain global and regional issues. Since its inception in 2016, the Dialogue has emerged as India's flagship conference on geopolitics and geo-economics and it is widely regarded as the Indian version of the Shangri-La Dialogue in Singapore, but it covers a much wider scope of issues that matter not only to the South Asian, IOR or Indo-Pacific Regions, but also all those concerns and issues on the UN agenda. By contrast, the organiser of the Shangri-La Dialogue is the International Institute for Strategic Studies in London with the staunch support of the government of Singapore. Since its debut in 2002, the Shangri-La Dialogue, held in Singapore, has been Asia's premier defence summit where heads of state or government, ministers from all stakeholders debate the region's most concerned defence and security challenges, engage in bilateral or multilateral talks with the hope of putting forward better solutions or ideas together. Furthermore, the Shangri-La Dialogue 'has become a vital Asia-Pacific security institution, helping governments to build mutual confidence and foster practical cooperation'.[51] It was on the occasion of the Shangri-La Dialogue that India's Prime Minister Narendra Modi delivered his keynote address in 2018 and shared his 'vision of an open, stable, secure and prosperous Indo-Pacific Region'.[52]

The 1st Raisina Dialogue was held in early March 2016. More than 100 speakers from over 35 countries were invited to speak on the theme: 'Asia: Regional and Global Connectivity'. The focus of the Dialogue that year was on the issues of Asia's physical, economic, human and digital connectivity. Dozens of panels and discussions were arranged for the invitees to explore the opportunities and challenges for the Asia-Pacific region, and the global partnerships which are much needed to develop common pathways in the 21st century.[53]

The 2nd edition of the dialogue in 2017 was held in mid-January on a larger scale. Over 120 speakers from 65 countries and more than 800 participants were invited to attend to discuss the theme of 'The New Normal: Multilateralism with Multipolarity' In mid-January 2018, the 3rd edition of The Raisina Dialogue was held with a theme of 'Managing Disruptive Transitions: Ideas, Institutions and Idioms'. And the 4th edition of the Dialogue took place in early January 2019 with 'New Geometrics | Fluid Partnerships | Uncertain Outcomes' as its theme. Then in mid-January, 2020, the 5th edition of the Dialogue was held to explore the theme of 'Navigating the Alpha Century'.

The Raisina Dialogue 2021, the 6th edition, took place digitally in April, considering the worsening COVID-19 pandemic across the world and locally in India. The decision for the 2021 edition to be conducted digitally was been taken as a measure of caution. As the Spokesperson of the MEA explained, "it underlines the strong sense of responsibility that the organisers feel towards the safety of all those involved with the Dialogue." While avoiding any COVID-19 related risk, the fully digital event utilised the advanced technology 'to allow participants an opportunity to engage and debate on the most pressing issues that confront the global community'. And the reasons and concerns of the change in format of the event has been appropriately represented in India's diplomatic engagements and the proper understanding and support of all the participants was won. I-Chung Lai, President of Prospect Foundation, Taiwan, again was invited to be one of the speakers in The Raisina Dialogue 2021.[54]

Taiwan's former Foreign Minister Hung-mao Tien was invited to make a low-key visit to Delhi, in the name of the President of Taiwan's Institute for National Policy Research, to participate in the 1st Raisina Dialogue in 2016. He attended the Dialogue as planned despite the presence of Li Zhaoxing, Chinese former Foreign Minister, and the situation was handled splendidly by the organisers, as commented by Namrata Hasija.[55] Subsequently, I-Chung Lai (Executive Director, The Prospect Foundation, Taiwan) and Bi-Khim Hsiao (Senior Adviser, The Prospect Foundation, Chinese Taipei) participated in the 2017 and 2018 Dialogues on behalf of Taiwan respectively.[56] There were no records from the Indian side with regards to who actually represented Taiwan in the 2019 and 2020 editions of the Raisina Dialogue, since no Taiwan participant's name was shown on the agenda or the official reports. It could be the case that the Taiwanese participants' names were not shown on all dialogue documents for certain undisclosed reason. In the 2021 edition of the Raisina Dialogue, I-Chung Lai (President of The Prospect Foundation) and Ketty W. Chen (Vice President of Taiwan Foundation for Democracy) were present while Ming-Shih Shen (Acting Deputy CEO, Institute for National Defence and Security Research) was invited to join the 2022 edition. Taiwan's Deputy Secretary-General of National Security Council, Szu-Chien Hsu attended the 2023 edition held from March 2 to 4, 2023 in his capacity of the Director of the Institute for National Defence and Security Research (INDSR). Again, Szu-Chien Hsu was present at the Raisina Dialogue 2024 from February 21-23, 2024 in his same capacity of INDSR, together with Hao Yang, the Executive Director of then Taiwan-Asia Exchange Foundation. Obviously, all the participants were strictly selected to represent think tanks in Taiwan, at the same time in recognition of their dual identity as either political party key members or high-ranking government officials without creating political implications.

From the background of the invitees from Taiwan since 2016, there were a former Foreign Minister, Hung-mao Tien, a former Member of Parliament, Bi-Khim Hsiao, and three Think Tank executives, I-Chung Lai, Ketty W. Chen and Ming-Shih Shen, and a current Deputy Secretary-General of the National Security Council, Szu-Chien Hsu, among other representatives from the academic community. However, for those who are familiar with the political development in Taiwan will appreciate the fact that they are all heavy-weight opinion leaders affiliated with the Democratic Progressive Party (DPP), the ruling party of Taiwan for the first time from 2000 to 2008 and again since 2016 till the present. Hung-mao Tien was appointed the Minister of Foreign Affairs in 2000 and served as Taiwan's 'Ambassador' to the UK from 2002 to 2004. He then was appointed a National Policy Advisor to Tsai Ing-wen, the President of ROC (Taiwan) and concurrently the Chairman and President of the Institute of National Policy Research (INPR), a notable think tank in Taiwan. Since 2016 he has been appointed twice as a Senior Advisor to the President of Taiwan. What attracted attention in The Raisina Dialogue 2016 was that Tien was invited and registered under the title of the 'Former Minister of Foreign Affairs, Taiwan', where the PRC's former Foreign Minister Li Zhaoxing was also present. Such a scenario is unprecedented in any other international conference, as it would typically prompt PRC's intervention or boycott, often leading the host to back down to accommodate the PRC's protest claiming it is against its 'One-China Principle' and the host country's 'One-China Policy'. Undoubtedly, India's MEA and the event organiser, the ORF, must have thought of that and were brave enough to face that possible challenge from the PRC on that occasion. Fortunately, it turned out to be a successful event with a happy ending.

It is equally noteworthy that the sole official invitee on the Agenda in 2018, Bi-Khim Hsiao, had long been DPP's Director of the Department of International Affairs and a Member of Parliament. Before she assumed the post of Taiwan's 'Ambassador' to the US in July, 2020, she was a Senior Advisor at the National Security Council, Taiwan. And more significantly, she was DPP's Vice Presidential candidate for the January 13, 2023, Presidential Election and was elected the Vice President of Taiwan, being sworn in on May 20, 2024. The invitee in 2017 and 2021, I-Chung Lai, a veteran political analyst for years, has been actively participating in international think tank events in Taiwan and abroad. He used to serve as the Director of Taiwan Think Tank, the Director of the Department of International Affairs of DPP, and now he is the President of the Prospect Foundation, a prominent Thank Tank in Taiwan. He has been invited to participate in The Raisina Dialogues at least twice as one of the speakers. There were many other Taiwanese participants in The Raisina dialogues as well, but they were sporadically reported only in certain Taiwanese local media. However, the goodwill and well-balanced approaches taken by the Indian government, especially the MEA, and the organiser, the ORF, are commendable and much appreciated by Taiwan.

Given Taiwan's contribution to India's current economy, technology, employment and potential to India's future ICT manufacturing capabilities and other areas of interest, India may as well approach more invitees from Taiwan to cover wider issues on the UN Sustainable Development Goals (SDGs), and share their expertise in public health insurance system, green energy, climate change, food security, waste water treatment and recycling, women empowerment, and experiences in international development, etc.

The Quad and Quad-Plus Dialogue

Composed of Australia, India, Japan and the US, the Quad emerged as Tsunami Core Group in the aftermath of the devastating 2004 Tsunami in Indian Ocean. It executed a credible *Humanitarian Assistance and Disaster*

Relief (*HADR*) response to the tsunami-affected countries. Subsequently, the members of the Quad jointly held the Malabar exercises which helped prepare the Quad with a high sense of synergy and interoperability for maritime missions like HADR, anti-piracy, etc. The four members through the Malabar exercises project themselves as committed stakeholders to an open and transparent mechanism which allows 'people, goods, capital, and knowledge to flow freely'.[57]

After the Quad resumed dialogue in 2018, a multi-layer communication structure began to develop. Against this background, the Quad-Plus is therefore an extension of the Quad with an aim to formulate preliminary consensus through brainstorming among think tanks. Taiwan was invited to participate in the first Quad-Plus Dialogue in Japan in March 2018, co-hosted by The Heritage Foundation from the US, The Japan Institute of International Affairs, Vivekananda International Foundation of India and ASPI. The participants from Taiwan included the Executive Directors of the INPR, Taiwan Foundation for Democracy and the Foundation on Asia-Pacific Peace Studies.[58]

The Quad's activities have always been seen, especially by China and Russia, as a grouping to counter a 'rising China'. The Quad is organised to be a constructive architecture of the Indo-Pacific region for the four democracies to work as a group and with like-minded countries to work out solutions and tackle issues on economics, technology, climate, and security. It has often been advised by officials, scholars, and experts that the Indo-Pacific should not function as a grouping of 'mini North Atlantic Treaty Organisation (NATO)' or 'Asian NATO', but it does provide a useful and convenient platform for democratic countries to brainstorm in areas of critical and common interests. Therefore, the first Quad Leaders' Summit held online on March 12, 2021, was a big step in the right direction as it is not just in the security realm where the rise and advancement of China is noticeable.[59] The first Quad Leaders' Summit ushered in the consensus on 'the importance of peace and stability across the Taiwan Strait'. In the Joint Statements of the US-Japan Summit, US-Korea Summit, EU-Japan Summit and Japan-Australia Summit 2+2 Foreign and Defence Ministerial Consultations, the Communiqués of G7 Foreign and Development Ministers Meetings, G7

Summit and the Statement of the EU-US Summit, in addition to the Quad senior officials virtual meeting in 2021, all 'underscore the importance of peace and stability across the Taiwan Strait and encourage the peaceful resolution of cross-Strait issues'. They imply that peace and stability in Taiwan Strait is now a global concern.[60] In the meantime, democratic countries around the world of different groupings are voicing their worries about the PRC's assertive military coercing activities toward Taiwan, and thus inconducive to the stability in the Indo-Pacific region.

The second Quad Leaders' Summit, in person, held on September 24, 2021, in Washington DC Three new Working Groups on infrastructure, space, and cyber issues were announced. Also launched were 100 STEM fellowships, 25 from each Quad country to US universities for graduate and doctoral students from Quad countries.

On April 14, 2021, India's Foreign Minister S. Jaishankar dismissed China's criticisms without naming it, saying that comparing the Quad to the NATO was a 'mind game that others are playing'. He added that the grouping was for 'national, regional and global benefit'. In defence of the Quad and the France-India-Australia trilateral meeting, Jaishankar further stressed that the Quad was "overcoming the Cold War, not reinforcing it". Furthermore, he remarked that "he cannot accept other people to have a veto about what and with whom he is going to discuss, and how much he is going to contribute to the world".[61]

The Quad has brought to observers a considerable optimism toward a dynamic and effective forum to counter China's ambitions in the Indo-Pacific and preserve a rule-based international order for the region. There are encouraging signs that the Quad could expand to become the Quad-Plus with the addition of South Korea, Vietnam, New Zealand, UK, France and Germany. France already has a formidable presence in the Indian Ocean, it could be a possible candidate to join the Quad-Plus Dialogue. Germany has expressed its position to increase its presence in the Indo-Pacific and did participate in joint military exercises in Australia in August 2022, possibly making another candidate for the Quad-Plus. The US has dismissed that the Quad is an 'Indo-Pacific NATO' as accused by China and Russia, but it may be happy to have this grouping to become a NATO-like status in the future. Practically speaking, partnerships like the Quad-Plus will have plenty of room to expand in the Indo-Pacific.

India, Australia, and Japan have committed to the Quad as they all are facing considerable military and economic challenges from China. For India, it may have to detour a little bit from its traditional reluctance for multilateralism in the name of strategic autonomy. India could further express to other Quad members that it is ready to enhance military cooperation with them, at least in certain areas and it is also willing to join the developmental initiatives of the Indo-Pacific infrastructure partnership established by the US, Japan, and Australia.

France, India and Australia have openly indicated they are determined to jointly to step up their presence in the Indo-Pacific to enhance their cooperation in maritime security, according to the remarks made by their foreign ministers at the mid-April Raisina Dialogue 2021. Indian External Affairs Minister S. Jaishankar further highlighted that the France-India-Australia trilateral meeting would next discuss 'something similar' to the topics on the agenda of the Quad, which means that they are going to cover vaccine cooperation, higher education, student mobility and emerging technology as well. In addition to the US, India is also an important partner to Europe and the Indo-Pacific Region holds 'great economic, strategic and geopolitical importance to Europe'. Essentially, India can engage NATO in many aspects, such as to consult, coordinate and take coordinated action to address the emerging challenges they commonly encounter.[62] S. Jaishankar reiterated that India's participation in the Indo-Pacific initiative delivers a clear message that India's presence will not be constrained between the Malacca Strait and the Gulf of Aden because India's national interests, influence and activities go way beyond.[63]

The third Quad Leaders' Summit was held virtually on March 3, 2022, to discuss the situation in Ukraine and its impact on the Indo-Pacific. A Quad Partnership on HADR was launched. The fourth Quad Leaders' Summit, also in-person, took place in Japan on 24 May, 2022. The Quad Satellite Data Portal was launched to provide regional countries with space-based data for climate and disaster forecasting and sustainable use of marine resources. A Q-CHAMP mechanism of practical cooperation on climate finance, and technology transfer was initiated for countries to meet their climate commitments on climate action. Furthermore, the leaders also launched the Quad Debt Management Resource Portal to address challenges of unsustainable debt financing and the Quad Partnership on HADR, which was initiated by India, to provide 'timely and effective assistance in the Indo-Pacific region' in the event of future incidents.

Speaking on 'India's Vision on the Indo-Pacific' in Thailand on August 19, 2022, S Jaishankar maintained that the Quad "is the most prominent plurilateral platform that addresses contemporary challenges and opportunities in the Indo-Pacific". He argued the entire Indo-Pacific region will benefit from the Quad and rebutted any reservations to the mechanism is possibly a "unilateral opposition to collective and cooperative endeavours", implying China's attitude.[64] Taiwan no doubt is within the Indo-Pacific region and the peace and stability in the region covers Taiwan, although India does not specifically mention the word–Taiwan—when it talks about Indo-Pacific.

The fifth Quad Leaders' Summit, also in-person, was held in Hiroshima, Japan on May 20, 2023. Together with the Leaders' Joint Statement, the 'Quad Leaders Vision Statement – Enduring Partners for the Indo-Pacific' was also announced, underscoring the Leaders' vision for 'a free, open, and inclusive Indo-Pacific, and upholding the principles of sovereignty, territorial integrity, and peaceful resolution of disputes'.[65] India is scheduled to be hosting the next Quad Leaders' Summit sometime in 2024.

Remark The 6th Summit in USA not covered

What and how can Taiwan play a part in the Quad-Plus Dialogues? From a pragmatic point of view, there is not much for Taiwan to do in the beginning. It takes a consensus of all the four members of the Quad to tackle the PRC's constant provocative military activities across the Taiwan Strait. However, if India would agree to invite Taiwan to meaningfully participate in the future Quad-Plus Dialogue, the other three members of the Quad will be much more likely to facilitate the invitation because they are already very close to Taiwan in many substantial aspects. And Taiwan's participation will highlight the Quad leaders' consensus of 'the importance of peace and stability across the Taiwan Strait'.

Global Cooperation and Training Framework

The US, Taiwan, and the Japan-Taiwan Exchange Association jointly sponsor the GCTF, which provides a convenient and effective template for Taiwan to share its expertise in many areas with partners across the globe. Benefiting from its innovation, human resource and strong policy support from the government, Taiwan has developed a wide variety of world-class expertise covering public health, disaster relief, green energy, environmental protection, women empowerment, cyber security, good governance and many others as far as an island is concerned. However, due to political constraints, Taiwan is not allowed to participate in many international institutions as a member or a sovereign state. Consequently, Taiwan is not able to share its specialised knowledge and experience to better the common goals of international community. Since June 2015, the GCTF allows people from other countries to learn what Taiwan can offer and to strengthen connections for them to tackle the problems across borders.[66] As of the end of 2023, over 70 online or physical workshops have been held under the GCTF Programs covering COVID-19 related public health, women's empowerment, law enforcement cooperation, media literacy, energy efficiency, cybersecurity, humanitarian assistance and disaster relief, digital economy, good governance, sustainable materials management solutions to marine debris, advancing international development through public private partnership, virtual engagement series for Latin America and the Caribbean: COVID-19 and digital economy, Austronesian languages revitalisation Forum, e-commerce facilitation, etc.[67] The accumulated number of participants and lecturers reached 7,500 from 127 countries across the globe, including India and others from South Asia, South East Asia, East Asia, and West Asia.[68]

The GCTF Programs, with the far-reaching expertise in resolving global issues, have gained more and more attention and interest from countries worldwide. As the most populous democracy, India, is supposed to have the unique privilege to share with other interested countries by means of the GCTF platform. India's participation in the GCTF Programs is so meaningful that deeper involvement and wider contribution from India's professionals and officials will make a big difference in all aspects. India's

NGO Voice of Healthcare hosted the first ever GCTF's hybrid conclave exploring collaborations in the digital healthcare space in South Asia on February 25, 2022, in New Delhi, bring together 300 participants, both in physical presence and online, including government officials, professionals, researchers, entrepreneurs and decision-makers from India, Taiwan, US, Japan and Australia. Efforts like this are encouraged to continue to better utilise expertise and technological know-hows in digital healthcare.[69] On December 11, 2023, a GCTF workshop on cybersecurity was held at the United Service Institution of India in New Delhi, in which high-profile participants from Taiwan, India and the US attended to discuss issues on artificial intelligence, cybercrime, the digital economy and ways to safeguard critical information infrastructure.

The 2022 GCTF conference on 'Ending Gender-based Violence', co-hosted by Japan, US, Australia, UK, Canada, EU, Israel and Taiwan, was held in May 2022, in which 13 foreign Representative Offices based in Taipei and over 200 participants from 22 countries were present.[70] More notably is that Indian presence was well recognised. Another workshop on 'Pursuing Inclusive and Gender-Equal Recovery: Empowering Women in the Post-Pandemic Era' was conducted in both virtual and physical modes in St. Lucia in the Eastern Caribbean on August 26, 2022.[71] A GCTF seminar on 'Building an Inclusive, Resilient And Secure Indo-Pacific Through Partnership Aimed at Accelerating the SDGs' was held on the sidelines of the 78th UN General Assembly on September 11, 2023 in which speakers from the four member countries, Australia, Japan, Taiwan, US, contributing their respective reports on the theme.[72]

South Asian Association for Regional Cooperation The South Asian Association for Regional Cooperation (SAARC), founded in 1985, is a regional inter-governmental organisation and geopolitical union of Afghanistan, Bangladesh, Bhutan, India, the Maldives, Nepal, Pakistan and Sri Lanka to promote peace, prosperity and partnership as the bedrock of regional cooperation. As of April 30, 2021, India has been generous enough to provide SAARC countries, except Pakistan, with nearly 20 million doses of made-in-India COVID-19 vaccine on the bases of grant, commercial and under the COVAX mechanism. The quantity of doses each country received is as follows: Afghanistan 968,000, Bangladesh 10.3 million, Bhutan 550,000, the Maldives 312,000, Nepal 2.448 million, Sri Lanka 1.264 million, in addition to those of Myanmar 3.7 million, Mauritius 400,000 and Seychelles 50,000 in India's neighbourhood. Altogether India has delivered 66.3698 million doses of vaccine to 95 countries and UN peacekeepers.[73]

When India witnessed a second wave of the COVID-19 pandemic in April 2021, several countries including Taiwan urgently mobilised their limited resources to donate oxygen concentrators and other materials to be airborne to India even without the latter's official lobbying. Earlier in 2020, Taiwan has donated 1 million medical masks to India through Indian Red Cross Society.

India launched the first South Asia Communication Satellite, GSAT-9, in May 2017 to boost connectivity among the SAARC nations, as an initiative proposed by India's Prime Minister Narendra Modi during the SAARC summit in Nepal in November, 2014.[74] India set up a satellite tracking and data reception centre in Bhutan to take advantage of the South Asia Satellite. The new centre also serves to counter a similar Chinese facility in Tibet.[75] India also helped train four space engineers from Bhutan in early 2021 as the phase one project. It was part of a program to jointly develop a small satellite for Bhutan.[76]

As the largest power in the IOR, India has committed to assisting its immediate neighbouring countries amidst the greater influence from the PRC's 'Belt Road Initiatives' to encroach India's traditional relations with them. Taiwan's government and NGOs over the years have engaged Nepal, Sri Lanka, Bhutan and Bangladesh and implemented water projects, public health, education, organic agriculture, poverty eradication and disaster relief on their own. If the government of India and its NGOs welcome to establish a tripartite collaboration and join forces with Taiwan's stakeholders to implement projects that can benefit the SAARC member states, the new synergy of efforts together would actually enhance the impact of India's 'Neighbourhood First' policy.

Since the inception of SAARC, there has been 18 summits hosted by different member states. In the aftermath of the 2016 Uri terror attack, India decided to cancel its participation in the 19th SAARC summit to be held in

Islamabad, alleging Pakistan's involvement in the terror attack. Bangladesh, Afghanistan, Bhutan, Maldives and Sri Lanka also decided to pull out of the summit. Therefore, the 19th summit did not take place, even at the end of 2023. There is little of hope that the summit is going to resume in the near future as the tension and security concerns between India and Pakistan have no sign of peaceful resolution.

SAARC has made steady progress in several agreed areas of cooperation, especially in poverty alleviation which has been described as the over-arching goal of SAARC by the leaders of its member countries. At least, one optimistic trend of the ongoing programs supported by Asian Development Bank, UN Economic and Social Commission for Asia and the Pacific, United Nations International Children's Emergency Fund, Japan, South Korea, are going full swing.

The SAARC has eight members and nine observers. Considering its areas of cooperation, Taiwan can at least contribute in human resource development, agriculture and rural development, environment, natural disasters and biotechnology, information and poverty alleviation, energy, transport, science and technology, education, security and culture. But in what capacity can Taiwan participate in the cooperation programs? The SAARC can invite Taiwan's application to become an observer, a status that is less politically sensitive if all members agree to enhance regional development with one more democratic country which has all capability to offer to elevate the livelihood and well-being of the people in the region.

Bay of Bengal Initiative for Multi-Sectoral Technical and Economic Cooperation established in 1997, the Bay of Bengal Initiative for Multi-Sectoral Technical and Economic Cooperation (BIMSTEC) has increased its membership in the following 25 years. Currently there are seven member states: Bangladesh, Bhutan, India, Myanmar, Nepal, Sri Lanka and Thailand. Each country emphasises different sectors of interest to cooperate, such as Bangladesh on trade, investment and development, blue economy; Bhutan on environment and climate change, mountain economy; India mainly on security, counter-terrorism and transnational crime, disaster management and energy; Myanmar on agriculture and food security, fisheries and livestock; Nepal on people-to-people contact, culture, tourism, poverty alleviation;

Sri Lanka on science, technology and innovation, health, human resource development; Thailand mainly on connectivity.

The BIMSTEC has made declarations to express its positions on the regional issues on many occasions as necessary. Countries around the Bay of Bengal are facing different difficulties and drastic changes by globalisation, financial crisis and, specifically, China's ambitious and affirmative strategy to launch the Belt-and-Road Initiative and the devastating COVID-19 pandemic. BIMSTEC's objectives to ensure shared and accelerated growth through mutual collaboration among member states, to utilise regional resources and geographical advantages for common interests have not been realised as they all have agreed to attain. They also have appreciated the importance of signing the FTA for their economic benefits; however, despite several rounds of talks and renewed attempts again and again, no FTA framework has been agreed upon. Therefore, its current focus is still on enhancing bilateral ties. Additionally, the ecological concerns and shared historical ties of the region have not received the attention they deserve. More efforts are needed to improve people-to-people connectivity across the region. Effective measures should be taken to facilitate tourism diplomacy, academic and student-exchange programs. More importantly, member states need to strengthen cross-border public health coordination and regional collaboration, especially in fight against any epidemic in the post-COVID-19 era.

Under the 'Neighbourhood First' Policy, India has resumed its leadership in rendering necessary assistance to other member states with regards to vaccines and financial aid at the most critical period of pandemic. The Bay of Bengal is a key transit route between the Indian and the Pacific Oceans., often neglected as a junction of Indian and Chinese strategic interests. Consequently, any initiative India undertakes to counter Chine's increasing influence will immediately affect all other BIMSTEC member states. Countries in this region have identified several urgent issues to be addressed, such as freedom of navigation, transnational threats, and the Bay's natural resource to improve people's livelihood. They generally believe that India's leadership in the region will help stabilise regional political and economic situations to counter external influence. Taking advantage of its 'Act East Policy', India can use its policy tools to consolidate South and Southeast Asian countries in unity socially and economically. Whatever India decides to do in the near future will have long-term impact on the well-being of the people that will strategically change the balance of power in the Indo-Pacific.[77]

The 5th BIMSTEC Summit was held on March 30, 2022, in a hybrid format in Sri Lanka. The main outcome was the adoption and signing of the BIMSTEC Charter that formalises the grouping into an organisation. Also, the adoption of the Master Plan for Transport Connectivity lays out a guidance framework for connectivity activities in the future. Indian Prime Minister Narendra Modi called upon all leaders "to strive to transform Bay of Bengal into a bridge of connectivity, prosperity, and security among the BIMSTEC member countries".[78] It has been agreed upon that 'the Head of Government Summit... will be held every alternative year and the Ministerial Meeting at the level of the Foreign Ministers would be held every year'. The 2022 Summit also agreed to have an annual consultative mechanism of the BIMSTEC National Security Advisors Forum.[79]

Thailand, in its role as the chairman of the BIMSTEC, has decided to reschedule the 6th BIMSTEC summit originally slated from November 27-30, 2023 to the year 2024 to allow for better preparation.

Taiwan started to dispatch agricultural technical mission to Vietnam in 1959 and to African countries in 1961 during the period of receiving economic aid from the US. Over the past seven decades, Taiwan has developed from a pure agricultural society into a high-tech democracy even with nearly nothing in its natural resource. Taiwan has been well-known for not only its ICT industries, but also for its expertise in agricultural, soil conservation, green energy, disaster prevention and early warning, quality higher education, public health and vibrant civil society which are one of the best examples to share with the BIMSTEC member countries. Mechanism of cooperation can be established with the help of India and endorsement from other member states if they so wish for Taiwan to contribute in whatever capacity. And Taiwan stands ready to render technical assistance to any BIMSTEC member country.

India Space Research Organisation[80]

India Space Research Organisation (ISRO) was established in Bangalore in 1972. Over the years, with a shining record of over 100 successful space missions, ISRO, being among the top six government space agencies in the world, has matured in experience and technological capabilities and the scope for international cooperation has become multifaceted. Under ISRO, there are 16 space centres offering training programs to personnel from numerous countries across the globe.[81] ISRO has signed MOUs or Framework Agreements with 55 countries, in addition to 5 international multilateral bodies. India is highly rated by space exploring nations as an emerging space power. It is capable of accomplishing its mission in a more cost effective and time-efficient manner, which has won ISRO global accolade. Many ambitious countries all over the world now approach India for assistance in building up their space technology.[82]

Dr K. Sivan, Chairman, ISRO/ Secretary, Department of Space and the Head of Australian Space Agency had a virtual meeting in mid-February 2021. They reviewed the status of several on-going programs in earth observation, satellite navigation, space situational awareness. They also discussed the establishment of transportable terminal in Australia to support India's Gaganyaan program.[83] On another occasion, Dr K Sivan met with his Japanese counterpart in mid-March 2021 virtually to review the on-going cooperation in earth observation, lunar cooperation and satellite navigation. In the end, they have agreed to further explore possible programs for collaboration in space situational awareness and professional exchange of visit. They also signed an implementing arrangement for projects to monitor rice crop area and air quality using satellite data.[84] Dr K Sivan also received his counterparts and minister from Saudi Arabia, Italy, Brazil, etc. to enhance international collaboration earlier in 2021.[85]

On the Taiwan side, two Taiwanese small and light-weighted satellites were successfully lifted off by a SpaceX rocket in Florida in late January 2021. SpaceX launched a rideshare mission carrying 143 small satellites in a single rocket, setting a new record.[86] Among the small satellites, the Flying Squirrel from Taiwan weighs only 4.5 kg and costs USD 1.43 million. It is designed to observe how plasma in the earth's ionosphere could affect the movement of radio waves that are used for 5G communication. The satellite uses a plasma sensor that is a miniature version of what was installed on Taiwan's FormoSat-5 satellite launched in 2017. By contrast, Taiwan's FormoSat-5 and 7 satellites weighed 450 and 300 kg respectively. Taiwan's National Formosa University has also designed a small satellite, the Nut, for flight tracking, and it will be launched later in 2021.[87]

The Formosat-7/COSMIC-2, jointly developed by the US and Taiwan, was launched in June, 2019 in the US, marking a milestone for Taiwan's space technology industry. The Formosat-7 is set to take over from another Taiwan-US product, the Formosat-3., The National Space Organisation (NSPO) was stablished in 1991 to be administered by the National Applied Research Laboratories under the Ministry of Science and Technology in Taiwan. It is designated to be an innovation centre for space science and to conduct space programs commissioned by Taiwan or from abroad.[88]

The year 2023 was a fruitful year for the ISRO. It successfully landed its Chandrayaan-3 Lander Module (Vikram) on the surface of the Moon on August 23, 2023. The world witnessed that the Lander successfully touched down in the Moon's southern polar region as planned, making India the first nation to achieve this remarkable feat of landing a spacecraft in such proximity to the lunar south pole. Furthermore, a Rover Module (Pragyan), a 6-wheeled solar-powered robotic vehicle with a life span of one lunar day (14 Earth days), carrying a suite of instruments exited from the Lander to study the lunar surface and subsurface for deriving the elemental composition in the vicinity of landing site. On September 2, 2023, the ISRO's Aditya-L1 was launched to study the Sun's activities, which marks the first of its kind by India.

Three critical launches are already scheduled by the ISRO for the first quarter in 2024, including the first polarimetry mission X-Ray Polarimeter Satellite (XPoSat), the launch of INSAT-3DS satellites, and the ISRO's collaborative mission with the National Aeronautics and Space

Administration (NASA). Two of them will be launched in January. The NASA-ISRO Synthetic Aperture Radar mission (NISAR), a low earth orbit (LEO) observatory, is "to map the globe in 12 days and provide spatially and temporally consistent data for understanding changes in Earth's ecosystems, ice mass, vegetation biomass, sea-level rise, groundwater and natural hazards, including earthquakes, tsunamis, volcanoes and landslides.[89]

As satellite communication is going to play a more significant role in communication technologies beyond 5G, the LEO satellites possess the considerable potential fill in the gaps in the coverage by ground network infrastructures.[90] As Taiwan is ready to issue licenses for the delivery of LEO satellite services, which normally operate below an altitude of 2,000 km and is not constrained by geographical features, it is widely expected to create great business opportunities for relevant industries to boost the satellite phone market and, to utilise the services for military purposes and to facilitate synergy with 5G mobile communications to relay 5G coverage.[91]

A prominent case in point between India – Taiwan collaboration is that ISRO's Polar Satellite Launch Vehicle carried Taiwan's INSPIREsat-1 (IS-1) satellite, developed jointly by India, Singapore, Taiwan and the US, into the orbit on February 13, 2022. Dr Priyadarshnam Hari commented on Taiwan's technological strength in engineering by saying that "Taiwan has a good space science group and excellent electronics manufacturing industry. Rapid prototyping and flight model realisations of the designs are very important for progressing rapidly in which Taiwan's industry can play a major role." He argued that universities in India and Taiwan could benefit from further space science collaboration, especially in the area of remote sensing and space science through student satellites by combining their strengths. "Regular exchange of students and faculty members can be used to improve both technical and cultural aspects", he added.[92]

There is spacious room for India's ISRO and Taiwan's NSPO to engage each other for future collaboration, both in training and projects of research and technology with an aim to deepen bilateral relations in space science and applied technology for peaceful usage. The officials from both Taiwan and India have agreed to engage each other.

World Health Organisation and World Health Assembly

India geographically belongs to the WHO South-East Asia Region, one of the six WHO Regions, and it covers over a quarter of the world's population. To serve nearly two billion people, WHO South-East Asia Region is based in New Delhi, India, and it has 11 member states—Bangladesh, Bhutan, Democratic People's Republic of Korea, India, Indonesia, Maldives, Myanmar, Nepal, Sri Lanka, Thailand, and Timor-Leste. The WHO works closely with all the member states to address and relieve persisting and emerging epidemiological and demographic challenges. Each year, WHO sets a few key priorities to enhance emergency risk management, to facilitate sustainable development, to promote universal health coverage and to set up robust health systems in member states. The South-East Asia Region currently are entrusted to implement eight flagship programs following the UN SDGs and WHO's global triple billion goals. WHO has country offices in all member states to monitor and coordinate the implementation of approved projects.[93]

Although at present Taiwan is not a member of WHO and theoretically is supposed to be covered by the WHO Western Pacific Region, it used to be invited to participate in the annual World Health Assembly (WHA) as an observer under the name of 'Chinese Taipei" from 2008 to 2016. In facing the COVID-19 pandemic, the 'Taiwan Model' of successfully containing the pandemic has earned global recognition and accolades for the effective actions it has taken; as a result, Taiwan has received unprecedented support for its participation in WHO and WHA activities in 2022-23. Leaders, high-level government officials and parliamentarians of more than 80 countries showed their staunch support to Taiwan in 2020. Taiwan is a busy transport hub for the Asia-Pacific Region. It handled more than 72 million inbound and outbound passengers in 2019. Despite the impact of the COVID-19 pandemic on tourism, it managed 19 million journeys in 2020. Thus, for the safety and health of all the passengers and workers at the airports, Taiwan should be allowed to conduct real-time information exchange with the world via WHO's International Health Regulations mechanism. It was exactly via this mechanism that Taiwan took the lead in reporting information to WHO in the very beginning of the COVID-19 pandemic break-out in late 2019 and early 2020. However, Taiwan somehow was unable to obtain information on the pandemic and related data issued by the WHO Western Pacific Regional Office (WPRO). In fact, Taiwan is not invited to participate in most of the meetings organised by the WPRO for obvious political reasons. Other technical meetings organised by WHO have refused 70 perecent of Taiwan's applications for participation. Even when the whole world was campaigning for a concerted effort to fight the COVID-19 pandemic in 2020, Taiwan, as one of the best performing countries, was only allowed to attend seven out of the 12 meetings it applied to.

Although Taiwan once again failed in its bid to be invited to participate in the WHA 2022, the Australian Office, Taipei, the British Office Taipei, the Canadian Trade Office in Taipei, Japan-Taiwan Exchange Association and American Institute in Taipei reaffirmed in a joint statement their countries' "support for Taiwan's meaningful participation in the work of WHO and Taiwan's participation as an observer in the WHA. In 2022, Taiwan received the support and backing of 71 governments, parliaments and parliamentary groups in total for Taiwan's participation in WHO bodies.[94]

At the WHA 2023, 12 of Taiwan's diplomatic allies proposed to invite Taiwan to participate in the WHA as an observer. During the General Committee debate, Belize and Nauru solemnly refuted the Chinese argument which inappropriately linked United Nations General Assembly Resolution 2758 and WHA Resolution 25.1 to the so-called 'One-China Principle'. Belize and Nauru stressed that prioritising politics over public health is unacceptable to the world. Eswatini and the Marshall Islands, during the plenary session debate, lauded Taiwan as a model for the world in fighting against the COVID-19 pandemic and called for Taiwan's participation in WHO and the WHA. Ultimately the proposal item was not included in the agenda, but Taiwan's diplomatic allies made the voice of justice heard at the WHA again.

In addition, 13 like-minded countries supported Taiwan at the WHA. The US, Japan, the UK, Canada, Australia, France, Germany, Lithuania, the Czech Republic, and Luxembourg spoke up for Taiwan. Estonia for the first time expressed its support in a direct reference to Taiwan. New Zealand and Latvia emphasised the goals of inclusiveness, avoiding politicisation, and leaving no region of the world behind to echo Taiwan's appeals for participation in WHO and the WHA.

India's Ministry of Ayush and the WHO South-East Regional Office signed a letter of exchange for the secondment or deputation of an Ayush expert to WHO's Regional traditional medicine program in New Delhi. And in February, 2021, India donated INR1.5 million to Taiwan's National Research Institute of Chinese Medicine to launch cooperation in traditional medicine.[95] On April 21, 2021, the World Medical Association council session in South Korea passed a motion overwhelmingly to support Taiwan's participation in the WHO activities with a vote of 22:1, China being the only dissenter, while it claimed it can cover Taiwan's need.[96] It is once again a clear indicator that the 'Universal Coverage' and 'Health for All' ideals are upheld by the medical associations all over the world to take care of the health of Taiwan's 23.5 million people. Since no country can fight an epidemic alone, closer international cooperation in a concerted manner is the only way to prevent and control an epidemic. As India is the leader in the WHO South-East Asia Region, it would be in all stakeholders' interest for Taiwan to share its experience and expertise in combating the COVID-19 pandemic, even with the 11 member states in the WHO South-East Asia Region. The momentum of Taiwan's bid to meaningfully participate in WHO and WHA will be further boosted if India is able to pronounce its support in the years to come.

Exercise Malabar

Exercise Malabar began as a bilateral exercise between India and the US in 1992 and later It evolved into a multilateral exercise with the addition of Australia and Japan. The 24th edition of the Malabar maritime exercise Phase 1 was conducted off Visakhapatnam in Bay of Bengal in early November, 2020, and Phase 2 was conducted in the Arabian Sea in mid-November, 2020, jointly by Indian Navy, United States Navy, Japan Maritime Self Defence Force and Royal Australian Navy. Essentially the agenda included advanced surface and anti-submarine warfare exercises, seamanship evolutions and weapon firings which were undertaken during the two phases of Malabar 2020, demonstrating the synergy, coordination and inter-operability between the four friendly navies. The Malabar series of exercises began as an annual bilateral naval exercise between India and the US in 1992. The 24th edition of Malabar, conducted in the backdrop of COVID-19 pandemic, was reflective of the commitment of the participating countries to support a free, open and inclusive Indo-Pacific as well as a rules-based international order.[97]

Taiwan is not a member of the Quad mechanism, but it shares similar strategic maritime concerns as Australia, Japan and the US in the West Pacific and the South China Sea. As the South China Sea carries an estimated one-third of global shipping, its waters are particularly critical for China, Taiwan, Japan, and South Korea, all of which rely on the Strait of Malacca, which connects the South China Sea and, by extension, the Pacific Ocean with the Indian Ocean.[98] The IOR is of strategic importance as it bridges the Indian Ocean to the Pacific and the Mediterranean and is a vital intersection of maritime trade through which more than two thirds of global oil and over 80 percent of China's and Japan's oil is shipped. So is Taiwan's. Notably, nearly half of global container shipments sail on these waters.

Exercise Malabar whether conducted in the Bay of Bengal or the Arabian Sea concerns the maritime security of Taiwan's oil tankers, cargo and container ships. With the support of all the participating countries, Taiwan would be interested in observing at least some parts of the exercise to enhance its own preparedness and strengthen international cooperation, should the situations across Taiwan Strait demonstrate signs of escalation.

The series of Malabar exercises provided a working platform for members of the Quad to enhance their maritime cooperation in technical terms. Since they all face similar maritime challenges, therefore, an urgent need for interoperability among their navies should be a priority task in making the South China Sea and the Indian Ocean free and open. Those key issues of improving intelligence sharing, secure communications, coordinated logistics, and smooth interoperability should all be better coordinated at one time outside the annual Malabar exercise. Recently, India has signed the Basic Exchange and Cooperation Agreement, the Logistics Exchange Memorandum of Agreement and the Communications Compatibility and Security Agreement with the US. They are all positive landmarks of coordination in that direction. In addition, India has signed agreements on military logistics with Australia and Japan as well.

The success of the Exercise Malabar in 2020 has sent a strong signal that China's ambition and affirmative behaviours will be checked jointly by the Quad members and by an increasing number of like-minded countries. Some scholars even advised that a powerful follow-up to Malabar Exercise in 2020 could be to conduct the next Exercise Malabar in the South China Sea.[99] The Exercise Malabar 2022 was conducted in September 2022 with the previous edition conducted in two phases in August off Guam in the Western Pacific and in October in the Bay of Bengal in 2021.[100]

Australia hosted the Exercise Malabar 2023 for the first time from August 10-21, 2023. Together with the Navies from India, Japan and the US, they joined in high-end training including air defence and anti-submarine exercises, aviation, communications and replenishment at sea between ships to face the complex challenges of the maritime domain.

If political barriers can be put aside, Taiwan can also be involved in the Exercise Malabar as an observer to witness the command system, coordination process and joint tactics in facing maritime challenges, since the free and open maritime navigation in the Indo-Pacific also matters so much to Taiwan's economic and security lifelines in the Taiwan Strait, the South China Sea and the Indian Ocean.

Section 4: Policy Recommendations

The physical size of Taiwan may not immediately convey its economic and strategic significance to India, especially under the 'One-China Policy' that India has long claimed to observe, either explicitly or implicitly manner. India's relationship with the PRC cannot be underestimated owing to the geographically proximity and politically sensibility between the two most populous neighbouring countries. Over recent decades, India's economic over-dependency on the PRC has led to the Indian wealth to flow into the PRC's economy. However, there are clear signs of a shift as the 'Make in India' and 'Atmanirbhar Bharat' initiatives begin to be implemented as intended. Indian Prime Minister Narendra Modi underlined trusted source, transparency and timeframe for improving global supply chains and committed that India is ready to play a role in the supply chain for clean technology.[101] Taiwan's Foreign Minister Jaushieh Joseph Wu echoed by saying: "As vibrant democracies, Taiwan and India share the universal values of freedom, respect for human rights and the rule of law. By working together with trust-worthy, like-minded partners, I have every confidence that our democratic supply chain will provide everyone with a more sustainable and undisrupted lifestyle."[102] Putting aside political considerations, Taiwan and India are natural partners to supplement each other's strengths and it is more so than ever after the COVID-19 pandemic.

To take advantage of the emerging ties of the relations between India and Taiwan over the past 29 years or so since the establishment of the two countries' representative offices in 1995, following recommendations are listed for India and Taiwan to take into account if both countries are determined to navigate political obstacles for a much closer collaboration in the scopes of economy, industries, education, investment, R&D on science and technology, health and vaccines, and NGOs:

To the Government of Taiwan

- The New Southbound Policy was launched by President Tsai Ing-wen in 2016. It is time to review the effectiveness of this policy after seven years of implementation, especially on the issue of whether it is appropriate to have targeted 18 countries including Southeast Asian, South Asian countries, Australia and New Zealand. Although Taiwan's bilateral trade with New Southbound Policy countries exceeded USD 180 billion *in* 2022, up 88 percent from 2016, The projected objectives and results in relations with Pakistan, Bangladesh, Nepal, Sri Lanka, Bhutan are far from satisfactory due to the absence of a permanent diplomatic representation of Taiwan Office in these countries. Therefore, the policy guidelines shall be strictly examined and reviewed thoroughly in order to revamp a new package of policy as the New Southbound Policy 2.0, which preferably should just focus on India, Southeast Asian countries, Australia and New Zealand. Substantial resources shall be allocated to enhance relations with India in mutually selected areas of interest, such as people-to-people interaction, higher education, employment of Indian talent and skilled workers, public health, science and technology and even agriculture, climate change, environment, UN SDGs, etc.

- The number of annual Taiwan Scholarships and Mandarin Enrichment Scholarships awarded to Indian college students for studying for Master or Doctoral degrees in Taiwan should be ambitiously increased. The current annual quota of under 100 is far too few, taking into account that the number of India's annual college graduates exceeds 11 million and the fact that Taiwanese first-tier universities can recruit many more Indian talents. The scholarship recipients should span a wider range of expertise, not necessarily focused on science and technology. Areas such as liberal arts, social science, tropical agriculture, intelligence property law, business administration, international development, traditional herbal medicine, music and dance are just some excellent areas for Indian students to pursue post-graduate degrees in Taiwan. Likewise, Taiwanese students should be encouraged to visit India, work or study in India with more substantial incentives.
- In order to retain more Indian talent in Taiwan, after being awarded Master's or Doctoral degrees, whether to start new enterprises or to work for local and foreign companies more easily, the current Employment Gold Card for Foreign Special Professionals regulations shall specifically target and encourage more qualified Indian professionals to apply, in close coordination with the India-Taipei Association, and the Indian Mission in Taiwan. Under this scheme, special professionals can legally stay in Taiwan up to three years, allowing them to work out plans and make informed decisions to contribute their expertise in Taiwan. In the long run, the Indian talents will become a highly qualified and efficient group of agents, significantly bridging mutually beneficial relations between India and Taiwan. Following the signing of the MOU on Labor Cooperation has been signed in Mid-February 2024, Taiwan is set to welcome more Indian professional and skilled migrant workers. Retaining Indian talents will become an imminent and far-reaching issue for Taiwan's high-tech and other industries.

- There are quite a number of Indian scholars specialising in India-China relations. While India's relations with Taiwan are on an upward trend, the number of Taiwanese scholars who are trained with India-related expertise are still far too few. Universities and think tanks in Taiwan should train and recruit more experts, both from local or India and other countries, in areas such as India's domestic policies, foreign policy, international relations, judiciary, agriculture, social and cultural aspects and Indo-Pacific Strategy. This will help analyse India's perspectives and its potential for engagement with Taiwan based on their respective national interests, fostering deeper mutual understanding and appreciation for each other's strengths to make both countries grow stronger together.
- Government policy guidance is essential for encouraging Taiwanese businesspeople who are looking for alternative investment destination in India. Hence, there should be more frequent lectures and accessible information on the evolving relations between India and Taiwan, along with advice on how Taiwanese companies can prepare to seize the golden opportunities and potential that India presents to the entrepreneurs. More importantly, systematic business and technology briefings should take place regularly to highlight the opportunities, explain how to do business in India and provide feasible solutions to the challenges they may encounter, in addition to the current support systems from both countries.
- Although there were 31 Taiwan Education Centres in India by the end of 2023, there remains a huge demand among the higher education institutions in India for high-quality Mandarin teachers provided by Taiwan. This number could smoothly increase to 50 sooner than expected in the coming years. Taiwan should have a talent pool of individuals willing to serve in India and redesign its entire employment package to ensure that Mandarin teachers receive favourable provisions for medical insurance, air travel and remuneration.. This would make Mandarin teaching opportunities in India can be competitive with similar vacancies offered by Taiwan's Ministry of Education in other countries or by other official institutions or agencies.

To the Government of India

- The 'One-China Policy' in India's foreign relations has been in place for over seven decades under which the relations with Taiwan have been strictly confined in areas of economic and investment projects, higher education, Mandarin Chinese training, and cultural exchanges. While all countries in the world have their own version of the 'One-China Policy', some are ambiguous and loosely followed, while others are strictly aligned with the PRC's preferences. India has prioritised balancing its China policy to support domestic economic development and manage foreign threats, extending its policy's boundaries to maximise its relations with countries like Taiwan, as well as Japan, South Korea and Singapore. India should tactfully engage with Taiwan to garner the economical and technological benefits without compromising its interest in managing relations with the PRC as it pursues policy goals like 'Make in India', 'Digital India', 'Skill India', 'Smart India' and 'Atmanirbhar Bharat', etc. in collaboration with suitable partners. Taiwan offers India suitable opportunities in terms of investment, scientific and technological advancements, food security and strategic collaboration. As major democratic powers are committed to maintain a free and open Indo-Pacific and the South China Sea, in line with India's foreign policy, India's specific endorsement of peace and stability across the as an essential component of a free and open Indo-Pacific, would add substantial weight. Definitely, the other member countries of the Quad would welcome such a stance.
- India is highly influential regionally and, with a capability to engage key stakeholders worldwide, in addition to the Indo-Pacific strategy. Taiwan has identified India as one with the most suitable destinations for Taiwanese companies looking to relocate from amid the US-China trade war and ongoing strategic conflicts between them. With the approval of the Semicon India program by India's Union Cabinet and the establishment of the India Semiconductor Mission and the Production Linked Incentive Scheme for large scale electronic manufacturing, the policy makers in India should think hard how best India can attract more substantial Taiwanese investments, in the fields like electric

vehicles, green energy, recycling waste water, high-tech agriculture and ICT manufacturing industries. Special consideration and policy support should be given to encourage collaboration in smart phone manufacturing and the establishment of semiconductor manufacturing facilities that some prominent Taiwanese companies are already on board. Improving the infrastructure to facilitate ease of doing business and to win over the staunch support from the US, Japan and Europe would help position India as a semiconductor manufacturing hub and restructure the global supply chain for strategic components that matter to defence, security and sensitive high-tech industries.

- Over the years, Taiwanese investors altogether have created hundreds of thousands of employment opportunities and have generally operated successfully in India, though a few of them did encounter social, cultural and management challenges. The most notable case is the riot that broke out at the Wistron iPhone plant in Bengaluru, Karnataka in December 2020, which directly or indirectly led to the company's decision to sell out its 100 percent equity stake in Wistron Infocomm Manufacturing (India) to the Tata Group in November, 2023. This sale enabled the Tata Group to become an iPhone assembler and join the Apple supply chain. Another noteworthy case is about the Continental Holdings Corporation, a well-known engineering and construction company, which claimed that it had about 20 pending cases for arbitration in 2018. If an effective mechanism had been available for the Indian government to render professional consultation to companies before reaching the arbitration stage, the negative impacts these setbackc could have been minimised. If a mechanism like that can be efficiently worked out, not only Taiwanese companies, but also Japanese, South Korean and Singaporean companies will welcome it.
- There is precedence for Taiwanese minister and vice minister level officials to visiting India, meeting with Indian counterparts and signing MOUs, though, these engagements have been largely limited to areas such as economy, education, science and technology. Reportedly, only an incumbent Education Minister, a Planning and Development Minister, a couple of Deputy Ministers of Foreign Affairs, a Deputy Defence

Minister, a couple of Deputy Ministers of Science and Technology and a Vice Minister of Economic Affairs from Taiwan have visited India over the past two decades. On the Indian side, before 2020, very few officials at the Secretary level from the Central government of India, or Principal Secretary level from the State governments were allowed to visit Taiwan, let alone Union Minister, Minister or Chief Minister from any State, due to political constraints. Even visits by parliamentarians visits to Taiwan have been carefully screened by the Indian government. Taiwan has been pragmatic in its quasi-diplomatic approach for decades, and is far from 'living in fantasy'. India has all the potential for Taiwan to enhance collaboration despite previously showing little interest in relations with Taiwan outside the economic sphere. In terms of bilateral relations are concerned, more frequent high-level visits from Taiwan and consultations across various sectors would be highly beneficial for Government of India to facilitate in order to address mutual concerns. Taiwan is ready to welcome high-ranking Indian officials for 'unofficial' or 'private' visits, or even online meetings if both sides agree to keep a low-profile in dealing with this essential but sensitive relationship with Taiwan. The pace of collaboration may be relatively slow, as time is needed to fully incorporate Taiwan into India's 'Act Indo-Pacific' and 'Atmanirbhar Bharat' ambitions.

- In February 2021, India donated funds to Taiwan to boost cooperation on traditional medicine, marking the first time in seven decades that Taiwan received a donation from India India's Ayurvedic medicine is one of the world's oldest medical systems and remains one of India's traditional health care. Ayurvedic treatment primarily uses products, mainly derived from plants, but may also include animal, metal, and minerals, alongside diet, exercise, and lifestyle practices. Meanwhile Taiwan preserves ancient treasured medical books from the Qing Dynasty, Forbidden City, and continues to innovate the tradition Chinese medicine into a modern form of medical science. Both India and Taiwan has university departments and research centres. The two governments should enhance exchanges in training on traditional medicine, either through degree programs or for professional practitioners with scholarships.

- India is the birthplace of Buddhism where Siddharth Gautam, the Buddha, was born, grew up, attained enlightenment, delivered his first and last sermons and attained Mahaparinirvana. Present day India holds all of Buddhism holiest pilgrimages sites, including Lumbini, Kapilvastu, Bodhgaya, Vajrasana, Mrigdava, Sarnath, Shravasti, Nalanda, Griddhkuta Hill, and Kushinagar For Buddhists and tourists worldwide, these holiest pilgrimages sites hold immense significance. The Indian government should take initiative to coordinate with the government of Nepal, private entrepreneurs, and NGOs to create a comprehensive system of pilgrimage route packages. These packages could that combine all the holiest sites, offering modern facilities and varied itineraries for the pilgrims and tourists to choose from. Taiwan, China, Japan, South Korea, the ASEAN countries and Sri Lanka are some of the top priority sources. From the point of view of promoting either Buddhism or Hinduism, India has a unique status to promote religious interactions with the rest of the world. If the tour packages are well organised and run by professionals, India can be ready to welcome millions more of pilgrims and tourists every year especially those interested in Buddhism. Additionally, religious and cultural conferences or seminars could be held more frequently to discuss the past, the present, and the future of Buddhism. Scholars, students from the Buddhist universities, associations, leaders of Buddhist sects and experts in Taiwan are some of the natural partners for such academic and religious events.
- It would be in all stakeholders' interest if India took a leading role, at least among South Asian countries, in maintaining a 'free and open' Indo-Pacific. With the support of participating countries, Taiwan could be invited to observe Exercise Malabar, regular meetings of SAARC and BIMSTEC, or to participate in training courses and professional meetings hosted by ISRO or WHO South East Asia Region to share Taiwan's expertise and experience in space science, technology, and public health, particularly its experiences in fighting the COVID-19 pandemic. Taiwan's bid to meaningfully participate in WHA as an observer and in its specialised meetings goes beyond political considerations and

deserves support from India and other Asian countries to uphold WHO's ideals of 'Universal Coverage' and 'Health for All'. The PRC's claim that it covers Taiwan's medical and public health needs is in reality, simply fictional. India has successfully overcome severe challenges of COVID-19 pandemic, and its efforts in combating the virus are valuable to the world community, as many countries are still under the shadow of encountering the threat again. Taiwan is among the few countries including the US, EU, the PRC and others to transport oxy-generators and other medical materials to India in early May, 2021 out of pure humanitarian concern. Taiwan has been ready to offer a helping hand wherever there is an urgent need. Likewise, Indian government may try to facilitate as much as possible Taiwan's involvement in certain pragmatic mechanisms like Quad Plus, UNFCCC, INTERPOL, and ICAO leveraging India's role as a key player on regional and global issues. This would allow Taiwan to meaningfully participate and contribute more than ever.

- The TaiwanICDF is Taiwan's official international development agency, which is implementing over 75 projects entrusted or supported by the Ministry of Foreign Affairs to conduct in more than 30 countries, partnering with Taiwan's diplomatic allies, friendly partner countries, international organisations, aid agencies and INGOs. The TaiwanICDF's operations cover six major contemporary development issues such as agriculture, public health and medicine, education, information and communications technology, environment, small and medium enterprises, with these projects conducted by its 20 technical missions in developing countries. Based on the discussions in an international conference focused on food security and rural development in New Delhi in November, 2023, projects on smart agricultural technical cooperation, women empowerment, Micro, Small, and Medium Enterprises, vocational training, and micro-financing can be encouraged to be explored and discussed by the governments of India and Taiwan, both at the central and state government to garner essential mutual benefits by fostering collaboration on agriculture and other areas of shared expertise.

Section 5: Future prospects for India-Taiwan Relations

The prospects for India-Taiwan relations under the leadership of Prime Minister Narendra Modi and President Ching-te Lai can be expected to include several key areas of collaboration, building on the foundations laid in recent years. Many essential and substantial developments are evolving and going to expand and strengthen:

- **Economic Cooperation and Trade**: India and Taiwan will continue to work together to diversify and strengthen supply chains, particularly in technology and electronics. Taiwan will continue to increase investments in India's technology, manufacturing and infrastructure sectors. India will continue to attract Taiwanese firms looking to relocate or expand in response to geopolitical tensions.
- **Technological Collaboration**: Taiwan's expertise in semiconductor manufacturing can complement India's ambitions in this sector. Collaboration will be bolstered by setting up more fabrication plants in India and sharing technological know-how; Joint R&D initiatives in areas like AI, 5G, and green technologies must be fostered.
- **Strategic and Security Cooperation**: Feasible ways will be identified by both countries to deepen cooperation in the Indo-Pacific region on maritime security, counterterrorism and ensuring freedom of navigation. Projects will be sought to deepen defence technology cooperation, joint exercises, and sharing intelligence on common security concerns.
- **Healthcare and Biotechnology**: Joint research initiatives in healthcare, particularly in biotechnology and pharmaceuticals will be enhanced. Taiwan's expertise in healthcare infrastructure can be utilised to aid India in improving its medical facilities and systems.
- **Bilateral and Multilateral Diplomacy**: More regular dialogues and communication will take place to facilitate high-level visits, and institutional mechanisms to address issues of mutual interest. Some forms of collaboration in multilateral forums with Taiwan's participation will be encouraged to address global challenges such as climate change, public health, regional security and international development.
- **Trade Agreement and Economic Partnerships**: More frequent discussions on a FTA or comprehensive economic partnership agreement

will resumed to facilitate easier trade and investment flows between the two countries; more business delegations, trade missions, and trade shows will be organised to explore new areas and opportunities and partnerships.

- **Educational and Cultural Exchanges:** Many more student and academic exchange programs will be established to enhance mutual understanding and foster long-term partnerships. Frequent cultural exchanges, including language programs and cultural festivals will strengthen people-to-people ties.

Given Prime Minister Modi's focus on economic growth and technological advancement, and President Lai's background in governance and his progressive stance on international cooperation, the relationship between India and Taiwan is more than likely to see significant advancements, fostering a mutually beneficial partnership across multiple domains.

The US factor

The US relations with India and Taiwan will essentially impact India's collaboration with Taiwan in several ways. Here are some key considerations:

- **Strategic Alignments:** The US has been promoting the Indo-Pacific strategy to counterbalance China's influence in the region. Stronger US-India and US-Taiwan relations can enhance trilateral cooperation, fostering a strategic alignment among the three nations. India's involvement in the Quad provides a platform for deeper collaboration on regional security and economic issues. While Taiwan is not a formal member, its interests often align with Quad objectives.
- **Economic and Technological Cooperation:** The US push for supply chain diversification away from China is driving India and Taiwan to collaborate more closely in sectors like semiconductors, electronics, and critical technologies. US support and investments in India and Taiwan can encourage greater economic cooperation between the two, with American companies facilitating joint ventures and partnerships.

- **Defence and Security:** The US plays a pivotal role in defence technology transfers and joint defence projects involving India and Taiwan. Enhanced US-India defence ties can indirectly benefit Taiwan through shared technological advancements and intelligence. The US commitment to ensuring regional security can provide a security umbrella, encouraging India and Taiwan to engage in more overt collaborations to jointly counter China's coercive and assertive threats.
- **Diplomatic and Political Support:** It is in US's interest to support India and Taiwan in international forums, advocating for their interests and helping them navigate geopolitical challenges. This support can create a more conducive environment for India-Taiwan collaboration. While the US does not officially recognise Taiwan as a sovereign state, its strong unofficial relations and support can encourage other countries, including India, to strengthen ties with Taiwan.
- **Trade agreement and economic partnerships:** The US can facilitate discussions on FTA or comprehensive economic partnerships agreements involving India and Taiwan, encouraging more robust economic ties. The US influence in the global business ecosystem can drive multinational companies to explore opportunities in India and Taiwan, fostering trilateral business collaborations.
- **Humanitarian and cultural exchange:** The US can promote education and cultural exchange programmes that involve India and Taiwan to enhance people-to-people ties and mutual understanding. Joint initiatives in healthcare, supported by US expertise and funding, can bring India and Taiwan closer in addressing global health challenges.

US relations with India and Taiwan are likely to have a positive impact on India-Taiwan collaboration by providing strategic, economic, and diplomatic support. This trilateral dynamic can lead to more robust partnerships, helping both India and Taiwan navigate regional and global challenges effectively.

The China factor

Reassessment of the One-China Policy: The PRC's assertive actions against India in the past few years could significantly impact India's stance on the

One-China Policy and potentially create more room for Taiwan to invest in India. Firstly, to counter China's persistent, unilateral assertiveness, which threatens India's sovereignty and territories, India is compelled to reassess its One-China Policy, whether it officially acknowledged or not, and adopt a more flexible interpretation of the One-China Policy unless the territorial disputes are resolved to India's satisfaction. While not officially recognising Taiwan as a separate state, India has to enhance its unofficial ties and engagements with Taiwan in response to Chinese assertiveness, especially, when India seeks Taiwan's investment and technological collaboration in semiconductor manufacturing and AI supply chains, effectively acknowledging Taiwan as a key player in the AI era. Furthermore, increased parliamentary exchanges, cultural events, and high-profile visits can signal a shift in India's approach, indicating a willingness to deepen relations with Taiwan.

Economic and Trade Opportunities: Amidst growing tensions with China, India must diversify its economic partnerships by attracting more Taiwanese investments in key sectors such as semiconductor manufacturing, AI technology and infrastructure, aligning with India's strategic goals of 'Make in India' and 'Viksit Bharat 2047'. India could offer incentives to Taiwanese companies looking to relocate or expand operations, especially in the context of global supply chain realignments, as India holds an advantageous position as one of the major stakeholders and players in the democratic camp.

Technological collaboration: Taiwan's expertise in semiconductors presents a critical area of collaboration. India's focus on becoming a semiconductor hub offers ample opportunities for Taiwanese investment and technology transfer. Joint R&D projects in emerging technologies such as 5G, AI, and renewable energy should be prioritised.

Strategic Partnerships: India's participation in the Quad and its Indo-Pacific strategy, with the consent of other members, could involve more coordinated efforts with Taiwan on maritime security, cybersecurity, and regional stability. While overt defence cooperation might be limited due to diplomatic sensitivities, backchannel communications and intelligence sharing could enhance India-Taiwan strategic understanding.

Impact of PRC's assertiveness: Ongoing border tensions with China, such as those seen in Ladakh, may push India to reconsider its strategic options. Closer engagement with Taiwan could serve as a counterbalance to Chinese actions. Rising anti-China sentiment among the Indian public, media and political leaders can further create a favourable environment for stronger India-Taiwan ties. This shift could lead to in more supportive policies and increased bilateral engagements.

Multilateral Diplomacy: India may consider lending more support to Taiwan's participation in international organisations and forums, advocating for its inclusion in bodies like the WHO, UNFCCC and the ICAO, where no one should be excluded for political reasons and statehood is not a prerequisite. Collaborating with other countries in the region that have similar concerns about China's assertiveness could create a network of support for Taiwan, indirectly strengthening India-Taiwan relations.

Bilateral agreements and frameworks: Bilateral economic agreements and frameworks are in the best interest of both countries. Building on the foundations laid over the past three decades, India may continue to negotiate a FTA or comprehensive economic partnership agreement with Taiwan to institutionalise economic cooperation and provide a framework for increased investment. More substantial MOUs and joint ventures in strategic sectors could formalise the economic relationship and attract Taiwanese investments.

PRC's assertive actions against India can prompt a strategic recalibration of India's One-China Policy, creating more space for Taiwan to invest in India. This shift could be driven by economic, technological, and strategic considerations, with both nations seeking to navigate the complexities of regional geopolitics to their mutual benefit.

Notes

1. Keoni, Everington, "Taiwan rated 2nd and freest in Asia by Freedom House, 7th in world", *Taiwan News,*athttps://taiwantoday.tw/news.php?unit=2&post=249388; "Freedom in the World 2024", Freedom House. https://freedomhouse.org/country/taiwan/freedom-world/2024, accessed on March 1, 2024.
2. Chen Yun-yu and Evelyn Kao, "Taiwan ranked top in Asia, 10th in world on EIU freedom index", *Focus Taiwan*, at https://focustaiwan.tw/politics/202402150018, accessed on February 15, 2024.

3. "Explained: What is 'Viksit Bharat 2047' and what does it aim to achieve?", *Deccan Herald*, at https://www.deccanherald.com/india/explained-what-is-viksit-bharat-2047-and-what-does-it-aim-to-achieve-2920441, accessed on March 4, 2024.
4. "Second advance estimates of national income 2023-24", *Ministry of Statistics, Government of India*, At https://pib.gov.in/PressReleasePage.aspx?PRID=2010223, accessed on February 29, 2024.
5. "India-China Bilateral Relations", *Ministry of External Affairs, Government of India, 7,* At https://mea.gov.in/Portal/ForeignRelation/china_brief_sep_2019.pdf, accessed on April 15, 2021.
6. Wikileaks, https://wikileaks.org/plusd/cables/04TAIPEI3845_a.html, accessed April 11, 2020.
7. "'Upswing In Levels Of Cooperation': Jaishankar On India-Taiwan's 'Substantial' Relations", ABP News, November 16, 2023. https://news.abplive.com/news/india/eam-jaishankar-on-india-taiwan-substantial-relations-1643038.
8. "Live: EAM S Jaishankar attends interactive session on Northeast India's Integration | Asia | Japan", *ANI News*, at https://www.youtube.com/watch?v=78OACqXVE7o, accessed on April 29, 2024.
9. D. P. Tripathi and B. R. Deepak, ed., *India and Taiwan: From Benign Neglect to Pragmatism*, (New Delhi: VIJ Books, 2016).
10. Pankaj Doval, "Foxconn chairman Liu eets PM Modi; looks at semiconductor manufacturing with Vedanta", *Times of India, June 23, 2022*. https://timesofindia.indiatimes.com/business/india-business/foxconn-chairman-liu-meets-pm-modi-looks-at-semiconductor-manufacturing-with-vedanta/articleshow/92419714.cms.
11. "PM participates in 'India's Techade: Chips for Viksit Bharat' program", *Narendra Modi*, at https://www.narendramodi.in/prime-minister-narendra-modi-participates-in-%E2%80%98india-s-techade-chips-for-viksit-bharat--580486, accessed on March 13, 2024.
12. Kuang-ying Liu, "Having worked hard in India for 15 years, why does Yin Chi stop playing?", *Commonwealth Magazine, Issue 649*, June 4, 2018. https://www.cw.com.tw/article/5090272, accessed on April 22, 2021.
13. Archana Chaudhary and Suvashree Ghosh, "India Aims to Spend $1.4 Trillion Building Infrastructure", *Bloomberg*, August 15, 2021. https://www.bloomberg.com/news/articles/2021-08-15/india-aims-to-end-energy-imports-boost-infrastructure-spending.
14. "India to unveil $1.35 trillion infrastructure plan, PM Modi says", *Daily Sabah*, August 15, 2021. https://www.dailysabah.com/business/economy/india-to-unveil-135-trillion-infrastructure-plan-pm-modi-says.
15. "COVID-19 INDIA", Ministry of Health and Family Welfare, Government of India. Accessed on August 17, 2021. https://www.mohfw.gov.in/.

16. "#IndiaFightCorona COVID-19", Government of India, September 4, 2022. https://www.mygov.in/covid-19/.
17. Sana Hashmi, "India-Taiwan Ties: A Case for Stronger Partnership", *Asie. Visions, Ifri, No 125*, November 2021. https://www.ifri.org/en/publications/notes-de-ifri/asie-visions/india-taiwan-ties-case-stronger-partnership, accessed on "Not yet time to conduct official FTA talks with India: MOEA", *Focus Taiwan*, March 8, 2011. https://focustaiwan.tw/business/201103080023.
18. Seema Guha, "India-Taiwan Business Cannot Be Built On An Anti-China Platform", *Outlook*, March 4, 2021. https://www.outlookindia.com/website/story/india-news-want-to-needle-china-woo-taiwan-say-experts/376117.
19. "Vedanta, Foxconn sign $20 billion Gujarat chip deal", *The Times of India*, September 13, 2022. https://timesofindia.indiatimes.com/business/india-business/vedanta-foxconn-sign-20-billion-gujarat-chip-deal/articleshow/94169496.cms.
20. "Foxconn submits application for setting up semiconductor unit: MoSIT", *Press Trust India, December 20, 2023.* http, at s://www.ptinews.com/home-detail/Foxconn-submits-application-for-setting-up-semiconductor-unit--MoS-IT/302314.
21. Danny D'Cruze, "Tata Electronics finalises 100% stake in Wistron India to become first Indian company to make Apple iPhones", *Business Today, Nov. 9, 2023*, https://www.businesstoday.in/technology/news/story/tata-electronics-finalises-100-stake-in-wistron-india-to-become-first-indian-company-to-make-apple-iphones-405176-2023-11-09.
22. Yu Nakamura, "TSMC to invest $2.8 bn in China to ramp up auto chip production", *Nikkei Asia, April 26, 2021*, at. https://asia.nikkei.com/Business/Tech/Semiconductors/TSMC-to-invest-2.8bn-in-China-to-ramp-up-auto-chip-production.
23. Lin Yu-li and Frances Huang, "Dresden ready to take on TSMC's water, power, housing needs: Mayor", *Focus Taiwan, October 29, 2023*, at https://focustaiwan.tw/business/202310290007.
24. Kathrin Hille, "TSMC: how a Taiwanese chipmaker became a linchpin of the global economy", *Financial Times, March 24, 2021*, at https://www.ft.com/content/05206915-fd73-4a3a-92a5-6760ce965bd9.
25. Chung Jung-feng, "3nm plants reportedly installed, TSMC: slated to start mass production in the second half of 2022", *Central News Agency, August 2, 2021*, at https://www.cna.com.tw/news/afe/202108020193.aspx.
26. "About TSMC Arizona", TSMC Arizona., at https://www.tsmc.com/static/abouttsmcaz/index.htm, accessed on June 2, 2024.
27. Supra, note 9.
28. "What are the five pillars of a self-reliant India?", *Narendra Modi, May 13, 2020,* at https://www.narendramodi.in/what-are-the-five-pillars-of-a-self-reliant-India-read-to-find-out-more-549630, accessed on "PM Modi shares 5 pillars that will

make India self-reliant in Covid-19 times", India Today, May 12, 2020. https://www.indiatoday.in/india/story/pm-modi-speech-5-pillars-atm-nirbhar-self-reliance-covid-19-lockdown-1677293-2020-05-12.

29. "Atmanirbhar Bharat is our path as well as our resolve: PM Modi", *ANI*, May 6, 2022. https://www.aninews.in/news/national/general-news/aatmnkrbhar-bharat-is-our-path-as-well-as-our-resolve-pm-modi20220506135926/.
30. "PM Modi's Independence Day speech: Key points", *The Times of India*, August 15, 2022. https://timesofindia.indiatimes.com/india/pm-modis-independence-day-speech-key-points/articleshow/93564760.cms.
31. Chiang Chin-yeh and Lee Hsin-Yin, "U.S., Japan reaffirm commitment to Taiwan Strait stability", *Focus Taiwan*, April 17, 2021. https://focustaiwan.tw/politics/202104170002.
32. Kelvin Chen, "Taiwan attends regional air force meeting", *Taiwan News, January 21, 2022*, at https://www.taiwannews.com.tw/en/news/4417177.
33. "ASEAN-India Foreign Ministers' Meeting and other related meetings", *Ministry of External Affairs, Government of India*, August 5, 2022. https://www.,mea.gov.in/press-releases.htm?dtl/35631/ASEANIndia_foreign_Ministers_Meeting_and_other_meetings; "U.S.-Australia-Japan Trilateral Strategic Dialogue", Office of the Spokesperson, the Department of State, the USA, August 5, 2022. https://www.state.gov/u-s-australia-japan-trilateral-strategic-dialogue/.
34. Vincent Ni, "Liz Truss summons Chinese ambassador over aggression towards Taiwan", *The Guardian*, August 10, 2022. https://www.theguardian.com/politics/2022/aug/10/liz-truss-summons-chinese-ambassador-over-aggression-towards-Taiwan.
35. "Taiwan-China crisis: India calls for de-escalation of tensions", *The Times of India*, August 12, 2022. https://timesofindia.indiatimes.com/india/taiwan-china-crisis-india-calls-for-de-escalation-of-tensions/articleshow/93522458.cms; Sachin Parashar, "One-China? No need to reiterate our consistent policies, says India", The Times of India, August 13, 2022. https://timesofindia.indiatimes.com/india/one-china-no-need-to-reiterate-our-consistent-policies-says-india/articleshow/93530107.cms.
36. Deeptiman Tiwary, "India, China troops begin disengagement from Gogra-Hotsprings in Ladakh", *The Indian Express*, September 9, 2022. https://indianexpress.com/article/india/india-china-troops-disengagement-ladakh-8139126/.
37. "Foreign Minister Wu gives interviews to India's media", *Taiwan Today*, August 25, 2022. https://taiwantoday.tw/news.php?unit=2,6,10,15,18&post=224105.
38. Helen Davidson, "India accuses China of 'militarisation of the Taiwan Strait' as row over navy vessel grows", *The Guardian*, August 29, 2022. https://www.theguardian.com/world/2022/aug/29/india-accuses-china-of-militarisation-of-the-taiwan-strait-as-row-over-navy-vessel-grows.

39. "Taiwan rejects China's protest over messages between Modi, Lai", *The Arunachal Times*, June 8, 2024. https://arunachaltimes.in/index.php/2024/06/08/taiwan-rejects-chinas-protest-over-messages-between-modi-lai/.
40. "'Part of diplomatic business': US on China's objection to Modi-Lai exchange on Indian polls", *Deccan Herald*, June 7, 2024. https://www.deccanherald.com/world/part-of-diplomatic-business-us-on-chinas-objection-to-modi-lai-exchange-on-indian-polls-3056304.
41. Brahma Chellaney, at *X*, June 6, 2024. https://x.com/Chellaney/status/1798687954262687835.
42. Vedika Sud, Barbara Starr, Sahar Akbarzai and Kathleen Magramo, "US to take part in military exercise near India's disputed border with China", *CNN*, August 6, 2022. https://edition.cnn.com/2022/08/06/india/india-us-military-exercise-line-of-actual-control-china-intl-hnk/index.html.
43. "China Claims India-US Exercise Would Violate Border Pacts, India Disagrees", *The Wire*, August 25, 2022. https://thewire.in/diplomacy/china-claims-india-us-exercise-would-violate-border-pacts-india-disagrees.
44. "Transcript of Weekly Media Briefing by the Official Spokesperson (September 22, 2022)", *Ministry of External Affairs, Government of India*, September 22, 2022. https://mea.gov.in/media-briefings.htm?dtl/35742/Transcript+of+Weekly+Media+Briefing+by+the+Official+Spokesperson+September+22+2022.
45. "The CHIPS Act of 2022: Section-by-Section Summary", *Senate Commerce Committee, the USA*. Accessed on August 8, 2022. https://www.commerce.senate.gov/services/files/592E23A5-B56F-48AE-B4C1-493822686BCB.
46. "President Biden Signs Executive Order to Implement the CHIPS and Science Act of 2022", *The White House*, August 25, 2022. https://www.whitehouse.gov/briefing-room/statements-releases/2022/08/25/fact-sheet-president-biden-signs-executive-order-to-implement-the-chips-and-science-act-of-2022/.
47. Eric Martin and Debby Wu, "U.S. and India plan to boost chips collaboration, Biden's commerce chief says", *The Japan times, March 10, 2023*, https://japantimes.co.jp/news/2023/03/10/world/us-india-chip-collaboration.
48. "99% Indian-made mobile phones in country today, says Union minister Ashwini Vaishnaw", *Hindustan Times*, November 27, 2023. https://www.hindustantimes.com/technology/99-indian-made-mobile-phones-in-country-today-says-union-minister-ashwini-vaishnaw-101701102725789.html.
49. Liam Gibson and Tridivesh Singh Maini, "How to 'de-hyphenate' Taiwan-India-China relations", *Taiwan News*, August 16, 2021. https://www.taiwannews.com.tw/en/news/4271069.
50. "Raisina Dialogue 2021 to be held digitally due to COVID-19", *The Economic Times*, April 5, 2021. https://economictimes.indiatimes.com/news/india/raisina-dialogue-2021-to-be-held-digitally-due-to-covid-19/articleshow/81909937.cms.

51. "IISS Shangri-La Dialogue", *The International Institute for Strategic Studies.* Accessed on April 10, 2021. https://www.iiss.org/events/shangri-la-dialogue/shangri-la-dialogue-2021.
52. "Prime Minister's Keynote Address at Shangri La Dialogue)", *Ministry of External Affairs, Government of India*, June 1, 2018. https://www.mea.gov.in/Speeches-Statements.htm?dtl/29943/Prime+Ministers+Keynote+Address+at+Shangri+La+Dialogue+June+01+2018.
53. *Raisina Dialogue 2016 Conference Report* (New Delhi: Observer Research Foundation, 2016). https://www.orfonline.org/wp-content/uploads/2016/10/Raisina2016_Report.pdf.
54. "Speakers", Observer Research Foundation. Accessed on April 11, 2021. https://www.orfonline.org/raisina-dialogue/speaker/.
55. Ibid. 26-27; Namrata Hasija, "India Quietly Enhances Ties With Taiwan – Analysis", *South Asia Monitor, February 6, 2017*, Accessed on March 20, 2021. https://www.eurasiareview.com/06022017-india-quietly-enhances-ties-with-taiwan-analysis/.
56. "Raisina Dialogue 2017 Conference Report", *New Delhi: Observer Research Foundation, 2017, 16*, https://www.orfonline.org/wp-content/uploads/2020/01/Raisina-Report-2017-WEB.pdf.; *Raisina Conference Dialogue 2018 Report* (New Delhi: Observer Research Foundation, 2018), 21. https://www.orfonline.org/wp-content/uploads/2018/09/ORF_Raisina_Final-Report.pdf.
57. S. B. Asthana, "Quad Summit 2021: Why is China Rattled?", *Financial Express*, March 12, 2021. https://www.financialexpress.com/defence/quad-summit-2021-why-is-china-rattled/2212544/.
58. "Diplomatic breakthrough: Taiwan was invited by the US, Japan, India and Australia for security dialogue", *The Liberty Times*, March 12, 2018. https://news.ltn.com.tw/news/focus/paper/1183169. (In Chinese)
59. Premesha Saha, "First Quad leaders meeting: An agenda beyond security", *Observer Research Foundation, March 16, 2021*, https://www.orfonline.org/expert-speak/first-quad-leaders-meeting-agenda-beyond-security/.
60. Matt Yu and Emerson Lim, "Peace in Taiwan Strait a global concern: Taiwan's foreign minister", *Focus Taiwan*, July 19, 2021. https://focustaiwan.tw/politics/202107190025; Stacy Hsu and Matthew Mazzetta, "Quad countries discuss 'peace and security' in Taiwan Strait", Focus Taiwan, August 13, 2021. https://focustaiwan.tw/politics/202108130005.
61. Kunal Purohit, "France, India and Australia step up Quad-style cooperation, with China on the horizon", *South China Morning Post*, April 14, 2021. https://www.scmp.com/week-asia/politics/article/3129564/france-india-and-australia-step-quad-style-cooperation-china.
62. Dinakar Peri, "Raisina Dialogue| ' Huge potential for India, NATO to collaborate,' says NATO Secretary General", *The Hindu*, April 14, 2021. https://www.thehindu.

com/news/national/raisina-dialogue-huge-potential-for-india-nato-to-collaborate-says-nato-secretary-general/article34314397.ece.

63. "Indo-Pacific Construct Reflects Overcoming Of Cold War: S Jaishankar", *NDTV*, April 14, 2021. https://www.ndtv.com/india-news/quad-reflects-contemporary-world-overcoming-of-cold-war-external-affairs-minister-s-jaishankar-at-raisina-dialogue-2413735.
64. "Eye on China, Jaishankar says Quad will benefit Indo-Pacific", *The Indian Express*, August 19, 2022. https://indianexpress.com/article/india/eye-on-china-jaishankar-says-quad-will-benefit-indo-pacific-8098617/.
65. "Quad", Ministry of External Affairs, Republic of India. Accessed on December 30, 2023. https://www.mea.gov.in/Portal/ForeignRelation/Quad_brief_October_2023.pdf.
66. "Global Cooperation and Training Framework (GCTF) Programs", *American Institute in Taiwan.* Accessed on April 13, 2021. https://www.ait.org.tw/our-relationship/global-cooperation-and-training-framework-programs-gctf/.
67. "Global Cooperation & Training Framework", Ministry of Foreign Affairs, the Republic of China (Taiwan). Accessed on April 13, 2021. https://www.gctf.tw/en/#.
68. "Participating Countries", *Global Cooperation & Training Framework, Ministry of Foreign Affairs, the Republic of China (Taiwan)*, Accessed on April 13, 2021. https://www.gctf.tw/en/Countries.htm.
69. "Global Conclave Promises Closer Collaboration in Healthcare", Voice of Healthcare, February 25, 2022. https://voiceofhealthcare.org/pressrelease.php?id=127.
70. "GCTF Conference on Ending Gender-based Violence in Taipei", *New Southbound Policy Portal*, May 24, 2022. https://nspp.mofa.gov.tw/nsppe/news.php?unit=370&post=219635.
71. "GCTF hosts workshop on Empowering Women in the Post-Pandemic Era in St. Lucia", *Ministry of Foreign Affairs, the Republic of China (Taiwan)*, https: www.mofa.gov.tw/News_Content.aspx?n=95&sms=73&s=98450. (In Chinese)
72. The author, in his capacity of the Secretary General of the Taiwan ICDF, had the privilege of making a speech on this occasion representing Taiwan.
73. "Vaccine Supply", Ministry of External Affairs, Government of India, April 30, 2021. https://www.mea.gov.in/vaccine-supply.htm.
74. Sandhya Dangwal, "ISRO SAARC satellite launch today: Here's how first South Asian satellite will benefit India's neighbours", India.com, May 5, 2017. https://www.india.com/business/isro-saarc-satellite-launch-today-heres-how-first-south-asian-satellite-will-benefit-indias-neighbours-2100691/.
75. Dipanjan Roy Chaudhury, "ISRO's new station in Bhutan to counter China's Tibet facility", *The Economic Times*, January 2, 2019. https://economictimes.indiatimes.com/news/politics-and-nation/isros-new-station-in-bhutan-to-counter-chinas-tibet-facility/articleshow/67343292.cms.

76. Dipanjan Roy Chaudhury, "Bhutan's space engineers to undergo 2-month training in India for joint development of satellite", *The Economic Times*, December 28, 2020, https://economictimes.indiatimes.com/news/science/bhutans-space-engineers-to-undergo-2-month-training-in-india-for-joint-development-of-satellite/articleshow/79993426.cms.
77. Rakhahari Chatterji and Anasua Basu Ray Chaudhury, *Reimagining BIMSTEC: Strengthening Regional Solidarity Across the Bay of Bengal, Observer Research Foundation (New Delhi: Observer Research Foundation*, February 22, 2021), *12-14*, https://www.orfonline.org/research/reimagining-bimstec-strengthening-regional-solidarity-across-the-bay-of-bengal/.
78. "5th BIMSTEC Summit", Ministry of External Affairs, Government of India, March 30, 2022. https://www.mea.gov.in/press-releases.htm?dtl/35093/5th+BIMSTEC+Summit.
79. Sripathi Narayanan, "5th BIMSTEC Summit", *Indian Council of World Affairs*, April 22,2022. https://icwa.in/show_content.php?lang=1&level=3&ls_id=7277&lid=4914.
80. "GSLV Successfully Launches South Asia Satellite", *Indian Space Research Organisation*, May 5, 2017. Accessed on April 13, 2021. https://www.isro.gov.in/update/05-may-2017/gslv-successfully-launches-south-asia-satellite.
81. Arun Rao, "India has the potential to be the next space hub of the world", The Economic Times, October 24, 2020. https://economictimes.indiatimes.com/small-biz/sme-sector/india-has-the-potential-to-be-the-next-space-hub-of-the-world/printarticle/78840533.cms.
82. "International Cooperation", Department of Space, *Indian Space Research Organisation*, Accessed on April 21, 2021. https://www.irro.gov.in/intertnational-cooperation.
83. "Dr. K. Sivan, Chairman, ISRO/Secretary, DOS had a meeting with the new Head of Australian Space Agency and signed an amendment to the existing India – Australia MoU for space cooperation", ISRO, February 17, 2021. https://www.isro.gov.in/update/17-feb-2021/dr-k-sivan-chairman-isro-secretary-dos-had-meeting-with-new-head-of-australian.
84. "Dr. K. Sivan, Chairman, ISRO/Secretary, DOS had a meeting with the President of Japan Aerospace Exploration Agency", *ISRO,* March 11, 2021. https://www.isro.gov.in/update/11-mar-2021/dr-k-sivan-chairman-isro-secretary-dos-had-meeting-with-president-of-japan.
85. "Brazilian Minister visited ISRO to witness the launch of Amazonia-1 satellite", *ISRO*, February 28, 2021. https://www.isro.gov.in/update/28-feb-2021/brazilian-minister-visited-isro-to-witness-launch-of-amazonia-1-satellite.
86. Amy Thompson, "SpaceX launches a record 143 satellites on one rocket, aces landing", *Space.com*, January 24, 2021. https://www.space.com/spacex-launches-143-satellites-transporter-1-rocket-landing.

87. "SpaceX rocket carries two Taiwanese satellites into space", *Focus Taiwan*, January 24, 2021. https://focustaiwan.tw/sci-tech/202101240019.
88. "SpaceX Falcon Heavy launches, Taiwan-US Formosat-7/COSMIC-2 deployed", Taiwan Today, June 26, 2019. https://taiwantoday.tw/news.php?unit=2,6,10,15,18&post=157599.
89. Soumya Pillai, "Three launches in Q1: ISRO's upcoming missions in 2024", *Hindustan Times*, December 22, 2023. https://www.hindustantimes.com/india-news/three-launches-in-q1-isro-s-24-plan-101703183805729.html.
90. "(Digitimes) iST takes early action to target non-terrestrial communication technologies beyond 5G to open a pathway to space communication for the Taiwan Industry", *Integrated Service Technology*, September 23, 2020. https://www.istgroup.com/en/media_20200923/.
91. "LEO satellites offer opportunities", Taipei Times, May 31, 2022. https://www.taipeitimes.com/News/biz/archives/2022/05/31/2003779036.
92. Emerson Lim, Pan Tzu-yu and James Lo, "Satellite of love: Taiwan-developed INSPIREsat-1 enters orbit", Focus Taiwan, February 14, 2022. https://focustaiwan.tw/sci-tech/202202140022.
93. "About WHO in the South-East Asia Region", *The World Health Organization*. https://www.who.int/southeastasia/about.
94. "Foreign missions issue joint statement supporting Taiwan's WHA bid", Focus Taiwan, May 21, 2022. https://focustaiwan.tw/politics/202205210008.
95. "India donates funds to Taiwan to boost cooperation on traditional medicine", *ANI, February, 27, 2021*, https://www.aninews.in/news/world/asia/india-donates-funds-to-taiwan-to-boost-cooperation-on-traditional-medicine20210227230435/.
96. Keoni Everington, "WHA votes in favor of Taiwan's participation in WHO", *Taiwan News*, April 21, 2021. https://www.taiwannews.com.tw/en/news/4182667.
97. "Exercise MALABAR 2020 Concludes in Arabian Sea", Indian Navy. Accessed on April 14, 2021. https://www.indiannavy.nic.in/content/exercise-malabar-2020-concludes-arabian-sea.
98. "How Much Trade Transits the South China Sea?", *ChinaPower, CSIS*. Accessed on April 22, 2021. https://chinapower.csis.org/much-trade-transits-south-china-sea/.
99. Manoj Rawat, "Quad 2.0 Is Off to a Good Start – It Must Keep Going", The Diplomat, November 23, 2020. https://thediplomat.com/2020/11/quad-2-0-is-off-to-a-good-start-it-must-keep-going/.
100. "Malabar exercise phase-II to kick off next week in Bay of Bengal", *The Economic Times*, October 10, 2021, https://economictimes.indiatimes.com/news/defence/malabar-exercise-phase-ii-to-kick-off-next-week-in-bay-of-bengal/articleshow/86907026.cms.

101. "Modi's supply chain mantra: trusted source, transparency and time frame", *IANS*, November 1, 2021. https://www.business-standard.com/article/current-affairs/modi's-mantra-at-supply-chain-summit-trusted-source-transparency-time-frame-121110100086_1.html.
102. "Remarks by Minister Jaushieh Joseph Wu at a reception to celebrate India's 75th Republic Day", *Ministry of Foreign Affairs, Republic of China (Taiwan),* January 27, 2022. https://en.mofa.gov.tw/News_Content.aspx?n=1575&s=97308.

Annexure 1

Country	India	Taiwan
National flag		
Population	1.436 billion	23.5 million
Area	3.3 million sq. km	36,000 sq. km

India and Taiwan

Annexure 2

Map of India

Source: Glance @ India, MEA, Government of India
https://www.mea.gov.in/india-at-glance.htm

Annexure 3

Map of Taiwan

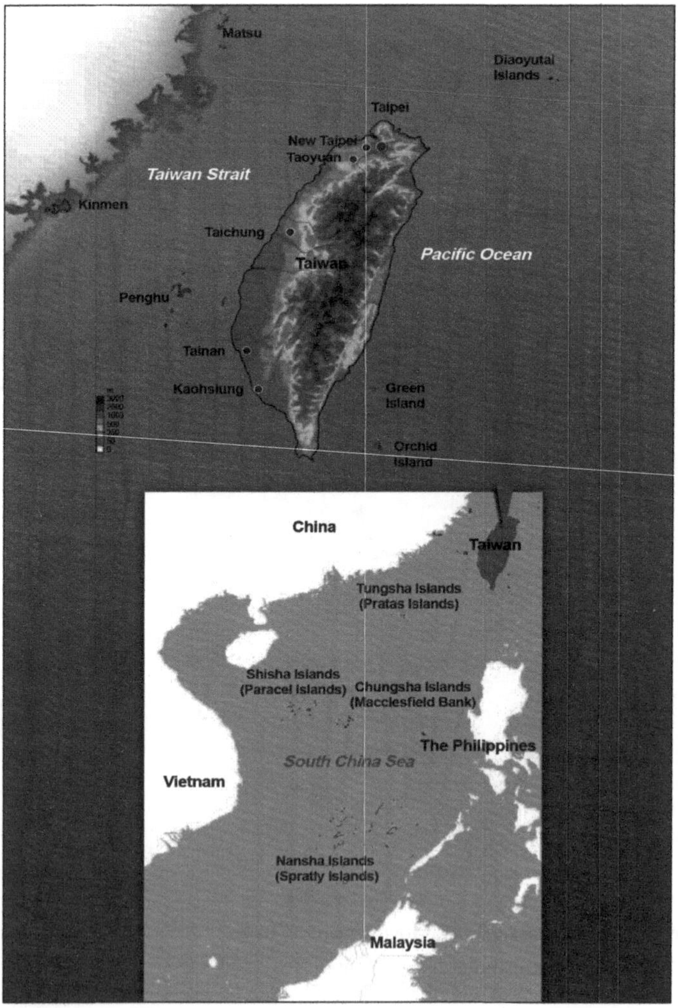

Source: 2020-2021 Taiwan at a Glance
https://multilingual.mofa.gov.tw/web/web_UTF-8/MOFA/glance2020-2021/2020-2021%20Taiwan%20at%20a%20Glance%20(English).pdf

Annexure 4

Faxian's Travels

Source: *Encyclopedia of India-China Cultural Contacts Vol I*, MEA, Republic of India (New Delhi: MaXposure Media Group, 2014), 290. http://www.mea.gov.in/images/pdf/India-ChinaEncyclopedia_Vol-1.pdf

Annexure 5

Xuanzang's and Yijing's Journey to India

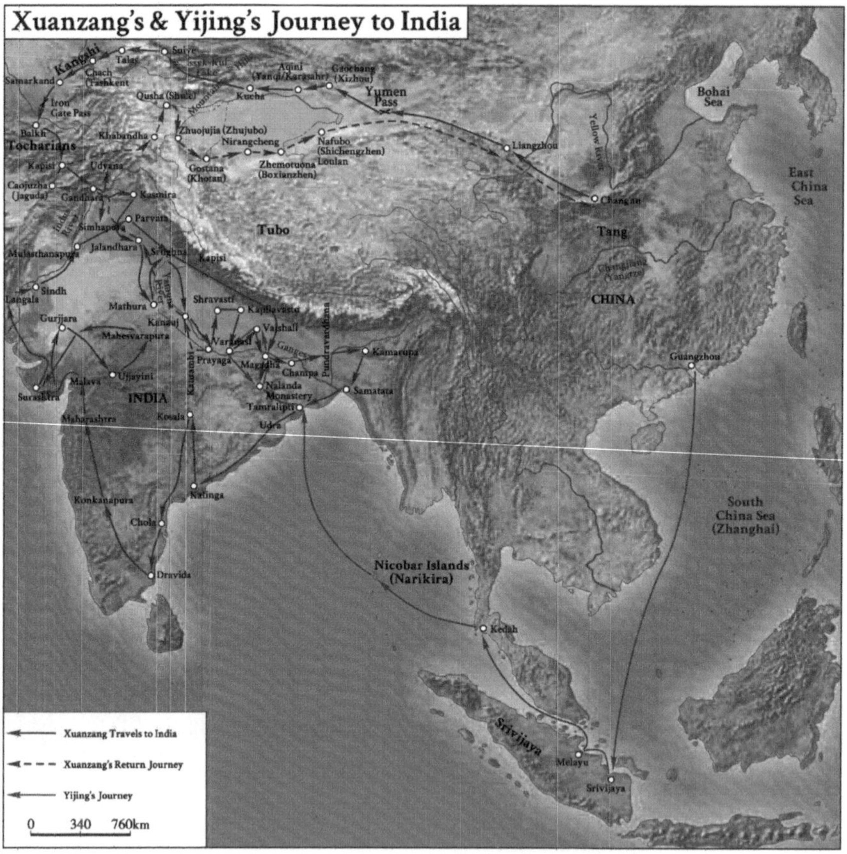

Source: *Encyclopedia of India-China Cultural Contacts Vol I*, MEA, Republic of India (New Delhi: MaXposure Media Group, 2014), 124.
http://www.mea.gov.in/images/pdf/India-ChinaEncyclopedia_Vol-1.pdf

Annexure 6

Heads of Mission of India-Taipei Association

Chinese Name	English Name	Tenure
康維諾	Vinod C. Khanna	1995-1997
溥達賢	L. T. Pudaite	1997-2000
谷南吉	Ranjit Gupta	2000-2003
顧凱傑	Vijay Keshav Gokhale	2003-2007
史泰朗	T. P. Seetharam	2007-2009
羅國棟	Pradeep Kumar Rawat	2009-2013
趙志恒	Manish Chauhan	2013-2016
史達仁	Sridharan Madhusudhanan	2016-2020
戴國瀾	Gourangalal Das	2020-2023
葉達夫	Manharsinh Laxmanbhai Yadav	2023-

Heads of Mission of Taipei Economic and Cultural Centre in India

Chinese Name	English Name	Tenure
鄧備殷	P. Y. Teng	1995-1998
錢剛鐔	K. T. Chien	1998-2003
高振群	Andrew J. Kao	2003-2007
夏立言	Andrew Hsia	2007-2008
翁文琪	Wen-chyi Ong	2008-2013
田中光	Chung-kwang Tien	2013-2020
葛葆萱	Bau-shuan Ger	2020-

Heads of Mission of Taipei Economic and Cultural Centre in Chennai

Chinese Name	English Name	Tenure
林明誠	Frank Lin	2012-2015
李朝成	Charles Li	2015-2020
王北平	Ben Wang	2020-2023
陳俊郎	Richard Chen	2023-

Annexure 7

New Southbound Policy Map

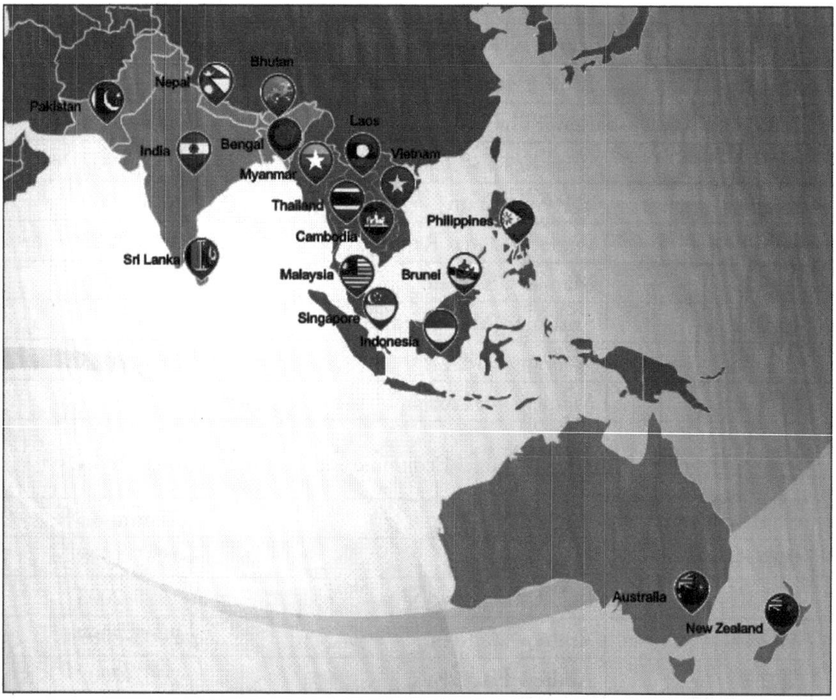

Source: New Southbound Policy Portal, Ministry of Foreign Affairs, Republic of China (Taiwan)
https://nspp.mofa.gov.tw/nsppe/

Annexure 8

The MOUs and Agreements Signed by TECC and ITA

Year	Name of Document	Taiwan Signatory	Indian Signatory	Remarks
July 2001	MOU on Civil Aviation	K. T. Chien	Ranjit Gupta	
October 2002	Agreement on the Promotion and Protection on Investment	K. T. Chien	Ranjit Gupta	
April 2007	MOU on Science and Technology Cooperation	Andrew J. Kao	T. P. Seetharam	
July 2011	Double Taxation Avoidance Agreement	Wen-chyi Ong	Pradeep Kumar Rawat	
July 2011	Customs Mutual Assistance Agreement	Wen-chyi Ong	Pradeep Kumar Rawat	
March 2013	Agreement on Temporary Admission for Goods	Chung-Kwang Tien	Pradeep Kumar Rawat	
December 2015	MOU on Small and Medium Sized Enterprises	Chung-Kwang Tien	Manish Chauhan	
September 2016	Air Services Agreement	Chung-Kwang Tien	Sridharan Madhusudhanan	
September 2016	MOU on Taiwan-India Agricultural Cooperation	Chung-Kwang Tien	Sridharan Madhusudhanan	
December 2016	Letter of Intent for Cooperation on Railway Heritage in Chiayi City of Taiwan	Chung-Kwang Tien	Sridharan Madhusudhanan	

Year	Name of Document	Taiwan Signatory	Indian Signatory	Remarks
October 2017	Mutual Recognition of the Respective Authorised Economic Operator Program	Chung-Kwang Tien	Sridharan Madhusudhanan	
December 14, 2017	MOU on Promotion of Industry Collaboration	Chung-Kwang Tien	Sridharan Madhusudhanan	
December 18, 2018	The Mutual Recognition Arrangement (MRA) of Authorised Economic Operator (AEO) between Taiwan and India	Chung-Kwang Tien	Sridharan Madhusudhanan	
December 18, 2018	Bilateral Investment Agreement	Chung-Kwang Tien	Sridharan Madhusudhanan	
June 22, 2019	MOU on Higher Education Cooperation	Chung-Kwang Tien	Sridharan Madhusudhanan	
May 18, 2022	MOU on Cooperation of Intellectual Property Rights	Baushuan Ger	Gourangalal Das	
May 18, 2022	Mutual Cooperation Agreement on Standardisation and Conformity Assessment Procedure	Baushuan Ger	Gourangalal Das	
October 22, 2021	Agreement on Standards and Conformity Assessment	Baushuan Ger	Gourangalal Das	
November 4, 2022	MOU on Cooperation of Traditional Medicine	Baushuan Ger	Gourangalal Das	
February 16, 2024	MOU on Labor Force Cooperation	Baushuan Ger	Manharsinh Laxmanbhai Yadav	
June 24, 2024	MOU on	Baushuan Ger	Manharsinh Laxmanbhai Yadav	

Annexure 9

The Significance of South China Sea Trade

For many of the world's largest economies, the South China Sea is an essential maritime crossroads for trade. Over 64 percent of China's maritime trade transited the waterway in 2016, while nearly 42 percent of Japan's maritime trade passed through the South China Sea in the same year. The United States is less reliant on South China Sea, with just over 14 percent of its maritime trade passing through the region.

Country	% Share of World GDP	Trade Value through South China Sea (USD billions)	South China Sea Trade As % of All Trade in Goods
United States	24.5	208	5.72
China	14.8	1470	39.5
Japan	6.53	240	19.1
Germanyx	4.58	215	9.00
UK	3.46	124	11.8
France	3.26	83.5	7.77
India	2.99	189	30.6
Italy	2.45	70.5	8.14
Brazil	2.37	77.3	23.4
Canada	2.02	21.8	2.67

Source: https://chinapower.csis.org/much-trade-transits-south-china-sea/
CSIS ChinaPower Project | International Monetary Fund

Annexure 10

Trade Volume between
Taiwan and New Southbound Policy Countries

Unit: US$ million

Country/Year	2020	2021	2022	2023
18 countries	61,075.99	82,580.52	180,242.86	152,354.99
Singapore	28,073.46	37,794.20	42,048.74	39,259.89
Malaysia	19,348.45	25,125.09	30,563.34	24,857.21
Australia	11,292.25	19,570.68	32,180.12	23,423.16
Vietnam	16,019.54	20,106.40	21,560.84	17,863.87
Thailand	9,833.82	12,984.48	13,841.75	16,238.12
Indonesia	6,785.05	10,970.73	14,427.26	10,404.41
India	4,795.56	7,698.92	8,460.55	8,224.65
Philippines	7,771.41	9,070.35	10,720.89	7,409.71
New Zealand	1,301.76	1,646.00	1,879.99	1,536.85
Bangladesh	939.59	1,334.21	1,915.40	1,068.37
Cambodia	788.21	975.97	1,031.12	730.95
Pakistan	524.58	887.18	832.22	455.60
Sri Lanka	369.86	489.13	411.37	318.83
Brunei Darussalam	213.70	172.68	51.07	295.43
Myanmar	269.49	234.57	284.94	212.74
Nepal	10.48	12.23	10.80	29.58
Laos	18.42	24.26	21.46	24.62
Bhutan	0.12	0.11	0.03	0.03

Source: From the statistics of the Customs, the Republic of China (Taiwan)

Annexure 11

Taiwan investment in India and ASEAN countries

Unit: US$ in Thousands

	2018		2019		2020		Total	
Country	Case No.	Amount	Case No.	Amount	Case No.	Amount	Case No.	Amount
India	21	361,224	11	70,375	8	152,624	111	941,167
Singapore	16	165,967	27	635,706	16	638,137	658	14,890,522
Indonesia	25	134,610	16	148,802	15	512,374	325	2,156,011
Malaysia	16	54,108	25	101967	15	40793	461	3,337,357
Philippines	15	149,703	12	106,725	11	92,111	247	2,236,272
Thailand	28	146,376	46	327,690	20	165,974	591	4,232,401
Vietnam	65	901,411	97	914,870	64	767,435	788	11,746,988
Laos	2	12,430	2	23,680	1	21,961	15	111,797
Myanmar	14	56,234	9	42,908	10	199,223	49	423,992
Cambodia	15	180,503	9	91,847	11	224,850	78	959,501
Brrnei	1	1,000	1	10,000	0	0	63	100,327

Source: Investment Commission, MOEA, ROC (Taiwan)
https://www.moeaic.gov.tw/english/news_bsAn.jsp

Annexure 12

India, ASEAN and Taiwan Offices

Country	Office in Taiwan	Taiwan's Office	Visa
India	India-Taipei Association	Taipei Economic and Cultural Centre in India Taipei Economic and Cultural Centre in Chennai	V
Brunei	Brunei Darussalam Trade and Tourism Office in Taipei	Taipei Economic and Cultural Office in Brunei	V
Indonesia	Indonesian Economic and Trade Office to Taipei	Taipei Economic and Trade Office, Jakarta, Indonesia Taipei Economic and Trade Office in Surabaya	V
Malaysia	Malaysian Friendship and Trade Centre, Taipei	Taipei Economic and Cultural Office in Malaysia	V
Myanmar	Myanmar Trade Office (closed)	Taipei Economic and Cultural Office in Myanmar	V
The Philippines	Manila Economic and Cultural Office	Taipei Economic and Cultural Office in the Philippines	V
Singapore	Singapore Trade Office in Taipei	Taipei Economic and Cultural Office in Singapore	V
Thailand	Thailand Trade and Economic Office	Taipei Economic and Cultural Office in Thailand	V
Vietnam	Vietnam Economic and Cultural Office in Taipei	Taipei Economic and Cultural Office in Vietnam Taipei Economic and Cultural Office in Ho Chi Minh City	V
Cambodia	–	–	
Laos	–	–	

Bibliography

Books

1. Allen, Charles. *The Buddha and the Sahibs.* London: John Murray, 2003.
2. Blackwill, Robert D. and Philip Zelikow. *The United States, China, and Taiwan: A Strategy to Prevent War*, Council Special Report No. 90. New York: Council on Foreign Relations, February 2021.
3. Cardenal, Juan Pablo, Jacek Kucharczyk, Grigorij Meseznikov, Gabriela Paleschova. *Sharp Power: Rising Authoritarian Influence.* Washington D.C.: National Endowment for Democracy, December 2017.
4. Chatterji, Rakhahari and Anasua Basu Ray Chaudhury. *Reimagining BIMSTEC: Strengthening Regional Solidarity Across the Bay of Bengal*, Observer Research Foundation. New Delhi: Observer Research Foundation, February 22, 2021. https://www.orfonline.org/research/reimagining-bimstec-strengthening-regional-solidarity-across-the-bay-of-bengal/.
5. Chu, Hung-yuan. "General Sun Li-jen's Political character demonstrated in the Battle of Yenangyaung." In *China-India Relations in First Half of the Twentieth Century*, edited by Hsieh Hsiao-chin and Fang Tien-sze, 129-165. Hsinchu, Taiwan: National Tsing Hua University Press, 2015.
6. https://brill.com/view/journals/jaer/25/3/article-p263_263.xml.
7. Deepak, B. R. *India and China: Foreign Policy Approaches and Responses*. New Delhi: Viji Books India, 2016.
8. Dongchu, Master. *Interaction of Buddhism between China and India* (中印佛教交通史), http://dongchu.dila.edu.tw/html/02/cwdc_03/cwdc_030374.html#d1e7703. (In Chinese)
9. Drun, Jessica and Bonnie S. Glaser, "The Distortion of UN Resolution 2758 and Limits on Taiwan's Access to the United Nations", The German Marshall Fund of the United States, March 24, 2022. https://www.gmfus.org/news/distortion-un-resolution-2758-and-limits-taiwans-access-united-nations.
10. Eekelen, W. F. Van. *Indian Foreign Policy and the Border Dispute with China.* The Hague: Martinus Nijhoff, 1964.
11. Fang, Tien-Sze. "An Assessment of Ambassador Luo Jialun's Mission to India: 1947-9." In *China-India Relations in First Half of the Twentieth Century*, edited by Hsieh Hsiao-chin and Fang Tien-Sze, 120. Hsinchu, Taiwan: National Tsing Hua University Press, 2015. (In Chinese)

12. Gokhale, Vijay. *The Long Game: How the Chinese Negotiate with India*. Gurugram: Penguin Random House India, 2021.
13. Gokhale, Vijay. *The Road from Galwan: The Future of India-China Relations*. New Delhi: Carnegie India, 2021. https://carnegieendowment.org/files/Gokhale_Galwan.pdf.
14. Gokhale, Vijay. *What Should India Do Before the Next Taiwan Strait Crisis?*, New Delhi: Carnegie India, April, 2023. https://carnegieindia.org/2023/04/17/what-should-india-do-before-next-taiwan-strait-crisis-pub-89515.
15. Guha, Ramachandra. *Jawaharlal Nehru and China: A Study in Failure?*, Harvard-Yenching Institute Working Paper Series. Cambridge, MA: Harvard-Yenching Institute, 2011. https://www.harvard-yenching.org/wp-content/uploads/legacy_files/featurefiles/Ramachandra%20Guha_Jawaharlal%20Nehru%20and%20China.pdf.
16. Nehru, Jawaharlal. "Cable to K. M. Panikkar", *Selected Works of Jawaharlal Nehru Second Series Vol. 15, October 1950–February 1951, Part 2*. New Delhi: Jawaharlal Nehru Memorial Fund, 1993. https://nehruselectedworks.com/pdfviewer.php?style=UI_Zine_Material.xml&subfolder=&doc=s2v15p2.pdf|10|592#page=472.
17. Panda, Jagannath P., ed. *India and China in Asia: Between Equilibrium and Equation*. London: Routledge, 2019.
18. Pandey, Utkarsh. "The India-China Border Question: An Analysis of International Law and State Practices," *ORF Occasional Paper No. 290*. New Delhi: Observer Research Foundation, December 2020.
19. Saklani, Avinash Mohan. "Nehru, Chiang Kai-shek, and the Second World War." In *India and China in the Colonial World,* edited by Madhavi Thampi, 167-183. New York: Routledge, 2017.
20. Sharma, Anita and Sreemati Chakrabarti, *Taiwan Today*. Delhi: Anthem Press, 2010.
21. Singh, Prashant Kumar *Transforming India-Taiwan Relations: New Perspectives IDSA Monograph Series no. 35*. New Delhi: IDSA, 2014.
22. Singh, Pashant Kumar, "Taiwan: A forgotten Frontier of India's 'Act East'?" In *India-Taiwan Relations in Asia and Beyond: The future,* edited by Jagannath P. Panda. New Delhi: Pentagon Press and IDSA, 2016.
23. Singh, Zorawar Daulet. *Power & Diplomacy: India's Foreign Policies During the Cold War*. Oxford: Oxford University Press, 2019.
24. Sikri, Rajiv. *Challenge and Strategy: Rethinking India's Foreign Policy*. New Delhi: Sage Publications, 2009.
25. Suri, Gopal. *China's Expanding Military Maritime Footprints in the Indian Ocean Region (IOR): India's Response*. New Delhi : Vivekananda International Foundation, 2017.

26. Tripathi, D. P. and B. R. Deepak, eds. *India and Taiwan: From Benign Neglect to Pragmatism*. New Delhi: VIJ Books, 2016.
27. Yang, Alan Yao and Sana Hashmi, eds. *Taiwan and India Strategizing the Relations.* Taipei: Taiwan-Asia Exchange Foundation, February 2022.

Books without Author

28. *Raisina Dialogue 2016 Conference Report*, New Delhi: Observer Research Foundation, 2016. https://www.orfonline.org/wp-content/uploads/2016/10/Raisina2016_Report.pdf.
29. *Raisina Dialogue 2017 Conference Report,* New Delhi: Observer Research Foundation, 2017, 16. https://www.orfonline.org/wp-content/uploads/2020/01/Raisina-Report-2017-WEB.pdf.
30. *Raisina Conference Dialogue 2018 Report,* New Delhi: Observer Research Foundation, 2018, 21. https://www.orfonline.org/wp-content/uploads/2018/09/ORF_Raisina_Final-Report.pdf

Journals

31. Chang, David W. "U.S. Aid and Economic Progress in Taiwan." *Asian Survey* 5, No. 3 (1965): 152. https://jstor.org/stable/2642405.
32. Clark II, Keith Allan. "Republic of China's 1955 Veto of Mongolian Membership in the United Nations", *Journal of American-East Asian Relations Volume 25: Issue 3.* n.l.: Brill (September 3, 2018): 263-295.
33. Hashmi, Sana. "India-Taiwan Ties: A Case for Stronger Partnership", *Asie. Visions*, Ifri, No 125, November 2021. https://www.ifri.org/en/publications/notes-de-ifri/asie-visions/india-taiwan-ties-case-stronger-partnership.
34. Khanna, Vinod C. "The India-Taipei Association: A Mission Extraordinaire", *Indian Foreign Affairs Journal Vol. 5, No, 2* (April-June 2010): 240-251.
35. Ladwig, Walter. "Delhi's Pacific Ambition: Naval Power, 'Look East,' and India's Emerging Role in the Asia-Pacific," *Asian Security*, Vol. 5, No. 2 (June 2009): 98-101.
36. Laskar, Rejaul. "Promoting National Interest Through Diplomacy", *Extraordinary and Plenipotentiary Diplomatist* 1 (9) (December 2013): 59-60.
37. Morris, Paul. "Asia's Four Little Tigers: A Comparison of the Role of Education in Their Development." *Comparative Education* 32, No. 1 (1996): 95-109. http://www.jstor.org/stable/3099602.
38. Liu, Kuang-ying. "Having worked hard in India for 15 years, why does Yin Chi stop playing?", *Commonwealth Magazine, Issue 649* (June 4, 2018). https://www.cw.com.tw/article/5090272. (In Chinese)

39. Pajtinka, Erik. "Between Diplomacy and Paradiplomacy: Taiwan's Foreign Relations in Current Practice", *Journal of Nationalism, Memory & Language Politics,* Volume 11: Issue 1 (April 2017).
40. Sen, Tansen. "The Spread of Buddhism to China: A Re-examination of the Buddhist Interactions between Ancient India and China", *China Report 48:1-2* (July 2012): 11-27.
41. Singh, Prashant Kumar. "India-Taiwan Ties: Can They Overcome Structural Challenge?", *Eurasia Border Review Vol 9, No.1* (2018 Fall): 1-28.
42. Thampi, Madhavi. "Indian Soldiers, Policemen and Watchmen in China in the Nineteen and Early Twentieth Centuries", *China Report 35:4* (Nov. 1999): 417-8.

Government Publications

43. Department of Foreign Affairs and Trade. *An India Economic Strategy to 2035.* Government of Australia, 2018. https://www.dfat.gov.au/geo/india/ies/overview.html.
44. Department of State. *People's Republic of China: Maritime Claims in the South China Sea, Limits in the Seas No.150,* Government of the United States of America, January 2022. https://www.state.gov/wp-content/uploads/2022/01/LIS150-SCS.pdf.
45. Ministry of External Affairs. *Encyclopedia of India-China Cultural Contacts Vol I,* Republic of India. New Delhi: MaXposure Media Group, 2014.
46. *The President's Annual Report of the Foreign Assistance Program of the United States for Fiscal year 1962.* Washington, D. C.: Govt. Printing Office, August 28, 1963.

EU

47. "Joint Communication to the European Parliament and the Council: The EU strategy for cooperation in the Indo-Pacific", European Commission and High Representative of the Union for Foreign Affairs and Security Policy of the European Union, September 16, 2021. https://eeas.europa.eu/sites/default/files/jointcommunication_2021_24_1_en.pdf.

UN

48. "UN Charter Article 6", United Nations. https://legal.un.org/repertory/art6.shtml.
49. "882nd Plenary Meeting, United Nations General Assembly Fifteenth Session Official Records", United Nations, October 3, 1960. https://undocs.org/en/A/PV.882.
50. "892nd Plenary Meeting, United Nations General Assembly Fifteenth Session Official Records", United Nations, October 7, 1960. https://undocs.org/en/A/PV.892.
51. "1875th Plenary Meeting, United Nations General Assembly Twenty-Fifth Session Official Records", United Nations, October 20, 1970. http://undocs.org/en/A/PV.1875.

52. "1959th Plenary Meeting, United Nations General Assembly Twenty-Sixth Session Official Records", United Nations, October 8, 1971. http://undocs.org/en/A/PV.1959.
53. "2758 (XXVI). Restoration of the lawful rights of the People's Republic of China in the United Nations", United Nations General Assembly.
54. file:///Users/charles/Downloads/A_RES_2758(XXVI)-EN.pdf.

Articles

55. A, Divya. "Looking forward to continuing people to people exchanges with Taiwan: India", The Indian Express, January 19, 2024. https://indianexpress.com/article/india/looking-forward-to-continuing-people-to-people-exchanges-with-taiwan-india-9116255/.
56. Asthana, S. B. "Quad Summit 2021: Why is China Rattled?", Financial Express, March 12, 2021. https://www.financialexpress.com/defence/quad-summit-2021-why-is-china-rattled/2212544/.
57. Bagchi, Indrani. "India should take the lead in the Quad", The Times of India, October 18, 2020. https://timesofindia.indiatimes.com/blogs/Globespotting/india-should-take-the-lead-in-the-quad/.
58. Bajpai, Kanti. "Back to the future: India's China policy has come full circle since Indira Gandhi", The Times of India, October 30, 2020. https://timesofindia.indiatimes.com/blogs/toi-edit-page/back-to-the-future-indias-china-policy-has-come-full-circle-since-indira-gandhi/.
59. Swati Bharadwaj, "India's 1st nasal Covid vaccine gets approval", The Times of India, September 7, 2022. https://timesofindia.indiatimes.com/city/hyderabad/indias-first-nasal-covid-vaccine-gets-approval/articleshow/94037891.cms.
60. Bhattacherjee, Kallol. "Indian media is free, says in MEA response to Chinese Embassy's note to press on Taiwan", October 8, 2020. https://www.thehindu.com/news/national/indian-media-is-free-says-in-mea-response-to-chinese-embassys-note-to-press-on-taiwan/article32806814.ece.
61. Bhaumik, Anirban. "Once probed for spying, China's Confucius Institutes now among models for India to learn lessons on soft power projections", Deccan Herald, August 14, 2023. https://www.deccanherald.com/india/learn-soft-power-lessons-from-confucius-inst-parliamentary-panel-tells-mea-2646355.
62. Blanchard, Ben and Yimou Lee. "Taiwan denies approval for UBI's COVID-19 vaccine candidate", Reuters, August 16, 2021. https://www.reuters.com/world/asia-pacific/taiwan-denies-approval-ubis-covid-19-vaccine-candidate-2021-08-16/.
63. Bose, Joydeep. "Dalai Lama was asked if he wants to visit Taiwan. Here's his answer", Hindustan Times, November 10, 2021. https://www.hindustantimes.com/world-news/dalai-lama-was-asked-if-he-wants-to-visit-taiwan-here-s-his-answer-101636521624751.html.

64. Bristow, Michael. "China encroaching along Nepal border - report", BBC News, February 9, 2022. https://www.bbc.com/news/world-asia-60288007.
65. Chai, Sze-chia and Joseph Yeh. "China has no right to interfere with Taiwan-Lithuania exchanges: MAC", Focus Taiwan, November 21, 2021. https://focustaiwan/cross-strait/202111210013.
66. Chan, K. C. "Britain's Reaction to Chiang Kai-shek's visit to India, February 1942", Online Library, August 1975. https://onlinelibrary.wiley.com/doi/abs/10.1111/j.1467-8497.1975.tb01141.x.
67. Chaudhury, Dipanjan Roy. "Bhutan's space engineers to undergo 2-month training in India for joint development of satellite", The Economic Times, December 28, 2020. https://economictimes.indiatimes.com/news/science/bhutans-space-engineers-to-undergo-2-month-training-in-india-for-joint-development-of-satellite/articleshow/79993426.cms.
68. Chaudhury, Dipanjan Roy. "ISRO's new station in Bhutan to counter China's Tibet facility", The Economic Times, January 2, 2019. https://economictimes.indiatimes.com/news/politics-and-nation/isros-new-station-in-bhutan-to-counter-chinas-tibet-facility/articleshow/67343292.cms.
69. Chaudhury, Dipanjan Roy. "India's one China policy may not be permanent future amid Beijing's aggression", The Economic Times, June 13, 2020. https://economictimes.indiatimes.com/news/defence/indias-one-chona-policy-may-not-be-permanent-feature-amid-beijings-aggression/articleshow/76351486.cms.
70. Chaudhury, Dipanjan Roy. "Rethink India's one-China Policy", The Economic Times, July 3, 2020. https://economictimes.indiatimes.com/news/defence/rethink-indias-one-china-policy/articleshow/76762670.cms.
71. Chellaney, Brahma. "Beijing's bendable principles", Japan Times, June 2, 2015. https://www.japantimes.co.jp/opinion/2015/06/02/commentary/world-commentary/beijings-bendable-principles/.
72. Chellaney, Brahma. at X, June 6, 2024, https://x.com/Chellaney/status/1798687954262687835.
73. Chen, Kelvin. "US president supports closer Taiwan-Lithuania relations", Taiwan News, November 4, 2021. https://www.taiwannews.com.tw/en/news/4334717.
74. Chen, Kelvin. "Taiwan attends regional air force meeting", Taiwan News, January 21, 2022. https://www.taiwannews.com.tw/en/news/4417177.
75. Chen, Mu-min. "Decoding secret diplomatic archives of Taiwan and India: Interactions between Taiwan and India post 1962 Sino-Indian war", The Reporter, June 6, 2020. https://www.twreporter.org/a/opinion-sino-indian-war-taiwan-secret-diplomatic-archives. (In Chinese)
76. Chen, Yun-yu. "Sridharan: India-Taiwan relations expand to fill the gap of industrial supply chains", CNA, January 22, 2020.
77. https://www.cna.com.tw/news/aipl/202001220320.aspx. (In Chinese)

78. Chen Yun-yu, "Lithuanian economic minister: representative office in Taiwan is set to open in early 2022", Central News Agency, October 27, 2021. https://www.cna.com.tw/news/firstnews/202110270301.aspx. (In Chinese)
79. Chen, Yun-yu and Frances Huang. "Lithuania set to open representative office in Taiwan in early 2022", Focus Taiwan, October 27, 2021. https://focustaiwan.tw/business/202110270021.
80. Chen Yun-yu and Evelyn Kao, "Taiwan ranked top in Asia, 10th in world on EIU freedom index", Focus Taiwan, February 15, 2024. https://focustaiwan.tw/politics/202402150018.
81. Cheng, Jassie Hsi. "The Taiwan-India 'Milk Tea Alliance'", The Diplomat, October 20, 2020. https://thediplomat.com/2020/10/the-taiwan-india-milk-tea-alliance.
82. Cheng, Ting-fang, Lauly Li and Kim Jaewon. "TSMC says it will make ultra-advanced 2nm chips by 2025", NikkeiAsia, June 17, 2022. https://asia.nikkei.com/Business/Tech/Semiconductors/TSMC-says-it-will-make-ultra-advanced-2nm-chips-by-2025.
83. Chiang, Chin-yeh and Lee Hsin-Yin. "U.S., Japan reaffirm commitment to Taiwan Strait stability", Focus Taiwan, April 17, 2021. https://focustaiwan.tw/politics/202104170002.
84. Chung, Jung-feng. "3nm plants reportedly installed, TSMC: slated to start mass production in the second half of 2022", Central News Agency, August 2, 2021. https://www.cna.com.tw/news/afe/202108020193.aspx. (In Chinese)
85. Chung, Yu-chen and Emerson Lim. "MOFA welcomes Lithuania's plan to set up trade office in Taiwan", Central New Agency, July 2, 2021. https://focustaiwan.tw/politics/202107020018.
86. Chung, Yu-chen, Lin Yu-li, Tang Pei-chun and Lee Hsin-Yin. "Taiwan thanks Slovakia for pledging COVID-19 vaccine donation", Focus Taiwan, July 16, 2021. https://focustaiwan.tw/politiocs/202107160008.
87. Crossley, Gabriel, Rozanna Latiff and Martin Petty. "Xi tells Southeast Asian leaders China does not seek 'hegemony'", Reuters, November 22, 2021. https://www.reuters.com/world/china/xi-says-china-will-never-seek-hegemony-summet-with-asean-2021-11-22/.
88. Dangwal, Sandhya. "ISRO SAARC satellite launch today: Here's how first South Asian satellite will benefit India's neighbours", India.com, May 5, 2017. https://www.india.com/business/isro-saarc-satellite-launch-today-heres-how-first-south-asian-satellite-will-benefit-indias-neighbours-2100691/.
89. Davidson, Helen. "India accuses China of 'militarisation of the Taiwan Strait' as row over navy vessel grows", The Guardian, August 29, 2022. https://www.theguardian.com/world/2022/aug/29/india-accuses-china-of-militarisation-of-the-taiwan-strait-as-row-over-navy-vessel-grows.

90. D'Cruze, Danny. "Tata Electronics finalises 100% stake in Wistron India to become first Indian company to make Apple iPhones", Business Today, November 9, 2023. https://www.businesstoday.in/technology/news/story/tata-electronics-finalises-100-stake-in-wistron-india-to-become-first-indian-company-to-make-apple-iphones-405176-2023-11-09.
91. Doval, Pankaj. "Foxconn chairman Liu meets PM Modi; looks at semiconductor manufacturing with Vedanta", Times of India, June 23, 2022. https://timesofindia.indiatimes.com/business/india-business/foxconn-chairman-liu-meets-pm-modi-looks-at-semiconductor-manufacturing-with-vedanta/articleshow/92419714.cms.
92. Dutta, Amrita Nayak. "With P8I aircraft, Navy takes part in Quad anti-submarine warfare exercise in Guam", The Print, January 22, 2021. https://theprint.in/defence/navy-takes-part-in-quad-anti-submarine-warfare-exercise-with-p8i-aircraft/590430/.
93. Dutta, Prabhash K. "How China captured Aksai Chin", India Today, June 22, 2020. https://www.indiatoday.in/india/story/how-china-captured-aksai-chin-1691562-2020-06-22.
94. Echols, William. "Whitewash: China Calls Invasion of Tibet 'Peaceful Liberation'", Poligraph.Info, May 25, 2021. https://www.polygraph.info/a/fact-check-china-tibet-1951-liberation/31273424.html.
95. Everington, Keoni. "Indians in Taiwan celebrate 75 years of Indian independence", Taiwan News, August 16, 2021." https://www.taiwannews.com.tw/en/news/4270886.
96. Everington, Keoni. "Taiwan rated 2nd and freest in Asia by Freedom House, 7th in world", Taiwan News. March 1, 2024. https://taiwantoday.tw/news.php?unit=2&post=249388.
97. Everington, Keoni. "WHA votes in favor of Taiwan's participation in WHO", Taiwan News, April 21, 2021. https://www.taiwannews.com.tw/en/news/4182667.
98. Goel, Shrishti. "Taiwan train Accident Leaves Over 50 Dead; MEA Expresses Condolence to Kin of Victims", Republic, April 3, 2021. https://www.republicworld.com/india-news/general-news/taiwan-train-accident-leaves-over-50-dead-mea-expresses-condolence-to-kin-of-victims.html.
99. Ghosh, Rudroneel. "Chinese Learning: If Confucius Institutes are a problem, Taiwan Education Centres can fill the void", The Times of India, August 6, 2020. https://timesofindia.indiatimes.com/blogs/talkingturkey/chinese-learning-if-confucius-institutes-are-a-problem-taiwan-education-centres-in-india-can-fill-the-void/.
100. Gibson, Liam and Tridivesh Singh Maini. "How to 'de-hyphenate' Taiwan-India-China relations", Taiwan News, August 16, 2021. https://www.taiwannews.com.tw/en/news/4271069.
101. Gordon, Peter. "'The Long Game: How the Chinese Negotiate with India' by Vijay Gokhale", Asian Review of Books, July 12, 2021. https://asianreviewofbooks.com/content/the-long-game-how-the-chinese-negotiate-with-india-by-vijay-gokhale/.

102. Ghoshal, Devjyot and Anand Katakam. "China Steps up construction along disputed Bhutan border, satellite images show", Reuters, January 13, 2022. https://www.reuters.com/world/china/china-steps-up-construction-along-disputed-bhutan-border-satellite-images-show-2022-01-12/.
103. Guha, Seema. "India-Taiwan Business Cannot Be Built On An Anti-China Platform", Outlook, March 4, 2021. https://www.outlookindia.com/website/story/india-news-want-to-needle-china-woo-taiwan-say-experts/376117.
104. Gupta, Shishir. "Taiwan President follows PM Modi, wishes Dalai Lama on his 86th birthday", Hindustan Times, July 6, 2021. https://www.hindustantimes.com/india-news/taiwan-president-follows-pm-modi-wishes-dalai-lama-on-his-86th-birthday-101625588047651.html.
105. Han, Ting-ting, Joseph Yeh, Chiang Yi-ching and Lee Hsin-Yin. "2nd Taiwanese COVID-19 vaccine maker applies for EUA", Focus Taiwan, June 30, 2021. https://focustaiwan.tw/sci-tech/202106300021.
106. Han, Ting-ting and Joseph Yeh. "Taiwan vaccine maker applies to conduct Phase 3 clinical trials in Paraguay", Focus Taiwan, July 6, 2021. https://focustaiwan.tw/sci-tech/202107060024.
107. Haqqani, Husain and Aparna Pande. "India needs to find a sweet spot between ignoring and provoking China", The Print, July 11, 2021. https://theprint.in/india-needs-to-find-a-sweet-spot-between-ignoring-and-provoking-china/694077/.
108. Hariharan, Sindhu. "Tata Electronics and SASTRA University to foster talent in electronics design and manufacturing", The Times of India, June 29, 2021. https://timesofindia.indiatimes.com/home/education/news/tata-electronics-and-sastra-university-to-foster-talent-in-electronics-design-and-manufacturing/articleshow/83848516.cms.
109. Hashmi, Sana. "India-Taiwan Ties: A Case for Stronger Partnership", *Asie. Visions*, Ifri, No. 125, November 2021. https://www.ifri.org/sites/default/files/india-taiwan_ties_since_the-1920s_a_classic_case_of_friendliness_mutual_neglect_and_redefining_ties.pdf.
110. Hasija, Namrata. "India Quietly Enhances Ties With Taiwan – Analysis", South Asia Monitor, February 6, 2017. https://www.eurasiareview.com/06022017-india-quietly-enhances-ties-with-taiwan-analysis/.
111. Hayton, Bill. "Two Years On, South China Sea Ruling Remains a Battleground for the Rules-Based Order", The Royal Institute of International Affairs, July 11, 2018. https://www.chathamhouse.org/2018/07/two-years-south-china-sea-ruling-remains-battleground-rules-based-order.
112. Hille, Kathrin. "TSMC: how a Taiwanese chipmaker became a linchpin of the global economy", Financial Times, March 24, 2021. https://www.ft.com/content/05206915-fd73-4a3a-92a5-6760ce965bd9.

113. Hiranandani, Niranjan. "Advantage India", The Hindu, October 8, 2020. Accessed March 31, 2021. https://www.thehindubusinessline.com/opinion/advantage-india-during-covid-scenario/article32785099.ece.
114. Hsu, Stacy and Matthew Mazzetta. "Quad countries discuss 'peace and security' in Taiwan Strait", Focus Taiwan, August 13, 2021. https://focustaiwan.tw/politics/202108130005.
115. Hsu, Szu-chien. Remarks at CSIS on June 10, 2019. https://www.csis.org/analysis/dr-szu-chien-hsu-deputy-minister-foreign-affairs-republic-china-taiwan-remarks.
116. Hui, Mary. "Semiconductors helped make Taiwan Asia's top-performing economy in 2020", Yahoo News, February 3, 2021.
117. Irish, John. "France summons Chinese envoy over 'unacceptable' insults", Reuters, March 23, 2021. https://www.reuters.com/article/us-france-china-idUSKBN2BF1MU.
118. Jacob, Jayanth. "Air India's decision consistent with international norms, India's position on Taiwan: MEA", Hindustan Times, July 6, 2018. https://www.hindustantimes.com/india-news/air-india-s-decision-consistent-with-international-norms-india-s-position-on-taiwan-mea/story-x6jr4PV2zX5ded0S9WPdGO.html.
119. Jacob, Rahul. "Why India needs to look east at Taiwan", Mint, March 18, 2021. https://www.livemint.com/tehnology/tech-news/why-india-needs-to-look-east-at-taiwan-11615996534314.html.
120. Jie, Shan. "Mainland pays tribute to victims of train crash in Taiwan island; netizens, experts calling for accountability", Global Times, April 3, 2021. https://www.globaltimes.cn/page/202104/1220166.shtml.
121. Joshi, Manoj. "How Beijing's New Maritime Rules in the South China Sea Will Affect India and Others", Observer Research Foundation, September 6, 2021. https://www.orfonline/research/how/beijings-new-maritime-rules-in-the-south-china-sea-will-affect-india-and-others/.
122. Kannan, Saikiran. "Tokyo 2020: China's social media trolls take aim at Taiwan and Japan's Olympic athletes", India Today, August 5, 2021. https://www.indiatoday.in/sports/tokyo-olympics/story/tokyo-2020-china-s-social-media-trolls-take-aim-at-taiwan-and-japan-s-olympic-athletes-1837376-2021-08-05.
123. Kao, Evelyn. "Taiwan reports eight new COVID-19 cases, four deaths", Focus Taiwan, August 9, 2021. https://focustaiwan.tw/society/202108090008.
124. Kesavan, K. V. "India's 'Act East' policy and regional cooperation", Raisina Debate, Observer Research Foundation, February 14, 2020. https://www.orfonline.org/expert-speak/indias-act-east%20policy-and-regional-cooperation-61375/.
125. Khan, Danish. "India must ensure basic infra to woo chip makers: NXP", The Economic Times, May 27, 2021. https://economictimes.indiatimes.com/industry/cons-products/electronics/india-must-ensure-basic-infra-to-woo-chip-makers-nxp/articleshow/82984540.cms.

126. Kondapalli, Srikanth. "Xi's Tibet visit: Bad Signal for India?", Rediff.com, July 24, 2021. https://www.rediff.com/news/column/srikanth-kondapalli-is-xi-jinping-tibet-visit-bad-signal-for-india/20210724.htm.

127. Kondapalli, Srikanth. "Taiwan election results — good for India, bad for China", The Indian Express, January 16, 2024. https://indianexpress.com/article/opinion/columns/taiwan-election-results-good-india-bad-china-9111841/.

128. Krishnan, Ananth. "BJP MPs praise Taiwan as 'democratic country as President Tsai Ing-wen begins new term', The Hindu, May 20, 2020. https://www.thehindu.com/news/national/bjp-mps-praise-taiwan-as-democratic-country-as-president-tsai-ing-wen-begins-new-term/article31635242.ece.

129. Krishnan, Ananth. "The Hindu explains: What are Confucius Institutes and why are they under the scanner in India", August 9, 2020. https://www.thehindu.com/news/national/the-hindu-explains-what-are-confucius-institutes-and-why-are-they-under-the-scanner-in-india/article32306693.ece.

130. Krishnan, Ananth. "Xi Jinping visits Tibet border region, first by Chinese leader in years", The Hindu, July 23, 2021. https://www.thehindu.com/news/international/xi-jinping-visits-tibet-border-region-first-by-chinese-leader-in-years/article35481755.ece.

131. Krishnankutty, Pia. "India should presume that China negotiates to deceive, says former foreign secretary Vijay Gokhale", The Print, July 19, 2021.. https://theprint.in/india/india-should-presume-that-china-negotiates-to-deceive-says-former-foreign-secretary-vijay-gokhale/698750/.

132. Laskar, Rezaul H. "India, Taiwan start talks on free trade agreement", Hindustan Times, December 16, 2021. https://www.hindustantimes.com/world-news/india-taiwan-start-talks-on-free-trade-agreement-101639673988033.

133. Laskar, Rezaul H. and Sutirtho Patranobis. "India, China diplomats discuss Ladakh faceoff, 16th round of military talks next", Hindustan Times, May 31, 2022,. https://www.hindustantimes.com/india-news/india-china-diplomats-discuss-ladakh-faceoff-16th-round-military-talks-next-101654011609131.html.

134. Lee, James. "Supply chains critical to Taiwan's security", *East Asia Forum*, March 10, 2021. https://www.eastasiaforum.org/2021/03/10/geoeconomics-and-the-security-of-taiwan/.

135. Li,Yu-li, Chung Yu-chen and Elizabeth Hsu. "Czech Republic pledges vaccines to Taiwan", Focus Taiwan, July 27, 2021. https://focustaiwan.tw/politics/202107270008.

136. Lim, Emerson, Pan Tzu-yu and James Lo. "Satellite of love: Taiwan-developed INSPIREsat-1 enters orbit", Focus Taiwan, February 14, 2022. https://focustaiwan.tw/sci-tech/202202140022.

137. Lin, Sing-chien. "Grand opening of Taiwan Expo India 2021 to strengthen industrial linkage in COVID-19 pandemic", Central News Agency, October 27, 2021. https://www.cna.com.tw/news/afe/202110270176.aspx. (In Chinese)

138. Lin, Tin-Hui. "Taiwan's Policy Evolution after the South China Sea Arbitration", The National Bureau of Asian Research, March 22, 2018. https://www.nbr.org/publication/taiwan-policy-evolution-after-the-south-china-sea-arbitration/.
139. Lin, Yu-li and Frances Huang. "Dresden ready to take on TSMC's water, power, housing needs: Mayor", Focus Taiwan, October 29, 2023. https://focustaiwan.tw/business/202310290007.
140. Lu, Kuo-chen. "Taiwan's Tesla Boom, and Looking for More", Commonwealth, August 27, 2020. https://english.cw.com.tw/article/article.action?id=2787.
141. Lum, Thomas and Hannah Fisher. "Confucius Institutes in the United States: Selected Issues", Congressional Research Service, May 20, 2022. https://crsreports.congress.gov/proiduct/pdf/lF/lF11180.
142. Martin, Eric and Debby Wu, "U.S. and India plan to boost chips collaboration, Biden's commerce chief says", The Japan times, March 10, 2023. https://japantimes.co.jp/news/2023/03/10/world/us-india-chip-collaboration.
143. Miglani, Sanjeev. "China tells Indian media not to call Taiwan a country, Taiwan says 'get lost'", Reuters, October 8, 2020. https://www.reuters.com/article/india-china-taiwan-idUSKBN26T1LE.
144. Myers, Steven Lee. "China's Aggressive Diplomacy Weakens Xi Jinping's Global Standing", New York Times, April 17, 2020. https://www.nytimes.com/2020/04/17/world/asia/coronavirus-china-xi-jinping.html.
145. Nakamura, Yu. "TSMC to invest $2.8 bn in China to ramp up auto chip production", Nikkei Asia, April 26, 2021. https://asia.nikkei.com/Business/Tech/Semiconductors/TSMC-to-invest-2.8bn-in-China-to-ramp-up-auto-chip-production.
146. Narayanan, Sripathi. "5th BIMSTEC Summit", Indian Council of World Affairs, April 22, 2022. https://icwa.in/show_content.php?lang=1&level=3&ls_id=7277&lid=4914.
147. Negi, Nanjeet. "India pushes for resolution in eastern Ladakh in 15th round talks with China", India Today, March 12, 2022. https://www.indiatoday.in/india/story/india-pushes-resolution-friction-points-china-15th-round-corps-commander-talks-1924473-2022-03-12.
148. Nguyen, Thanh Trung and Le Ngoc Khanh Ngan. "Cidifying Waters and Reshaping Orders: China's Strategy for Dominating the South China Sea", Center for Strategic and International Studies, September 27, 2021. https://amti.csis.org/codifying-waters-and-reshaping-orders-chinas-strategy-for-dominating-the-south-china-sea/.
149. Ni, Vincent. "Liz Truss summons Chinese ambassador over aggression towards Taiwan", The Guardian, August 10, 2022. https://www.theguardian.com/politics/2022/aug/10/liz-truss-summons-chinese-ambassador-over-aggression-towards-Taiwan.

150. Niraj, Shruti. "AICTE and Taiwan join hands to push academic collaboration between the two countries", The Times of India, April 30, 2019. Accessed on March 25, 2021. https://timesofindia.indiatimes.com/home/education/news/aicte-and-taiwan-join-hands-to-push-academic-collaboration-between-the-two-countries/articleshow/69114396.cms.

151. Owen, Glen. "Chinese teachers in British classrooms are to be replaced by recruits from Taiwan after Commons spy scandal", Daily Mail, September 16, 2023. https://www.dailymail.co.uk/news/article-12526631/Chinese-teachers-British-classrooms-replaced-recruits-Taiwan-Commons-spy-scandal.html.

152. Panag, H. S.. "LAC disengagement done. India, China can now return to old love-hate routine", The Print, March 18, 2021. https://theprint.in/opinion/lac-disengagement-done-india-china-can-now-return-to-old-love-hate-routine/623812/.

153. Pant, Harsh V. "The strategic signal of an Indian presence in the South China Sea", Observer Research Foundation, September 2, 2021. https://www.orfonbline.org/research/strategic-signal-indian-presence-south-china-sea/.

154. Pant, Harsh V. and Premesha Saha. "The Taiwan Question in Indian Foreign Policy", *Raisina Debates*, Observer Research Foundation, May 16, 2020. https://www.orfonline.org/expert-speak/taiwan-question-indian-foreign-policy-66249/.

155. Parashar, Sachin. "One-China? No need to reiterate our consistent policies, says India", The Times of India, August 13, 2022. https://timesofindia.indiatimes.com/india/one-china-no-need-to-reiterate-our-consistent-policies-says-india/articleshow/93530107.cms.

156. Patranobis, Sutirtho. "China in 70 years has not occupied an inch of foreign land: Beijing", Hindustan Times, September 1, 2020. https://www.hindustantimes.com/world-news/china-in-70-years-has-not-occupied-an-inch-of-foreign-land-beijing/story-eVxbF0U7ZL8GZPVZmqt9xI.html.

157. Peri, Dinakar. "Raisina Dialogue| ' Huge potential for India, NATO to collaborate,' says NATO Secretary General", The Hindu, April 14, 2021. https://www.thehindu.com/news/national/raisina-dialogue-huge-potential-for-india-nato-to-collaborate-says-nato-secretary-general/article34314397.ece.

158. Phartiyal, Sankalp and Aditi Shah, "Exclusive: A billion for every chip-maker who 'makes in India,' sources say", Reuters, March 31, 2021. https://www.reuters.com/article/india-semiconductor/exclusive-a-billion-for-every-chip-maker-who-makes-in-india-sources-say-idUSKBN2BN12H.

159. Pillai, Soumya. "Three launches in Q1: ISRO's upcoming missions in 2024

160. "Hindustan Times, December 22, 2023. https://www.hindustantimes.com/india-news/three-launches-in-q1-isro-s-24-plan-101703183805729.html.

161. Purohit, Kunal. "France, India and Australia step up Quad-style cooperation, with China on the horizon", South China Morning Post, April 14, 2021. https://www.

scmp.com/week-asia/politics/article/3129564/france-india-and-australia-step-quad-style-cooperation-china.

162. Rao, Aprameya. "India, Taiwan natural partners: Envoy Tien", Deccan Chronicle, October 25, 2019. https://www.deccanchronicle.com/business/in-other-news/251019/india-taiwan-natural-partners-envoy-tien.html.
163. Rao, Arun. "India has the potential to be the next space hub of the world", The Economic Times, October 24, 2020. https://economictimes.indiatimes.com/small-biz/sme-sector/india-has-the-potential-to-be-the-next-space-hub-of-the-world/printarticle/78840533.cms.
164. Rawat, Manoj. "Quad 2.0 Is Off to a Good Start – It Must Keep Going", The Diplomat, November 23, 2020. https://thediplomat.com/2020/11/quad-2-0-is-off-to-a-good-start-it-must-keep-going/.
165. Rej, Abhijnan. "In 'Historic' Summit Quad Commits to Meeting Key Indo-Pacific Challenges", The Diplomat, March 13, 2021. https://thediplomat.com/2021/03/in-historic-summit-quad-commits-to-meeting-key-indo-pacific-challenges/.
166. Roy, Nabarun. "Why did Nehru want the People's Republic of China in the United Nations?", The Diplomat, April 7, 2018. https://thediplomat.com/2018/04/why-did-nehru-want-the-peoples-republic-of-china-in-the-united-nations/.
167. Saha, Premesha. "First Quad leaders meeting: An agenda beyond security", Observer Research Foundation, March 16, 2021. https://www.orfonline.org/expert-speak/first-quad-leaders-meeting-agenda-beyond-security/.
168. Sanyal, Shreyashi. "China slams the U.S. for interfering in Arunachal Pradesh border dispute with India", CNBC, March 22, 2024. https://www.cnbc.com/2024/03/21/us-rejects-chinas-claim-to-arunachal-pradesh-says-it-is-a-part-of-india.html.
169. Shepherd, Christian, Katherin Hille and Richard Milne. "China recalls ambassador to Lithuania over Taiwan office", Financial Times, August 10, 2021. https://www.ft.com/content/a8d2b571-0b8e-4c9c-858b-f1b56aec1af4.
170. Simhan, T. E. Raja. "China Steel Corp to invest $178 m in new plant in Gujarat", The Hindu, August 25, 2011. https://www.thehindubusinessline.com/companies/China-Steel-Corp-to-invest-178-m-in-new-plant-in-Gujarat/article20327566.ece.
171. Singh, Mayank. "Hindi-Chini bhai bhai is history, and a poor one at that", The Times of India, March 15, 2019. https://timesofindia.indiatimes.com/blogs/voices/hindi-chini-bhai-bhai-is-history-and-a-poor-at-that/.
172. Singh, Sushant. "India's China Policy Is Confused", Foreign Policy, June 14, 2022. https://foreignpolicy.com/2022/06/14/india-china-policy-ladakh-border-clash-quad-modi/.
173. Slodkowski, Antoni and Elaine Lies, "Dalai Lama: China's leaders 'don't understand variety of cultures'", Reuters, November 10, 2021. https://www.reuters.com/world/china/dalai-lama-says-prefers-india-since-taiwan-china-relations-delicate-2021-11-10/.

174. Su, Ssu-yun, Chang Ai and Frances Huang. "Taiwan's forex reserves hit new high at end of 2023", Focus Taiwan, January 6, 2024. https://focustaiwan.tw/business/202401060008.

175. Sud, Vedika, Barbara Starr, Sahar Akbarzai and Kathleen Magramo. "US to take part in military exercise near India's disputed border with China", CNN, August 6, 2022. https://edition.cnn.com/2022/08/06/india/india-us-military-exercise-line-of-actual-control-china-intl-hnk/index.html.

176. Suneja, Kirtika and Deepshjikha Sikarwar. "New FDI rules not for Taiwan inflows", The Economic Times, April 30, 2020. https://economictimes.indiatimes.com/news/economy/policy/new-fdi-rules-not-for-taiwan-inflows/articleshow/75479443.cms.

177. Tang, Pei-chun and Joseph Yeh. "European Parliament passes report on enhancing Taiwan-EU relations", Focus Taiwan, October 21, 2021. https://focustaiwan.tw/politics/202110210012.

178. Tang, Pei-chun and Teng Pei-ju. "As Lithuania faces China intimidation, EU leaders vow to push back", Focus Taiwan, October 29, 2021. https://focustaiwan.tw/politics/202110290008.

179. Tang, Pei-chun and Teng Pei-ju. "Dutch parliament passes motion backing Taiwan's participation in Interpol", Focus Taiwan, November 24, 2021. http://focustaiwan.tw/politics/202111240006.

180. Tankersley, Jim and Ana Swanson. "Amid Shortfalls, Biden Signs Executive Order to Bolster Critical Supply Chains", New York Times, February 24, 2021. https://www.nytimes.com/2021/02/24/business/biden-supply-chain-executive-order.html.

181. Textor, C. "GDP growth rate in Taiwan 2010-2021", Statista, February 22, 2021. https://www.statista.com/statistics/328535/gross-domestic-product-gdp-annual-growth-rate-in-taiwan/.

182. Thompson, Amy. "SpaceX launches a record 143 satellites on one rocket, aces landing", Space.com, January 24, 2021. https://www.space.com/spacex-launches-143-satellites-transporter-1-rocket-landing.

183. Tiezzi, Shannon. "How Are Taiwan's Diplomatic Allies Faring in the Great Vaccine Race?", The Diplomat, July 9, 2021. https://thediplomat.com/2021/07/how-are-taiwans-diplomatic-allies-faring-in-the-great-vaccine-race/.

184. Tiezzi, Shannon. "Taiwan – Sorry, 'Chinese Taipei' – Is Having a Fantastic Olympics", The Diplomat, August 5, 2021. https://thediplomat.com/2021/08/taiwan-sorry-chinese-taipei-is-having-a-fantastic-olympics/.

185. Tiwary, Deeptiman. "India, China troops begin disengagement from Gogra-Hotsprings in Ladakh", The Indian Express, September 9, 2022. https://indianexpress.com/article/india/india-china-troops-disengagement-ladakh-8139126/.

186. Wen, Kuei-hsiang. "The President wishes the Dalai Lama on his 86th birthday, thanking him for sharing wisdom of facing the pandemic" (In Chinese), Central

News Agency, July 6, 2021. https://www.cna.com.tw/news/aipl/202107060175.aspx.

187. Westcott, Ben and Steven Jiang. "China is embracing a new brand of foreign policy. Here is what wolf warrior diplomacy means", CNN, May 29, 2020. https://edition.cnn.com/2020/05/28/asia/china-wolf-warrior-diplomacy-intl-hnk/index.html.
188. Wu, Chia-jung and Elizabeth Hsu. "Taiwan records historical high in exports in 2020", Focus Taiwan, January 8, 2021. https://focustaiwan.tw/business/202101080019
189. Wu, Chia-jung and Frances Huang. "Taiwan becomes world's No. 15 largest exporter", Focus Taiwan, April 3, 2021. https://focustaiwan.tw/business/202104030010
190. Wu, Chia-jung, Pan Tzu-yu and Frances Huang. "American development bank opens first office in Asia in Taiwan", Focus Taiwan, July 6, 2021. https://focustaiwan.tw/business/202107060011.
191. Wu, Jui-chi, Yu Kai-hsiang, Sophia Yeh and James Lo. "Slovakia-donated COVID-19 vaccines arrive in Taiwan", Focus Taiwan, September 26, 2021. https://focustaiwan.tw/society/202109260003.
192. Wu, Ming-yen. "The Speech delivered by Madame Chiang Soong Mei-ling to the US House of Representatives in 1943", National Policy Foundation, June 30, 2008. https://www.npf.org.tw/2/4398.
193. Yeh, Joseph. "Europe is standing with Taiwan in defending freedom: EP delegation", Focus Taiwan, November 4, 2021. https://focustaiwan.tw/politics/202111040006.
194. Yeh, Joseph. "Lithuania looks to open trade office in Taiwan in September", Focus Taiwan, June 15, 2022. https://focustaiwan.tw/politics/202206150023.
195. Yu, Matt and Emerson Lim. "Peace in Taiwan Strait a global concern: Taiwan's foreign minister", Focus Taiwan, July 19, 2021. https://focustaiwan.tw/politics/202107190025.

Articles without Author

196. "2023 IMD World Digital Competitiveness: Taiwan Has Advanced to the 9th Position Globally, With the Leading Position in Five Key Indicators Worldwide", Ministry of Digital Affairs, Republic of China (Taiwan). https://moda.gov.tw/en/press/press-releases/9089.
197. "5th BIMSTEC Summit", Ministry of External Affairs, Government of India, March 30, 2022. https://www.mea.gov.in/press-releases.htm?dtl/35093/5th+BIMSTEC+Summit.
198. "99% Indian-made mobile phones in country today, says Union minister Ashwini Vaishnaw", Hindustan Times, Nov. 27, 2023. https://www.hindustantimes.com/technology/99-indian-made-mobile-phones-in-country-today-says-union-minister-ashwini-vaishnaw-101701102725789.html.
199. "About TSMC Arizona", TSMC Arizona. https://www.tsmc.com/static/abouttsmcaz/index.htm.

200. "About WHO in the South-East Asia Region", The World Health Organization. https://www.who.int/southeastasia/about.
201. "Act East", Reconnecting Asia, CSIS. https://reconnectingasia.csis.org/database/initiatives/act-east/b17b6a1c-5c17-40f0-a2ec-c6a8ce802ab9/.
202. "Agreement On The Maintenance Of Peace Along The Line Of Actual Control In The India-China Border", The Stimson Center. September 7, 1993. https://web.archive.org/web/20150924110627/http://www.stimson.org/research-pages/agreement-on-the-maintenance-of-peace-along-the-line-of-actual-control-in-the-india-china-border/.
203. "An Indian doctor in China", Mumbai Mirror, March 6, 2020. https://mumbaimirror.indiatimes.com/opinion/city-columns/an-indian-doctor-in-china/articleshow/74502883.cms.
204. "ASEAN-India Foreign Ministers' Meeting and other related meetings", Ministry of External Affairs, Government of India, August 5, 2022. https://www.,mea.gov.in/press-releases.htm?dtl/35631/ASEANIndia_foreign_Ministers_Meeting_and_other_meetings.
205. "Asia University and Yuan Ze University assist nurturing India's semiconductor talent", Central News Agency, August 19, 2021. https://www.cna.com.tw/news.ait/202108190246.aspx. (In Chinese)
206. "Atmanirbhar Bharat Abhiyaan", Invest India, Ministry of Commerce and Industry, Government of India. https://cdnbbsr.s3waas.gov.in/s3850af92f8d9903e7a0559a98ecc857/uploads/2020/05/2020051717.pdf.
207. "Atmanirbhar Bharat is our path as well as our resolve: PM Modi", ANI, May 6, 2022. https://www.aninews.in/news/national/general-news/aatmnkrbhar-bharat-is-our-path-as-well-as-our-resolve-pm-modi20220506135926/.
208. "B. Singapore 3294, Public Library of US Diplomacy", WikiLeaks. Accessed April 11, 2020. https://wikileaks.org/plusd/cables/04TAIPEI3845_a.html.
209. "Brazilian Minister visited ISRO to witness the launch of Amazonia-1 satellite", ISRO, February 28, 2021. https://www.isro.gov.in/update/28-feb-2021/brazilian-minister-visited-isro-to-witness-launch-of-amazonia-1-satellite.
210. "Cabinet okays India-Taiwan investment pact", Business Standard, October 24, 2018. https://www.business-standard.com/article/news-ians/cabinet-okays-india-taiwan-investment-pact-118102400924_1.html.
211. "Carbis Bay G7 Summit Communiqué: Our Shared Agenda for global Action to Build Back Better", Foreign, Commonwealth and Development Office, the United Kingdom, June 12, 2021. https://www.consilium.europa.eu/media/50361/carbis-bay-g7-summit-communique.pdf.
212. "China Claims India-US Exercise Would Violate Border Pacts, India Disagrees", The Wire, August 25, 2022. https://thewire.in/diplomacy/china-claims-india-us-exercise-would-violate-border-pacts-india-disagrees.

213. "China says Arunachal Pradesh 'inherent part' of its territories", Business Standard, December 31, 2021. https://www.business-standard.com/article/international/china-says-arunachal-pradesh-inherent-part-of-its-territory-121123100627_1.html.
214. "Confucius Institute U.S. Center' Designation as a Foreign Mission", Office of the Spokesperson, U.S. Department of State, August 13, 2020. https://2017-2021.state.gov/confucius-institute-u-s-center-designation-as-a-foreign-mission/index.html
215. "Constitution of the Republic of China (Taiwan)", Ministry of Justice. January 1, 1947. https://law.moj.gov.tw/ENG/LawClass/LawAll.aspx?pcode=A0000001.
216. "COVAXIN – India's First Indigenous COVID-19 Vaccine", Bharat Biotech. https://www.bharatbiotech.com/covaxin.html.
217. "Cutting Ties with Confucius Institutes", In the Name of Confucius, https://inthenameofconfuciusmovie.com/cutting-ties-with-confucius-institutes/.
218. "Dalai Lama is welcome to visit Taiwan", The Hindu, July 6, 2021.
219. https://www.thehindu.com/news/international/dalai-lama-is-welcome-to-visit-taiwan/article32006648.ece.
220. "Digital Competitiveness Ranking, Taiwan, China, 2020", IMD. https://worldcompetitiveness.imd.org/countryprofile/TW/digital.
221. "(Digitimes) iST takes early action to target non-terrestrial communication technologies beyond 5G to open a pathway to space communication for the Taiwan Industry", Integrated Service Technology, September 23, 2020.
222. https://www.istgroup.com/en/media_20200923/.
223. "Diplomatic Allies", Ministry of Foreign Affairs, Republic of China (Taiwan). https://www.mofa.gov.tw/AlliesIndex.aspx?n=167&sms=33. (In Chinese)
224. "Diplomatic breakthrough: Taiwan was invited by the US, Japan, India and Australia for security dialogue", The Liberty Times, March 12, 2018. https://news.ltn.com.tw/news/focus/paper/1183169. (In Chinese)
225. "Documentary highlights Swami Vivekananda's less known visit to China", The Hindu, September 22, 2020. https://www.thehindubusinessline.com/news/variety/documentary-highlights-swami-vivekanandas-less-known-visit-to-china/article32667578.ece.
226. "Dr. K. Sivan, Chairman, ISRO/Secretary, DOS had a meeting with the new Head of Australian Space Agency and signed an amendment to the existing India – Australia MoU for space cooperation", ISRO, February 17, 2021. https://www.isro.gov.in/update/17-feb-2021/dr-k-sivan-chairman-isro-secretary-dos-had-meeting-with-new-head-of-australian.
227. "Dr. K. Sivan, Chairman, ISRO/Secretary, DOS had a meeting with the President of Japan Aerospace Exploration Agency", ISRO, March 11, 2021. https://www.isro.gov.in/update/11-mar-2021/dr-k-sivan-chairman-isro-secretary-dos-had-meeting-with-president-of-japan.

228. "Electronic Systems", Taiwan Plus, Invest India, Ministry of Commerce and Industry, Government of India. https://www.investindia.gov.in/country/taiwan-plus.
229. "Economic Survey 2018: 5 states show the way with 70% of exports, enjoy higher standard of living", The Indian Express, January 30, 2018. Accessed on March 30, 2021. https://indianexpress.com/article/business/economy/economic-survey-five-states-show-the-way-with-70-of-exports-enjoy-higher-standard-of-living-union-budget-5044319/.
230. "Election results 2019: Xi Jinping, Putin, Netanyahu congratulate Narendra Modi", The Hindu, May 23, 2019. https://www.thehindu.com/elections/lok-sabha-2019/election-results-2019-reactions-foreign-international-leaders-narendra-modi-bjp/article27218189.ece.
231. "English rendering of PM's remarks at the East Asia Summit, Nay Pyi Taw", PMINDIA, Government of India, November 13, 2014. https://www.pmindia.gov.in/en/news_updates/english-rendering-of-pms-remarks-at-the-east-asia-summit-nay-pyi-taw/.
232. "European Parliament resolution of 9 March 2022 on foreign interference in all democratic processes in the European Union, including disinformation (2020/2268(INI))", European Parliament, March 9, 2022. https://www.europarl.europa.eu/doceo/document/TA-9-2022-0064_EN.html.
233. "Exchange of views between Generalissimo Chiang Kai-shek and President Roosevelt regarding situation in India", Foreign Relations of the United States: Diplomatic Papers, 1942, China. https://history.state.gov/historicaldocuments/frus1942China/comp17.
234. "Exercise MALABAR 2020 Concludes in Arabian Sea", Indian Navy. https://www.indiannavy.nic.in/content/exercise-malabar-2020-concludes-arabian-sea.
235. "Explained: The offer that Zhou made, and Nehru rejected…the lessons from it", The Indian Express, June 19, 2020. https://indianexpress.com/article/explained/india-china-border-dispute-jawaharlal-nehru-zhou-enlai-6466231/.
236. "Explained: What is 'Viksit Bharat 2047' and what does it aim to achieve?", Deccan Herald, March 4, 2024. https://www.deccanherald.com/india/explained-what-is-viksit-bharat-2047-and-what-does-it-aim-to-achieve-2920441.
237. "Eye on China, Jaishankar says Quad will benefit Indo-Pacific", The Indian Express, August 19,2022. https://indianexpress.com/article/india/eye-on-china-jaishankar-says-quad-will-benefit-indo-pacific-8098617/.
238. "Foreign Exchange Reserves as of the End of February 2021", Central Bank of the Republic of China (Taiwan), March 5, 2021. https://www.cbc.gov.tw/en/cp-448-132390-947a7-2.html.
239. "Foreign Minister Wu gives interviews to India's media", Taiwan Today, August 25, 2022. https://taiwantoday.tw/news.php?unit=2,6,10,15,18&post=224105.

240. "Foreign missions issue joint statement supporting Taiwan's WHA bid", Focus Taiwan, May 21, 2022. https://focustaiwan.tw/politics/202205210008.
241. "Foxconn submits application for setting up semiconductor unit: MoSIT", Press Trust India, December 20, 2023. https://www.ptinews.com/home-detail/Foxconn-submits-application-for-setting-up-semiconductor-unit--MoS-IT/302314.
242. "Freedom In The World 2022", Freedom House. https://freedomhouse.org/ciuntry/taiwan/freedom-world/2022.
243. "Freedom In The World 2023", Freedom House. https://freedomhouse.org/country/taiwan/freedom-world/2023.
244. "Freedom in the World 2024", Freedom House. https://freedomhouse.org/country/taiwan/freedom-world/2024.
245. "Full text of Xi Jinping's speech on the CCP's 100th anniversary", Nikkei Asia, July 1, 2021. https://asia.nikkei.com/Politics/Full-text-of-Xi-Jinping-s-speech-on-the-CCP-s-100th-anniversary.
246. "Full Text: Tibet Since 1951: Liberation, Development and Prosperity", Xinhuanet, May 21, 2021. http://www.xinhuanet.com/english/2021-05/21/c_139959978.htm.
247. "GCTF Conference on Ending Gender-based Violence in Taipei", New Southbound Policy Portal, May 24, 2022. https://nspp.mofa.gov.tw/nsppe/news.php?unit=370&post=219635.
248. "GCTF hosts workshop on Empowering Women in the Post-Pandemic Era in St. Lucia", Ministry of Foreign Affairs, the Republic of China (Taiwan). https: www.mofa.gov.tw/News_Content.aspx?n=95&sms=73&s=98450. (In Chinese)
249. "Global Conclave Promises Closer Collaboration in Healthcare", Voice of Healthcare, February 25, 2022. https://voiceofhealthcare.org/pressrelease.php?id=127.
250. "Global Cooperation and Training Framework (GCTF) Programs", American Institute in Taiwan. https://www.ait.org.tw/our-relationship/global-cooperation-and-training-framework-programs-gctf/.
251. "Global Cooperation & Training Framework", Ministry of Foreign Affairs, the Republic of China (Taiwan). https://www.gctf.tw/en/#.
252. "GSLV Successfully Launches South Asia Satellite", Indian Space Research Organisation, May 5, 2017. https://www.isro.gov.in/update/05-may-2017/gslv-successfully-launches-south-asia-satellite.
253. "G7 Foreign and Development Ministers' Meeting Communiqué", Foreign, Commonwealth and Development Office, the United Kingdom, May 5, 2021. https://assets.publishing.service.gov.uk/government/uploads/system/uploads/attachment_data/file/983631/G7-foreign-and-development-ministers-meeting-communique-london-5-may-2021.pdf.
254. "G7 United Kingdom 2021 Chair's Statement", Foreign, Commonwealth and Development Office, the United Kingdom, December 12, 2021. https://assets.publishing.service.gov.uk/government/uploads/system/uploads/attachment_

data/file/1040131/G7_Foreign_and_Development_Ministers_Meeting_December_2021_-_Chair_s_Statement.pdf.

255. "Helsinki University closes China-funded Confucius Institute", Yle News, June 18, 2022. https://yle.fi/news/3-12500430.
256. "Henley Passport Index: Q1 2021 Global Ranking". January 5, 2021. https://www.henleypassportindex.com/assets/2021/Q1/HENLEY_PASSPORT_INDEX_2021_Q1_INFOGRAPHIC_GLOBAL_RANKING_201209_1.pdf.
257. "Henley Passport Index: Q1 2022 Global Ranking". January 11, 2022. https://cdn.henleyglobal.com/storage/app/media/HPI/HENLEY_PASSPORT_INDEX_2022_Q1_INFOGRAPHIC_GLOBAL_RANKING_211221_1.pdf.
258. "How Much Trade Transits the South China Sea?", ChinaPower, CSIS. Accessed on April 22, 2021. https://chinapower.csis.org/much-trade-transits-south-china-sea/.
259. "IISS Shangri-La Dialogue", The International Institute for Strategic Studies. https://www.iiss.org/events/shangri-la-dialogue/shangri-la-dialogue-2021.
260. "Inaugural address of ROC 15th-term President Tsai Ing-wen", Office of the President, Republic of China (Taiwan), May 20, 2020. https://english.president.gov.tw/News/6004.
261. "India-China Bilateral Relations", Ministry of External Affairs, Government of India. https://mea.gov.in/Portal/ForeignRelation/china_brief_sep_2019.pdf.
262. "India donates funds to Taiwan to boost cooperation on traditional medicine", ANI, February, 27, 2021. https://www.aninews.in/news/world/asia/india-donates-funds-to-taiwan-to-boost-cooperation-on-traditional-medicine20210227230435/.
263. "India facilitates, promotes interactions with Taiwan: MEA on Taipei Economic and Cultural Centre in Mumbai", ANI, July 6, 2023. https://theprint.in/world/india-facilitates-promotes-interactions-with-taiwan-mea-on-taipei-economic-and-cultural-centre-in-mumbai/1657791/.
264. "India's GDP growth estimated to be in range of 7.5-12.5%: World Bank", The Hindu. March 31, 2021. https://www.thehindubusinessline.com/news/national/india-gdp-growth-estimated-to-be-in-range-of-725-125-says-world-bank/article34203804.ece.
265. "India's 24th Taiwan Education Centre – TEC comes up in Bengaluru", Asian Community News, December 28, 2021. https://www.asianommunitynews.com/indias-24th-taiwan-education-centre-tec-comes-up-in-bengaluru/.
266. "Indo-Pacific Construct Reflects Overcoming Of Cold War: S Jaishankar", NDTV, April 14, 2021. https://www.ndtv.com/india-news/quad-reflects-contemporary-world-overcoming-of-cold-war-external-affairs-minister-s-jaishankar-at-raisina-dialogue-2413735.
267. "India reiterates its stand, says South China Sea a part of global commons", The Business Standard, July 16, 2020. https://www.business-standard.com/article/

current-affairs/india-reiterates-its-stand-says-south-china-sea-a-part-of-global-commons-120071601917_1.html.

268. "India to unveil $1.35 trillion infrastructure plan, PM Modi says", Daily Sabah, August 15, 2021. https://www.dailysabah.com/business/economy/india-to-unveil-135-trillion-infrastructure-plan-pm-modi-says.
269. "International Cooperation", Department of Space, Indian Space Research Organisation. https://www.irro.gov.in/intertnational-cooperation.
270. "Introduction", Hanban, August 9, 2020. http://english.hanban.org/node_7880.htm.
271. "Joint Press Release of the 16th Round of India-China Corps Commander Level Meeting", Ministry of External Affairs, Government of India, July 18, 2022. https://www.mea.gov.in/press-releases.htm?dtl/35496/Joint+Press+Release+of+the+16th+Round+of+IndiaChina+Corps+Commander+Level+Meeting.
272. "Kelsang Gyaltsen Bawa takes charge as new Representative of Office of Tibet, Taiwan", Central Tibetan Administration, April 22, 2021. https://tibet.net/kelsang-gyaltsen-bawa-takes-charge-as-new-representative-of-office-of-tibet-taiwan/.
273. "Ladakh standoff: India, China 14th round of military talks lasted for 13 hours", Livemint, January 13, 2022. https://www.livemint.com/news/india/ladakh-standoff-india-china-14th-round-of-military-talks-lasted-for-13-hours-11642041819914.html.
274. "Largest countries in the World 2021", World Population Review. Accessed on July 7, 2021. https://worldpopulationreview.com/country-rankings/largest-countries-in-the-world.
275. "LEO satellites offer opportunities", Taipei Times, May 31, 2022. https://www.taipeitimes.com/News/biz/archives/2022/05/31/2003779036.
276. "List of countries by foreign-exchange reserves", Wikipedia. https://en.wikipedia.org/wiki/List_of_countries_by_foreign-exchange_reserves.
277. "Mainland Policy and Work, 2002", Mainland Affairs Council, Republic of China (Taiwan). September 2, 2002. https://www.mac.gov.tw/en/News_Content.aspx?n=0D58AA484DB9A9B1&sms=35503662D9CE6DD9&s=5F761BAF31A2E3F4.
278. "Malabar exercise phase-II to kick off next week in Bay of Bengal", The Economic Times, October 10, 2021. https://economictimes.indiatimes.com/news/defence/malabar-exercise-phase-ii-to-kick-off-next-week-in-bay-of-bengal/articleshow/86907026.cms.
279. "Modi's supply chain mantra: trusted source, transparency and time frame", IANS, November 1, 2021, https://www.business-standard.com/article/current-affairs/modi's-mantra-at-supply-chain-summit-trusted-source-transparency-time-frame-121110100086_1.html.
280. "MOFA expresses appreciation to over 600 dignitaries and friends from 80 countries and International Organizations who have extended condolences and sympathies

to the Taiwan Rail accident", Press Release No. 048, Ministry of Foreign Affairs, Republic of China (Taiwan), April 3, 2021. https://www.mofa.gov.tw/News_Content.aspx?n=95&sms=73&s=95618.

281. "MOFA expresses appreciation to 780 dignitaries and friends from 94 countries and International Organizations who have extended condolences and sympathies to the Taiwan Rail accident", Press Release No. 052, Ministry of Foreign Affairs, Republic of China (Taiwan), April 5, 2021. https://www.mofa.gov.tw/News_Content.aspx?n=95&sms=73&s=95624.

282. "MOFA expresses appreciation to 846 dignitaries and friends from 97 countries and International Organizations who have extended condolences and sympathies to the Taiwan Rail accident", Press Release No. 055, Ministry of Foreign Affairs, Republic of China (Taiwan), April 6, 2021.

283. "MoU signing between Taipei Economic and Cultural Center in India and Amity University Haryana", Amity University, February 26, 2021. https://www.amity.edu/gurugram/events/10948/mou-signing-between-taipei-economic-and-cultural-centre-in-india-and-amity-university-haryana.

284. "Not yet time to conduct official FTA talks with India: MOEA", Focus Taiwan, March 8, 2011. https://focustaiwan.tw/business/201103080023.

285. "'Part of diplomatic business': US on China's objection to Modi-Lai exchange on Indian polls", Deccan Herald, June 7, 2024.

286. https://www.deccanherald.com/world/part-of-diplomatic-business-us-on-chinas-objection-to-modi-lai-exchange-on-indian-polls-3056304.

287. "Participating Countries", Global Cooperation & Training Framework, Ministry of Foreign Affairs, the Republic of China (Taiwan). https://www.gctf.tw/en/Countries.htm.

288. "Peace in the South China Sea, National Territory Secure Forever: Position Paper on ROC South China Sea Policy", Ministry of Foreign Affairs, ROC Taiwan, 2016. https://en.mofa.gov.tw/Upload/WebArchive/1989/Position%20Paper%20on%20ROC%20South%20China%20Sea%20Policy%20(illustrated%20pamphlet%20PDF).pdf.

289. "PM Modi's Independence Day speech: Key points", The Times of India, August 15, 2022. https://timesofindia.indiatimes.com/india/pm-modis-independence-day-speech-key-points/articleshow/93564760.cms.

290. "PM Modi pushes for self-reliant India with 'Make for World' call," The Times of India, August 16, 2020. Accessed on March 30, 2021. https://timesofindia.indiatimes.com/india/pm-modi-pushes-for-self-reliant-india-with-make-for-world-call/articleshow/77568558.cms.

291. "PM Modi shares 5 pillars that will make India self-reliant in Covid-19 times", India Today, May 12, 2020. https://www.indiatoday.in/india/story/pm-modi-speech-5-pillars-atm-nirbhar-self-reliance-covid-19-lockdown-1677293-2020-05-12.

292. "PM participates in 'India's Techade: Chips for Viksit Bharat' program", Narendra Modi, March 13, 2024. https://www.narendramodi.in/prime-minister-narendra-modi-participates-in-%E2%80%98india-s-techade-chips-for-viksit-bharat--580486.
293. "President Biden Signs Executive Order to Implement the CHIPS and Science Act of 2022", The White House, August 25, 2022. https://www.whitehouse.gov/briefing-room/statements-releases/2022/08/25/fact-sheet-president-biden-signs-executive-order-to-implement-the-chips-and-science-act-of-2022/.
294. "Press release on Taiwan's International Investment Position (2019)", Central Bank of the Republic of China (Taiwan), June 15, 2020. https://www.cbc.gov.tw/en/cp-448-113959-289ff-2.html.
295. "Prime Minister's Keynote Address at Shangri La Dialogue (June 01, 2018)", Ministry of External Affairs, Government of India, June 1, 2018. https://www.mea.gov.in/Speeches-Statements.htm?dtl/29943/Prime+Ministers+Keynote+Address+at+Shangri+La+Dialogue+June+01+2018.
296. "Public Library of US Policy", WikiLeaks. Accessed April 11, 2020. https://wikileaks.org/plusd/cables/04TAIPEI3845_a.html.
297. "Quad", Ministry of External Affairs, Republic of India. Accessed on December 30, 2023. https://www.mea.gov.in/Portal/ForeignRelation/Quad_brief_October_2023.pdf.
298. "Quad Leaders' Joint Statement: 'The Spirit of the Quad'", White House, USA. March 12, 2021. https://www.whitehouse.gov/briefing-room/statements-release/2021/03/12/quad-leaders-joint-statement-the spirit-of-the-quad/.
299. "Raisina Dialogue 2021 to be held digitally due to COVID-19", The Economic Times, April 5, 2021. https://economictimes.indiatimes.com/news/india/raisina-dialogue-2021-to-be-held-digitally-due-to-covid-19/articleshow/81909937.cms.
300. "Rally held in Taipei to commemorate Tibet National Uprising Day", Focus Taiwan. March 7, 2021. https://focustaiwan.tw/politics/202103070009.
301. "Recent Investment", Taiwan Plus, Invest India. https://www.investindia.gov.in/country/taiwan-plus.
302. "Remarks by Minister Jaushieh Joseph Wu at a reception to celebrate India's 75th Republic Day", Ministry of Foreign Affairs, Republic of China (Taiwan), January 27, 2022. https://en.mofa.gov.tw/News_Content.aspx?n=1575&s=97308.
303. "Russia using ROC to participate in the Olympics misled UK's The Guardian to think it is Taiwan", Central News Agency, July 2, 2021. https://www.cna.com.tw/news/aspt/202107240252.aspx. (In Chinese)
304. "Second advance estimates of national income 2023-24", Ministry of Statistics, Government of India, February 29, 2024. https://pib.gov.in/PressReleasePage.aspx?PRID=2010223.

305. "Sino-India Relations Including Doklam, Border situation and Cooperation in International Organizations", Twenty Second Report to the Committee on External Affairs (2017-18)(Sixteenth Lok Sabha) by the Ministry of External Affairs, presented to Honourable Speaker on September 4, 2018.
306. http://164.100.47.193/lsscommittee/External%20Affairs/16_External_Affairs_22.pdf.
307. "Sino-Indian War", Wikipedia. https://en.wikipedia.org/wiki/Sino-Indian_War.
308. "South China Sea Issue", Ministry of Foreign Affairs, Republic of China (Taiwan). https://en.mofa.gov.tw/theme.aspx?n=1462&s=40&sms=294.
309. "SpaceX rocket carries two Taiwanese satellites into space", Focus Taiwan, January 24, 2021. https://focustaiwan.tw/sci-tech/202101240019.
310. "SpaceX Falcon Heavy launches, Taiwan-US Formosat-7/COSMIC-2 deployed", Taiwan Today, June 26, 2019. https://taiwantoday.tw/news.php?unit=2,6,10,15,18&post=157599.
311. "Speakers", Observer Research Foundation. https://www.orfonline.org/raisina-dialogue/speaker/.
312. "Statistics of the Investment Commission December 2020", Ministry of Economic Affairs, the Republic of China on Taiwan. https://www.moeaic.gov.tw/english/index.jsp.
313. "Sushma Swaraj tells Indian envoys to Act East and not just Look East", The Economic Times, August 26, 2014. https://economictimes.indiatimes.com/news/politics-and-nation/sushma-swaraj-tells-indian-envoys-to-act-east-and-not-just-look-east/articleshow/40907671.cms.
314. "Taiwan approves $140 million Pegatron investment in India", World News, WION News, published on January 29, 2021. YouTube video, 01:55, https://www.youtube.com/watch?v=6_4yA-yv2f0.
315. "Taiwan-China crisis: India calls for de-escalation of tensions", The Times of India, August 12, 2022. https://timesofindia.indiatimes.com/india/taiwan-china-crisis-india-calls-for-de-escalation-of-tensions/articleshow/93522458.cms.
316. "Taiwan-Country Commercial Guide: Information and Telecommunications Technology", International Trade Administration of USA, September 25, 2020. https://www.trade.gov/country-commercial-guides/taiwan-information-and-telecommunications-technology.
317. "Taiwan Education Center – Introduction and Structure", Foundation for International Cooperation in Higher Education of Taiwan. https://www.fichet.org.tw/en/what-we-do/taiwan-education-centers/.
318. "Taiwan, Nauru end diplomatic relations", Focus Taiwan, January 15, 2024. https://focustaiwan.tw/politics/202401150008.
319. "Taiwan India Relations", Taipei Economic and Cultural Center in India. Accessed on August 16, 2021. https://www.roc-taiwan.org/in_en/post/39.html.

320. "Taiwan is an opportunity to be grasped: Madahav Nalapat", The News 21, October 13, 2020. https://thenews21.com/taiwan-is-an-opportunity-to-be-grasped-madhav-nalapat.
321. "Taiwan is to establish 'The Taiwanese Representative Office in Lithuania' opening new page for cooperation and communication", Ministry of Foreign Affairs, the Republic of China (Taiwan), July 20, 2021. https://www.mofa.gov.tw/News_Content.aspx?n=73&s=96170. (In Chinese)
322. "Taiwan jumps to 11th in IMD World Digital Competitiveness Ranking 2020-Achieves maximum performance", National Development Council, Republic of China (Taiwan). https://www.ndc.gov.tw/en/nc_8455_34453.
323. "Taiwan message: New Delhi-Taipei cooperation is both mutually beneficial and a pointed signal to China", The Times of India, April 4, 2021. https://timesofindia.indiatimes.com/blogs/toi-editorials/taiwan-message-new-delhi-taipei-cooperation-is-both-mutually-beneficial-and-a-pointed -signal-to-china/.
324. "Taiwan Plus, Invest India", Ministry of Commerce and Industry, Government of India. https://www.investindia.gov.in/country/taiwan-plus.
325. "Taiwan rejects China's protest over messages between Modi, Lai", The Arunachal Times, June 8, 2024. https://arunachaltimes.in/index.php/2024/06/08/taiwan-rejects-chinas-protest-over-messages-between-modi-lai/.
326. "Taiwan's semiconductor industry sets new output milestone in 2020", Focus Taiwan, February 22, 2021. https://focustaiwan.tw/business/202102220012.
327. "Taiwan Strait", Global Security. July 21, 1995 to March 23, 1996. https://www.globalsecurity.org/military/ops/taiwan_strait.htm.
328. "Taiwan world's 16th largest trading economy ibn 2021: MOF", Focus Taiwan, April 15, 2022. https://focustaiwan.tw/business/202204150008.
329. "Tata Joins hands with PSMC to build India's first 12-inch fab", TSMC, February 29, 2024. https://www.powerchip.com/en-global/insights/press-releases/content/20240229.
330. "The CHIPS Act of 2022: Section-by-Section Summary", Senate Commerce Committee, the USA. https://www.commerce.senate.gov/services/files/592E23A5-B56F-48AE-B4C1-493822686BCB.
331. "The First India–Taiwan Bilateral Forum on Mandarin Chinese Course Materials for Indian Learners held in Jawaharlal Nehru University (JNU), New Delhi", Ministry of Education, Republic of China (Taiwan), March 10, 2017.
332. https://english.moe.gov.tw/cp-13-17102-0013B-1.html.
333. "The Fourth India-Taiwan Bilateral Forum on Mandarin Chinese Teaching Materials for Indian Learners", Taiwan Education Center, https://www.tecindianthu.tw/edcontent_d.php?lang=tw&tb=7&cid=5&id=1000.
334. "The global economy is picking up slowly, Taiwan's four major manufacturing industries are all growing", Market Prospects, January 13, 2021.

335. https://www.market-prospects.com/articles/taiwan-major-manufacturing-industries-are-all-growing.

336. "The New Southbound Talent Development Program", Ministry of Education, the Republic of China (Taiwan). https://www.edunsbp.moe.gov.tw/overview_students_en1011.html.

337. "Top Indian envoy discusses priority areas of cooperation with Taiwan", Focus Taiwan, January 9, 2021. https://focustaiwan.tw/politics/202101090002.

338. "Transcript of Weekly Media Briefing by the Official Spokesperson (September 22, 2022)", Ministry of External Affairs, Government of India, September22, 2022. https://mea.gov.in/media-briefings.htm?dtl/35742/Transcript+of+Weekly+Media+Briefing+by+the+Official+Spokesperson+September+22+2022.

339. "Treaties Handbook", Treaty Section of the Office of Legal Affairs, United Nations, 71-72. https://treaties.un.org/doc/source/publications/THB/English.pdf.

340. 'Upswing In Levels Of Cooperation': Jaishankar On India-Taiwan's 'Substantial' Relations, ABP News, November 16, 2023. https://news.abplive.com/news/india/eam-jaishankar-on-india-taiwan-substantial-relations-1643038.

341. "U.S.-Australia-Japan Trilateral Strategic Dialogue", Office of the Spokesperson, the Department of State, the USA, August 5, 2022. https://www.state.gov/u-s-australia-japan-trilateral-strategic-dialogue/.

342. "Vaccine Supply", Ministry of External Affairs, Government of India, April 30, 2021. https://www.mea.gov.in/vaccine-supply.htm.

343. "Value of Export & Import by Country", Bureau of Foreign Trade, Ministry of Economic Affairs, the Republic of China (Taiwan). Accessed on August 17, 2022. https://cuswebo.trade.gov.tw/FSCE040F/FSCE040F.

344. "Vedanta, Foxconn sign $20 billion Gujarat chip deal", The Times of India, September 13, 2022. https://timesofindia.indiatimes.com/business/india-business/vedanta-foxconn-sign-20-billion-gujarat-chip-deal/articleshow/94169496.cms.

345. "Visa-Exempt Entry and Landing Visa", Bureau of Consular Affairs, Ministry of Foreign Affairs, Republic of China (Taiwan). https://www.boca.gov.tw/1p-149-2.html.

346. "Wang Yi Delivers a Speech at the French Institute of International Relations", Ministry of Foreign Affairs, the People's Republic of China, August 30, 2020. https://www.fmprc.gov.cn/mfa_eng/zxxx_662805/t1811319.shtml.

347. "What are the areas of China's 14 Dynasties: the smallest is 5 times larger than Japan, and the largest is 87 times larger than that of Japan" (In Chinese). https://www.sohu.com/a/343624093_679063.

348. "What are the five pillars of a self-reliant India?", Narendra Modi, May 13, 2020. https://www.narendramodi.in/what-are-the-five-pillars-of-a-self-reliant-India-read-to-find-out-more-549630.

349. "Where is India on the One China Policy?", The Diplomat. March 6, 2017. https://thediplomat.com/2017/03/where-is-india-on-the-one-china-policy/.
350. Wikileaks, Accessed April 11, 2020. https://wikileaks.org/plusd/cables/04TAIPEI3845_a.html.
351. "Wolf Warriors and a crazed hyena French researcher not intimidated after clash with China Envoy", France 24, March 23, 2021. https://www.france24.com/en/europe/20210323-wolf-warriors-and-a-crazed-hyena-french-researcher-not-intimidated-after-clash-with-china-envoy.
352. "#IndiaFightCorona COVID-19", Government of India, September 4, 2022. https://www.mygov.in/covid-19/.
353. "財団法人交流協会と亜東関係協会との間の在外事務所相互設置に関する取り決め", 政策研究大學院大學 (National Graduate Institute for Policy Studies). https://worldjpn.grips.ac.jp/documents/texts/JPCH/19721226.O1J.html. (In Japanese)

TV and Social Media

354. Berman, John and John Avlon, anchored. *New Day*. Aired August 6, 2021 on CNN. http://edition.cnn.com/TRANSCRIPTS/2108/06/nday.02.html.
355. "Live: EAM S Jaishankar attends interactive session on Northeast India's Integration | Asia | Japan", ANI News, April 29, 2024.
356. https://www.youtube.com/watch?v=78OACqXVE7o.

Miscellaneous

Constitution of a Special Investment Promotion Task Force under the Chairmanship of Chief Secretary to Attract Investors-Orders-Issued, G.O. (Ms) No.123, Industries (MIB.1) Department, Tamil Nadu, India, 29.04.2020.